The Indian Frontier, 1763–1846

HISTORIES OF THE AMERICAN FRONTIER

Ray Allen Billington, General Editor
Coeditors:
William Cronon, University of Wisconsin
Howard R. Lamar, Yale University
Martin Ridge, The Huntington Library
David J. Weber, Southern Methodist University

The Indian Frontier 1763-1846

R. DOUGLAS HURT

UNIVERSITY OF NEW MEXICO PRESS

ALBUQUERQUE

For Mary Ellen,
Adlai, and Austin

LIBRARY OF CONGRESS CATALOGING-IN-PUBLICATION DATA

Hurt, R. Douglas.
The Indian frontier, 1763-1846 / R. Douglas Hurt.—1st ed.
300 p. cm.—(Histories of the American frontier)
Includes bibliographical references and index.
ISBN 0-8263-1965-3 (cloth : alk. paper)—ISBN 0-8263-1966-1
(pbk. : alk. paper)
1. Indians of North America—Government relations—1789-1869.
2. Indians of North America—Government relations.
3. United States—Ethnic relations—History.
4. Indians of North America—Wars—1750-1815.
5. Indians of North America—Wars—1815-1875.
I. Title. II. Series.
E93 .H95 2002
970'.00497—dc21
2002002098

DESIGN: MINA YAMASHITA

Contents

List of Maps

Foreword

When Ray Allen Billington launched the Histories of the American Frontier series in 1963, he envisioned that future volumes would be written by "a recognized authority who brings to his task an intimate knowledge of the subject he covers and a demonstrated skill in narration and interpretation." With Billington's words in mind the current editors of this series are confident that R. Douglas Hurt's *The Indian Frontier, 1763-1846*, would more than satisfy Billington's highest expectations.

Douglas Hurt is not only the author and editor of more than a dozen books on American agriculture, the frontier, and the West, two of his most recent studies, *Indian Agriculture in American History: Prehistory to the Present* (1987), and his acclaimed *The Ohio Frontier: Crucible of the Old Northwest 1720-1830* (1996), reveal an extraordinary knowledge of North American Indian nations and their cultures. His writings also demonstrate an equally full understanding of the Indian nations' and tribes' often turbulent relations with the British, American, French, Spanish, and Mexican governments and peoples.

Indeed, in *The Indian Frontier,* Hurt has followed the grand continental vision of two of the earlier volumes in the series: W. J. Ecles *The Canadian Frontier, 1534-1760* (1969), and John Francis Bannon *The Spanish Borderlands Frontier, 1513-1821* (1970), by making a broad study of the hundred years from the Treaty of Paris (1763), which resulted in the most far-reaching changes of political power in North America since its first European settlements, to the Mexican War when the United States assumed full possession of the coast to coast regions that became the forty-eight continental states.

Even so, how was one to portray in one volume the relations of the British and the Americans to the nation-tribes of the Old Northwest and the Southeast, the early experiences of the Spanish in the American Southwest and California, and the competition of Britain, France, Spain, and the United States for the Pacific Northwest? This also meant covering the troubled history of Americans and the five Southern Nations in the Southeast, as well as the later encounters of the Mexicans

with the Comanches and other Indian groups in the southern Great
Plains and with California Indians during the mission period. Not content
with these large challenges, Hurt then decided to tell the violent story of
the Texas Republic's hostile relations with the Comanches.

Hurt persuasively reassures his readers that he can handle these
challenges by explaining in a superbly clear and delightfully written
preface how he would accomplish this task. There he not only acquaints
the reader with the disparate even unique history of each of these
regions and its native peoples, but explains that rather than the usual
story of westward moving frontiers, it is "a cross-sectional look at
many frontiers, that is, zones or regions of encounter, and the cultural
interactions between whites and Indians within them." Hurt then goes
on to remind us that the history of one region relates to the others in
both subject and time and assists our understanding of the complex
relationships by providing a comparative chronology for the reader.
This chronology reminds us, for example, that while Daniel Boone
was leading settlers to Kentucky in the 1770s, Juan Bautista de Anza,
Spain's Daniel Boone of the Southwest, was leading settlers to future
San Francisco at the same time.

Perhaps the most distinctive contribution of *The Indian Frontier,*
however, is that the focus of each chapter is in the Indian country itself
and records the Indians' perceptions of events and changes in their
relationship with Euroamerican whites. Hurt finds that the Indians were
always negotiator-participants with strategies for dealing with both whites
and other Indian groups, and were never passive victims.

Inevitably the topics of some of the nine chapters in the volume cover
familiar ground, for example, the turmoil in the Old Northwest between
Pontiac's Rebellion in 1763 and the role of the Southern Indians in the
American Revolution; yet each contains fresh information and voices
new interpretations. In the chapter on British America we learn that the
British never really controlled the Old Northwest for the Indians were
still pro-French and considered most of the various treaties they signed
to be dead letters. By the eve of the Revolution, the enemies of the Ohio
Indians were not the British Government but aggressive American
settlers. Yet at the end of the Revolution, Indian tribes still held the lands
north and west of the Ohio River.

Far from portraying a successful imperial Spain, his chapter on the

Spanish Southwest reminds us that "simply put, trade, treaties and toleration became the essential principle of Spanish frontier Indian policy instead of military force," because as the Spanish themselves admitted the Comanches, Apaches, and the nations to the north essentially controlled the borderlands frontier and continued to do so in the Mexican period. Similarly, Hurt's candid treatment of the authoritarian Franciscan missionaries, whom he feels hated the Indians, and the effects of European diseases on the mission Indians, go far to explain the rise of a strong resistance movement on the part of both mission and interior valley Indians. Once again he challenges the idea of California Indians being passive and defeatist.

In tracing the history of the Europeans in the Pacific Northwest fur trade, Hurt finds that women played a far more central role in the trade than has been assumed and that both Indians and whites believed that they controlled the trading process. In the end, however, white diseases and American settlers determined the future of the Northwest Indians.

In Hurt's account of the trans-Appalachian frontier and the story of the Southern Nations we find a familiar story of American occupation, the battles of William Henry Harrison and his land grabbing, and the belief of every president from Jefferson to Jackson in Indian removal. But here again Hurt sets the scene of action with the Indians themselves rather than with Washington, and we watch with dismay as each Southern Nation is forced to remove to Indian Territory. Hurt's retelling of the Indian removal story both in the South and after the Black Hawk War in Illinois, constitutes two of the most moving chapters in the book. The narrative is particularly effective because of his unforgettable character-izations of scores Indian leaders such as Red Eagle, Pushmataha, John Ross, Black Hawk, and Keokuk.

Hurt brings his compelling narrative to a climax in two lively final chapters: "The Great Plains" and the "Far West" between 1821 and 1846. In the former he traces the extraordinary role of the Comanches in the Spanish Southwest and the brutal encounter of that tribe with Texans in these years. The "Far West" is one of the most original chapters in the volume for it traces in careful detail the failed Mexican Indian policy on its northern border. "By the eve of the Mexican War," writes Hurt, "the Comanches, Apaches, Navajos, and Utes essentially controlled the Mexican frontier in New Mexico and Arizona." Even in California Indian resistance to Mexican authority was so great that by the 1830s the Indians of the interior valleys were called "horse-stealing Indians." Hurt's dramatic narrative ends where Robert M. Utley's *The Indian Frontier of the American West 1846-1890* begins.

Hurt's volume concludes with the observation that Indians everywhere were far more successfully resistant to white invasion than we have assumed, but that neither side had a monopoly on morality and virtue; rather the story is one of self-interest on both sides.

Hurt is not only to be congratulated for his eminently readable and original history of the Indian frontier between 1763–1846 but for organizing the narrative so that it can be used as a text for classes in Indian, Western, and American history courses. His efforts to reach both students and the general reader again reflect one of the chief aims of Ray Allen Billington. A superb bibliography and many illustrations enhance this important new addition to the Histories of the American Frontier series.

Howard R. Lamar, *Yale University, for the editors of the Histories of the American Frontier series,*

CO-EDITORS:
William Cronon, *University of Wisconsin*
Martin Ridge, *the Huntington Library*
David J. Weber, *Southern Methodist University*

Preface

The history of North American frontiers is the story of the interaction of many peoples over time and within the context of place. It is a complex story not easily told. In fact, it cannot be completely told with one broad stroke of the pen, because it involves a host of issues, such as race, class, gender, politics, economics, culture, religion, and military affairs, to name only a few of the more salient matters that historians grapple with to give form, substance, and explanation to the broader subject of frontiers.

My purpose is to provide a historical synthesis of the interaction between Indians, Europeans, and Anglo-Americans, primarily in the area of the present-day United States west of the Appalachians from the end of the French and Indian War in 1763 until the beginning of the Mexican War in 1846. This book is designed for general readers and students of Indian-white relations who are coming to the subject for the first time. It is admittedly selective, even impressionistic, in its coverage, but my intent has been to discuss Indian affairs in terms of interactions between cultural groups within particular areas or regions.

Although the national government consistently sought to acquire Indian lands by both treaties and force, the Indian nations with whom it dealt used traders, agents, and the military for their own advantages, and they, too, pursued their own policies toward the Europeans and Anglo-Americans. By so doing, they made their own decisions and took responsibility for their own affairs and did not merely react as backward, warlike, or culturally deprived people when confronted with a supposedly superior civilization.

This book, then, is the story of conflict and cooperation between Indians and whites in areas that both claimed. It is also the story of cause and consequence, because the actions of Indians and whites had meaning for the present and future. Often it is more the story of the struggle for power by Indians and whites, rather than a history of cooperation, but it is always the story of cultural interaction over time and space. Yet, it is not a simple story of whites versus Indians. Indian culture was too complex for the creation of a monolithic force to prevent the acquisition, if not seizure, of Indian lands. Just as the Spanish, French, British, and Americans formulated and executed different policies for dealing with the Indian nations within the territory that each claimed, the Indian nations also had different policies or plans for not only dealing with the Europeans and Americans, but also for dealing with each other. Frequently the Indians, such as the Creeks, Comanches, and Potawatomies, acted more independent than unified, but their actions always reflected their own economic and political needs as well as cultural traditions. But, those actions invariably were designed to deal with other Indian and white nations to their own advantage. Indians and whites, then, constantly calculated how best to deal with the other to get what they wanted—trade, land, war, or peace. As a result, in the case of the Spanish, tribal enmity made it difficult for the Spaniards to make peace with one nation without ruining peaceful relations with others, such as in the case of the enmity between the Comanches and Apaches.

While this book, then, is the story of self-interest, violence, and dispossession, it is not the story of a linear progression of the frontier as a boundary line of westward movement. Rather, it is a cross-sectional look at many frontiers, that is, zones or regions of encounter and the cultural interactions between whites and Indians within them. In other words, this is the study of Indian and white interactions at the same time in several frontier areas where Indian societies occupied the region, usually for several generations, and where Europeans and Anglo-Americans intruded to control trade and land for the purpose of expansion and empire. Ultimately, it is the story of conflict and eventual conquest, although that outcome was never predetermined. Consequently, this is a study of Indian and white relations based on the multisided negotiations of each for influence, domination, and control of regions that are nothing less than simultaneous frontiers in what is now the continental United States.

One should speak, then, in terms of "frontiers," rather than of a "frontier." The plural or multiple nature of frontiers in American history is never more evident than when studying the relationships between Indian and European and Anglo-American cultures on the North American continent. Moreover, even if the frontier can be considered a neutral region for interaction, the participants, both Indian and white, who competed for that space and place were not homogenous, monolithic groups. The Creeks, for example, were a single people in name only, and the Upper and Lower Creeks claimed different lands. At the same time, white representatives of national and state governments disagreed about which political entity controlled specific lands that these Indians also considered their own. As a result, Creeks and whites contested among themselves as well as with other cultural groups to define and control the southern frontier. Between whites and Indians as well as among their respective people, the frontier remained an identifiable yet amorphous region. Both Indians and whites, then, had specific needs and policies or plans to achieve their goals, but even within a specific culture individuals and groups competed to determine which course of action would prevail. Indeed, the frontier has never been a single place in time and space. Rather, many frontiers have existed simultaneously, and they have changed constantly.

I use the concept of frontiers in the historical, that is, contemporary sense of the European and Anglo-American cultures that interacted with the Indian nations in both commerce and war. Although the concept of a "frontier" remains controversial among historians, the term must be used in the context that gave it meaning in the past. Certainly, definitions depend on cultural perspective and the geographical region and the spatial relationships of the groups in question, the latter here meaning Indians and whites. The French, British, and Spanish used the term "frontier" as an unsettled or slightly populated area that both Indians and whites used, if not shared, and an area that each culture wanted as its own, but also one in which both made accommodation for the other based on their own cultural, economic, political, and military needs.

The French, who essentially left the continent at the point where this book begins, pursued a policy of friendship and cooperation based on trade, gifts, and intermarriage. The French did not want Indian lands for agriculture, but rather sought wealth through the fur trade while claiming a vast portion of the continent for empire. They did not recognize Indian title to land, particularly for nomadic tribes, but they respected the possessory right of the Indians to the soil, that is, their right to claim certain lands for villages and hunting. Even so, the French never recognized "official" Indian title to land, although the French could acquire ownership of those lands by following certain governmental procedures.

The Spanish at first followed a paternalistic pacification policy that treated the Indians as subjects for integration into Spanish society to expand the empire in contrast to the inclusionary policy of the French or the exclusionary policy of the Americans. The Spanish also followed specific regulations for the settlement of Indian lands, but the practice of acquiring those lands differed from region to region. In Upper Louisiana, Spain continued to use the French system based on trade and gifts to make the Indians dependent on them and to win their friendship. As a result, the forts that Spain built in the Mississippi Valley were designed for trade rather than defense, in contrast to many other posts on the frontier. Moreover, in Upper Louisiana no Indian nation received written title to land until the late eighteenth century, and individual titles usually went to mixed-bloods because of their white parentage. After 1763, the Spanish also invited the Shawnees, Delawares, and other Indians from the Old Northwest to settle in Upper Louisiana in order to use them to block Anglo-American expansion west of the Mississippi River. Spain judged that these Indians already harbored ill feelings against the Americans who had driven them from their lands on the trans-Appalachian frontier, and Spain could use its experience to Christianize and acculturate these Indians and manipulate them to serve Spain as a foil to Anglo-American expansion. By the late eighteenth century, however, Spain had adopted the French policy of accommodation and reciprocity with the Indians in the Southwest to foil aggressive American expansion into the region, but without sufficient skill or financial commitment to succeed.

The Americans had a far different concept of landholding. They had a strict concept of separate space and soon after the War of Independence pursued a policy of extinguishing Indian title to lands with cession treaties that gave them legal title to specific lands that white settlers could purchase as their own. Often, violence initiated by white settlers who squatted on Indian lands preceded the cession treaties designed to protect those settlers and drive the Indians away. American frontier policy, based on assumptions of racial and cultural superiority as well as an insatiable desire for land, expansion, and empire, then, emphasized exclusion of Indian people from white society rather than inclusion and integration.

Whether considering trade relations with the French, diplomacy with the Spanish and British, or war with the Anglo-Americans, the Indians, Europeans, and Anglo-Americans lived on an interactive frontier. Their lives were mutually, reciprocally, and inextricably linked. Over time, the Anglo-American and Indian frontiers changed from inclusive zones of encounter between civilizations to exclusionary regions dominated by the major military power as white settlement expanded and as the Indians lost control of their lands. These changes depended on the cultures involved as well as demography, administration, and economics. But "power" is the most important determinant in terms of ideological will, population numbers, and military prowess.

Without question the men and women of European or Anglo-American descent who lived between the French and Indian and the Mexican American Wars used the term "frontier," and they knew what it meant. In their mind's eye they could see regions where Indian and white cultures contested for space, often defined as land, and more importantly for power. All of which is to say that the frontier was and is a cultural construct, but that does not make it either unreal or invalid. Although the concept of a frontier correctly involves an understanding of the term within the context of social process, it was and is a state of mind. But, significantly, those men and women who lived between 1763 and 1846 understood in their own minds what frontiers meant to them. It is in this context of time and place, where Indians and whites struggled for power, then, that I use the term Indian frontiers.

As a cultural construct, frontiers had different meanings for the Indian nations. They had contested for space with one another across several frontiers for generations by the time of white contact. The Iroquois, for example, extended their domination into their own frontier of the Ohio Valley, where they demanded subordination from the Shawnees and Delawares, among others, but those nations did not consider themselves under Iroquois hegemony and acted accordingly in their contacts with the British on their own frontier. Moreover, the Indians had more than a century of experience dealing with the French, British, and Spanish across changing frontiers over matters of trade and land as well as peace and war by 1763. Both Indians and whites, then, contested for control of land and resources and, according to their own cultural traditions, ownership of the frontiers on the North American continent.

White contact, however, resulted in unmitigated disaster for the Indian nations. War and disease reduced and in many cases decimated and nearly annihilated some Indian cultures, but many of these Indian nations on the frontiers of concern here may well have been on the way to major environmental or ecological crises of their own making, in part due to the white introduction of horses. The coming decline of the bison population offers a suggestive example of disastrous change not entirely the making of whites.

Always the interactions between Indians and whites on the frontiers of the North American continent changed each people, sometimes quickly, usually slowly, but nonetheless decisively. For the Europeans, contact with Indian nations often meant changing military procedures to meet the abilities of a new and unconventional enemy in an environment for which their armies proved unprepared. For the Indians, it meant cultural change in the form of Spanish, French, and English languages, trade goods that became necessities, and religion, all at least as great an influence on their lives as military defeat. For the Anglo-Americans, it meant expanding a legal procedure to acquire lands and remove Indian populations, both backed by force.

Above all, the history of Indian and white frontiers is the story of people in motion. It is the story of interaction and negotiation over a host of issues—

trade, land, peace, and war. This motion and interaction involved Indians as well as whites, and, indeed, many of the Indian bands and nations, such as the Shawnees, Delawares, and Kickapoos, were as mobile as whites who moved west of the Mississippi River from Ohio and Georgia, and the movement of the Indians and whites for hunting and trade differs only in the details. Certainly, the frontiers involved in this study were continually changing for all of the people who lived in those regions. The Indian frontiers were porous, never fixed, where many people intermingled, cooperated, and coexisted as well as competed, divided, and fought across cultural boundaries. If anything, a frontier by definition is a dynamic region, which undergoes continuous reorganization and renegotiation as the economic, social, political, and military needs of people change.

In this study, I use the term Indians to refer to the Native Americans because that is the term that they most often use to identify themselves. I use the term Americans as shorthand for Anglo-Americans (many of whom were not "Anglo"). Each term is readily recognizable and understandable to the general reader, and this is not the place to debate academic fine points about identity, ethnicity, and labels. Space limitations, however, permitted only the citation of quoted material. These citations refer to printed primary sources, such as the *American State Papers,* or to secondary sources that quote primary materials in foreign archives or sources that are not easily available to the general reader or introductory student of Indian and white relations. The bibliography, however, will take readers to the next level of study.

I am grateful to Howard Lamar for inviting me to contribute a synthesis designed for the general reader to the Histories of the American Frontier series and for David Holtby's help and encouragement. During the course of the research a number of people at a host of institutions provided essential aid, and I would be remiss if I did not acknowledge them for this support. They are John Powell, Newberry Library; Joan Stahl, Smithsonian American Art Museum; John Lovett, Western History Collections, University of Oklahoma; Duane Sneddeker, Missouri Historical Society; Elaine Miller, Washington State Historical Society; Trevor Bond, Washington State University Library; Carolyn Marr, Museum of History and Industry, Seattle; Ellen Westhafer, State Historical Society of Iowa; Keshia Whitehead, Chicago Historical Society; Mary Michaels, Illinois State Historical Society; Susan Sutton, Indiana Historical Society; Mikki Tint, Oregon Historical Society; Jeffrey Rogers, Mississippi Department of Archives and History; Larry Miller, University of New Mexico; Karina McDaniel, Tennessee State Library and Archives; Fae Sotham, State Historical Society of Missouri; Angelika Tietz, University of Oklahoma Press; Rebecca Jordan, Susan Congdon and Mary Jane Thune, Parks Library, Iowa State University; Charles Brodine at the Navy Historical Center; and the curators of the Peabody Museum of Archaeology and Ethnology, Harvard University. Jeff Thomas at the University of Missouri prepared the maps. Cynthia Potter served as my research assistant. I am thankful for the help of all.

Howard Lamar, Martin Ridge, and David Weber provided substantive evaluations of the manuscript that enabled me to improve this book beyond measure. I am appreciative for their help and support.

THE INDIAN FRONTIER, 1763–1846

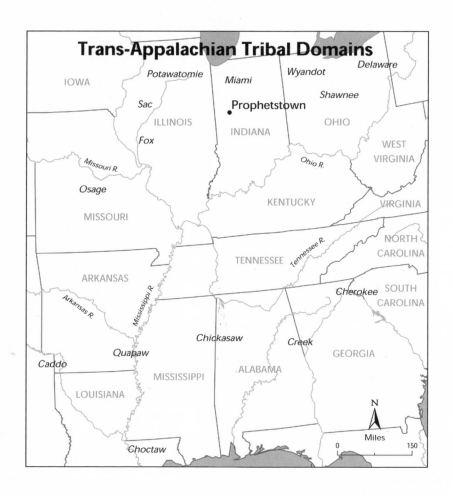

Trans-Appalachian Tribal Domains

IOWA

Potawatomie

Miami

Wyandot

Delaware

Sac

Shawnee

•Prophetstown

ILLINOIS

INDIANA

OHIO

Fox

WEST
VIRGINIA

Missouri R.

Ohio R.

Osage

KENTUCKY

VIRGINIA

MISSOURI

NORTH
CAROLINA

TENNESSEE

Tennessee R.

ARKANSAS

Cherokee

SOUTH
CAROLINA

Arkansas R.

Mississippi R.

Chickasaw

Creek

GEORGIA

Quapaw

Caddo

ALABAMA

MISSISSIPPI

LOUISIANA

N

Choctaw

Miles

0   150

CHAPTER 1

British America

News that the French and the British had stopped fighting reached the Indian nations west of the Appalachians between November 1762 and January 1763. The word spread to the Delaware villages on the Tuscarawas and to the Shawnees camped along the Scioto. The Wyandots near Sandusky, the Miamis in northwestern Indiana, and even the Kickapoos and Potawatomies in the Illinois country heard it. To the south the Chickasaws and Creeks learned of it as well, colored by Spanish interpretation from New Orleans about what it meant. Many of the trans-Appalachian Indians considered the Treaty of Paris, signed on February 10, 1763, which ended the French and Indian War and transferred all French claims on the North American continent to the British, as bad news and a harbinger of difficult days to come.

By 1763 the Indian nations west of the Appalachians had relied on either French or British traders for a long time. Goods, such as blankets, knives, guns, and cooking utensils, that had once been luxuries now served as necessities. The Indians satisfied their wants by exchanging deerskins for the items that the traders brought to their villages. The British American traders who operated out of Pennsylvania, Virginia, and the Carolinas sought economic gain, but both the British and colonial governments that supported or regulated their ventures desired influence with the western nations more than profits. Both wanted to control the trans-Appalachian frontier or backcountry that Britain now claimed by right of conquest. Control, of course, meant power, and power meant empire, which involved the acquisition and settlement of Indian lands. But neither Britain nor the colonies that had aspirations for western expansion marshaled the strength to seize those lands. Instead a host of Indian nations, such as the Shawnees and Delawares, who lived north of the Ohio River, and the Creeks and Chickasaws who lived to the south, occupied those lands, and they did not intend to abdicate sovereignty to either Britain or the Americans.

At the end of the French and Indian War, the Shawnees and Delawares were the most important Indian peoples who lived north and west of the Ohio River.

They had migrated into the Ohio country from Pennsylvania and the Delaware River valley, respectively, between the late 1730s and the early 1750s, and they claimed the Ohio country as their own. While their women cultivated corn, beans, and squash near their villages in the river valleys, the men hunted and developed their own economic network with the Pennsylvania and Virginia traders. By the 1750s, the Shawnees and Delawares had distanced themselves from the Iroquois who also claimed the Ohio country, and the men of both nations earned reputations that recognized their war-making ability, such as "Shingas the Terrible," chief of the Delaware's Turkey division.[1]

Politically, the Indian nations in the Ohio country had a loose unity. The Shawnees divided into five groups—the Chillicothe, Hathawekele, Kispoko, Mequachake, and the Piqua, which became the most complex political organization north of the Ohio. Among the Shawnees, the chiefs inherited their positions patrilineally through the Chillicothe division while the warriors predominately came from the Kispoko. Similarly, the Delawares organized through the Turtle, Wolf, and Turkey divisions. Matrilineal succession through a particular lineage determined the village chiefs, who essentially exercised only ceremonial powers. Among the Ohio nations, each band had a peace and a war chief, but the latter could be earned only through bravery. Above all, the Shawnees and Delawares had been forced into the Ohio country either directly or indirectly by westward moving white settlers. By 1763, they had no intention of moving again.

South of the Ohio River, the Creeks held the reputation as the major Indian nation west of the Appalachians. At the end of the French and Indian War, they essentially occupied present-day Alabama. They were less a nation than a loose confederation of people with enough similarities to foster unity. These Muskogean-speaking natives had organized for mutual support by the time of European contact in the mid-sixteenth century. They shared a common culture and a network of related, matrilineal clans. The Creeks divided into two geopolitical divisions, called the Upper and Lower Towns, in part resulting from two main trade routes to South Carolina. The Upper Creeks and Lower Creeks held separate councils, claimed their own lands, and often pursued different diplomatic policies. From the end of the Yamasee War in 1717 to the American Revolution, the Creeks enjoyed a reliable trade with the British colonies. Between 1763 and 1783, the foundation of British policy toward the Creeks involved regulating the deerskin trade to bind them to the empire, keeping the Creeks from American influence, and treating both white and Indian traders equitably.

The Chickasaws lived north and west of the Creeks, primarily in northern

Mississippi and western Tennessee. Like the Choctaws, with whom they had a close cultural affiliation, they too spoke Muskogean. One contemporary called the Chickasaws the "Spartans" of the Lower Mississippi Valley because they honored "martial virtue, and not riches" as a cultural standard. The war-like spirit of the Chickasaws differentiated them from the other Indian nations in the trans-Appalachian southwest. They readily kept the French at bay, in part by refusing to accept missionaries during the early eighteenth century, but they welcomed British traders who came among them as early as 1698. By 1705, Chickasaw men had become commercial hunters to supply deerskins as well as captives for trade goods, horses, and black slaves. When French traders arrived in their villages, the Chickasaws invariably complained that they offered shoddy and overpriced goods compared to British traders. By 1706, the French considered the Chickasaws their enemies, because of their close trading relations with the British. Consequently, the French began to arm the Choctaws, who lived between the Chickasaws and the Gulf Coast, against them. By so doing, the French began a nearly perennial war between the Chickasaws and the Choctaws. When the French and Indian War ended with the Treaty of Paris, the Chickasaws had been friends with the British and enemies of the French for a long time. Thereafter, the British worked to keep the Creeks and Chickasaws loyal through trade. Pensacola and Mobile became the major trading centers in West Florida, which served the southwestern trans-Appalachian frontier.[2]

Newcomer, head of the Delawares, was "[s]truck dumb for a considerable period of time" when he learned of the peace treaty in 1763. The French father had abandoned his children. George Croghan, the British trader and Indian agent operating out of Pennsylvania, reported that the Ohio Indians on learning the news angrily contended that the "French had no Right to give away their Country; as, they Say, they were never Conquered by any Nation." While the new British father assured the Indians that he would treat them well, they were not convinced. The western Indians, who had been largely tied to the French through trade, but who had never been opposed to playing off one side against the other for their own advantage, now felt isolated and reliant on an enemy to meet their needs for European goods. They worried most, however, about the insatiable demands of the British Americans for land. Indeed, while the French had come among them to trade for furs, they did not stay in great numbers, and they made no personal claims to lands for private use. The British Americans, personified by the Pennsylvanians and the Virginians, whom they fearfully called the "long knives," already spilled over the Appalachians and claimed lands for their own use and built cabins with the intent to stay. Even so, most Indians were not willing to continue the war. Instead, they recognized that the British were few in number, traders still entered the backcountry, and the French might return. For the moment they would wait and see what the Treaty of Paris really meant.[3]

They did not wait long. By early 1763, the British clearly signaled a new relationship with the western Indians that involved both restricted trade and exclusive land ownership west of the Appalachians. Soon the Indians complained that the British had not replaced the French traders on the scale that their needs required. Goods offered by British traders always proved insufficient and the prices high. At Detroit they complained about shortages of lead and powder, unaware that the British, in contrast to the French, deliberately restricted the distribution of munitions as a matter of defense, while the Indians considered them necessities for providing food for their families and deerskins for trade. At the same time, settlers continued to cross the mountains and claim Indian lands as their own. Early thoughts of peace and cooperation quickly gave way to arguments for resistance and war.

Some of the Indians in the Ohio country registered their displeasure with the new British order and loss of their lands to whites by raiding across the Ohio River to steal horses and livestock from garrisons and settlers, and they plundered and sometimes killed traders who came among them. Others turned to spiritual revival to counter the British threat, achieve intercultural harmony, and improve their lives. Neolin, a Delaware prophet who mixed Christianity with native religion, led the spiritualists or nativists and urged all who would listen to reject European goods and return to their traditional cultural practices and thereby purify themselves of "sins and vices." Cultural separation rather than accommodation as well as belief in an all-powerful creator or Master of Life would enable the Indians to lead a good life on earth and in the next world. In the spring of 1763, Neolin's teachings spread quickly through the Ohio and Illinois country. Among the Ottawa, Pontiac, whom a French contemporary called "[a] proud, vindictive, war-like and easily offended man," combined Neolin's call for spiritual purification and a return to traditional ways of living with his own, urging them to mobilize a pan-Indian uprising and forcefully resist all British attempts to upset the generations-old social and political order in the trans-Appalachian West. Increasingly, those such as Tamaqua among the Delaware, who sought accommodation with the British, lost influence. Instead, Indian leaders who demanded resistance to the British, whose presence west of the Appalachians threatened native sovereignty and security, gained the attention of the young men. They agreed that the British had become "too great a People," and that the whites could only be stopped from taking their lands by war.[4]

By the spring of 1763, many of the Indians west of the Appalachians believed that military power, not accommodation, offered the best response to the new order created by the Treaty of Paris. Although many tribal members realized that a complete return to past cultural practices would be impossible because they had become dependent on both the French and British for trade goods, they could still use military power to drive white settlers from their lands. Consequently, when Pontiac counseled the need for war the Indians listened. He reportedly said the "Master of Life put Arms in our hands" and that "[i]t is important for us, my brothers, that we exterminate from our lands the nation which seeks only to destroy us." In May 1763, when the Ottawas, Potawatomies, and Hurons, known as Pontiac's Confederacy, attacked Detroit, they were taking responsibility for their own affairs by an act of war that the British called the "conspiracy of Pontiac."[5]

The Shawnees, Delawares, Wyandots, Munsees, and Senecas followed the Ottawa leader by forming an alliance that they called the "Five Nations of Scioto." Acting alone and together these tribes struck white settlements east of the Ohio River, killing more than six hundred Pennsylvanians. By the autumn of 1763 the Indians had destroyed or captured every British post west of the Appalachians except Detroit, Fort Niagara, and Fort Pitt, even though they lacked tribal unity and adequate munitions, and they had essentially stopped westward expansion by the British Americans. George Croghan held the Shawnees responsible, reporting that they had "[m]ore to Say with the Western Nations then any othe[r] [nation] this Way." Whether led by Pontiac, who sought a return of the French, or by the Shawnees, who fought for the control of their lands and cultural autonomy, the Indians essentially engaged in a defensive war designed to protect their own interests.[6]

While British officials worked to formulate a rational, effective, and equitable Indian policy, and while the frontier people claimed Indian lands whenever possible, the army had the responsibility of keeping the peace and defending the frontier. It did not do its job effectively or well. Prior to the Treaty of Paris, Sir Jeffrey Amherst, commander-in-chief of the British Army in America, had great difficulty recruiting soldiers and keeping an army in the field. The defense of Detroit against Pontiac's siege and the Canadian garrisons took most of his men, trained or otherwise, and Amherst necessarily turned to Pennsylvania militia and a ragtag collection of soldiers at Fort Pitt to bring peace to the Ohio country. But, during the spring and summer of 1763, the Indians held firm in the Ohio River valley, and the army had neither the men nor the resources or the will to strike west of the river and inflict a decisive defeat. By July 1763 desperation laced with racial hatred now motivated Amherst to ask Colonel Henry Bouquet, commander of the Southern Department of the British Army in North America, "Could it not be contrived to send the Small Pox among those disaffected tribes of Indians[?]" Given the inadequacy and failure of British military power, he contended, "We must, on this occasion, Use Every Stratagem in our power to Reduce them." Bouquet agreed and responded, "I will try to inoculate the [Indians] with Some Blankets that may fall in their Hands." When a party of Indians arrived at Fort Pitt for trade and negotiations on June 24, 1763, they were given two blankets and a handkerchief from the Small Pox Hospital at the fort. William Trent, who engaged in the Indian trade from Fort Pitt, hoped they would have the "desired effect." Smallpox soon devastated many Indian communities in the Ohio country, but it may have been brought home by the Indians who had attacked white settlements that suffered from the disease. By casting morality and ethics aside, however, Amherst revealed the all-pervasive hatred of Indians by whites on the trans-Appalachian frontier, which, when combined with the insatiable lust for land by the frontier people, jeopardized, if not prevented, a realistic and equitable Indian policy.[7]

By the autumn of 1763, the Shawnee, Delaware, and Mingo villages in the Ohio country suffered from both sickness and deprivation. Their attacks on settlements east of the river had depleted their supplies of powder and lead, and they hungered for a restoration of trade. As the Ohio tribes began to think of peace, if not accommodation, General Thomas Gage, newly appointed commander at Fort Pitt, scavenged enough men to form a 1,500-man force under Henry Bouquet to march deep into the Ohio country. Before Amherst departed from the colonies in November 1763, he intended to break Pontiac's insurgency and gain control of the Ohio country. Bouquet's expedition fit his plans either to coerce the Indians into submission or inflict sufficient casualties for them to accept peace. When confronting the Indians, Amherst had told Bouquet as early as the summer of 1763, "I Wish to Hear of *no Prisoners,* should any of the Villains be met with in Arms." Bouquet also considered the Indians to be nothing less than rebels who inhabited their domain by the grace of the conqueror, that is,

Great Britain, after the French and Indian War. For him, they had the choice of submitting to British rule or annihilation.[8]

Bouquet departed for the Tuscarawas River valley on October 3, and he reached the Delaware and Mingo villages in mid-October. There, he met with a Delaware by the name of Beaver, chief of the Turkey clan and a few Shawnees and Senecas. Bouquet told them that the Ottawas, Ojibwas, and Wyandots had already made peace and that the French Canadians were not coming back because they were now "subjects of the king of Great-Britain." Speaking on behalf of the king, Bouquet told the Tuscarawas villagers that the British would grant them a truce if they returned all of their prisoners. Then they could discuss peace terms. If they refused, he would destroy them. But, Bouquet told his audience, "the English are a merciful and generous People, averse to shedding the Blood, even of their most cruel Enemies. And if it was possible that you could convince us, that you sincerely repent of your past conduct, and that we could depend on your good behavior for the future, you might yet hope for Mercy and Peace."[9]

Bouquet's expedition of intimidation and his threats achieved greater success than anyone expected because he caught these Ohio Indians at the right time. Weakened from smallpox, low on powder and lead, and impressed with the number of soldiers who had come among them, the Shawnees, Delawares, Mingos, and Senecas realized that they could not drive the British away and that their villages lay at considerable risk. Consequently, they agreed to return their captives and make peace, or at least accept an armed truce, pending a formal treaty in the spring. By so doing they could protect their villages and avoid any land cessions, although the Shawnees reportedly were "very crabby" about the whole affair.[10]

By the time spring came the Shawnees, Delawares, and Senecas had thought about the terms of peace throughout the winter. Although they had been surprised by Bouquet's march to the Tuscarawas and intimidated by his large expedition, they understood that they could not decisively defeat Bouquet's force so they asked for and received important concessions. As a result, the peace negotiated in the spring obligated the British to protect Indian lands from the relentlessly westward-moving settlers and reopen the Indian trade. In turn, the Ohio Indians agreed to end their attacks on frontier settlements and send intermediaries to the Illinois country to represent the goodwill of the British among the Kickapoos and Potawatomies. Simply put, however, in 1764, the peace negotiated with the western Indians essentially returned the Ohio Valley to the status quo prior to

Pontiac's war, that is, to a stalemate in which the Indians north of the Ohio could not drive white settlers from the trans-Appalachian frontier and the British army could not defeat the Indians. The British won the return of many white captives, control of the French posts, and the right of passage through the region, as well as recognition of title to all lands south of the Ohio to the Tennessee River, but they did not gain the right to claim Indian lands north and west of the Ohio River. Most important, while the Ohio Indians technically became British subjects, William Johnson, superintendent of Indian affairs for the Northern District, understood that this designation applied only "so far as the same can be consistent with the Indians['] native rights," particularly regarding lands. Without the ability to decisively defeat the other, diplomacy and accommodation by the Indians, British, and Americans remained essential to maintaining the peace and the intercultural affairs that followed. Pontiac's Rebellion, however, proved the need for imperial supervision of the trans-Appalachian frontier. Whether the Americas would be willing to finance a new Indian policy and accept British administration and regulation remained an important, but unanswered question.[11]

While the army and frontier people reeled from Indian attacks, British officials had already formulated a new Indian policy for implementation after the French threat to the continent had ended. As early as 1761, the British government planned to temporarily restrict trading and settlement west of the Appalachians to bring system, order, and efficiency to both the Indian trade and the acquisition of tribal lands. The British particularly worried that if settlers occupied Kentucky, the Indians would attack and military expenditures would be exorbitant to restore the peace. Better to keep the peace first, the ministers decided, than to reestablish it later. Formally announced as the Proclamation of 1763, this royal policy sought to gain British control of the West by licensing traders and restricting them to specific garrisoned posts in order to control pricing and restrict the liquor trade. No longer would traders be able to freely visit the Indian villages whenever they pleased, far from the watchful eyes and regulations of their superiors. In this proclamation, the British also prohibited settlement beyond the crest of the Appalachians until officials could purchase Indian lands, survey "fixed boundaries," and thereby permit an orderly, peaceful settlement of the backcountry.[12]

British officials, however, miscalculated the obedience of their white subjects. The Proclamation of 1763 proved to be nothing more than a paper barrier, and it had little effect except on land companies and large-scale speculators who could not claim and settle western lands without a legal title that involved securing a government grant.

Individuals acting on their own could go wherever their courage let them and claim lands with the authority of their long rifles. Indeed, white settlers and traders paid little attention to the proclamation. One contemporary observed that "not even a second Chinese wall, unless guarded by a million soldiers, could prevent the settlement of the lands on the Ohio and its dependencies."[13]

The frontier people, then, who aggressively seized Indian lands contributed most to the continuing hostility of the western nations, and British officials could do little to restrain them. In the autumn of 1763, General Thomas Gage, who replaced Jeffery Amherst as commander-in-chief of the British forces, considered them "a Sett of People . . . near as wild as the country they go in, or the People they deal with, & by far more vicious & wicked." The frontier people demanded the right to seize unoccupied Indian lands, that is, those lands not settled and under cultivation, and they proved as dangerous as the young men in the Indian villages who championed war against the Americans. Still, the Indians in the Ohio country were not without blame. They had killed traders, hunters, and settlers for revenge, and they met every violent act by whites with similar retribution.[14]

While the British grappled with the problems of enforcing the Proclamation of 1763 and defending settlers in the Ohio Valley, the argumentative and restive colonists along the eastern seaboard increasingly challenged the authority of Parliament, including its avowed power to tax them to pay for their defense. After the Stamp Act crisis in 1765, the British government began to withdraw troops from the trans-Appalachian frontier because it could not support them or enforce the provisions of the Proclamation of 1763 without additional funds, the receipt of which became increasingly problematic with every colonial rejection of a new taxing scheme. It also shifted soldiers from the western posts to the increasingly volatile eastern cities to help maintain the peace. The government also contended that the colonists could best manage the Indian trade because the British army could not enforce Parliament's trade regulations or evict the settlers who moved in great numbers onto Indian lands in the Ohio Valley and as far west as the Illinois country. At the same time, Pennsylvania and Virginia proved unable or unwilling to administer British Indian policy, that is, protect tribal sovereignty to the land, promote equitable trade, and provide for their own defense. As the years passed, the Shawnees increasingly became the spokesmen for Indian demands in the Ohio country, and their words carried influence westward to the Wabash and Upper Mississippi River country and south to the Tennessee River valley.

Insufficient support for the army, colonial unrest, and an unenforceable Indian policy brought paralysis to government affairs west of the Appalachians after 1765. The British could not raise sufficient revenue to support garrisons in the trans-Appalachian West and white settlers encroached on Indian lands with impunity. At the same time, the Ohio Indians bitterly complained that the British did not honor their agreements and keep settlers off of their lands. Scalp hunters brought fear to the Indian villagers, and the chiefs demanded that the British control their young men. In several respects, however, the Indians had won Pontiac's war, because they learned the British could be coerced, if not defeated. By the time the fighting ended in 1765, the British had repealed every policy that the trans-Appalachian nations opposed. The British reinstituted the diplomatic policy of gift giving, renewed limited trade of guns, powder, and lead, as well as liquor. The Indians also learned that the British could not stop white settlers from spilling over the mountains and taking their lands. Moreover, continued violence, committed by both Indians and whites in the Ohio Valley, threatened to deteriorate into a full-fledged war the British could not afford in terms of men or money. Consequently, the Crown attempted to try, once again, to establish a boundary that both Indians and whites would respect and thereby prevent the seemingly never-ending attacks and festering grievances of each culture against the other. As a result, the Treaty of Fort Stanwix in 1768 became the last desperate effort of the British to create order west of the Appalachians.

By the spring of 1768, the Indians in the Ohio country had begun to stiffen their resistance to white settlement beyond the Appalachians by making specific land claims that they intended to maintain by either diplomacy or war. When the major tribes met at Fort Pitt in late April and early May, Tamaqua of the Delawares told George Croghan that "the Country lying between this River [the Ohio] and the Allegheny Mountains, has always been our Hunting Ground." Among the Shawnees, Nymwha blamed the British for the violence in the Ohio country because the army had failed to keep settlers east of the mountains and had abandoned their forts. Indian leaders also demanded that the British prevent settlers and hunters from going into Kentucky, which the Shawnees considered their major hunting grounds. Nymwha put it simply, saying that the Ohio Valley "is the Property of us Indians."[15]

The British, however, asserted that the Iroquois, not the Shawnees, owned the land south of the Ohio River by right of conquest. The Six Nations, however, had not been active in the region since the outbreak of the French and Indian War. By 1768, they exercised only rhetorical control of the Ohio country and the lands south of the river, and they understood that further white settlement would bring full-fledged war to the Ohio River valley. Although they enjoyed British friendship and trade, they made it clear to William Johnson, superintendent of Indian affairs for the Northern District, and trader and emissary George Croghan that they would not support the British in a war against the western tribes. With the Six Nations favoring a peaceful resolution of the land problem, Johnson recognized the opportunity to seize as much territory as possible under the guise of Indian support. Consequently, he issued a call for the Six Nations and their "dependents," that is, the Ohio tribes, to meet at Fort Stanwix in New York State in October to resolve a boundary that would meet the needs of both sides.[16]

Following Johnson's lead, land speculators, traders, and political representatives from New York, Pennsylvania, and Virginia, as well as more than two thousand Indians opened the treaty congress on October 24. The Shawnees and Delawares found themselves outnumbered and outvoted. The result proved less a negotiated than a British-imposed treaty. By accepting the fiction that the Six Nations controlled the land south of the Ohio, the British recognized the confederacy's cession of that area for a land adjustment in the Mohawk Valley. As result, the Six Nations astutely gave up lands that they claimed but neither controlled nor possessed for land accommodations closer to home. By so doing, they also reinforced their position as Britain's major Indian allies. At the same time, they washed their hands of potential troubles between white settlers and the Indians in the Ohio country.

Although the Shawnees and Delawares could not prevent the Six Nations from crafting an agreement with the British based on their seniority in an extensive alliance or covenant chain that linked the Indians from New England to the Ohio country, they had no intention of accepting a treaty that did not protect their interests. Red Hawk, a Shawnee leader, succinctly expressed this position by saying that the Six Nations were like an "elder brother" who often offered good advice, but who had no power over them. As a result, when the Ohio Indians learned about the Treaty of Fort Stanwix they immediately rejected it, because the Iroquois had no right to cede their lands. Negotiation and diplomacy had failed to safeguard their interests; only war remained to guarantee their security and lands. But war required both unity and strength. As the months following Pontiac's rebellion faded into years, the Shawnee leaders in the villages along the Scioto River valley planned to use the promise of spiritual renewal and a pan-Indian confederacy to marshal both the strength and will of the western nations to drive the British Americans from the trans-Appalachian frontier. General Thomas Gage, commander of the American forces, considered this plan "a very dangerous Event."[17]

In the spring of 1769, the Shawnees, Delawares, and Mingos sent emissaries to the Miamis, Piankishaws, Weas, and Misquetons living along the Wabash and Miami Rivers to form an alliance. They also contacted the Creeks, Chickasaws, and Choctaws south of the Ohio. If these nations could unify against the Americans, they would form the largest and strongest Indian confederacy ever created. The far western and southern nations, however, were too divided to form such a confederacy. The Creeks and Choctaws fought a grueling war among themselves between 1765 and 1771 that claimed more than six hundred lives. Moreover, nearly all the southern nations considered at least one of the northern tribes to be their enemy, and as George Croghan reported to William Johnson, many of the western Indians were "very averst to Makeing paice with ye Southern Nations." Consequently, Indian raids across the Ohio River against other Indians gave the Americans their best protection from a general Indian attack. Even so, the Shawnees, Delawares, and Mingos believed they could fashion a confederacy, because the time was right. The Indian nations west of the Appalachians, they believed, wanted to stop the settlement of the "Virginians," the term they used for all white settlers. A nativist movement now smoothed differences while emphasizing common grievances. By 1770, most nations north of the Ohio had extended peace offerings to all tribes south of the river and west of the Appalachians to the Mississippi. Although no grand Indian confederacy emerged, the Shawnees, Delawares, and Mingos used their diplomatic skills to make the Treaty of Fort Stanwix a dead letter for more than a decade.[18]

The tribes west of the Appalachians, however, could do little more at first than continue their isolated attacks on white settlements because they lacked unity for a confederacy that would enable them to marshal their strength in numbers against British soldiers, American militia, and white settlers. The Shawnees remained divided for nearly a decade after the Treaty of Fort Stanwix concerning a commitment to outright war, while the Miamis in the Wabash River valley preferred to campaign against the Cherokees, their enemy to the south. In turn, the Cherokees and Chickasaws attempted to form a confederacy with the Ohio tribes against the Miamis. While the western Indians, then, fought among themselves, Virginia long hunters continued to decimate their hunting grounds south of the Ohio and endanger their food supplies and way of life. The Virginians also jeopardized Indian safety. Missionary David McClure called them "white Savages," who took Indian lives as easily and willfully as they killed deer.[19]

By 1774, approximately fifty thousand whites had crossed the Appalachians, and the British had neither the desire nor the ability to control them. General

Gage understood the impossibility of keeping them from infringing on Indian lands, saying they were "too Numerous, too Lawless and Licentious ever to be restrained." Gage reflected that they were "almost out of Reach of Law and Government; Neither the Endeavors of Government, or Fear of Indians has kept them properly within Bounds." McClure also noted that they seemed "freed from the restraining influence of religion." By the eve of the American Revolution, then, the British were no longer the major enemy of the Ohio Indians; instead, their major adversaries were the incessantly westward-moving Americans.[20]

Confronted with these aggressive, pressing settlers, George Croghan reported that the Indians did not consider themselves safe even north of the Ohio. He also reported to William Johnson that the settlers in western Pennsylvania "thought it a meritorious act to kill Heathens whenever they were found." Johnson observed that this attitude seemed to be "the opinion of all the common people." Many of the young Shawnee and Delaware men who lived in the villages along the Muskingum and Scioto Rivers eagerly returned the hostility and willfully crossed the Ohio on raids into western Pennsylvania in an effort to maintain control of their Kentucky hunting grounds and slow the encroachment of settlers on their lands. Frequently, the Pennsylvania militia responded and the killing intensified.[21]

By the eve of the American Revolution, mutual reciprocity between whites and Indians based on trade and friendship had degenerated to exchanges of violence. On October 10, 1774, Cornstalk led a force of approximately one thousand Shawnees across the Ohio to strike an equal force of Virginia militia at the mouth of the Kanawha where they were building a fort. This engagement, perhaps the hardest fighting along the Ohio River, became known as the Battle of Point Pleasant. Neither side could claim a battlefield victory, but the Shawnees eventually withdrew and the Virginians pursued them across the Ohio and up the Hocking Valley, where, on the Pickaway Plains, Lord Dunmore, governor of Virginia, negotiated a truce. Known as the Treaty of Camp Charlotte, it required the Shawnees to accept the Treaty of Fort Stanwix, abide by British trade regulations, return all white captives, and stop attacking immigrant barges floating down the Ohio. For their part, the Virginians promised not to hunt north of the river. Colonel William Crawford boasted that "[w]e have made them sensibler of their villainy and weakness." Dunmore agreed, contending that he had "impressed an Idea of the power of the White People, upon the minds of the Indians." Many whites, both officials and settlers, hoped that the Indian problem had now been solved.[22]

In reality Dunmore's War occurred because the Virginians, whom competing

Pennsylvanians called "men without character and fortune," planned to use a militia force to seize Kentucky for themselves and displace both Indians and Pennsylvanians who also had aspirations to claim the area as their own. Indeed, Dunmore's War was little more than a preemptive strike against the Indians in order to claim Kentucky and keep non-Virginian speculators and settlers at bay, and it did not persuade the increasingly hostile Shawnees to accept the continued seizure of their hunting lands south of the Ohio River. Most important, however, Dunmore's War marked a turning point in Indian-white relations in the Ohio country, because the fighting occurred in the Indians' home territory, and because it resulted in the first land cession by the Shawnees. It also proved that the colonials, in this case the Virginians, would act as they thought best in order to seize Indian lands. British power over the Americans clearly waned, especially west of the Appalachians where land-hungry and Indian-hating settlers did as they pleased. By the mid-1770s, they began to crowd the very banks of the Ohio River and looked longingly and aggressively at the vast Indian lands to the north and west. By the eve of the American Revolution, then, Indian-white relations in the Ohio country centered only on one issue—control of the land. Both Indians and whites were determined that their people alone would exclusively exercise that power.[23]

By the summer of 1775, however, both Indians and whites in the Ohio country had learned about the fighting between British soldiers and colonists east of the mountains. Although many of the Shawnee leaders saw war impending between the British and Americans and counseled neutrality, the young men saw the conflict as an opportunity to strike the Americans in a time of weakness and thereby regain their lands south of the Ohio and ensure the defense of their villages north and west of the river. Moreover, the British were quick to encourage them to "take up the hatchet" against the Americans. If they did not, the British argued from Detroit, they would not only lose more land, but their way of life as well as their lives. Still, the British, in contrast to the French during the previous war, were unwilling to commit to a full-fledged Indian war merely to guarantee Indian land claims. Consequently, the Indians in the Ohio country could not use them as a counterweight to stop American expansion. If the Ohio Indians chose to stand against the Americans, they would essentially stand alone.[24]

Throughout the summer of 1775, the Shawnees remained divided over casting their fate with the British to keep the Americans at bay. Although the Wyandots near Sandusky had remained hostile to the Americans since the French and Indian War, many Delawares and Shawnees along the Tuscarawas, Muskingum, and

Scioto River valleys worried that war between the British and Americans would sweep them into the conflict. The members of the Continental Congress worried too, but they feared the western Indians would join the British. As a result, on July 12, 1775, Congress authorized Indian commissioners to "treat with the Indians in their respective departments, in the name and on behalf of the united colonies, in order to preserve peace and friendship with the said Indians, and to prevent their taking part in the present commotions." Congress also drafted a message for the commissioners to deliver to the tribes. It urged them to stay out of their quarrel with Great Britain and to "love and sympathise with us in our troubles; that the path may be kept open with all our people and yours, to pass and repass, without molestation." Traders operating out of Fort Pitt with the intent of keeping the Shawnees and Delawares neutral if not allied to the American cause reported that "the Women all seem very uneasy in Expectation that there would be war."[25]

In an attempt to keep the Indians in the Ohio country neutral, the Americans held a general council at Pittsburgh in the autumn of 1775. The Shawnees, Wyandots, Delawares, Mingos, Senecas, and Potawatomies attended and pledged friendship with the Americans and reaffirmed the Treaty of Fort Stanwix. The American representatives also pledged to keep their people south of the Ohio. But considerable acrimony and argument plagued the peace meeting. White Eyes, a Delaware leader, used the proceedings to cast off the long-recognized subservience of his people to the Iroquois, and dramatically claimed tribal lands to the west by pointing to the Allegheny River, saying, "All the country on the other side of that river is mine." White Eyes's pronouncement carried a less-than-veiled threat. If the Americans did not guarantee Delaware lands, he would lead his people into the British camp. Moreover, among the Ohio tribes, British agents operating from Detroit now began supplying the Indians with a host of trade goods in both quantity and at the right prices. In contrast, the Americans struggled with their own political organization, and they had little money to buy Indian friendship or keep them neutral. Consequently, the Ohio Indians drifted toward the British camp.[26]

By 1777, war parties of Shawnees, Delawares, Wyandots, and Mingos regularly crossed the Ohio to strike frontier settlements from Wheeling to Boonesborough. The Americans could not marshal sufficient force to march deep into the Ohio country and strike the hostile villages because their war with the British consumed their time and military resources. The Indian problem could not be resolved by force until the British had been defeated. In the meantime, they attempted to win

Indian neutrality by persuasion. In March 1778, for example, Colonel George Morgan met with the Delawares at Coshocton on behalf of the governor of Pennsylvania. Morgan urged the Delawares to stay out of the war. "The Tempest," he told them, "will be over in a few Months. You will then enjoy the Sweets of Peace whilst your restless Neighbors are suffering the Punishment due to their evil deeds."[27]

Soon thereafter the Delawares asked Congress to consider them friendly to the United States, with their leaders saying that their young men who had sided with the British were similar to the Tories. The Delawares sought peace and asked Congress to "make a proper Distinction between our nation and Individuals— who, on Account of their Conduct have become Outcasts from it and whom we will never receive as Friends untill you agree to receive them as your Friends or you obtain full satisfaction for the Injuries they have done you." Ultimately, however, peace for the Indian nations proved impossible, because both the British and Americans pressured them for a commitment, or at least neutrality. Daniel Broadhead, the American commander at Fort Pitt, for example, told the Shawnees that the British had come only "to rob & Steal & fill their Pockets."[28]

While Henry Hamilton, the British lieutenant governor at Detroit, urged the Ohio Indians against the Americans and provided them trade goods and munitions for their raids and money for white scalps, Morgan asked them to be patient. If they kept the peace and remained out of the fight, he told them, "your wants shall be all supplied by and by." If they did not keep the peace, however, they would suffer destruction. The Delawares listened apprehensively and ultimately signed a peace treaty on September 17, 1778, at Fort Pitt (the first between whites and Indians and the only one approved during the American Revolution) that proclaimed a "perpetual peace and friendship" between them and the United States and mutual aid against the British. But it soon collapsed after the murder of White Eyes by frontiersmen, and the Delawares cast their fate with the British. In the meantime, the Shawnees, Wyandots, and Mingos resolved to drive the Americans from the Ohio country with or without British aid.[29]

The American Revolution, then, meant little to the Shawnees, Wyandots, and Mingos in the Ohio country other than the continuation of war with the whites, particularly the Virginians, to stop settlers from seizing their lands. By the spring of 1778, they looked north to Detroit for leadership and supplies to fight the Americans, and they began to strike the settlements south and east of the Ohio with impunity. The Shawnees also sent emissaries to the Creeks and Chickasaws to gain their support against the Americans throughout the trans-Appalachian frontier. American militia retaliated in kind, crossing the Ohio and killing villagers, both peaceful and hostile, burning towns, and destroying crops. Yet, despite their raids across the Ohio, the Americans particularly feared the Shawnees, because they believed in total war. By 1780, they no longer adopted their white captives into their villages and families to replace loved ones lost in battle. Now they marked them for torture and death by painting their faces black. The Shawnees also remained elusive and out of reach by American forces. In August 1780, when George Rogers Clark led a personal army of volunteers against the Shawnee villages in the Miami River valley, he burned several towns and destroyed crops, but the Shawnees melted away before him. After the Americans departed, they rebuilt their homes and continued to rely on British supplies to cover their losses. By September 1782, the Shawnees remained in control of the Ohio River valley. At that time, Colonel William Christian informed Virginia Governor Benjamin Harrison that if the war continued for another year the settlers in Kentucky would be killed, held captive in Detroit, or forced to flee.

Between 1763 and 1783, most of the Indian nations between the Great Lakes and the Gulf Coast had united, at least in spirit, against the Americans, while giving tacit support to the British. South of the Ohio River and Kentucky, the Chickasaws, Creeks, Choctaws, and Chickamaugas particularly resisted American expansion. In 1763, the British, of course, wanted to ensure peace with the southern nations as well as those north of the Ohio River, but the pressure of white settlers made peace through diplomacy difficult to achieve. In May 1765, the British met with the Creeks in a council known as the Congress of Pensacola. Emisteseguo, Mortar, and The Wolf of the Upper Creeks, and Captain Allick, White Cabin, and Escochabey of the Lower Creeks, and some two dozen other leaders met with Governor George Johnstone and John Stuart, superintendent for Indian affairs in the Southern District. The British convinced them that the French would not return, and they promised to trade at Pensacola and Mobile at fair prices. The Creeks, in turn, agreed to a boundary running between Pensacola and Mobile and to the execution of all Creeks who killed whites. The Creeks were not happy about the agreement, but they did not want war. They quickly learned, however, that the British could not enforce treaty obligations and violations by the young men of both sides went unpunished. Persistent settlement of Creek lands by whites, who also stole their horses, kept relations tense. On November 2, 1771, Emisteseguo responded to Stuart's request for a land cession by saying, "My nation is numerous and every child in it has an equal property in the land with the first warriors[;] making any alteration in the boundary without the consent of the whole is improper." But their ongoing war with the Choctaws affirmed their need to keep the peace with the British. Moreover, Creek relations with the Spanish, operating from New Orleans, remained uneasy, because the Spaniards pressed them to accept Christianity and offered few trade goods, while the British sought trade and allegiance.[30]

Among the Indian groups in the Old Southwest, however, the Chickasaws had the reputation as the most skilled in the art of war. In 1775, the Chickasaws marshaled approximately 475 fighting men in a nation of 1,900 men, women, and children. Despite their small number, however, the other southern Indian nations, particularly the Choctaws, feared them. One observer noted that the Chickasaws were "arrogant and conseited [*sic*], high minded[,] touchy as tinder," and John Stuart recorded that they were "esteemed the bravest Indians on the Continent." The confident and often hostile spirit of the Chickasaws made them a nation of consequence and, in the words of Piomingo, chief of Techoukafala (the most populous village), they talked and fought to remain independent as a "people to our Selves."[31]

During the French and Indian War, the Chickasaws had relied on British trade to keep their enemies, both Indian and French, at bay. The British considered their allegiance "as Strong as Iron," and British Superintendent John Stuart always used the Chickasaws as a model of fidelity. When the war ended the British worked to keep the Chickasaws loyal and crafted an administrative system to help maintain mutual reliance. In 1764, the British divided Florida at the Chattahoochee River into East and West Florida. West Florida extended to the Mississippi River and bordered the thirty-first parallel on the north. Governor George Johnstone, along with John Stuart, administered British Indian policy from Pensacola, the capital of West Florida, for the territory south of the Ohio River. The Chickasaws were most concerned about protecting these lands from white encroachment and maintaining trade. To do so, they had to rely on the British to protect them from settlers whom they called Virginians. The Chickasaws, led by full-bloods Payamataha and Piomingo, particularly feared encirclement by whites, and they demanded the British survey a boundary and enforce it. After 1763, however, whites rushed into the Lower Mississippi Valley via the Ohio and Tennessee Rivers and crossed Chickasaw lands. Some did not leave. Traders also came among them and sometimes tampered with tribal politics. The British traders also wrought havoc in Chickasaw villages by exchanging rum for deerskins. The Chickasaws, then, were dependent on the British for trade and the guarantee of their lands, and they hoped the British would fulfill both responsibilities in reciprocity for

Chickasaw loyalty. In 1765, Payamataha, the leading war chief and prophet, told the British during a council at Mobile that "My Heart & the Superintendents are as one, it is well known I never deserted the British Interest and I never will. Tho' I am a Red Man my Heart is white from my Connections with & the Benefits I have received from the white People, I allmost [*sic*] look upon myself as one of them." Even so, the Chickasaws thought their own thoughts and acted in their own interests, not those of the British.[32]

On the eve of the American Revolution, the Spanish began their attempts to lure the Chickasaws away from the British as part of their plan to regain West Florida. At the same time, the Chickasaws refrained from getting involved in the conflict between the Shawnees and Virginians that led to Dunmore's War, and they maintained their British loyalty. In Detroit, commander Henry Hamilton planned to enlist the Chickasaws and the other tribes in the Lower Mississippi Valley, along with the Cherokees farther east, with the Shawnees and Delawares to strike the Americans. General Thomas Gage, in October 1775, ordered Superintendent Stuart to rally the tribes and "when opportunity offers . . . make them take arms against his Majesty's Enemies." Stuart responded in December 1775 by sending arms and ammunition to the Indian nations under his charge, including three thousand pounds of powder and lead to the Chickasaw villages to help them halt any American attack on British posts along the Gulf Coast. Gage, however, only wanted to use the southern Indians in coordination with his army to gain the best results, rather than encourage independent attacks that would endanger Loyalists while striking traitors. Essentially, then, the British offered trade, friendship, and limited military action, while the Americans sought neutrality. Neither, however, offered a guarantee of Indian lands. To the surprise of the British, however, the Chickasaws hesitated to give them their support by scouting along the Mississippi and Tennessee Rivers in order to report Spanish activities. The Choctaws also refused to act until the Chickasaws made a commitment to the British, Americans, or Spanish. For the moment, they, too, would wait and see.[33]

Superintendent Stuart, who had long advocated the importance of controlling the Indian trade to tie the southern nations to Great Britain and foil American and Spanish overtures, now gained authority to control all facets of that trade to bring and keep the Indians in the British camp. Stuart especially believed that if the British did not control the Indian trade, the rebels would use it to gain Indian allies and send them against the British. Stuart used Indian contacts, trade goods, tribal dependency, and American hostility, exemplified by violence and land grabbing, to strengthen the British presence in the South. The efforts of Stuart and his agents proved successful. In the spring of 1777, the Chickasaws told a British trader they could not "look upon them [the Americans] as brothers as they are surrounding them on all Sides, and debar[r]ing them from all Necessaries and Destroying their friends." At the same time, Stuart called for the Chickasaws, Choctaws, and Creeks to send delegates to a council in Mobile where the British would then gain their support against the Spanish and Americans. Beginning on May 1 and continuing into June, some 2,800 villagers listened to the British agents, who told them about the relentless American theft of Indian lands. Thereafter, American initiatives among the Chickasaws met rejection. Later that year, Stuart told a delegation of Lower Creeks at Pensacola that "if the Rebels should prove victorious you may be certainly assured that they would immediately endeavour to possess themselves of all your lands and extirpate you."[34]

The southern Indians did not doubt that the Americans wanted their lands, and they knew their needs for trade goods could only be met by the British, not the Americans, while both made war. This assessment proved correct because rebel traders had difficulty acquiring goods, but British agents at Pensacola had considerable supplies received by sea. Moreover, many southern Indian leaders trusted Stuart, and he encouraged them to side with the British for trade and protection. As a result, in 1778, George Rogers Clark sent couriers to the Chickasaws, whom he considered the "most potent southern nation," to make peace, but he reported, "[T]heir conversation on the subject was cool and answered no great purpose."[35]

A year later in May 1779, Virginia sent a message to the Chickasaws that offered them either peace or war. War leaders Mingo Houma, Payamataha, and Tuskau Pautaupau responded that the Ohio Indians constantly warned them that the Americans would stop at nothing to take their lands, so peace and friendship was an impossibility. The Chickasaw leaders clearly and emphatically also told the Virginians that "[w]e desire no other friendship of you but only desire you will inform us when you are Comeing and we will save you the trouble of Coming quite here for we will meet you half Way. . . . Take care that we don't serve you as we have served the French before with all their Indians, send you back without your heads." Clearly the Chickasaws could not be intimidated by the Americans. "We are," they said, "a Nation that fears or Values no Nation as long as our Great Father King George stands by us for you may depend as long as life lasts with us we will hold him fast by the hand." Then, the chiefs asked the Virginians to print their message in the newspapers so "that all your people may see it and know who it was from. We are men & Warriors and don't want our Talks hidden." When the Americans built Fort Jefferson five miles below the mouth of the Ohio on the Mississippi River, the Chickasaws and Choctaws made it too dangerous to occupy, and the fort was abandoned in June 1781. Thereafter, the Americans remained content with the Ohio River as their line of conquest.[36]

When Spain declared war on Great Britain in June 1779, Governor Bernardo de Galvéz at New Orleans also attempted to strike an alliance with the Creeks and Choctaws to remove them as British auxiliaries and enhance his chance to seize Natchez and Pensacola and occupy West Florida. But when Payamataha learned about these overtures, he warned the Choctaws to "return immediately to the English," or he would send the Chickamaugas, the pro-British Cherokees who had recently settled west of the Appalachians, and the Shawnees against them, which Alexander Cameron, agent for the Chickasaws and Choctaws, reported "had a good effect upon them." Improved trade also encouraged the Creeks and Choctaws to help the British defend Pensacola in April 1780. At that time, some 1,500 Creeks, led by Alexander McGillivray, assistant British commissary in the Upper Creek towns, who also had blood ties to the Creeks through his mother, helped the British discourage the Spanish from attacking. Several months later on September 14, the Creeks helped foil an American attack on Augusta in a sharp fight in which 250 Creeks joined British regulars in driving back 600 Americans. Creek losses, however, proved heavy, and they executed the captured Americans in retribution. This engagement was the only major Indian contribution to the war in the Southwest, in part because the British focused their effort in Georgia and the Carolinas. Even so, the war bitterly divided the Creeks, whose factions remained hostile within the nation as well as against the Americans long after the conflict ended.[37]

By the early 1780s, British supply of trade goods had become parsimonious for reasons of political economy. As British trade goods declined, Chickasaw leaders increasingly turned their attention to accommodation with the Americans and the Spanish, the latter of whom had captured Baton Rouge, Natchez, and, on May 9, 1781, Pensacola, the last British stronghold and Indian supply center in West Florida. The Chickasaws, however, remained loyal and struck Spanish positions in West Florida and closed the Mississippi River to shipping between New Orleans and St. Louis, even capturing Donā Anicanora Ramos, the wife of Francisco Cruzat, lieutenant governor of Spanish Illinois, and her four children. The Spanish could not muster sufficient strength to invade Chickasaw territory and ultimately negotiated for the return of these high-priced captives. By the end of the American Revolution, however, factions emerged with the anti-British

Chickasaws supporting the Spanish, while the old British allies transferred allegiance to the Americans. During the last eighteen months of the war, then, British influence over the southern Indians declined rapidly and the Americans gave all the nations west of the Appalachians little attention, because they were preoccupied with the British army to the east. At best, the British could only encourage the southern nations to make peace with the Spanish in order to strike the Americans. In the end, Great Britain's strategy to use the southern Indians against the settlers in the backcountry drove those villagers into the American camp for the want of needed trade goods on which they depended, and both the British and the Indians lost the war on the trans-Appalachian frontier.

In the summer of 1783, the Shawnees, Delawares, Chickasaws, Creeks, and other tribes west of the Appalachians learned that the British and Americans had inexplicably made peace. The British told their Indian allies that they had ceded all lands south of the Great Lakes, but that the Americans would respect the Ohio River as the boundary with the Indian nations to the north as provided by the Treaty of Fort Stanwix. The Treaty of Paris, however, offered no such guarantees, and it did not even mention the Indians. The Shawnees, Delawares, and Munsees were "thunder struck" by the terms of the Treaty of Paris, because the British essentially had given away Indian lands that the Americans had neither held nor won, and they doubted the frontier people would respect their lands north of the Ohio. The northern and western Indian people, however, believed the Treaty of Fort Stanwix should be respected by the whites, whether British or American. They may not have liked the treaty when the Iroquois negotiated it in 1768, but they had come to accept it, and they thought the American government should also honor it. Frederick Haldimand, governor of Canada, understood their apprehension and unwillingness to forfeit more land, because the Americans said they were entitled to the land for defeating the British. In November 1783, Haldimand told Lord North, who headed the British government during the war, that the tribes would not give up easily because "these People my Lord, have as enlightened Ideas of the nature & Obligations of Treaties as the most Civilized nations have, and know that no Infringement of the Treaty of 1768 ... Can be binding upon them without their Express Concurrence & Consent." Peace for the British, however, was now more important than war, and although the British intended to maintain friendly relations with the Indians in order to use them as auxiliaries against the United States if war came again, they considered the Indians expendable in 1783. To the south, the Creeks called the news a "Virginia Lie."[38]

While the British had been swift to give away Creek, Chickasaw, and Choctaw lands, the Americans had been even quicker to take it. Although the Indians did not consider themselves defeated, officials of the republic considered the United States a conqueror and acted accordingly by dictating, blustering, and ordering about the Indians as a defeated people. Almost immediately they antagonized the western nations with their victory. At a prisoner exchange in July 1783 near the falls of the Ohio (present-day Louisville), an officer told the Shawnee that "Your Fathers the English have made Peace with us for themselves, but forgot you their Children, who Fought with them, and neglected you like Bastards."[39]

To the southwest, the Chickasaws somewhat ambivalently accepted the news that the British and Americans had made peace. In November 1783 many Chickasaw chiefs met in council with the Americans at French Lick near Nashville and agreed to a treaty. There, they pledged to return their prisoners and expel the enemies of the United States from the Chickasaw territory. Mingo Houma and Tuskau Pautaupau (referred to as the Red King in the treaty) received a promise from the American commissioners that whites would respect Chickasaw boundaries, stop settling on their lands, and recognize the Cumberland-Tennessee divide from the Ohio to the Duck River as the boundary between them.

The Chickasaws firmly reminded the commissioners that they would never cede their land and that they had no power to sell it. After the treaty council, the majority of the Chickasaws drifted into the American camp because they were most like the British, and they hated the Spanish for sending the Kickapoos against them during the war. Spain, however, moved quickly to counter American influence and signed its own treaty with the pro-Spanish Chickasaws in June 1784, at Mobile. Here these Chickasaws pledged loyalty to Spain and promised to release their captives. They also accepted Spanish protection and traders. Spain, in turn, pledged to expel white settlers and provide abundant goods at fair prices.

In the days ahead, however, the friendly association of the Chickasaws with the Americans caused the Creeks to worry about their security. Alexander McGillivray quickly saw the Chickasaws as a danger to his plans for the creation of a pan-Indian alliance against the Americans. Soon the Creeks responded to the Treaty of Paris by making war on both the Americans and the Chickasaws. Led by McGillivray and supported by the Spanish at New Orleans, the Creeks held firm against the Americans, who considered all lands west of the Appalachians theirs by right of conquest after defeating the British. By the mid-1780s with the British gone and the Americans pressing onto Creek lands, McGillivray sought a marriage of convenience with the Spanish to ensure trade and recognition of their sovereignty. McGillivray did not believe the American government would be able to restrain land-hungry settlers from seizing Creek lands, but he thought the Spanish might be interested in helping them keep those lands from the Americans. McGillivray intended to encourage the Spanish to guarantee Creek lands as a buffer between Spain and the Americans and thereby help the Spanish press their claims north of the Tennessee River.

The Spanish proved receptive because they planned to extend the disputed northern boundary of West Florida as far north as possible, and they intended to use the Indian nations to help consolidate their claims to the Mississippi River valley. In the spring of 1783, Don Esteban Miró, governor of Florida, met with the Creeks, Chickasaws, Choctaws, and Chickamaugas at Pensacola. Miró opened the council by telling them: "Do not be afraid of the Americans. You our brothers the red men, are not without friends. The Americans have no King, and are nothing of themselves."[40]

Meanwhile, the Confederation Congress gave the Indians little thought, and it did not authorize a commission to negotiate peace treaties with them until March 15, 1785. By that time, however, McGillivray and the Creeks had asserted leadership among the southwestern tribes. As a result, on July 10, 1785, the Creeks, Chickasaws, and Choctaws met in council at Little Tallahassee in the Creek Nation and agreed to support McGillivray in rejecting the British land cession to the Americans west of the Appalachians, because they were not party to the Treaty of Paris. At that time, McGillivray, speaking for the assembled nations, warned that "as we were not partys, so we are determined to pay no attention to the Manner in which the British Negotiators has drawn out the Lines of the Lands in question Ceded to the States of America—it being a Notorious fact known to the Americans, known to every person who is in any ways conversant in, or acquainted with American affairs, that his Brittannick Majesty was never possessed either by session purchase or by right of Conquest of our Territory . . . which the Said treaty gives away." McGillivray, who had a quick mind and skillful prose, further proclaimed: "On the contrary it is well known that from the first Settlement of the English colonys of Carolina and Georgia up to the date of the Said treaty no tittle has ever been or pretended to be made by his Brittanic Majesty to our lands except what was obtained by free Gift or by purchase for good and valuable Considerations."[41]

Yet, the Chickasaws remained divided and on January 10, 1786, Piomingo, Mingatushka, and Latopoia signed a treaty with the American commissioners at Hopewell, South Carolina. In the Treaty of Hopewell, the Chickasaws agreed to peace and placed themselves "under the protection of the United States of America, and of no other sovereign whatsoever." In a little understood, but ominous clause, these Chickasaws also agreed "for the benefit and comfort of the Indians" that the United States would manage their affairs as the government officials "think proper." To the north the Ohio Indians prevented the Americans from seizing their lands and overrunning Detroit during the war, but they had been too far from the major fighting to affect the outcome of the American Revolution. Yet during the war they had fought for their independence as much as the white American patriots. Once the war ended, however, they collectively became the enemy of the new nation. In addition, many villages relocated to escape American pressures and the inhabitants suffered dislocation, and polyglot communities formed, often under new leaders. At the same time, white outsiders increasingly interfered with tribal politics, and British, American, and Spanish emissaries cultivated client chiefs to help them work their will against the others. The war also made the tribes increasingly dependent on the Americans for trade goods. Certainly, the American Revolution did not bring peace to the Indians west of the Appalachians, but no one could foresee that both Indians and whites would contest for the trans-Appalachian frontier militarily and politically to gain exclusion and power over the other for another thirty years.[42]

Still, no American soldiers occupied Indian lands north of the Ohio when the war ended, nor did they occupy the Illinois country or the Mississippi River valley, and the Shawnees, like the Creeks and other tribes, were unwilling to accept defeat based on a piece of paper. The war had ended, not because the Americans had forced the Indians to surrender, but because the British decided to make peace and urged the Indians to stop fighting. They had not lost militarily, but they had been defeated diplomatically. At the same time, the American Revolution created a greater sense of pan-American identity. So far as the Indians in the Ohio country were concerned, even though the great tide of white settlement had cost them their lands south of the river, the land north of the Ohio belonged to them. Anyone who claimed Indian land would pay a high price in blood to take it. Soon after the war, in 1785, Captain Johnny or Kekewepelethe, a Shawnee war leader, told the Americans at a council, "You are drawing so close to us that we can almost hear the noise of your axes felling our Trees and settling our Country." If white settlers crossed the Ohio, he warned, "[W]e shall take up a Rod and whip them back to your side." The future loomed ominously for both Indians and whites north and south of the Ohio.[43]

CHAPTER 2

The Spanish Southwest

In 1763 government officials in New Spain greeted the Treaty of Paris with considerable apprehension. The French provision for the transfer of Upper and Lower Louisiana west of the Mississippi River to Spain, as compensation for its partnership against Great Britain during the French and Indian War, required redrawing its northern and eastern boundaries on the North American continent. Spain's land windfall, however, brought more problems than advantages, only a part of which involved the threat of territorial acquisition by the British or Americans. Although the addition of French Louisiana to the Spanish Empire considerably increased its colonial territory by untold thousands of square miles and provided a sweeping buffer between the "silver provinces" of northern Mexico and British America, the drawbacks were enormous, and all of them related to the Indians in this newly acquired territory, as well as to those whom the Spanish had been trying to Christianize and Hispanicize for nearly a century in present-day Texas, New Mexico, and Arizona.[1]

The Spanish did not worry about the relatively prosperous agricultural people whom they called Pueblos because they lived in settled, compact villages, where flat-roofed, adobe houses of several stories formed plazas or squares. Although the Pueblos had rebelled against the Spanish in 1680 and drove them south into Mexico, the soldiers and government officials reasserted control in the 1690s. Thereafter, the Pueblos lived peacefully under Spanish rule and selectively integrated Iberian with native cultural practices.

The Pueblos, who descended from the Anasazi, formed a complex cultural group and divided into western and eastern branches. The Hopis in present-day Arizona and the Zunis, Acomas, and Lagunas in New Mexico comprise the Western Pueblos. Most of the Eastern Pueblos reside in the watershed of the Rio Grande in New Mexico and include more than a dozen groups. The Western and Eastern Pueblos spoke mutually unintelligible languages and organized matrilineally by clan, but the Eastern Pueblos relied on moieties, such as Winter and Summer among the Tanoans or Squash and Turquoise for the Keresans, to provide social structure for their villages. Both Western and Eastern Pueblos used a host of

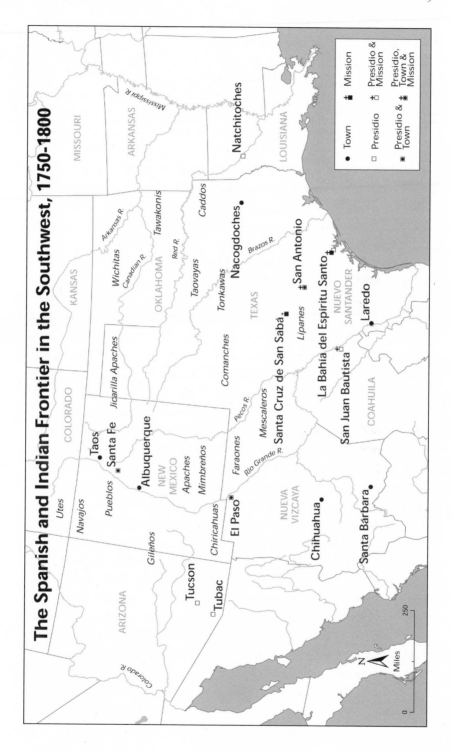

The Spanish and Indian Frontier in the Southwest, 1750-1800

societies or organizations to conduct various aspects of strictly village business. Although the Pueblos had many similarities, they did not unify politically, but religious societies appointed individuals to various offices created by the Spanish, such as pueblo governor, to represent the village to civil authorities and help give system and order to Spanish rule. The Pueblos prized conformity to community social traditions and values rather than individual achievements. By 1763, the Pueblos had accommodated Spanish political authority and gave nominal allegiance to the Catholic Church, while secretly maintaining their own religious practices. Pueblo men and women worked in the fields and raised corn, beans, squash, and cotton, and traded for desired goods with the Spanish. The Pueblos had ceased to pose a threat to the Spaniards.

In contrast, Spanish authorities feared the aggressive British and Americans, whom they believed would ally with the Indians to the north and use them to endanger Spanish mining villages and ranches or seize Spanish territory. Indeed, the Comanches and Apaches rather than European powers or American settlers primarily threatened the northern frontier of New Spain, and the Spanish hoped to use the Pueblos as auxiliary troops under the command of their own war leaders, subject to overall supervision by Spanish officers to defend New Mexico from the nomadic tribes that raided from the north and east.

By the mid-eighteenth century the Spanish particularly feared the Comanches. This Indian nation, known for its ferocity and love of war, occupied widely scattered villages south of the Arkansas with its eastern range extending to Louisiana, while the western boundary of the Comanchería faded into New Mexico. Hunting and fighting helped create a strong sense of identity, although they readily adopted captives to help regenerate their bands due to losses from disease and war. Custom and a consciousness of their likeness bound the Comanche nation together rather than political structure. A council of elders, each representing a family, gave the Comanche bands a loose political organization and structure. Peacetime leaders or chiefs represented the councils in broader tribal discussions. They held only advisory powers and met in council with the chiefs of the other bands to decide civil matters. In contrast to the peace chiefs, who gained their positions with their generosity, wisdom, and temperament, the war chiefs earned their leadership positions by demonstrating bravery on a raiding or war party, and Comanche males preferred death in battle to dying of old age. War brought honor, respect, and status, as well as wealth from stolen horses and other booty. Horses served as the Comanches' principal medium of exchange, especially for firearms purchased from traders.

In 1776, Father Francisco Atanasio Domínguez observed the Taos trade fair where the Comanches sold "buffalo hides, 'white elk skins,' horses, mules, buffalo meat, pagan Indians . . . good guns, pistols, powder, balls, tobacco, hatchets, and some vessels of yellow tin." He also reported, "They acquire these articles, from the guns to the vessels, from the Jumanas Indians," a clear indication of the extensive trade network on the southern Great Plains that linked the Indians with the French to the east. Much of this exchange had symbolic and cultural meaning. Medals obtained from Europeans became symbols of authority, and European dyes for face paints had ceremonial importance. The Comanches also proved to be skillful traders who set market prices or the exchange rate. They were not mere consumers of manufactured goods from outside traders. Father Domínguez reported: "If they sell a pistol its price is a bridle."[2]

The Comanches measured prestige in horses and valor, both of which could be best gained by making war. Their horse herds, with individuals owning from ten to forty, often expanded under the management of forced labor, and the Comanches exchanged captive women among themselves, other nations, and the Spanish, for improved breeding stock. In September 1807, John Sibley, Indian agent for Western Louisiana, reported to Thomas Jefferson that the Comanches had "a large number of very fine horses and mules mostly raised by themselves." From the broad expanse of the southern Great Plains, they used their horses to strike at will against Hispanic settlements and missions in Texas and New Mexico.[3]

By the 1730s, the southward-moving Comanches had begun to push the Apaches into southwestern Texas and eastern New Mexico, and they increasingly raided Spanish missions and settlements to meet both cultural and economic needs. Neither the Spanish nor the Apaches could stop them, and while raids against the Apaches always proved challenging, the Spanish were almost too easy an enemy for the young men who needed to earn honor in war. When not taking advantage of Spanish weakness, the Comanches often traded with the Wichitas along the Arkansas for French and later British and American goods, especially exchanging Spanish horses and Apache captives for guns, knives, cloth, needles, awls, and paint. By 1763, the Comanches had deprived the Apaches of the buffalo range on the southern Great Plains, and the Apaches had fallen back by necessity to the Spanish frontier, where they could steal livestock from the missions and ranches for food, as well as horses to replace those that the Comanches had taken from them, particularly near San Antonio. The Comanches, then, were a powerful, aggressive, even arrogant people who ranged from the Missouri River to the Rio Grande in Texas and to the Sangre de Cristo Mountains in New Mexico. The

Comanches also often allied with other Indian nations to the north, and Spain had neither the men nor the money to fight them.

Apaches were also a diffuse people, who lived in loose divisions rather than unified tribes. The Apaches did not recognize any national or tribal government and their chiefs held authority only during war, thereby making contacts and peace negotiations difficult. The Apache nations divided into tribes or bands that included the Gileños, Jicarilla, Chiricahuas, Mescaleros, and Lipanes. The Chiricahuas lived in southwestern New Mexico and the Jicarilla in northeastern New Mexico, while the Mescaleros and Lipanes resided along the Rio Grande and Pecos River valleys. The Gilenōs camped in present-day Arizona and raided across southern New Mexico and Arizona. As early as 1720, the eastern Apache nations had made a regular practice of attacking San Antonio and running off the livestock, especially the horses of the missions and presidios. A dozen years later, Apache attacks had nearly overrun San Antonio and the garrison commander pleaded with the governor of Texas to negotiate a peace. "Otherwise," he said, "this Presidio with its towns and Missions will be exposed to total destruction." In contrast, the cultural needs of the Spanish, which shaped Indian policy, emphasized the spread of Christianity, territorial expansion, and exploitation of natural resources—all of which required peace and stability.[4]

Another Apache group, the Navajos, lived west of New Mexico. The Navajos were the most recent Athapaskan migrants to the Southwest, arriving only a few centuries before the Spanish. They developed a close economic and social relationship with the Pueblos, selectively adopting agricultural and ceremonial practices. They lived atop well-guarded mesas in round houses, called hogans, made from brush and poles covered with earth. A complicated clan system and matrilineal extended families gave order and meaning to their lives. They did not have a unified governmental structure, although the Spanish attempted to impose an elected governor and lieutenant governor from among them, while leaving local control to the headmen. Although the Navajos lived in peace with the Spanish by 1763, relations deteriorated during the 1780s when the Spanish insisted that they join the war against the Apaches.

The Utes lived northwest of New Mexico across the San Juan River. They met their food needs by hunting and gathering. The Utes gave primary allegiance to the band but did not recognize any authority that could link the bands politically. Mutual language, friendship, and marriage across the bands helped give them unity. Leadership within the band depended on gaining and keeping reputations in war and through generosity. Leaders constantly attended to the matters of organizing hunting and war parties, which became more productive after the adoption of the horse, to maintain political power, which entitled them to lead by persuasion. Although the Utes preferred peace with the Spanish, they considered Hispanic livestock theirs for the taking.

Although the Spanish missionaries had some success at Hispanicizing Pueblo Indians, they had failed to teach nomads European agricultural practices and settle them near missions where the Franciscan fathers could monitor their behavior with the help of presidial soldiers. Nomads, in contrast to farming peoples, would not stay put at the missions, and Spain lacked sufficient force to subdue them. In early January 1773, Pedro Fermín de Mendinueta, governor of New Mexico, reported what most Spanish officials already knew. The Indians could not be attracted to the "tranquil magnificence" of the Catholic Church, he wrote, unless God "enlightens their understanding."[5]

While Spain had tried to convert plains peoples, French Indian policy, emanating from New Orleans and executed through Natchitoches, had emphasized the purchase of peaceful tribal behavior in East Texas and Louisiana. Traders bought peace as a matter of government policy by exchanging guns, powder, and lead, as well as a host of other consumer goods that kept the nations satisfied and dependent on the French. Spanish officials in Mexico City had considered French Indian policy dangerous, and refused to furnish Indians with firearms, but now they had inherited a vast and unwanted territory with uncounted Indian nations that had become accustomed to trading for guns and whose members would easily turn to the British if Spain did not meet their needs and wants. Rather than unarmed Pueblos, Spanish officials faced well-armed, hostile Comanches and other Indians from the interior, especially the Kiowas, Wichitas, and Pawnees, whom they called the Nations of the North. These *indios bárbaros* attacked their missions and presidios, stealing horses and cattle, and killing the Indian converts or "neophytes."[6]

British traders and French smugglers supplied guns that reached the southern tribes through an elaborate and systematic trading system. The western Comanches, for example, sold guns to the Pueblos in New Mexico for horses and livestock, while the Wichitas, Pawnees, and other nations often served as middlemen and traded firearms to the Comanches in Texas for stolen Spanish horses. The eastern Comanches, cut off from their firearms supply in French Louisiana, began trading Spanish horses to the western Comanches for guns. The Comanches then traded their horses to the northern tribes for more firearms, powder, and lead. The Omahas and Poncas controlled the weapons trade from

British Illinois and kept their trading partners to the south well supplied with guns for horses and hides. Often the Indians had more supplies and better firearms than those possessed by presidial soldiers. The Indians also usually had more ammunition for target practice, and they proved better marksmen than the Spanish soldiers and militiamen.

In 1763, then, Spanish soldiers on the northern frontier were not only outnumbered but poorly armed compared to the Indians whom they were expected to control, and Indian allegiance went to the British and French traders who supplied them with guns, powder, and lead. Consequently, Spain could not realistically hope to gain administrative control of its new territorial possession or expand settlements north of San Antonio and east of Santa Fe. Even a defensive position presented considerable problems. The presidial line that guarded the two-thousand-mile frontier, that is, the northernmost boundary that Spain tried to claim with force, extended far beyond its military capabilities to guarantee. In Texas and New Mexico alone, approximately ten thousand Indian fighting men confronted fewer than two thousand Spanish soldiers and militiamen. The presidios remained isolated, exposed, and undermanned. Comanche and Apache raiders swept through the line and around the presidios without danger to steal horses, mules, and cattle. Often the Apaches struck deep into the province of Nueva Vizcaya (today's Chihuahua and Durango in present-day Mexico), and they essentially controlled southern Arizona, southern New Mexico, and southwestern Texas. The Comanches, Utes, and the Nations of the North controlled much of the remaining interior territory claimed by Spain.

Confronted by a well-armed and mobile enemy, many soldiers and some government officials advocated retreat from the northern missions and posts and a reevaluation of Spanish Indian policy. In 1758 the commander at the presidio at La Bahía del Espíritu Santo on the Gulf Coast southeast of San Antonio agreed and reported, "The enemy [is] so superior . . . in firearms as well as in numbers that our destruction seems probable." Indeed, the recent attack by two thousand well-armed, Comanche-led raiders on the newly founded Franciscan mission of San Sabá about 175 miles northwest of San Antonio killed eight people, including the priest, and led to more disaster upon retaliation. Although the Comanches may have contributed only eight hundred to the raiding party, this attack marked the first major conflict between this Indian nation and the Spanish, and it proved a harbinger of difficult days to come. Indeed, a Spanish expedition bent on revenge under the command of Colonel Diego Ortiz Parrilla resulted in fifty-two soldiers killed or wounded at a fortified Wichita village on the Red

River, where the Comanches and their allies proved expert marksmen with French guns. The attack on San Sabá and the army's failure to extract retribution halted Spanish attempts to expand its control north and west of San Antonio with missions and presidios. Clearly then, by 1763, Spanish Indian policy smoldered in ruins. The army could not protect the missions, and its soldiers were outmanned, outgunned, and outfought. Spain could not control the northern territory that it had claimed for more than a century, let alone marshal the resources to bring the Louisiana Territory and its Indian peoples under Spanish jurisdiction.[7]

As a result, in 1765, Carlos III, king of Spain, sent the marqués de Rubí, a distinguished veteran officer, to inspect the northern frontier defenses and propose necessary reforms. Rubí arrived in December, by which time Comanche and Apache attacks on Spanish settlements had become a nightmare, and the British saw the Spanish Southwest as an attractive possibility. On March 10, 1766, after delays of every sort, Rubí rode north with a small entourage to inspect the presidios that marked, if not protected, the northern frontier. Rubí's tour covered 7,600 miles and took two years to complete. His findings were not encouraging. First, he learned that the Apache nations firmly held the lands that stretched from southwestern Texas to California, an area the Spaniards called Gran Apachería. Here, the Apache bands, after being driven south and west by the Comanches, developed a taste for cattle, horses, and mules, in the absence of buffalo, which they eagerly and appreciatively took from the Spanish with such a vengeance that they had earned a reputation for "extreme cruelty." Rubí also found upon reaching Santa Fe on August 19, that the only presidio in New Mexico was surrounded by hostile Apaches to the south and southwest, Navajos to the west, Utes to the north, and Comanches to the east, and in the words of his engineer Nicolás de Lafora, "incapable of defense." Rubí then traveled west to the presidio of Tubac about forty miles south of Tucson. This unfortified and exposed presidio could not provide more than a minimal Spanish presence on this portion of the northern frontier. When the Gileño Apaches struck it during his visit, Rubí observed that these Apache raiders were the "most feared" by the soldiers, and he considered the abandonment of Tubac the best course of action.[8]

Lafora considered the presidial officers and soldiers here and elsewhere on the northern frontier nothing less than incompetent. The poorly trained and equipped soldiers, he reported, were "totally ignorant of how to handle a musket," while the officers were, "for the most part, more ignorant and less accustomed to fighting than the men." Lafora also wrote, "[T]he enemy knows perfectly well how to take advantage of this. The enemy are amazing in their conduct, vigilance, speed, order, and endurance when they are raiding and retreating with their prizes. They use stratagems which always deceive our men."[9]

A year had now passed since Rubí began his reconnaissance, but he turned back toward Texas. In July 1767, he reached the presidio of San Sabá, which he considered "of no advantage whatever." Little more than a week later he arrived at the presidio of San Antonio de Béjar, founded in 1718 and the largest settlement in Texas. There some eight hundred Indians huddled near five missions and lived in terror of the Comanches and Nations of the North, who frequently raided the area. He also found the other missions, scattered as far east as the Louisiana border, virtually "useless" and a waste of money and troops.[10]

Rubí also learned that the Comanches and other plains tribes were better armed and thus more dangerous than the Apaches. Lafora agreed, and wrote, "[O]ur safety in that province [Texas] is entirely dependent upon their fidelity. They have little respect for the Spanish and we are admitted only as friends, but without any authority." Lafora felt helpless and embarrassed, and he lamented, "How disrespectful to the honorable forces of his Majesty, supposed to maintain law and order! . . . Here they are in the shameful position of supplicants." Rubí believed, however, that these nations could be allied with Spain against the Apaches. Moreover, the Comanches and the Nations of the North pressed hard on the presidios and missions, in part, because the Spanish offered protection to some of their Apache enemies. The Comanches and Nations of the North, however, had proven that they could honor peace treaties with New Mexico and Louisiana respectively, and they had not tried to use their superior numbers and firearms to overrun New Mexico. As a result, Rubí believed the Spanish had to pursue a more realistic Indian policy.[11]

By the time that Rubí returned to Mexico City on February 23, 1768, he had inspected twenty-three of twenty-four frontier presidios and seen firsthand "the tremendous damage His Majesty's subjects suffer daily from the barbarians." He had also observed poorly located presidios, garrisons inadequately trained and equipped, and commanders who made corruption with payrolls and supplies a way of life. Rubí recognized as clearly as any Spanish frontier official that the mission system had utterly failed to pacify Indians on horseback. With notes in hand and observations in mind, Rubí then drafted his general report to the king, which he submitted on April 3, 1768, to Julián de Arriaga, minister of the Indies. A month later he recommended basic changes to Spain's haphazard Indian policy. Rubí informed the king that Spain could not control the regions that it did not occupy. Most of present-day Texas, New Mexico, and Arizona really were only "imaginary dominions" of the king because hostile Indians controlled those lands. Indeed, Rubí's recommendations officially recognized that Spanish expansion northward had ceased. The Apaches and Comanches had halted the Spanish advance and even pushed back the frontier. In short, Rubí recommended that Spain abandon its efforts to expand the empire, draw a realistic frontier line, that is, boundary, and keep the hostile Indians north of it with well-manned and equipped garrisons.[12]

Specifically, Rubí first called for the construction of a "cordon of Presidios," fifteen in all, each with fifty well-equipped soldiers, located at one-hundred-mile intervals, stretching from the Gulf of Mexico to the Gulf of California, running roughly along the present border of the United States and Mexico. The presidios of Santa Fe and San Antonio, which stood far north of the line but whose population, property, and converts could not be written off, would be protected by eighty men each. These presidios would create a "separate frontier" north of the line for the protection of the Hispanic settlers and Christian Indians who lived nearby as well as serve as the first line of defense for the settlers and presidios to the south. He also recommended presidial design and structural changes as well as ways to make the frontier soldiers more efficient, the system less corrupt, and the army better able to pursue a "continuous offensive war" for the extermination of the Apaches and any other hostile tribes.[13]

In these recommendations Rubí essentially posed European solutions for American frontier problems. He failed to realize that a chain of presidios created a porous line at best for mounted Apache and Comanche raiders and that the Indians never assaulted a presidio because their goal was to capture the horse herd and inflict enough casualties to revenge a particular grievance. Even so, Rubí recognized that Spain had overextended its ability to possess its northern frontier to say nothing of its newly acquired Louisiana Territory or keeping the tribes peaceful. Moreover, he realistically urged Spain to retreat temporarily to a fortified position along the thirtieth parallel for the purpose of asserting control of the territory that it actually occupied, an area he said, that should be considered the "dominion and true possession of the king." Instead of pursuing "the rule of pushing domination forward," Rubí contended that Spain needed to consolidate its position and populate the lands that it controlled. Then, Spain could expand north to Canada and colonize Alta California. Rubí also proposed a corollary to this policy of retrenchment with a recommendation for Spain to form alliances with the Comanches and Nations of the North to enable a joint campaign against the Apaches, whom he considered the most troublesome of the Indians on the Spanish frontier.[14]

Indeed, Rubí recommended the expulsion of the Apaches from nearly every mission, presidio, and settlement on the frontier. By cutting the Apaches adrift from Spanish protection and commitments, the Comanches and the Nations of the North could wage relentless war against them. The Spanish would then join with those powerful and allied tribes to threaten the destruction of the Apache people. Caught in a pincher, the Apaches could either surrender unconditionally or face extermination. Those captured in war would be dispersed deep in Mexico where they would be Christianized and assimilated with the peaceful Indians. Those tribes that sought peace would be required to prove their sincerity through a prisoner exchange, then they could settle near a presidio. At the same time, Spain would overlook minor transgressions, such as occasional horse stealing and murders by the peaceful tribes. By so doing, Rubí recognized that a purely military solution could not be applied to all the Indian tribes given their numerical superiority and mobility. Still, military force remained an essential feature of Spanish policy for its dealings with the Indians on the northern frontier.

Rubí's suggestions, however, did not become policy until the king gave them official sanction on September 10, 1772, as the *New Regulations of Presidios*, also known as the *Royal Regulations*. These royal regulations included Rubí's recommendations as well as a provision for a new frontier office of commander-inspector to implement those instructions and direct all military affairs (instead of the governors) in the northern provinces. The commander-inspector would realign the presidios, make strategic plans, and coordinate attacks against the Indians. Viceroy Antonio María de Bucareli appointed Lieutenant Colonel Don Hugo O'Conor to that office in September 1772. O'Conor, a professional soldier who spoke Spanish with an Irish accent, had served on the northern frontier since 1765, including as provisional governor of Texas from 1767 to 1770. His red hair earned him the nickname "Captain Red" among the Indians. O'Conor had an eye for terrain and a mind for strategy and tactics as well as energy and will. He would need all of these strengths to achieve two tasks: relocate the presidios and launch an offensive against the Apaches.[15]

By the spring of 1773, O'Conor had begun the realignment of the presidios. Little more than two years later, he had moved or closed all presidios north of the present-day, U.S.-Mexican border, except Santa Fe, San Antonio, and La Bahía, and he moved the garrison from Tubac in Sonora to the Pima village of Tucson. North of that line, the Apaches, Comanches, and other tribes had free rein as Spain attempted to consolidate its defenses. In New Mexico alone, the Apaches took advantage of the Spanish retreat to attack settlements and peaceful Indian communities, killing at least 243 Hispanics by the end of the decade. Apaches found Hispanics especially vulnerable because they insisted on living on scattered ranches and farms. Other raids went unanswered. In present-day Arizona, the soldiers could not protect the missions, such as Tumacácori or San Xavier, which the Apaches destroyed, or the presidial horse herd at Tubac.

On March 5, Father Bartolomé Ximeno wrote from Tumacácori that the government had failed to provide "prompt, active, and efficacious measures to contain the Apaches." He particularly blamed the military for permitting Apache attacks on the missions by inaction, which made the Papagos afraid to settle near them and convert to Spanish ways. Father Ximeno sarcastically observed: "I think that on these frontiers gunpowder has lost all the power and effectiveness the Author of Nature bestowed on it. In so many murders, robberies, and atrocities committed by the Apaches since I have been at this mission, I have never heard it said that our men killed a single Apache." Little changed and Apache attacks continued against Hispanic and friendly Indian settlements, such as the Pima, Papago, and Yuma, and the loss of lives, horses, and cattle mounted.[16]

In September 1775, however, O'Conor set 1,500 presidial and provincial troops against the Apaches and drove them to the headwaters of the Gila in western New Mexico where he continued to harass the bands until winter forced the soldiers to withdraw, but not before they had killed 138 warriors and captured 104 men, women, and children, and nearly two thousand horses and mules in fifteen engagements. O'Conor, however, achieved even greater success against the Apaches through the Comanches, who between September and December 1776, killed more than three hundred families caught buffalo hunting along the Colorado River in Texas. O'Conor made no attempt to make peace with the Apaches. Instead, he followed the established policy of extermination, a policy that Spain would pursue for another decade before giving it up in vain.

At the same time, the Spanish lost approximately six lives for every Comanche killed in New Mexico and Texas. As O'Conor said of the presidio of San Sabá, all of the presidios on the northern frontier provided as much protection to the interests of the king "as a ship anchored in mid-Atlantic would afford in preventing foreign trade with America." In 1776, he reported that the Comanches were the "lords of the broad country lying between the mountains of New Mexico and the Missouri River. They are as a people of such number and hardiness that they consider themselves as numerous as the stars." Even so, he considered the Apaches the greater problem on New Spain's northern frontier. The Apaches, he wrote, "commit bloody insults; and among all the nations . . . are the most fearsome not only because of the firearms that they now have acquired from the English which they can use skillfully but also for their valor and intrepidity and because they are not accustomed to flee, preferring to win the engagement or die." By 1776, however, the presidial line recommended by Rubí had been established and the Apaches forced back, but Spain had gained little security on the northern frontier.[17]

In January 1777, O'Conor resigned as commander-inspector after Carlos III reorganized the governing structure of New Spain on May 16, 1776, which placed him under Teodoro de Croix, the first commander-general of the interior provinces, who wielded civil, military, and judicial powers dependent only on the viceroy for troops and supplies. Upon O'Conor's departure, much still needed to be done to conquer the Apaches. Yet, little had changed, because officials remained committed to a military solution to the Indian problem on the frontier. Croix had nearly thirty years of experience in the Spanish army as governor of Acapulco and inspector of troops. He, too, believed, as Rubí and O'Conor, that only force would compel the Indians to keep the peace on the frontier. After arriving in Mexico City on December 22, 1776, he began planning a major offensive against the Apaches, but with fewer than two thousand men to guard a two-thousand-mile frontier from a few isolated presidios, he could do little more than plead for more troops and make essential adjustments in frontier defenses.

As commander-general, however, Croix adopted Rubí's recommendation to make peace with the Comanches through alliances in order to marshal his troops, the Comanches, and the friendly Nations of the North against the Apaches, whom Spanish officials still considered the most dangerous and untrustworthy of all the tribes on the frontier. Croix planned to make war on the Apaches from Texas to California with his allies, stopping only when they sued for an unconditional peace and settled near a presidio where they would practice agriculture and accept the Christian faith or cease to exist as a people. He quickly found, however, that on the northern frontier little had changed. The presidios remained poorly located, in-adequately garrisoned, and ill-equipped. The soldiers still lacked sufficient horses, firearms, gunpowder, musket balls, and adequate clothing. Croix particularly feared the loss of New Mexico to the Comanches, Apaches, Utes, and Navajos. Santa Fe provided a weak defense of the province at best, and Croix informed José de Galvéz, secretary of the Indies, that: "I am persuaded that if we lose the important barrier of New Mexico which I pray God may not happen, the Indians would be masters of that immense country, and accustomed to living by robbery would indubitably approach us." He further wrote, "If today an army is needed only to make war on the numerous Apache, what force would be necessary to curb the other nations[?]"

1. Teodoro de Croix served as the first commander-general of the interior provinces. Upon arrival in Mexico in late December 1776, he worked to establish a strong line of presidios on the northern frontier from Texas to California as well as make peace with the Comanches and defeat the Apaches. Croix, however, never had sufficient resources to achieve these goals of Spanish Indian policy. (Courtesy, University of Oklahoma Press.)

In Texas, he reported that the Comanches and their allies, the Nations of the North, had essentially overrun the province and "not a foot of land is free from hostility." Settlers had abandoned their farms and ranches in terror for the relative safety of the villages. To the west at Tucson, the presidio endured without meat, butter, or candles. Overall, the supply system had completely broken down.[18]

While Croix worked to solve these problems as well as plan an offensive against the Apaches, the American colonies declared independence and provided Spain the opportunity to strike Great Britain, its perennial enemy. As a result, in July 1779, Croix received word from José de Gálvez, secretary of the Indies, dated February 20, that he would not receive reinforcements for an offensive against the Apaches, because war with Great Britain was imminent and paramount. In fact, Spain had already declared war on Great Britain on June 21. Peaceful persuasion was now required rather than war to pacify the Apaches. Major offensives must wait. Indeed, Spain would soon be committing troops to Louisiana for the purpose of retaking Florida. Even so, Croix continued to readjust the presidial line, strengthen the garrisons by using local militia, and plan an offensive against the Apaches.

By 1779, however, Gálvez was prepared for this turn of international events. He believed the Apaches could not be defeated any time soon because they did not have a vital center that could be attacked and destroyed. Instead, they were highly mobile and able to live on little food in the rugged mountains and parched desert. Militarily superior in ability and numbers, knowledge of their terrain, horsemanship, and use of weapons, they could not be defeated by the small number of poorly equipped presidial and militia troops, and the Spanish treasury could not provide the resources necessary to force a peace. Instead, Galvéz informed Croix that the king preferred that he pursue a defensive action by using diplomatic accommodation, gifts, and trade rather than military force as the best Indian policy. By gaining peace and stability through trade, preventing Indian alliances, and overlooking minor offenses, Spain would incur far less cost than waging war against the tribes at a time when its resources were needed elsewhere. This realistic reassessment and redirection of Spanish policy recognized the success of the French trade in the Louisiana Territory in keeping peace with the tribes. Rather than destroy them militarily, which remained impractical and impossible, Galvéz now planned to initiate the proven policy of gaining peace through such lucrative trade that the Indians would become utterly dependent on Spain for their existence.

In 1785, Bernardo de Galvéz, previously the governor of Spanish Louisiana and nephew of José de Galvéz, became viceroy of New Spain. He also had responsibility for executing Spain's new Indian policy. Galvéz had considerable experience with Indian affairs, and he believed that Spain alone could not defeat the Apaches. Although the younger Galvéz recognized that Indian cultures could not be quickly changed by trade, he believed trade would achieve and maintain peace with far less expense than war and the continued threat of force. Indeed, he contended that through trade, "the King would keep them very contented for ten years with what he now spends in one year making war upon them." Accordingly, Galvéz redirected Spanish Indian policy with his *Instructions of 1786*. The result was a new Indian policy with three essential features. First, the army would maintain persistent military pressure against the Indians and destroy the Apaches, particularly the Mescaleros, if necessary. Second, officials would continue to forge alliances with the tribes and play them against each other, and he noted, "[T]he vanquishment of the heathen consists of obligating them to destroy one another." Third, gifts and trade would be used to make the Indians dependent on the Spanish, and remove any need to attack Spanish settlements. If this policy succeeded, Galvéz believed the Indians "may be attracted gently to the advantages of rational life and to commerce by discreet and opportune gifts." But, he contended, "If peace is broken . . . we shall rightly return to incessant and harsh war, alternating war and peace as often as the haughty or humble behavior of the barbarous Indian requires." Essentially, Galvéz proposed to make either peace or war with the Indians, but he preferred the former alternative as a matter of fiscal responsibility, practicality, and realism.[19]

2. Juan Bautista de Anza gained extensive military experience campaigning against the Apaches and Comanches. He led several expeditions to California that resulted in the founding of Monterey and San Francisco. In 1786, as governor of New Mexico, he negotiated a peace treaty with the Comanches that lasted for a generation. (Courtesy, Vargas Project, University of New Mexico.)

Trade goods cost less than garrisons and would enable Spain to achieve "peace by deceit." Galvéz intended to introduce alcohol as a trade item, contending that: "After all the supplying of drink to the Indians will be a means of gaining their goodwill, discovering their secrets, calming them so that they will think less often of conceiving and executing their hostilities, and creating for them a new necessity which will oblige them to recognize their dependence upon us more directly." Spanish traders would also furnish guns to the tribes, but the firearms would be long and difficult to maneuver on horseback and poor in quality so they would often break, thereby making the Indians dependent on the Spaniards for repair or replacement. In time, the Indians would "begin to lose their skill in handling the bow," which he considered a more effective Indian weapon. The result would be another facet of cultural destruction that would make them even more dependent on the Spanish for survival. The Indians that sought peace could have it, even if it meant for the Spanish to make a bad peace, given their weakness on the frontier, because those that violated it could always be struck again or be subjected to incessant war. Brigadier General Jacobo Ugarte, who became commander-general of the interior provinces on April 20, 1786, had responsibility for implementing this sophisticated, brutal, and deceptive new Indian policy of divide and conquer and peace by purchase, or the extermination of those who rejected it.[20]

Simply put, trade, treaties, and toleration became the essential principles of Spanish frontier Indian policy instead of military force. But the articulation of this policy by Galvéz was not entirely new. Juan Bautista de Anza, governor of New Mexico (1778–1787), with a full beard, hatchet nose, and a mind that cut to the essentials, had already applied these principles to gain a lasting peace with the Comanches, although he had laid the groundwork for this success with the application of considerable military pressure. By 1777, the Comanches under war chief Cuerno Verde (Green Horn), the most successful and aggressive war chief, had led many devastating attacks against the Spanish. Anza considered Cuerno Verde, whose father the Spanish had killed in battle on October 30, 1768, "[a] scourge of the kingdom who has exterminated many pueblos, killing hundreds and making many prisoners whom he afterward sacrificed in cold blood." In response, Anza developed a policy of making persistent attacks against the Comanches. In late August 1779, Anza led a force of 573 soldiers and militia men as well as 259 Pueblo and Ute auxiliaries into southeastern Colorado along Fountain Creek where they destroyed a Comanche camp of 120 lodges, killed 18 villagers, and captured 34 women and children and 500 horses. He missed Cuerno Verde, however, who had left the camp to attack Taos. Cuerno Verde had retreated from Taos over the Sangre de Cristo Mountains and crossed the Arkansas River where Anza ambushed his war party on September 2. Cuerno Verde and his men fought through Anza's troops with little difficulty, but he died the next day when leading a mounted attack by 50 Comanches against Anza's column of nearly 600 men. Anza considered Cuerno Verde's death "as brave as it was glorious." Cuerno Verde's eldest son and 4 leading war chiefs also died with him. In all, Anza's soldiers and auxiliaries had killed nearly 50 men and captured 63 women and children. The Indians also lost 600 horses and most of their provisions for the coming winter. Anza, however, refused to make peace with the western Comanches until all bands agreed to cease their attacks.[21]

By spring 1780, most western Comanches had grown tired of war and its cost in lives and lost trade. They could no longer meet their trade needs at the Wichita and Pawnee villages, because the supplies of those nations soon diminished after the French defeat. As a result, friendly relations deteriorated into hostilities. Moreover, other tribes now began crossing the Mississippi River and competed with the Pawnees and Osages for hunting grounds and these nations, in turn, pressed the Comanches and Wichitas. With enemies to the north and south, the Comanches needed friends and trade, and the bands began asking for peace.

Although Cuerno Verde's death significantly calmed the New Mexico frontier, the eastern bands continued their attacks unabated, in part because Spain reduced its troops on the northern frontier from 1779 to 1783 to assist the Americans in their War of Independence. In 1781, Croix reported that the "incessant" Comanche attacks in Texas since the previous July were "so horrible and bloody, that, if they continue with the same steadfastness, the desolation of the province will be consequent, irremediable and immediate, and (as the governor believes) very few vassals of the king may remain to contemplate this misfortune." Indeed, Croix reported, "[A]t the moment not a foot of land is free from hostility. Its fruits of the field are despoiled, cattle ranches and farms . . . are rapidly being abandoned, and the settlers in terror are taking refuge in the settlements, nor do they venture to leave their neighborhood without a troop escort." In December 1784, the Comanches took further advantage of Spain's weakness and raided into the outskirts of San Antonio, stealing horses from the civilian and presidio corrals. Renewed Spanish attacks after the American Revolution, however, eventually convinced many Comanches to seek peace, and because a smallpox epidemic in 1780–1781 had weakened the bands. For these reasons, as much as from defeat, the Comanches sought peace, which guaranteed consistent access to Spanish goods via gifts and trade, as well as an absence of war.[22]

In November 1785 the western bands agreed to negotiate peace, and they chose Ecueracapa (Leather Jacket), a well-respected war chief of the Cuchanec Comanches (Buffalo-Eaters) as their spokesman, on the advice of the Spanish. On February 25, 1786, Ecueracapa, whom the Spaniards called Cota de Malla because he wore a shirt of mail in battle, arrived in Santa Fe and agreed to Anza's peace terms, which included the immediate cessation of hostilities against the Spanish, settlement near the Hispanic towns, renewed attacks (including by the eastern bands in Texas) against the Apaches, his assumption of the position of principal chief for all Comanches, and reconciliation with their traditional enemy, the Utes.

After adjourning to Pecos, three days later the Comanche, Ute, and Spanish officials formally agreed to peace, pending ratification by all the bands, and Anza opened the annual trade fair for the Comanches at Taos, with regulations designed to prevent unscrupulous Spanish and Pueblo traders from cheating them as they had customarily done in the past. Ecueracapa gave his own sign of sincerity by attacking the Apaches in southern New Mexico. Ugarte, who had become the new commander-general, accepted the preliminary peace, but instructed Anza to gain its ratification by all Comanche bands, which he achieved on April 21, 1787. In the meantime, Domingo Cabello, governor of Texas, had made peace with the eastern Comanches, because he could not defeat them. He signed a treaty with the bands in the autumn of 1785, which resulted from his diplomatic ability to form alliances with the Nations of the North to threaten the Comanches unless they stopped attacking Spanish settlements.

The peace treaties with the Comanches soon bore important results. On November 5, 1787, thirty-four Comanches, including Ecueracapa, riding Spanish horses and carrying Spanish guns, joined presidio soldiers, settlers, and Pueblo auxiliaries against the Apaches who lived southwest of the Moqui Villages (Hopi) in New Mexico, primarily to impress them with the Spanish-Comanche alliance. Thereafter, Fernando de la Concha, governor of New Mexico (1787–1793), supplied the Comanches with horses, guns, and other provisions for independent attacks against the Apaches. The Comanches then reported their attacks against the Apaches to the presidial commanders on "tally sheets," which listed the number killed and captured and horses seized. De la Concha was so pleased with the results that when a severe drought began in the autumn of 1787 and caused the buffalo to migrate beyond Comanche lands, he provided corn for the next two years to help alleviate their hunger. He also continued to lavish the Comanche bands with gifts of cloth, knives, mirrors, scissors, lead, sugar, and soap, and he believed "the disposition of the Comanche Nation is such that it will embrace any proposal made to them with gentleness, affection, and a few gifts." Spain considered this military aid to be humanitarian relief and gifts a small price to pay for friendship and peace with the Comanches.[23]

Moreover, as late as 1799, the Spanish continued to overlook Comanche transgressions, such as the occasional theft of cattle, horses, and mules, which Pedro de Nava, commander-general of the interior provinces, considered little more than "small disorders and robberies" and "petty thefts." He could do no more than reprimand the chiefs and urge them to control their young men and return the stolen livestock to San Antonio under the threat of losing their trading privileges. He did not, however, have sufficient military strength to enforce these demands. Nava also noted that while the chiefs sometimes made restitution, the settlers did little to help themselves because they neither fenced nor watched their livestock. Simply put, without the military assistance of the Comanches, the Spanish could not defeat the Apaches, and officials looked the other way when the Comanches made minor violations of the peace.[24]

Anza and Cabello, then, succeeded in gaining reconciliation with the Comanches because they offered peace and extensive trade, and the Comanches accepted it because the Spanish now agreed to meet their needs in the form of guns, powder, lead, and other essentials such as clothing, tobacco, and sugar, and because Anza marshaled sufficient forces to prevent them from trading at

Taos and other locations. The Comanches could have these goods in quantity and relatively easily and without a fight, if they made peace. At the same time, the Comanches did not forsake their cultural need to win honor by attacking their enemies, because Anza urged them to make war against their traditional enemy, the Apaches. This rapprochement was nothing less than realpolitik for both the Spanish and the Comanches. The Spanish could not have peace by defeating the Comanches and the Comanches could not gain needed trade goods while making war on the Spanish. Accommodation met the needs of both the Spanish and Comanches and allied tribes. Anza also achieved peace with the Comanches without alienating the friendly Jicarilla Apaches in northern New Mexico or the Utes to the northwest, both of whom considered the Comanches their enemy. Essentially, then, the Spanish bought the friendship that they could not coerce or win.

Still, the Spanish-Comanche peace, recommended by Rubí and achieved by Anza, Cabello, and Ecueracapa, depended on reciprocity to work and endure, and the cultures of both sides frequently stood in the way. Spanish settlers often preferred force, if not extermination, when dealing with the Comanches, and presidio commanders had to keep the peace between them. At the same time, Comanche treaty commitments depended on the persuasion of their leaders because the chiefs did not wield coercive power. Moreover, Comanche culture honored the theft of horses, contrary to Spanish civil law and Christian morality, and the bands never functioned as a unified people. Fortunately, both Spanish and Comanche leaders recognized that peace meant that mutual violations would be resolved by diplomacy, negotiation, and law, rather than war. Both would police their own people and make restitution for crimes or other infractions, and Spain would exercise tolerance until the Comanches learned to function as a single political entity.

The Spanish-Comanche peace worked best in New Mexico where the western bands developed important trade with Hispanic villages. The eastern Comanches in Texas had greater difficulty keeping the peace because they often pursued their traditional enemy, the Lipan Apaches, and war parties that passed Hispanic settlements often caused trouble by stealing horses. By the end of the eighteenth century, however, Comanches traded regularly at San Antonio, and the thievery had decreased. Moreover, the western Comanches worked to maintain the peace between their eastern relatives and the Spanish so war would not ruin the peace for them, and by the early nineteenth century, trade at San Antonio had become as important to the eastern Comanches as to the western Comanches in New

Mexico. The American occupation of Natchitoches in April 1804, four months after the Louisiana Purchase, placed this fragile peace in jeopardy, however, because the Americans began talking about the Rio Grande as the western boundary and to trade firearms to the Wichitas, Osages, and Pawnees, thereby weakening Comanche power.

The Spanish had more difficulty pacifying the Apaches. Neither Spanish officials nor soldiers could always distinguish among the bands, especially during raids. Only the Navajos, who lived in fixed villages, raised crops, and grazed sheep, agreed to make peace with Anza under threat of attack by a combined force of Pueblo and Ute auxiliaries and Spanish soldiers. The Spanish gave the Navajos little pause, but the threat to send the Utes against them caused considerable alarm, because the Navajos had lost many lives to them in the past.

On March 30, 1775, Governor Mendinueta reported that: "In order to curb the Navajos, no better expedient has been found than of protecting ourselves with the arms of the Yutas, and it is sufficient that they may declare war for the Navajos to desist from what they do to us, notwithstanding the fact that in the midst of peace they do commit small robberies and are accustomed to mix in the incursions of the other Apaches who cannot subsist without robbing because of their great sterility of the country where they live." In 1784, Governor Anza threatened to deny the Navajos the right to trade in New Mexico if they did not join the Spanish against the Gileño Apaches. He also threatened to send the Utes against them. The Navajos depended on the New Mexico trade, and they feared the Utes. As a result, on June 5, 1785, a force of 150 Navajos and 94 Pueblos attacked the Gileño Apaches, killing 40 and demonstrating their loyalty to Spain. Anza urged more attacks to ensure a break between these two Apache peoples, and he sent traders to the Navajo towns in the spring of 1786 with promises of extensive trade for an alliance.[25]

With the Comanches, Utes, and Navajos allied, the Spanish struck hard and persistently at the Apaches to the West. Ugarte led this offensive. Following Galvéz's *Instructions of 1786*, which superseded the *Regulations of 1772*, Ugarte pursued a ruthless war against the Apaches and he gave no quarter, because they neither asked nor offered it themselves. As early as 1787, the Spanish offered a bounty on Apaches killed, proof of payment on exhibit of their ears. By the 1790s they customarily sent Apache prisoners, including women and children, to Havana or distributed them among private citizens in Mexico as slaves in order to Christianize them, destroy their culture, and eradicate their existence from the northern frontier.

Gradually, the Apache bands agreed to peace and to settle in designated areas, called *"establecimientos de paz,"* that essentially resembled later reservations in the United States. There, they received Christian teachings and agricultural instruction, all under the watchful eye of soldiers rather than priests. Designated officers also served as Indian agents and distributed the weekly rations of food and maintained good communication with their charges. The Spanish believed that the Apaches who enjoyed freedom from want would lure the hostile bands to the establecimientos. Sooner rather than later, Governor Concha believed the remaining hostile bands would "solicit peace in order to enjoy the same benefits as their companions." Concha, however, had far less success gaining peace with the western Apaches than with the Comanches, Utes, Navajos, and Jicarillas, in part because the Comanches objected, claiming that peace with the Apaches would leave them with no enemies to fight.[26]

In November 1786, Manuel Antonio Flores, who became viceroy on the death of Galvéz, divided the military responsibility for the northern frontier, assigning Ugarte to the western provinces of Sonora, Baja California, and Alta California; José Rengel to Nueva Vizcaya and New Mexico; and Colonel Juan de Ugalde to the eastern provinces of Coahuila and Texas. Flores preferred Ugalde's propensity for search-and-destroy missions against the Apaches rather than Ugarte's preference to offer war or peace in keeping with the *Instructions of 1786,* because the Apaches often remained at peace in one province in order to draw supplies and trade booty while they raided in another. And, on January 19, 1787, Flores sent Ugarte on a campaign against the Apaches. By early spring the Mescaleros and Membreños sought peace. The Mescaleros, however, rejected his demand to live in fixed villages and farm because they prized their freedom. As a result, Ugarte compromised by permitting the peaceful bands to keep the presidio commanders informed about the location of their villages, required them to refrain from entering settled areas without permission, and encouraged their children to learn agriculture. Ugarte realistically sought peace with the Apaches, not their annihilation.

Only the Gileño Apaches in Arizona remained hostile, and Spain now intended to use troops from Texas and New Mexico along with Comanche, Ute, Navajo, and Apache auxiliaries against them. By late April 1787, however, this tentative peace had collapsed, because Flores considered the Mescaleros still hostile and ordered Ugarte to attack them in the province of Nueva Vizcaya, while Ugalde declared war on them in Texas. The Mescaleros could have peace, but not voluntarily. Flores and Ugalde insisted on defeating them first.

Ugarte, who hated Ugalde more than he disliked the Mescaleros because the Apaches were merely the enemy while Ugalde was a rival, felt betrayed and complained to Flores. By siding with Ugalde, Viceroy Flores had violated Galvéz's *Instructions of 1786*, which required him to wage war against the Apaches only until they asked for peace and to grant peace every time and place the Apaches sued for it (even though they likely would violate it), essentially accepting a bad peace for a good war. Ugarte had agreed with Galvéz that the Apaches would learn the advantages of peace, become reliant on Spanish goods, food, and gifts, and eventually ask for peace and keep it. Flores, however, continued to favor Ugalde, because he would not accept peace just because the Mescaleros asked for it. Flores believed the Apaches only sought peace when they needed it after the game became scarce to gain needed goods, or to regroup militarily. He argued that peace would come only after the Apaches had been decisively beaten in war. Flores also believed that Ugarte should tend to executing Spanish Indian policy west of the Rio Grande, and leave the eastern tribes to Ugalde.

Ugalde did not disappoint Flores. Soon persistent attacks on the Mescaleros had destroyed any chance of peace. Ugalde wantonly captured chiefs during peace negotiations and intentionally killed women and children during attacks. In the autumn of 1789, however, Ugalde's fortunes changed when Conde de Revillagigedo succeeded Flores as viceroy of New Spain. Revillagigedo considered Ugalde's methods bloodthirsty, removed him from command in April 1790, and placed Ugarte back in charge of the eight frontier provinces. Ugarte then sought to restore the peace with the Mescaleros after Ugalde left Texas in June 1790. In July many of the bands appeared at El Norte and accepted the peace terms offered before, including the demand for them to settle fixed villages along the Rio Grande and join the Spanish against the hostile Apaches to the west. By late 1790, Ugarte had regained the peace that Ugalde had lost. When Ugarte left his post on December 30, 1790, the Indian policy devised by Galvéz governed Spanish and Indian relations on the northern frontier.

By the early 1790s, many Apache bands had located in reservation-like villages or establecimientos near the presidios. In 1793, Arivaipa Apaches began settling near the presidio at Tucson, although the Pima practice of bringing captured Apaches there to sell as slaves to the Papagos threatened the tranquility of this settlement. Moreover, the local priest, Franciscan Father Diego Bringas, complained that instead of accepting Christianization, the Apaches learned to gamble, swear, and drink from the soldiers. They did not, however, break the peace. In all, eight reservations had become home to several thousand Apaches in the Southwest. Spanish commissioners or agents worked to prevent settlers from harming or cheating them, and band chiefs served as judges for their own people. The Indian agents also dispersed food rations to all Apaches living within ten miles of their presidio and allotted farming plots. This reservation policy foreshadowed that developed by the United States during the nineteenth century. The Gileños, the most hostile Apaches, however, still raided into New Mexico, but the Navajos waged consistent war against them, and, except for an uprising in 1796, the Navajos remained peaceful.

By 1796, most Apache bands had sued for peace and agreed to settle near presidios. This reservations system had become an essential feature of Spanish Indian policy, but it proved costly. Provisions of food, gifts, and agricultural seeds and tools mounted, and presidio soldiers spent considerable time watching their charges. Taxes increased for Hispanic settlers to help meet these costs. Even so, from 1790 to 1810 the reservation system for the Apaches reduced the military problem of frontier defense to routine patrols and police actions.

At this same time, the Comanches also remained at peace with the Spanish and continued to aid them by attacking hostile Apache bands. By ignoring minor transgressions against Hispanic settlers, such as the theft of cattle in Texas, Spain remained committed to keeping the peace in order to marshal its resources against the Apaches. Moreover, the Spanish had now come to view the Comanches as a buffer between Hispanic settlements in New Mexico and Texas and the Sioux, Pawnee, and other potentially hostile tribes to the north.

Tribal customs, however, proved hard to change, and the Comanches as well as the Apaches had difficulty living in fixed locations or refraining from striking their traditional enemies in order to meet their economic and cultural needs. The Apache cultural practice of destroying a house after the death of a family member also continued to pose problems for resettlement in fixed villages near the presidios, and the Apaches who would not submit fled northward beyond Spanish jurisdiction. Yet, during the 1790s the Spanish essentially did not interfere with Apache cultural practices, including religious beliefs and the selection of native leaders. Instead, they merely insisted that the Apaches live in designated areas near a presidio, draw their rations, and refrain from raiding as an economic activity or making war as a cultural necessity. Moreover, the Apaches added Spanish cultural practices rather than abandoning their own. They also learned to negotiate, and the Apaches became familiar with the Spanish language as well as military, agricultural, and domestic technology. And, as long as the Spanish remained a threat, Apache thoughts and preparations for war ensured the preservation of the essential features of Apache life, such as male prestige, ranking, and leadership based on war, as well as religious beliefs and rites associated with war and the avenging of slain kinsmen—all of which helped maintain a strong bond and moral order among the Apache people.

Although Spanish soldiers and Hispanic settlers periodically murdered Indian people, the Spanish brokered peace lasted for twenty years, largely because Spanish officials and tribal leaders preferred to overlook isolated transgressions, and because peace was more advantageous to both sides than war. As a result, the frontier became safer for Spaniards and Indians, and relatively secure trade routes opened between San Antonio, Santa Fe, and Tucson. In 1810, however, with the beginnings of the Mexican War of Independence, Spanish Indian policy slowly collapsed. Troops and funds went to quelling the rebellion, and Spanish officials provided fewer gifts, trade goods, and rations, which made the bought peace difficult to keep. As the trade goods disappeared, the alliances with the tribes on the northern frontier disintegrated. Once again, the Apaches became subjected to exploitative trade practices by commanders who also reduced their rations. The Apaches soon began fleeing their assigned villages. The eastern Comanches also increased their trade with the Americans, because they offered goods at better prices, and the Comanches began stealing more horses from Hispanic settlers for that trade, all with American encouragement. Royalists and insurgents appealed to the Comanches and Lipan Apaches for help against the other, but the tribes took advantage of Spain's weakness to renew their raiding, and the peace dissolved.

When Nemisio Salcedo, commander-general of Texas, learned in March 1812 that the Comanches intended to attack San Antonio, he did nothing, fearing a preemptive attack by Spanish troops would make the situation worse. He argued that a declaration of war against the Comanches had always been considered the "greatest evil that could befall the province." Instead, he urged conciliation. No one paid any attention, however, because the Mexican War of Independence made the San Antonio area a battleground. As a result, Hispanic settlers began to flee Texas. By 1814, San Antonio, which had a population of 3,417 in 1794, had become "almost abandoned." Moreover, with Mexican independence in 1821, American traders began to influence the tribes, and any hope for peaceful relations with the Indians on the northern frontier lay in the distant past.[27]

Spain's Indian policy formulated after 1763 achieved a relative peace and accommodation with the Indians, but it collapsed in far less time than needed to achieve it. In the absence of significant discoveries of precious metals to exploit, Spain had little reason to commit the funds and men necessary to subdue the native population and control the land area of the northern frontier. Certainly, Spain had no desire to provide more than minimal military control and a system of alliances to keep the peace among the Indian nations and protect isolated Hispanic settlements and ranches. Although Spain claimed a vast and ill-defined northern empire, it did not need to negotiate the acquisition of land from the Indians through a cession treaty process in the American tradition, because those lands were not needed for immediate settlement. Instead, the Spanish wanted peace on the northern frontier while the Indians often wanted trade. Expediency then dictated a mutual relationship, particularly regarding peace or war, and determined the formulation of policy for interaction by both sides.

Eventually, American officials would prove that they learned nothing from the Spanish experience as they went about executing an Indian policy based on force to claim lands that they neither occupied nor controlled. Nor would they understand Mexico's renewal of Spanish Indian policy that sought a mutually useful, though imperfect, peace to a devastating war. In the meantime, the Comanches, Apaches, and the Nations of the North essentially controlled the old Spanish and now Mexican borderland frontier, just as they had for more than a century.

CHAPTER 3

Spanish Alta California

The Seven Years' War marked the end of the French and British struggle to control the eastern half of the North American continent, but the peace that followed also brought new opportunities for colonial expansion along the Pacific Coast where Spain feared encroachment by both Russia and Great Britain. When the marqués de Grimaldi, the Spanish minister of state, learned in late January 1768 about a Russian landing somewhere along the West Coast, he urged the marqués de Croix, viceroy of New Spain, to "observe such attempts as the Russians may make there, frustrating them if possible." By that time, however, José de Galvéz, special emissary from Carlos III to New Spain, had already given considerable thought to the extension of Spain's northern frontier into Alta or Upper California. Although the frontier area of present-day New Mexico and Arizona occupied much of his time, Galvéz proposed the occupation of Monterey Bay on the Pacific Coast to block Russian expeditions from the north, and in May 1767, he sought royal authorization for an expedition into Upper California.[1]

Galvéz's plan to seize Monterey Bay to ensure Spanish claims to California by right of discovery was hardly new. Spanish officials had discussed occupying California for more than sixty years, and they had always rejected the idea because the estimated expenses did not seem to be justified by the benefits to be gained. When the Spanish ambassador to Moscow learned about a Russian landing on the California coast, however, Galvéz's proposal received quick approval, and Grimaldi ordered Galvéz to find some means of "thwarting them however possible." Spain, however, had neither the funds nor the men to support a colonizing expedition that could secure the California coast south of Monterey Bay.[2]

In the absence of adequate soldiers, backed by Spanish gold, who would occupy designated outposts and thereby strengthen Spain's claim to California by right of possession, Galvéz turned to the Franciscan order of the Catholic Church for help. Although Carlos III broke the power of the Jesuits in Spain and its colonies in 1767 by removing them from positions of power and expelling them from the empire because they exercised too much influence in daily affairs and resisted secular change, the Franciscans were different. Galvéz knew that the

Franciscans had considerable experience "saving" souls and managing Indians at low cost. The Franciscan priests required little financial and military support if they established missions and used converted Indians to till the land. By establishing self-supporting mission communities the Franciscans zealously made conversions their life work and personal deprivation a badge of honor. They would provide a cost-efficient means to incorporate the Indians into Spanish society and help lay claim to California. By using two clerics, a half dozen soldiers, and a few artisans and settlers at each mission to congregate the Indians, the priests could teach them European-style agriculture and other skills such as textile production, leather working, and Spanish, as well as indoctrinate them in Catholicism. Eventually this training would enable the Indians to be acculturated and assimilated into Spanish society, and become productive workers as well as needed taxpayers. Moreover, these Indians would then serve as Spain's main colonizing force, where Spaniards proved insufficient in number and will to expand the empire themselves. Self-supporting missions and the nearby Indian communities would give Spain the claim to California that it needed to block colonial incursions by other powers and thereby protect the rich mines of northern New Spain. Hispanicized Indians also would be peaceful people and therefore cheaper to govern, particularly with the aid of the missions, than to coerce into submission with an expensive military presence in California. Galvéz, of course, knew little about the Indian peoples who lived along the coast and occupied the interior valleys, but he had no doubt that they would be used to meet Spain's imperial needs, and they would also become Christians.[3]

Some three hundred thousand Indians, divided into more than one hundred cultural groups with as many dialects, occupied Upper California when Galvéz planned his expedition. The cultural groups in the Central Valley included the Nisenan, Maidu, Konkow, Miwok, and Yokuts, while the Indians of the northwest included the Tolowa, Yurok, Karok, Hupa, Shasta, Chimariko, and Whilkut. Along the coast the Chumash, Salinan, Esselen, Costanoan, Coast Miwok, Pomo, Gabrielino, and Ipai, among other cultures, established their villages. These tribes might be composed of fewer than thirty people in several villages or as many as thirty villages totaling 1,000 people, although the villages averaged about 250 residents. More tribelets than tribes, these groups were related by blood and marriage. Economic and political alliances as well as intermarriage linked these cultural groups through twenty-one "nationalities." They lived in scattered villages that often served as little more than seasonal settlements, where they might plant a few crops of corn, squash, and beans (especially in the Colorado River region), hunted, gathered, and fished for a living. Marriage and kinship defined an individual's place in the community and determined personal actions. Families controlled specific hunting-and-gathering territories. In addition, these tribelet groups also organized a loose political structure that centered on the village, where chiefs (who might be women) from wealthy families administered daily affairs. These Indian groups also practiced polygamy.

In contrast to the Comanches and Apaches, the Indian cultures in Upper California neither organized powerful warrior societies nor used horses and guns at the time of Spanish contact. Moreover, the California Indians were generally peaceful, and they had little history of organized and prolonged warfare in the European sense of conquest and exploitation. Therefore, the California Indians could neither defend themselves as well as the tribes in Texas, New Mexico, and Arizona, nor attack the Spanish with the strength, boldness, and expectation of victory as the southwestern nations. Still, the California Indians had no reason to expect brutal treatment by the Spanish, but they confronted an invading people accustomed to an authoritarian state and church where tolerance came only after social and religious conformity.

On January 9, 1769, Galvéz began the "sacred expedition" to occupy Upper California and foil the Russian threat when the *San Carlos* set sail from La Paz on the Baja Peninsula for Monterey Bay. The *San Antonio* followed on February 15. Bad weather and scurvy among the crews, however, made Monterey Bay an impossible goal, and on April 11 the *San Antonio* dropped anchor in San Diego Bay, followed by the *San Carlos* two weeks later. Meanwhile, in late March two parties of soldiers began an overland trek up the Baja. The first, led by Captain Fernando de Rivera y Moncada with twenty-five soldiers, forty-two Christian Indians, and three mule drivers, reached San Diego Bay on May 14 and rendezvoused with the soldiers and crews of the *San Carlos* and *San Antonio,* all of whom one officer reported were "immobilized and in so unhappy and deplorable a state as moved my deepest pity."[4]

While the few healthy and strong members of the expedition went about the task of building fortifications, the nearby Ipai Indians, whom the Spanish called "friendly and tractable," left them alone but could not help observing that the cemetery expanded faster than the presidio and mission buildings. For the moment, however, the Ipai and the other coastal tribes were content to watch the Spaniards from afar, including the expedition under Gaspar de Portolá that left San Diego on July 14 in search of Monterey Bay. Although Portolá missed his destination, he discovered and claimed San Francisco Bay for Spain before

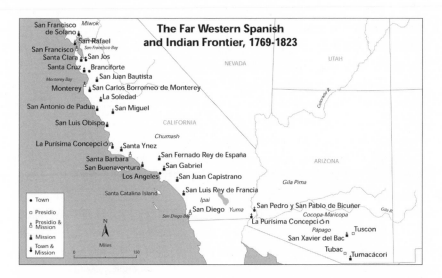

The Far Western Spanish and Indian Frontier, 1769-1823

returning to San Diego with his exhausted and starving men on January 24, 1770.[5]

But the Spanish did not rest. Between the founding of San Diego in 1769 until the early 1820s, the Franciscans established twenty-one missions along the coast, stretching beyond San Francisco Bay. Spain also constructed presidios at San Diego (1769), Monterey (1769), San Francisco (1776), and Santa Barbara (1782), and the three civilian towns of Los Angeles, San José, and Branciforte (Santa Cruz). In all, approximately five hundred soldiers and several dozen priests controlled nearly seventy thousand Indians.

Spanish officials in Mexico City assigned lands to the missions for the development of agriculture and livestock raising, but the Franciscans had complete responsibility for the development of the mission economy, including land use and Indian labor. By employing Indians and using their lands for agriculture, Galvéz believed the missions could subsidize military operations in California. The presidios, that is, military garrisons, constituted the single largest expense for the Spanish occupation of Upper California, at a time when officials in Madrid sought greater bureaucratic efficiency for administration and defense of the empire. By training the Indians to become farmers, Galvéz contended, the presidios could trim their expenses and reduce, if not eliminate, their reliance on food supplies transported from central Mexico. Moreover, Indian workers could be taught masonry and carpentry and assigned to the presidios for the repair and construction of buildings, thereby freeing the soldiers for other duties.

At the same time, the Franciscans believed the Indians could be taught to raise wheat, vegetables, and cattle to provide a consistent food supply that would draw other Indians to the missions where they could then begin the Christianization and acculturation process. The Franciscans also planned to use their earnings from supplying food to the presidios to purchase needed supplies in Mexico City, where officials reconciled the accounts of church and state. Both military and church officials also believed that Indian workers could be hired out to help settlers expand their agricultural lands and increase production, which would, in turn, strengthen the presidios, missions, and Spanish claims to California. In return, the Spanish Crown would provide an annual stipend for each priest and a small garrison to protect the mission and enforce discipline among the Indians who settled nearby.

The Spanish, then, intended the missions to control the Indians, provide economic support for the soldiers, and convert the Indians to Catholicism. To do so with the greatest speed and efficiency, military and church officials intended to congregate the Indians in communities, called *reducciones* or *congregaciones*, where they would deny them their "free, undisciplined," and traditional lifestyle and introduce them to a new economic and labor system. Essentially, the Spanish practiced a policy of divide and rule by separating the Indians who seemed willing to accept Christianity and reside near the missions from those who rejected Spanish culture and remained independent. By so doing, the Spanish missions became an authoritarian, even a totalitarian, political as well as economic and religious institution, because they were designed to destroy Indian culture, achieve acculturation, and forcibly gain converts.[6]

The Franciscans lured the Indians to the missions with food and gifts of cloth and clothing. Gifts of food and clothing appealed to many Indians because such support by the missions made their lives easier and helped free them from hunger and want. At the same time, the acceptance of these gifts made many Indians feel obligated to the priests based on their cultural beliefs about sharing and reciprocity, which, in turn, enabled the Franciscans to increase their influence over them. When a band moved to the mission and set up camp to take advantage of these benefits, the Franciscan missionaries used the opportunity to convert them or at least their children through baptism. By converting the children and indoctrinating them with Spanish ways, the priests believed they could ultimately and perhaps quickly achieve the destruction of Indian culture, including religion, while weakening the authority of parents and tribal leaders. The reluctance of the missionaries to learn any of the many Indian languages, however, slowed their work until their charges gained a working knowledge of Spanish, because many of the Indian languages did not have the equivalent words for God,

Trinity, and Sacrament. The priests, then, required the baptized neophytes or converts and their parents to reside at the mission, because they believed the converts would reject their vows and return to their former way of life if they returned to their villages. At the missions, then, the Franciscans dictated all daily activities and worked to suppress native religious practices and cultural traditions that did not meet Spanish views of appropriate behavior. Little wonder that the Indians slowly and often reluctantly accepted religious instruction.

Although light field work characterized farming at the missions, compulsory work violated Indian cultural traditions, as well as their sense of right and self-worth. Moreover, the Indians did not believe they should labor to feed the soldiers. Consequently, the priests necessarily resorted to coercion to ensure completion of daily tasks. In 1786, a French visitor to Mission San Carlos wrote, "The men and women are assembled by the sound of the bell, one of the religious conducts them to their work, to church, and all other exercises . . . [W]e saw men and women loaded with irons, others in stocks; and at length the noise of the strokes of a whip struck our ears." Indeed, the temporal and spiritual power of the priests over the mission Indians was absolute and often cruelly enforced. Those who fled or failed to meet the labor expectations of the Franciscans were subject to physical punishment, such as whipping, hobbling, solitary confinement, mutilation, branding, and execution upon their capture and forcible return.[7]

Occasionally, the gentiles or unchristianized Indians protected the converts who fled the missions. In July 1797, for example, the priests and soldiers at Mission San José learned about a Miwok village to the north that harbored runaways and encouraged neophytes to rebel. When a force of twenty-eight soldiers and civilians moved on the village to retrieve the neophytes, the Miwok fought back. Sergeant Pedro Amador reported that: "Although we repeatedly told them that we did not wish to fight but only to take away the Christians, they . . . began to shoot so as to kill one of our horses and wound two others. Seeing this opposition, we used our weapons in order to subdue them so that they would surrender. Some were killed, for they refused for two hours to give up. Finally, it was necessary to dismount and throw them back with swords and lances." In the end, the Spaniards returned to Mission San José with eighty-three neophytes and nine gentiles. By forcibly maintaining control over the Indian converts, the Franciscans enabled the missions to meet military needs by raising sufficient grain, vegetables, and cattle for the presidios, and thereby reduce their drain on government coffers and ease the supply problem from Mexico.[8]

The Indians felt degraded and resentful when the priests flogged or imprisoned them for a host of transgressions, such as adultery and theft. In 1786, a French visitor at Monterey observed, "Corporal punishment is inflicted on the Indians of both sexes who neglect the exercises of piety, and many sins which in Europe are left to divine justice, are here punished by irons and stocks." In November 1800, however, another observer at San Francisco noted that the priests practiced patience and moderation when dealing with transgressions by their Indian charges. No matter the seriousness of the violation, he wrote, "it is never ordered to give anyone more than twenty-five lashes and with an instrument incapable of drawing blood or of causing notable contusions. . . . The fugitives, despite absences of long duration, and although they may have committed mischief during their absence, are forgiven if they voluntarily surrender. And finally, no penalties are ever applied other than those solely correctional, even though the Indian insists on manifesting himself as incorrigible." He believed that "the treatment generally given the Indian is very gentle."[9]

The severity of corporal punishment, of course, was relative to Spanish culture. The Spaniards used the lash, fetters, stocks, or shackles on their own men or women to guarantee obedience, force cultural conformity (if not acceptance), and ensure social order. Spanish cultural practices included the corporal punishment of individuals for the good of the community, particularly as a deterrent to others. Only the governor or presidio commanders, however, could mete out punishment for grave crimes such as murder and robbery, because those violations mandated heavy whipping over the course of many days and probably ended with the death of the Indian. Above all, Spanish Indian policy demanded subjugation of the tribes and tranquility for the government to enforce its claims to California and marshal its attention toward potential European invaders along the coast.

Although the Franciscans believed that they could acculturate and convert the Indians with relative ease, these tasks quickly proved difficult to achieve, because the Franciscans sent too few priests to spread Spanish culture through secular and spiritual work. At best, the priests provided rudimentary instruction in Catholic doctrine at the mission schools, and the Indians learned to repeat prayers and hymns by rote memory. The Franciscans also stressed the importance of worshiping the single Christian deity and the rejection of native ceremonies, rituals, and beliefs. But, as on other frontiers, the Indians decided personally and privately what new religious and cultural practices to adopt and when and where they would cooperate with the Franciscans. Usually the Indians made those decisions based on perceived gains, such as material benefits in the form of food and trade goods, the acquisition of spiritual power and physical protection, or the avoidance of corporal punishment. Often the weaker Indian societies adopted Spanish cultural and religious practices or merged them with their own more readily than Indian groups capable of resistance.

In the beginning the Spanish government and the Franciscans planned the conversion of the Indians to Catholicism to be voluntary. They believed that moral suasion, reasoning, and social or economic inducements would attract the Indians to and help keep them near the missions. And, during the first twenty years of Spanish occupation of coastal California, the practice of kindness and persuasion drew many Indians to the missions, particularly for food, clothing, and shelter. After the Indians near the missions had been theoretically converted, or at least baptized, the Franciscans felt compelled to locate other potential converts in the interior and thereby give the government additional claim to California by right of possession as well as save additional souls.

Moreover, the death rate among the mission Indians from exposure to European diseases, especially smallpox, measles, and cholera, kept the population of converts low in proportion to the unacculturated Indians who lived in the villages beyond mission lands. Mission Indians probably lived little more than a decade due to exposure to European diseases. One Franciscan reported, "They live well free but soon die as we reduced them to a Christian and community life ... [T]hey fatten, sicken, and die." Still, the missionaries preferred dead Christians to live heathens, and they took comfort in their achievement to save as many souls as possible before death intervened. By concentrating Indian populations on mission lands and confining the women to small, locked, and unsanitary rooms at night to regulate sexual behavior in order to preserve chastity until marriage, the Spanish inadvertently ensured the rapid and often devastating spread of disease. Without immunity to European diseases, periodic epidemics sometimes killed as many as 60 percent of a mission's population, because disease spread so rapidly in crowded conditions. In addition, the stress of relocation and the disruption of traditional living patterns reduced fertility and contributed to a declining birth rate among the mission Indians. Overall, the death rates at the missions exceeded birth rates. As a result, the Franciscans continually recruited unconverted Indians from beyond mission lands.[10]

The Franciscans, then, with the aid of the military, ventured away from the coast to visit the villages, where they attempted to convince the residents to accept baptism, and they sent neophytes to urge distant tribes to move to mission lands. These villagers balked, however, because the Franciscans made little effort to learn Indian languages or teach the natives Spanish to facilitate communication.

In fact, most of the Franciscans apparently despised Indian culture and considered learning about it a waste of time. In 1816, a French visitor noted this contempt, writing, "[N]one of them appear to have troubled themselves about their history, customs, religions or languages." Moreover, recruitment proved difficult even at the missions because the priests delivered their sermons in Latin to the Indian congregation, and because many Indians believed that evil could only be kept away by performing various ceremonial dances rather than by merely making the sign of the cross, all of which convinced the missionaries that the Indians were "irrational savages."[11]

Usually, the Indians who gathered near the missions lived within a fifteen-mile radius. The tribal groups residing beyond that distance invariably proved reluctant to relocate on mission lands and convert. Many of those who did soon fled. The Franciscans customarily called upon the military to keep the converts from fleeing the missions and returning to their pagan villages as well as to capture baptized natives and return them to the missions for punishment and re-education. The presidial commanders, however, soon grew tired of pursuing runaways because the Indians often fled again. After 1810, the War of Independence prevented Spanish authorities from providing even rudimentary supplies to the missions and presidios. As a result, Indian labor became more important than ever to increase agricultural productivity to meet the needs of the soldiers and missionaries; military expeditions to capture runaways increased and violence escalated between the Indians and Spanish.

The Franciscans, however, had greater success in altering gender roles that governed work than saving souls. In California, as in most other areas of the North American continent, gender strictly divided daily activities. The men had the responsibility for hunting, fishing, and war, while women's duties involved collecting seeds and plants, preparing food, and conducting other family-related domestic tasks. At the missions the priests successfully changed work patterns by making agricultural tasks, such as plowing, planting, cultivating, and harvesting, as well as herding livestock, male responsibilities, while maintaining women's responsibilities for food processing, cooking, and the production of cloth and clothing. At the missions, then, Indian men and women essentially exchanged their labor as tribute for food, clothing, and shelter. By so doing, the Franciscans used the Indians to meet both mission and military food needs, reduce the drain on government coffers, and ease the supply problem from Mexico.

Spanish Indian policy, which depended on abduction, confinement on mission lands, forced conversions through baptism, and the capture of fugitives, brought two general responses from the Indians: acceptance and resistance. First, some villages and tribal groups, particularly those located within a few miles of the missions, accepted Spanish domination, settled on church lands, and accepted Christianity. The Costanoans, Salinans, Esselen, Chumash, and Coast Miwok, who lived in the "mission strip," that is, from the coast eastward to the western edge of the San Joaquín and Sacramento valleys and including all of the San Francisco Bay area, came under the control of the Franciscans. The majority of the California Indians, however, did not passively accept the Spanish incursion, and they resisted the mission acculturation program from the beginning to maintain their territorial sovereignty, ensure their traditional food supply, and protect their women. Many Indians also resisted the Spanish teachings and their god because the Franciscans could not prevent the spread of strange new diseases. The Spanish seemingly brought sickness and death. The Indians' own ways proved better for their lives.[12]

Indian resistance to Spanish occupation and subjugation took several forms. First, flight from the missions, or fugitivism, became the most widespread form of active resistance. The mission Indians in central and northern California usually fled to the villages in the Central Valley, an area that one priest called "a republic of hell and diabolical union of Apostates." In contrast to the Indians along the coastal area, the Spanish could not easily reach the tribes in the Central Valley with sufficient force to make them submit to the mission system. In general, the periodic expeditions into the valley to subjugate these tribes failed miserably, with no more than an estimated 250 Indians captured during twenty-nine expeditions between 1800 and 1830. Indeed, the Indians of the Central Valley strongly resisted Spanish incursions into their territory, and they often took the offensive.[13]

Many Indians used passive resistance to thwart Spanish control by obstructing the mission system through disobedience, theft, and the refusal to work or learn Spanish. In 1814, one priest at San Diego reported that to get the Indians to learn Spanish "we exhort and threaten them with punishment, and in the case of the young, we punish them from time to time." At San Juan Capistrano, the priests complained that "these Indians retain all the customs of their ancestors," particularly religious practices that they carefully guarded. Moreover, it appears that the California Indians only adopted Christianity superficially, and many often refused to confess, take communion, or attend mass, while still observing traditional religious ceremonies and rituals, such as dancing. Occasionally, they also poisoned and killed cruel priests.[14]

In addition to flight and passive resistance, the Indians resisted Spanish incursion by rebellion, that is, fighting. Indeed, the Spanish found it far easier to claim specific land areas than to control the Indian people who lived there. At first, armed resistance came from villages located near the newly established missions and presidios, where individual village chiefs led the early attacks usually without intervillage cooperation or coordination. As early as August 1769, Ipai leaders near Mission San Diego, who had expected gifts from the Spanish for the use of their lands but received less than they expected, turned hostile and mobilized their people to take what they considered their due. Since the arrival of the Spanish during the spring, the Ipai had become demanding neighbors more interested in the material wealth of the Spaniards than spiritual salvation. Ipai groups frequented the Spanish compound, begged for gifts, particularly cloth, as they believed the food caused the Spaniards considerable sickness (especially scurvy), and proved to be skillful thieves. When a group of Ipai entered the presidio and mission compound to take what they wanted, the Spanish resisted and a fight broke out, during which one Spaniard and three Indians were killed and several wounded on each side. Thereafter, the Spanish and Ipai observed an uneasy peace, but the Ipai continued to reject Franciscan offers of religious education and baptism.

The California Indians particularly resented the Spanish soldiers because they violated their women. After repeated occurrences, in a report to his superiors, Father Luis Jayme wrote, "At one of these Indian villages near this mission of San Diego . . . the gentiles therein many times have been on the point of coming here to kill us all, and the reason for this is that some soldiers went there and raped their women, and the other soldiers who were carrying their mail to Monterey turned their animals into their fields and there ate up their crops. Three other Indian villages have reported the same thing to me several times." Father Junípero Serra, leader of the Franciscan missions system, also noted that the Indians fled whenever they saw soldiers approaching on horseback. He reported, "[T]he soldiers, clever as they are at lassoing cows and mules . . . catch Indian women with their lassos to become prey of their unbridled lust. At times some Indian men would try to defend their wives, only to be shot down with bullets." In 1772, one priest wrote that many of the soldiers "deserve to be hanged on account of the continuous outrages which they are committing in seizing and raping women." The absence of Hispanic women, then, often created problems for the Franciscans, and they frequently considered the soldiers a detriment rather than an aid to their work.[15]

From the beginning of Spanish contact, then, the destruction of food resources and sexual abuse contributed to Indian resistance either by flight or fight. In the autumn of 1771, for example, several Indian bands attacked San Gabriel twice in response to the rape of their women by the soldiers assigned to the mission. After continued abuse, two Indian leaders near Mission San Diego by the name of Francisco of Cuyamac and Zegotay of Matamo organized eight hundred fighting men from nine villages, including Ipai, to launch a simultaneous attack on the presidio and mission located several miles away. On November 4, 1775, Cuyamac and Zegotay divided their army for the attacks. The Ipai surprised the mission, burned the buildings, killed three, including the priest, and wounded others. After the Spanish barricaded themselves in an adobe building, the Indians withdrew. In the meantime, the second attack failed because the mission had been struck before the Ipai were in place to attack the presidio, and they feared that the sound of gunshots and the sight of fire and smoke would alert the soldiers and ruin their opportunity for surprise. Even so, the Ipai had demonstrated, once again, that they were not passive recipients of Spanish will, and when faced with a ruthless attack on their way of life, they fought back. Indeed, one Ipai leader, whom the Spanish captured during the following punitive campaigns, confessed that the Indians wanted to kill the priests and soldiers "in order to live as they did before." Despite the failed attacks and the ruthless efforts of the Spanish to punish those involved, however, the Ipai continued to taunt and strike the Spanish. When the Spanish tried four village leaders— Aachil, Aalcuirin, Aaaran, and Taguagui—before a military court and then executed them for trying to "kill Christians," they merely ensured the continuation of the Ipais' violent resistance to Spanish plans for acculturation. The Ipai and other Indian groups would not meekly accept the loss of their freedom, land, and culture.[16]

Indeed, in addition to resistance and flight, many Indians in California also used a sophisticated combination of acquiescence to Spanish policy and native tradition to reconcile life among a people that they could not drive away. The Spanish accepted this accommodation because they needed the Indian leaders to make their imperial policy work. Usually, only two priests and four to five soldiers administered and protected between five hundred and one thousand Indians that comprised a mission community. In order to organize and regulate life and work at the missions, the Franciscans made considerable efforts to gain the support of the Indian leaders as well as selected individuals whom they believed showed a willingness to work with them in leadership positions, particularly as emissaries between the missions and the natives. These Indian leaders, called *alcaldes*, chosen in annual elections, worked under the direction of the Franciscans to manage the labor force, maintain discipline, and mete out punishment, such as whipping runaways and thieves. Essentially, then, the church and army authorities attempted to control their mission charges through Indian leaders. By using Indians to carry out religious and military policy the Spaniards compensated for an insufficient number of priests and soldiers.

Although the Franciscans gained considerable authority over the elections to choose the Indian leaders at the missions by controlling the nomination of candidates, which, in turn, guaranteed the election of Indians supportive of the missions and work of the Franciscans, they did not entirely dominate the elected Indian officials. While the priests exercised paternalistic authority over the Indian officials, requiring them to attend mass, "keep guard" of the village at night, "lead the people to prayer and work," inform the priests about native activities, and communicate information from the missions to the villages, Indian officials often purposefully lagged in the execution of their responsibilities. In 1814, for example, the priests at Mission San Francisco complained that the elected alcaldes did not supervise the work around the mission when asked. Instead, they reported, "[N]ot infrequently the alcaldes and the men spend their time in play and away [from the mission] for another day despite the fact that their task is an urgent one."[17]

Indian leaders also did a better job of conveying information to their villages than reporting tribal affairs to the priests, and they primarily served as protectors of their people rather than informers. The Franciscans particularly found them remarkably unhelpful when they asked them to report crimes in their villages. The Indians, however, never respected the position or authority of the alcaldes, and they continued to follow the leadership of their traditional chiefs at the mission communities. Some forty years after the founding of Mission San Carlos in 1770, for example, the Franciscans complained that: "The missionaries strive to humor them [chiefs], because the contentment of the Indians depends on this." The missionaries stationed at San Miguel also reported that: "The Indians respect only those who were the chiefs of their rancherías in paganism."[18]

By the end of the Spanish reign, Indian leaders at the missions, however, occupied powerful positions as intermediaries between both cultures, and their authority came from the Spanish and tribal kinship and lineage networks, where leadership usually descended patrilineally. These Indian leaders, then, used tribal qualifications to increase their political opportunities and power among the Spaniards. The Franciscans helped increase their authority and prestige by selecting them from tribal hierarchies as worthy candidates for mission affairs, while the tribes gave their leaders legitimacy by electing them annually to mission offices. By so doing, these Indian leaders served Spain, the Franciscans, and their villages as intermediaries in a world where cultures clashed more than harmonized.

The Ipai did not stand alone against the Spanish. In order for José de Galvéz and the Franciscans to extend Spanish power northward into Upper California, the Quechan Indians, who controlled a bottleneck ford, known as the Yuma Crossing, at the junction of the Colorado and Gila Rivers between present-day Arizona and California, had to acquiesce. The Quechans had known about the Spanish for more than two centuries, and they had acquired horses from them indirectly through trade with the Papagos. In contrast to the many Indian societies along coastal California, the Quechans honored war as a way of life, like the Comanches and Apaches, in part to capture their enemies, whom they sold as slaves to the Papagos and Pimas for European goods, food, and horses. Consequently, when Father Francisco Garcés made contact with the Quechans in August 1771, both peoples anticipated considerable benefits from mutual association.

Galvéz understood that the fledgling missions and presidios in California required continuous support via an overland supply route from northern Mexico, because the sea route already proved too long and dangerous. At the same time, the Franciscans saw an ideal opportunity to save thousands of souls among an Indian people on "the rim of Christendom" who had remained beyond their grasp. By establishing missions along the Colorado and Gila Rivers, the crossing could be secured, thereby ensuring the viability of Spanish expansion into California and eventually linking the missions in California with those in New Mexico. Viceroy Antonio María de Bucareli, however, did not authorize Juan Bautista de Anza and Father Garcés to open a road from Sonora to Monterey via the Yuma Crossing until September 9, 1773. Little did they know that the expansion of New Spain's northern frontier, the defense of California, and the establishment of a major link in the mission system chain depended on winning the friendship and support of the Quechans, especially the leader Olleyquotequiebe, who had visited the mission of Caborca several times, and whom the Spanish called Salvador Palma.[19]

On January 8, 1774, Anza led a thirty-four-man expedition from the presidio at Tubac bound for California via the Yuma Crossing and the Quechan villages. Anza's packhorses were laden with gifts for the Quechans and the sixty-five cattle promised food for both Indians and soldiers on the long route to California, which Father Garcés called El Camino del Diablo—The Devil's Road. When

Anza reached the junction of the Colorado and Gila Rivers on February 7, Salvador Palma and a large gathering of Quechans met him. Anza knew that Salvador Palma held considerable power among the Quechans, but he did not know the extent of that authority. Therefore, in an attempt to single out a supreme Quechan leader, Anza designated Salvador Palma as the leader of his people and distributed beads and other trinkets among the Quechans to gain their friendship.

Anza had chosen correctly. Salvador Palma was both a civic and war leader, whom the Quechans called *kwoxot,* or "the good." Prior to the arrival of the expedition, the Quechans had wanted to attack Anza's force, but Salvador Palma argued that the Spanish could be used to supply them with a host of European goods that they did not have or could only acquire through trade with the Papagos, and he threatened to fight any man who did not agree. When Anza departed for California on March 2, Palma protected Father Garcés and the soldiers, horses, and cattle left behind for which Anza promised him great rewards in the form of trade goods. Trade would also enhance Salvador Palma's power among the Quechans. When Anza returned from California in mid-May, he affirmed Palma's power by ceremonially bestowing him with a staff symbolizing the authority of office and admonished the Indians to follow his leadership. Both the Spanish and the Quechans relished the use of the other for their own benefit. Even so, Anza realistically wrote to Viceroy Bucareli that: "If the peoples who dwell along this great river are attached to us, we will effect its passage. . . . [I]f they are not, it will be almost impossible to do so."[20]

In late October 1775, Anza returned to Quechan territory on another trip to California. Upon arrival at the Yuma Crossing, Palma asked the Spanish to establish a settlement, and Anza told him they would settle among them "in due time." Before Anza left on his journey that would result in the founding of San Francisco, he distributed clothing, cloth, glass beads, and tobacco, which proved to most Quechans that the Spaniards had played into their hands. Some, however, opposed the settlement of Fathers Garcés and Thomas Eixarch among them, because Anza had left horses, mules, and cattle, and the livestock ate and trampled the Quechans' wheat crop. Father Eixarch reflected a sense of responsibility in his diary, writing, "These damages which these poor people . . . suffer might be in justice . . . made good with some equivalent. On whom does this obligation rest?" Neither he nor anyone else besides the Quechans could provide an answer. Moreover, Christianity had become considerably less appealing to the Quechans because, Father Eixarch observed, "[S]ome old Indians entertain the foolish notion that those who are baptized immediately die." This problem arose because the Franciscans did not want to baptize the Quechans until they understood the meaning of this sacrament, and because they baptized several adults and an infant on the verge of death in order to save their souls at the last minute. While these troubles brewed, Anza returned from California, distributed presents, and pledged that the Spanish would soon establish a settlement, thereby reassuring the Quechans that they had made the right decision to show friendship because they would soon be rewarded with European goods, horses, and tools from Spanish settlers and traders.[21]

But the Spanish did not come quickly to settle among the Quechans as promised. The delay occurred because the Spaniards considered the Comanche and Apache threat to the northern frontier their most serious problem, and because the crown placed frontier military activities on the defensive because all available resources were needed for Spain's impending war with Great Britain. By October 1777, however, Fathers Garcés and Juan Marcelo Díaz had founded the mission of La Purísima Concepción on the west bank of the Colorado River and began baptizing all Quechans who came to them for salvation. But, the Quechans now began experiencing the disappointment and betrayal of unfulfilled expectations, because the Spanish had presented them with far fewer gifts than Palma had led them to expect. Sergeant José Darío Arguello, commander of the military detachment, correctly reported that the "principal motive" of the Quechans in requesting missionaries was their desire for European goods, especially clothes. And, while the Quechans' hostility grew, Palma's authority began to slip away because he had been unable to deliver on his promises. In February 1780, Teodoro Croix, the commander general, responded by sending fifty soldiers and militiamen and their families to establish two "military colonies" among the Quechans. The military, not the Franciscans, would exercise direct control over the Indians, in contrast to the mission system along the California coast.[22]

While the soldiers worked to establish their colonies, grievance festered among the Quechans. In September 1780, Father Garcés warned Croix that the Quechans "already irritated by so many delays and evil influences . . . were becoming every day more restless and could not be controlled except by superior force," and rumors circulated among them that the priests and soldiers would be killed. In November Father Díaz informed Croix that because too few soldiers had been stationed at the mission "the Indians are losing their fear and respect and doing what they wish without our being able to remedy their disorders." Both fathers Garcés and Díaz felt safer when, on December 27, 1780, Ensign

Santiago Yslas arrived with more than a hundred settlers and a large force of soldiers along with several hundred cattle, horses, and mules to shore up the failing mission on the Colorado River and secure the Yuma Crossing.[23]

Yslas selected the site of La Purísima Concepción for reinforcement with both soldiers and settlers, but after consultation with Father Garcés he also decided to establish a second "military colony" approximately ten miles northeast of the Yuma Crossing on the same side of the Colorado River as La Purísima Concepción. On January 7, 1781, Yslas christened this new settlement San Pedro y San Pablo de Bicuñer. Unfortunately, the Spanish settlers now began to claim lands that the Quechans had cleared for crops and pasture. Father Juan Domingo Arricivata later wrote, "A grievous error it was for the Spaniards to think that the best lands should be for them." Moreover, forage and grazing acres proved insufficient. "The result was," Father Arricivata reported, "that much damage was done by this multitude of animals in the maize-fields and sown lands of the Indians." The Quechans complained to Yslas, but he did nothing to stop the encroachment on Indians lands. The Franciscan priests also failed to respect Quechan culture, particularly their practice of polygamy. Father Garcés reported, "These people are the wildest on the frontier and too stupid to be attracted by spiritual things, and so, few can be baptized of those that reach twenty years and are under sixty, because of the concubines that they habitually take and leave."[24]

By early 1781, Salvador Palma and his brother Ygnacio had lost all hope that the Spanish would supply their needs and wants for European goods and horses. Instead, the Spaniards had drained tribal food reserves and seized croplands and ruined others by letting their livestock graze unattended. Ygnacio particularly argued that the Spanish efforts to force the Quechans to accept Christianity was destroying their culture and leading to the enslavement of his people. The Palma brothers and other Quechans also believed the Spanish intended to send more soldiers among them to arrest tribal leaders and attack the Quechans. Trouble seemed imminent by the spring of 1781. Indeed, it had become unavoidable.

In June 1781, relations between the Quechans and the Spanish deteriorated further when Fernando Rivera y Moncada arrived with nearly a hundred soldiers, a group of California-bound settlers, and a thousand cattle, horses, and mules, all of which further taxed Quechan lands and food supplies. Quickly the Quechans turned insolent. After most of the soldiers and settlers left for California, Rivera remained encamped with a small force on the south side of the Colorado across from the town of Concepción. The Spanish were now separated into three camps, and Salvador Palma, Ygnacio, and the other Quechan leaders saw the opportunity to strike the divided and weakened Spanish settlements and encampment. During late June and early July the Quechans sent emissaries to other tribes seeking support, and a large number of Mohaves agreed to join the attack.

It came at dawn on July 17. Salvador Palma had planned a simultaneous assault on Concepción and Bicuñer. When the sun slipped over the mountains, several hundred Quechans and Mohaves attacked Bicuñer from all sides. They caught many Spaniards already working in the fields to avoid the daytime heat, as well as some sleeping in their houses off the plaza. The Quechans quickly killed nearly every Spaniard that they could find, breaking into houses and dragging the people outside for execution with war clubs and arrows. At Concepción, the Quechans infiltrated the town and plaza and upon the signal of a dropped bundle of firewood, launched their attack. Here, the fighting proved less bloody, because so many settlers barricaded themselves in their houses, but it proved no less devastating. During the pandemonium several women and children ran to the church and barricaded the doors. There, Father Garcés consoled them by saying the attack was "God's punishment for our sins." The screams of both victor and vanquished sounded across the Colorado River from La Concepción to Rivera's camp. Rivera, however, chose not to cross the river but ordered his men to dig entrenchments and prepare for an attack. While he waited, the Quechans and Mohaves looted Bicuñer and La Concepción, ransacking the houses and churches for valuables and supplies, stripping clothing from the dead, securing prisoners, and burning buildings. When night fell, the Quechans crossed the Colorado and surrounded Rivera's small force, and the next day swept over the breastwork and killed Rivera and his men.[25]

In the days that followed, Palma's followers rounded up the cattle, horses, mules, and sheep from La Concepción, Bicuñer, and Rivera's camp, as well as collected the firearms, lead, and powder from the dead soldiers, settlers, and caches. He counted approximately one hundred Spanish men, women, and children killed. His followers reported seventy-six hostages, mostly women and children. Quechan losses remain unknown, but were not numerous enough to prevent them from celebrating the restoration of their lands to tribal control, the capture of a large number of horses and cattle, and the annihilation of their enemy, as well as the seizure of hostages whom they could sell into slavery.

On August 5, 1781, the news of the Quechan attack reached the presidio at Tucson via a Pima messenger through San Xavier del Bac. The Papagos, who traded regularly with the Quechans, confirmed the report that the priests, soldiers, and settlers on the Colorado had been killed and that the women and children had been taken captive. One party of Papagos also reported, "Salvador Palma was the instigator of the whole massacre." In early September, upon confirmation of the Quechan attack and the Spanish losses, Croix ordered Lieutenant Colonel Pedro Fages to lead a force known as the Catalonian Volunteers, presidial troops, and Indian auxiliaries to avenge the loss of Rivera and the Spanish settlements of La Concepción and Bicuñer and rescue the hostages. Although Croix hoped to avoid war, he demanded that Palma and the other leaders of the attack undergo "a public and exemplary capital punishment . . . in the presence of the rest of the tribe . . . as a warning to prevent them . . . in the future . . . [from] committing like offenses." Croix also instructed Fages to send word to Felipe de Neve, governor of California, to send troops for an expedition against the Quechans.[26]

Fages reached the Yuma Crossing on October 18 with a force of more than two hundred soldiers and Pima and Papago auxiliaries. Across the river, Palma waited with a force of more than five hundred men, all heavily armed with bows, arrows, spears, and a few guns. Outnumbered, Fages preferred negotiating to fighting, and he shouted across the river to Palma that he wanted a truce to negotiate the release of the Spanish captives. Palma agreed, and the trading of cloth, blankets, beads, and tobacco won the release of more than sixty men, women, and children during the next two days. Further efforts to gain the release of other captives, however, ended when a large force of Gila Pimas, Maricopas, and Halchidomas attacked the Quechans, and Fages withdrew. Croix, however, ordered Fages to return to the Colorado River and "attack without losing an instant the faithless and stubborn Yumas, punishing them as their treachery and sedition deserve . . . and seize Captain Salvador Palma and the other ring leaders, . . . that they may immediately suffer capital punishment." Fages reached the Yuma Crossing on November 29 and ransomed a few more captives, but he could not entrap or otherwise decisively engage the Quechans, and he retreated on December 13. Although Croix sent other expeditions against the Quechans in the spring, summer, and fall of 1782, the Spaniards could not engage the Indians in decisive combat. By January 1783, Croix decided that the Quechans could not be defeated easily or cheaply, and without peace with these Indians, missions could not be established at the Yuma Crossing. Moreover, he believed the lands along the Colorado could not support Spanish settlements, missions, and presidios, and the maintenance of such a colony would severely tax the royal treasury. In addition, Croix contended that presidial soldiers were still needed against the Apaches, whom he considered the primary enemy on Spain's northern frontier. Simply put, Croix believed that all efforts to establish a base at the Yuma Crossing or punish the Quechans should be abandoned. José de Galvéz and Charles III agreed, and in August the war against the Quechans ended. It was a feeble conclusion to an ill-advised and poorly prepared attempt to control the Yuma Crossing, where the Spanish had been both outcommanded and outfought by the Quechans and their Indian allies.[27]

Other resistance to Spanish encroachment periodically occurred. Indian attacks continued throughout the early nineteenth century. In October 1813, for example, Lieutenant Luis Argüello led thirteen soldiers and one hundred neophyte auxiliaries from the presidio at San Francisco and Mission San José in search of runaways who had sought refuge in several villages in the Sacramento River valley. Instead of locating cowering fugitives, an angry force of approximately one thousand Yokuts found the expedition and attacked. Lieutenant Argüello reported that the Indians "attacked with such fury that all the valor of the soldiers was necessary in order to repulse them. This was accomplished by heavy fire, the hostile Indians maintaining their offensive for a long time and holding their position on all sides without perceiving the damage which their obstinacy caused them." After three days of fighting during which both sides kept the other at bay with either guns or arrows, the Indians withdrew and the Spanish retreated without recapturing any fugitives.[28]

By 1819, the Indians in the San Joaquín Valley blocked Spanish penetration at will, and they constantly stole cattle and horses from the missions. In September Father Marino Payeras at Mission Santa Barbara reported to Governor Pablo Vicente de Solá that the Christian Indians had become insubordinate. "A considerable number," he wrote, "have withdrawn from the mild rule of the friars, and have become one body with the savages with whom they carry out whatever evil their heart and malevolent soul dictates.... From day to day the danger of an attack from the united apostates and gentiles is growing." Similarly, Father Narciso Durán reported that the Muqueleme "give shelter to numerous Christian fugitives who are their friends and neighbors. We do not dare to demand their return, for the heathen are very refactory and according to the account of our Indians are disposed to fight and try to kill the Christians, the soldiers, the priests and others who may go there. It is said to be the common refrain of the wild Indians that they are still unbeaten, for they have many bows, arrows and horses."[29]

Throughout the early nineteenth century, then, the Indians held the Spanish to the coast and prevented the establishment of either presidios or missions in the interior, despite numerous military expeditions that inflicted a heavy loss of life and destroyed a host of villages. Not only did the Yokuts, Miwoks, and other Central

Valley tribes resist Spanish attacks, but they also took the offensive, particularly raiding to steal cattle and horses, the latter of which they then used to enhance the force of their raids. Simply put, the valley tribes had the security of distance from the Spanish and quickly adopted Spanish military techniques to prevent their subjugation.

The Indian uprisings against the San Diego and San Gabriel missions and the settlement along the Colorado River were organized and led by individuals whose authority came from their tribal villages. Other resistance came from individual Christianized leaders whose authority came from their ability to mobilize followers, that is, neophytes, within the mission system. Lupugeyun, a Coast Miwok, whom the Spanish called Pomponio, was one such leader, who after baptism fled the forced confinement and servitude of the missions. He then joined other neophytes who also escaped, but who were no longer welcome among their own people. Beginning in 1818, Pomponio led this band in raids against the scattered missions and ranches from Soledat to Sonoma. He eluded the Spanish for five years until his capture and imprisonment at Mission Carmel in 1823 where he awaited execution by a firing squad on February 6, 1824.

Yet, compared to the Southwest, violent confrontations between Indians and the Spanish occurred only occasionally, and each served as exceptions to the general peaceful relations between these two civilizations, and they should be considered exceptional moments rather than examples of commonplace events. The Franciscans and the soldiers were not all cruel and all Indians did not always act heroically to oppose them.

Still, the seizure of Indian lands, forced removal to mission estates, sexual assaults on Indian women, forced labor, corporal punishment, and increased chances of death from disease after association with the Spanish brought covert forms of Indian resistance from the beginning of contact. Although neither the coastal nor the interior tribes unified politically to resist Spanish expeditions designed to force their residence on mission lands, those who fled and those who fought actively asserted their independence and unwillingness to passively accept Spanish domination. In fact, the Spanish neither founded nor maintained any missions in California without soldiers.

The Spanish retreat from California, however, did not restore the Indians to their pre-contact ways of living. By 1821 only 200,000 Indians remained, a loss of 100,000 lives during little more than fifty years due to a high death rate from disease and a declining birth rate due to sterility caused by syphilis. Along the coast the Indian population had been reduced from approximately 70,000 in 1769 to about 20,000 in 1821. Ironically, then, the Spanish significantly reduced the Indian population while Hispanicizing it. Many Indians must have realized that by accepting Christianization and mission life they had agreed to a quick and certain death. Moreover, between 1769 and 1821, the coastal Indians between San Diego and San Francisco had been moved from their villages and relocated near the missions. During the mission period these tribes became the most acculturated. They had learned weaving, tanning, and blacksmithing, as well as the making of pottery, saddles, wine, and soap. They also learned to plant Spanish crops, such as wheat, and herd horses, cattle, and sheep. By 1821, Indians cultivated approximately 10,000 acres on mission lands, and they tended nearly 400,000 cattle, 60,000 horses, and more than 300,000 hogs, sheep, and goats. They had become sedentary agriculturists or farm workers in a way none could have imagined when the Spanish established the first mission and presidio at San Diego in 1769.

Toward the end of the Spanish era, then, the maintenance of labor rather than the Christianization of the natives had become the most important aspect of Spanish policy. The Franciscans served as little more than estate managers who devoted more of their time to overseeing Indian workers on mission lands and maintaining discipline and order among the converts who gathered near the missions, than to the saving of souls. Indeed, as early as 1787, Father Fermín Francisco de Lasuén reported that the people of San José used the Indians at Mission Santa Clara "indiscriminately for all their house and field work. They are an immense hindrance to the conversion of the pagans, for they give them bad example, they scandalize them, and they actually persuade them not to become Christians, lest they would themselves suffer the loss of free labor." In the end, however, Spanish policy seldom remade the Indians into "useful vassals of the King." The Spanish always needed the missions to convert the Indians and the soldiers to enforce their loyalty and thereby keep them from foreign influences, but the process of cultural change proved slower than anyone had imagined. Still, the Spanish never abandoned their goal of acculturation by "denaturalizing" the Indians. After 1810, however, Spanish authorities necessarily directed military and economic resources to help suppress the revolution in Mexico, thereby forcing the missions to rely on their own resources for survival. As a result, the rebellion as well as the Indians prevented the Spanish Crown from extending its empire to California on a strong and lasting basis.[30]

Cultural change, however, is complex. The missions provided greater availability of food for some Indians, but decreased food variety and quality for others. The Spanish fractured Indian political structures and religious systems while only partially remaking Indian society in their own image. Under the Spanish, the Indians exchanged independence and sovereignty for subservience and dependency, after succumbing to coercion and force. Some Indians found many benefits and much to gain by collaborating with the Spaniards; others resisted all efforts to force them to accept Spanish culture. Some Spanish officials considered the conditions at the missions appalling and intolerable; others believed the Indians needed firm, disciplined guidance until they learned to accept superior Spanish culture and Christianity. Some foreign observers who criticized Spanish policy were men of the Enlightenment who opposed clerics and communal societies, such as those found at the missions, and no doubt expressed bias in their reports.

Some Spaniards correctly claimed considerable success. Roughly 70,000 Indians had been baptized in the twenty years preceding the Spanish collapse in 1821, and Indians far exceeded the number of Spaniards at the missions. In 1821, approximately 21,750 Indians lived at the missions compared to 3,400 settlers and soldiers. Put differently, mission Indians outnumbered the soldiers by a ratio of five to one and civilians by six to one. These Indians congregated in villages near the missions, worked the fields raising Spanish crops and livestock, practiced crafts, nominally worshiped the Christian god, offered themselves and their children for baptism, attended the Catholic church, and adopted many Spanish social and cultural practices. Indian cultural life had declined, and individuals had been saved while native society had been weakened, if not destroyed. The safety, security, and material benefits of the missions had their effect on the Indians, and many could tolerate the religious instruction and expectations of the Franciscans. If the Indians were not yet Spaniards in 1821, they had made a start. The Spanish, then, could claim remarkable achievement for a small group of missionaries outnumbered by the people they sought to change and save.

By 1821, California and its garrisons remained isolated on a separate Spanish and Indian frontier. The presidios existed as much to defend the coast against foreign intruders as to protect the settlers from the Indians. At the same time, the Franciscans remained beyond the reach of Spanish officials and successfully resisted efforts to secularize the missions, that is, divide communal property among the Indians and place the missions under parish priests who would not be dependent on the government for support. They never relented in their belief that the missions were needed to save the Indians spiritually and prepare them for and protect them from the outside world. The missions, then, served as the major institution that affected Indian lives and determined Indian policy within the larger parameters determined in Madrid and Mexico City, because neither the military nor civil authorities had the means to establish their own dominance over Indian affairs on the California frontier. In the end, however, neither Spanish nor Indian civilizations survived, but the Spanish left a legacy of cruelty and exploitation that for some remains known as the "Black Legend."[31]

CHAPTER 4

The Pacific Northwest

On July 18, 1774, Juan José Pérez Hernández sighted land near the present border between Canada and Alaska. He had been sent north from Monterey by Antonio María de Bucareli, viceroy of New Spain, to scout the coast of present-day Oregon, Washington, and British Columbia to learn about Russian and British activities. Bucareli had also authorized him to locate and claim potential sites for Spanish settlements and fortifications in order to help maintain Spain's vast territorial claims and aspirations. Spain especially wanted to keep the northwest coastal area as a buffer to thwart foreign encroachment against California and Mexico. With reports that the Russians had already begun explorations from the North as well as knowledge that the British sought a Northwest Passage, Bucareli wanted the Spanish claim to the Northwest firmly established so that "any establishment by Russia, or any other foreign power, on the continent ought to be prevented, not because the king needs to enlarge his realms, as he has within his known dominions more than it will be possible to populate in centuries, but in order to avoid consequences brought by having other neighbors [there] than the Indians." Bucareli believed his responsibilities to Spain included ensuring her claim not only to its "vast domains, but also of trying to augment them insofar as possible, by means of new discoveries in unknown areas, so that numerous Indian inhabitants drawn into the sweet, soft, desirable vassalage of His Majesty may be bathed in the light of the Gospel by means of spiritual conquest, to separate them from the utter darkness of the idolatry in which they live and show them the road to eternal salvation, which are the true intentions of these undertakings which animate the pious heart of His Majesty."[1]

Bucareli accurately stated the motives of his king, which the crown had consistently expressed and which had been codified in the *Laws of the Indies,* regarding the purpose of Pérez's mission. Bucareli also proved correct in recognizing that the Indians would become a vital part of European and American policy for claiming, holding, and exploiting the Pacific Northwest. Accordingly, Pérez had instructions to treat any Indians that he encountered with "kindness and gentleness," giving them gifts while making friendly inquiries about their customs and neighbors,

The Pacific Northwest Coast

Haida

Haisla

Queen
Charlotte
Islands

BRITISH
COLUMBIA

Kwakiutl

C o a s t
S a l i s h

Vancouver
Island

Nootka
Sound

ALBERTA

Makah
Quileute
Quinault

Chinook

Clatsop

WASHINGTON

Yakima

Tillamook

The Dalles

Columbia R.

Nez Perce

OREGON

Klamath

N

Miles

0   200

Yurok

CALIFORNIA

NEVADA

and whether they had seen other Europeans. This policy, Bucareli instructed, would be "the most efficacious means of gaining and firmly establishing their esteem," which, in turn, would help ensure friendly treatment if Spain decided to later establish settlements along the coast.[2]

On July 19, a day after Pérez anchored off the Queen Charlotte Islands, which is now part of British Columbia, he met a group of Haida Indians who paddled out to his ship in canoes and spread feathers in the water as a sign of peace. Juan Crespi, a friar on board, concluded they were a "peaceful and very docile people," who soon offered sea otter skins in a manner that indicated they wanted to trade. The sailors, in turn, offered knives, beads, and clothes, which the Haida eagerly accepted for their furs. Pérez reported that "they are very adept at trading and commerce, judging by the briskness with which they dealt with us, and because before they would give any trifles they had to hold those things they wanted in their hands, examining them and satisfying their fancy with a look." Pérez also noted, "If pleased with them they ask for more, making it clear that without giving more they will not pay." Pérez then departed to the South and, on August 8, he sighted Vancouver Island and entered Nootka Sound the following day, where natives from the nearby villages soon approached his ship wanting to trade.[3]

The Indians with whom Pérez made contact comprised part of a complex Northwest Coast culture of peoples who occupied present-day Oregon, Washington, and British Columbia west of the Cascade Mountains and coast range, and southeast Alaska. This distinctive native Northwest culture includes the Tlingit, Haida, Kwakiutl, Nootka, Coast Salish, and Chinooks. Autonomous local kinship groups, social status derived from heredity and wealth, the practice of slavery, the observance of elaborate ceremonies (particularly involving the potlatch), and detailed woodworking as an art form characterized Indian society along the Northwest Coast. They lived close to the sea in large, rectangular, split-log houses that often provided shelter for several families. The Klamath in present-day Oregon, however, constructed round earth lodges over a pit. The coastal natives crafted dugout canoes from large spruce trees, and they skillfully worked copper. They did not, however, have ceramics or domesticated plants or animals other than "a multiplicity of dogs," which they ate or from which they clipped the hair for weaving blankets, as among the Coast Salish. The men and women wore earrings and nosepieces crafted from copper and shells. The men seldom wore clothing in warm weather, but the women clad themselves in skirts and shirts of deerskin or a cloth made from the wool of mountain goats and dog hair, and they wove a variety of cedar bark baskets. These Indians fished in the rivers and coastal waters, particularly for salmon, hunted deer and other small game, collected berries, and dug roots in nearby meadows, particularly the Kalapuyans and Molalas of the Willamette Valley. The Northwest Coast Indians also exhibited several subregional traits such as practicing the potlatch and carving totem poles. The northwestern Indians also spoke a variety of languages belonging to the Na-Dene, Wakashan, Salishan, and Penutian peoples, and the Penutian language of the Chinook, who lived along the Columbia River and dominated the Oregon-Washington coast, became the lingua franca of the Northwest Coast.[4]

The coastal people organized politically along family lines and local groups and lived in autonomous villages. Among the Chinooks, authority lay with the kin groups that could replace chiefs, and women sometimes held positions of leadership in the absence of qualified men. In general, chiefs, either men or women who claimed mystical or historical lineage, governed the villages, but, with the exception of the Puget Sound Salish, a political culture did not exist beyond the village level to provide strong cultural alliances. The senior men of the village lineages sat on the town council and, along with older women, determined the group's economic activities. Women participated in village council debates and played a more influential role in village affairs than other Indian women to the south and east.

The Indians who lived near the Pacific Northwest Coast were highly conscious of social standing, particularly compared to the Indians in California, and they used marriage to enhance the rank of families. Chinook men also took multiple wives. The Chinooks practiced the custom of flattening the foreheads of their infants from nose to top of the head by using a board fastened to the cradleboard and head. Among the Chinooks, a flattened head signified status and separated them from the more round-headed slaves. The coastal Indians also used slaves acquired in war or purchased from other tribes in Oregon and California for menial tasks around their villages and as concubines. The chiefs and upper-class villages practiced the potlatch ceremony, which involved feasting and gift giving to enhance their political and social standing and to mark special occasions such as marriage. The chiefs also lived aristocratic lives of special privilege, and heredity and wealth determined social position. They often wore sea otter capes as a sign of wealth, power, and prestige. The coastal Indians may have practiced ceremonial or symbolic cannibalism, although the maritime fur traders believed the chiefs commonly ate slaves and captive children.

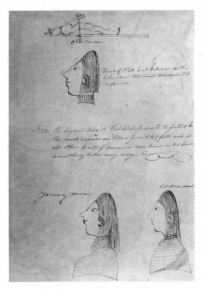

3. The Clatsop Indians flattened the heads of their children by using a board press. They considered a flattened forehead a sign of status and a visual separation of themselves from their slaves. At Fort Clatsop, William Clark made this drawing of the technique used and the results. (Courtesy, Missouri Historical Society, St. Louis.)

4. The Indians who lived near the Pacific Northwest Coast wore little clothing during warm weather, but the chiefs or leaders draped their shoulders with sea otter capes as a sign of wealth, power, and prestige. (*Man of Nootka Sound.* Painting by John Webber, 1778. Courtesy, Peabody Museum, Harvard University.)

5. Chinook, Clatsop, and other women along the Pacific Northwest Coast wore knob-top hats that were woven from cedar and beargrass and decorated with geometric figures representing whaling scenes. These hats were made on Vancouver Island and along the Washington coast and traded as far south as the Columbia River region. In addition to the utility of these hats, they served as status symbols and indicated a complicated and far-reaching trade network. (*Woman of Nootka Sound.* Painting by John Webber, 1778. Courtesy, Peabody Museum, Harvard University.)

The northwest Indians also engaged in extensive trade along the coast and into the interior prior to European contact. On the Columbia, where the river narrowed and became unnavigable, called the Dalles, a large Indian marketplace developed. In 1805, William Clark called it the "great mart of trade," and Alexander Ross, an employee of the Pacific Fur Company at Astoria, considered it the "great emporium or mart of the Columbia, and the general theatre of gambling and roguery." The Chinooks especially played key roles as traders at the Dalles, and their trade networks extended to the Nez Perce and other tribes in the northern Rockies. The reputation of the Chinooks as traders was so great that they felt they controlled the Columbia. By European contact, then, the Northwest Coast peoples were skilled traders and the dupes of none, and the coastal population totaled approximately two hundred thousand, which made the region one of the most densely populated nonagricultural areas of the world.[5]

Despite locating Vancouver Island and the most important port north of San Francisco, Pérez disappointed Bucareli because he did not map the coast north of Monterey or make many attempts to land, plant the cross, and leave documents to ensure Spain's claim to the region. Consequently, in 1775 Bucareli planned to send another expedition northward to strengthen Spain's claim to the Northwest Coast, including the eviction of all settlements found north of California. On March 16, Bruno de Hezeta sailed on the *Santiago,* leading an expedition northward from Monterey. Although Hezeta ultimately provided more geographical information for Spain, he had fewer friendly contacts with the Indians than Pérez. On July 13, off the coast of Washington near the mouth of the Quinault River, Hezeta and Francisco de la Bodega y Quadra, who commanded the *Sonora,* met some friendly Indians who came out to their ships to trade fish and otter skins for beads, earrings, and handkerchiefs. But, when Bodega sent a party of seven sailors to shore to refill water casks they were attacked by some three hundred Indians and hacked to pieces in view of the men aboard ship. Before Bodega could hoist sail, nine or ten canoes with nearly thirty Indians each approach his ship and tried to board, but Bodega's crew fired on them with the swivel gun and muskets and killed a half dozen with the initial volley. Bodega then departed for Monterey while Hezeta continued north before turning southward on August 11. Six days later, he became the first European to record sighting the entrance to the Columbia River. The strong current prevented him from entering the river, and he concluded that the opening was "the mouth of some great river, or of some passage to another sea." Hezeta, however, made no attempt to explore it and returned to Monterey. Not until seventeen years later when Robert Gray sighted the river and named it after his ship did the Columbia come into common parlance and the basis of the American claim to the region.[6]

News of the Spanish expeditions along the Pacific Northwest Coast reached England as early as April 1775, a time during which the British experienced other difficulties on the North American continent. A year later the British responded by sending Captain James Cook to foil Spain's attempts to extend its empire. Although Cook departed from Plymouth, England, in July 1776, he did not reach the Pacific Northwest until March 7, 1778, when he sighted Cape Flattery at the northwest tip of present-day Washington State. Cook had instructions to determine the economic and strategic importance of the area and search for a Northwest Passage. Cook's instructions authorized him to claim territory wherever possible as long as he did not interfere with Spanish claims. He was also to distribute among the Indians such things as would remain "traces and testimonies" that he had been along the Northwest Coast. As early as Cook's instructions, then, British policy mandated the use of the Indians along the coast to help expand the empire.[7]

Bad weather and chance brought Cook to Nootka Sound and Friendly Cove on March 29 where he learned of the Spanish visit when he purchased two silver spoons on Vancouver Island from the Indians who came to trade with him. Cook's ships were soon approached by canoes bearing members of the Mowachaht tribe, who, with faces and hands painted red and black and clothed in hides, wanted to trade sea otter skins for iron goods of any kind. Soon the sailors had traded away their knives, buckles, nails, and buttons. Cook and his men probably knew about the value of sea otter skins from reports of Russian expeditions to the Northwest Coast, and he realized that the 1,500 sea otter pelts that they acquired from the Indians marked the beginning of an aggressive and prosperous maritime trade with the natives that would reach from London and Boston to the Pacific Northwest Coast and on to Macao. Cook certainly understood the possibilities for profits and empire when he dispassionately reported: "The fur of these animals, as mentioned in the Russian accounts, is certainly softer and finer than that of any others we know of; and therefore, the discovery of this part of the continent of North America, where so valuable an article of commerce may be met with, cannot be a matter of indifference."[8]

After exploring the coast as far north as the Aleutian Islands, Cook's expedition wintered in Hawaii, where he was killed in 1779. Before returning to England, his ships stopped at Macao, where the crewmen were astonished to learn that the

6. Captain James Cook reached the Pacific Northwest Coast in early March 1778. He anchored at Nootka Sound where his men traded with nearby Indians for sea otter pelts, which they sold in Macao for high prices. The potential of the sea otter trade for British merchants remained unknown, however, until 1784 with the publication of Cook's record of the voyage. (Courtesy, Museum of History and Industry, Seattle.)

7. Nootka Sound served as a safe haven for ships engaged in the sea otter trade during the late eighteenth century. The Indians preferred to trade on land where they could control the process more than aboard a ship. About 1778, a trader made this drawing of a Nootka village. It shows two European traders with guns bargaining for a large black stack of sea otter hides. (*A Nootka Village, 1778*. Negative No. 70–072. Courtesy, Washington State University Libraries.)

sea otter pelts in their ships' holds brought as much as 120 Spanish dollars per hide, and totaled more than 2,000 pounds sterling, which in the years ahead would be a pittance for trading vessels. Immediately the crews wanted to return to the Northwest Coast to trade with the Indians for furs, but they sailed for England instead in October 1779 in a state "not far short of mutiny." News about the economic potential of the Northwest Coast based on furs, however, did not become generally known until 1784 with the publication of Cook's account of the voyage. The next year, the first British fur-trading vessel, named the *Sea Otter*, sailed into Nootka Sound on August 18, under the command of James Hanna, whose backers had profits and the extension of national power in mind, the repercussions of which would forever change the lives of the Indians in the Pacific Northwest.[9]

Spain could do little to block the British incursion along the Northwest Coast. War with Britain, as Spain took the side of the English rebels during the American Revolution, weakened Spain's ability to protect her interests along the Pacific Coast. The Revolution offered opportunity, but it also required major resources of men and material for an attempt to retake Gibraltar, and Spain had other valuable interests to protect in the Caribbean and the Philippines. Without sufficient soldiers, sailors, and money, Spain could not keep the Northwest Coast against all challengers, and her claims to the Pacific Northwest, reinforced by trade with the Indians, necessarily had to wait. Soon after the war ended, in 1785, the British set sail first for the Northwest Coast, and a host of merchant vessels bent on earning great wealth from the sea otter trade soon reached the area well ahead of the Spanish.

At the same time, the Americans began to take an interest in the Northwest Coast and the sea otter trade, and two ships financed by businessmen in Boston and New York City, under the commands of John Kendrick and Robert Gray, arrived at Nootka Sound in September 1788. Now unrestricted by British mercantile policy or war, Yankee merchants sought new markets, particularly Asian and Pacific, but in the absence of substantial manufactured goods, they needed something to trade for Chinese tea, silk, and porcelain that would bring substantial earnings on the Boston and New York markets. Quickly, the Yankee merchants recognized the great potential of sending goods, such as cloth, beads, and iron pots, to the Pacific Northwest to trade for sea otter pelts from the Indians. These sea otter skins could then be exchanged in Canton for Chinese goods, which, in turn, could be sold to American consumers—essentially a global triangular trade. Soon, they sent the best ships and sailors in the world to the treacherous waters off the Northwest Coast to earn their fortunes. The Americans would essentially dominate the maritime fur trade between 1790 and 1810, when British-American relations began to deteriorate and, with the decline of the sea otter population, the trade began to ebb.

British and American trade with the Indians for sea otter pelts alarmed the Spanish, who now recognized that such exchanges could be used to promote settlement, knowing full well that possession was the best claim to territory, while the Christianization and acculturation of the Indians would help establish a human bulwark to protect Spanish claims. One Spanish official recommended treating the Indians of the Pacific Northwest with "gentleness and affability," and thereby to "secure control of a rich and powerful commerce to which other strong nations now aspire and to which, if we are negligent, they may perhaps gain sole rights while we are still making plans." The abundance of sea otters along the California coast and the willingness of the Indians to provide them, even though the natives along the Northwest Coast were better hunters and the sea otters there had better pelts, however, discouraged most Spanish traders from venturing into the more dangerous waters along the Oregon and Washington coast. Moreover, Spain levied high export fees on furs, and the Franciscans in California wanted the Indians to give their attention to agriculture and the missions. As a result, Spain essentially forfeited the sea otter trade north of California to the British and Americans, except to contest its claim and occupation of the Nootka Sound area and to trade with the Indians there in 1789 by seizing several British trading ships at Nootka Sound. The capture of the British vessels involved more than prize and ransom money. It signified the clash of two great empires in the Pacific Northwest. Before the crisis ended in 1790 with Spain backing down because it stood alone in any military opposition to Great Britain, it caused Britain and the United States to reassess their diplomatic policies in relation to each other. This conflict between two international powers engaged in the sea otter trade forced the United States to begin clarifying its position on neutrality. It also made the British aware of their vulnerability to American opportunism in times of preoccupation or weakness elsewhere.[10]

British and American competition for the sea otter trade and the territorial claims that went with it, then, encouraged Spain to pursue an Indian policy based on friendship and peace. In 1791, Viceroy Conde de Revillagigedo instructed Francisco Antonio Mourelle, who had been selected to explore the channels off the Juan de Fuca Strait near Vancouver, to deal with any Indians he encountered with a "spirit of humanity." He hoped that "gifts, gentleness, and possibly pretending not to notice offenses they commit, as well as vigilance over your people so they do not insult the Indians in the slightest way, will be the bonds to link you with them, laying the foundation for friendship perhaps very useful in the future to religion and the sovereign."[11]

Revillagigedo also instructed Mourelle to collect as much information as possible about the natives, and "to neither take from the Indians nor permit taking anything belonging to them unless agreed upon and offered by their hand. It is of concern to observe this so they may always comprehend that we profess good faith and are truthful, thus removing from their imagination any idea that we are capable of deceiving them." Moreover, Mourelle's crew was to "bear whatever treachery the natives commit," if it did not interfere with his mission. Spain, then, would strengthen its claims to the Northwest Coast by establishing friendly contacts with the Indians as well as by attempting to occupy and fortify Nootka. Indeed, Spain could do little more because she did not have the power to make her claims and hold them by force. If she could lure the Indians into her base at Nootka to trade, British and American traders and their territorial claims might be weakened.[12]

By 1792, however, the Indians on Vancouver Island and along the Northwest Coast had become increasingly sophisticated in dealing with the Spanish, British, American, Russian, and French fur traders who visited the area. John Kendrick worked to gain competitive advantage by giving them gifts in larger quantities than other traders, speaking their language, wearing Indian dress, and most important, trading guns, powder, and lead for pelts and teaching the Indians how to use firearms. One Spaniard observed, "I cannot say whether it was self-interest or rivalry with the English that suggested to the Americans the perverse idea of teaching the savages the handling of firearms—a lesson that could be harmful to all humanity." Soon, many Indians would not trade sea otter pelts for anything but guns and ammunition, and, in 1799, British traders, known as "King George's men," complained that during the past decade the "Boston men" had increased the cost of otter skins from one to five muskets per hide and from one to six yards of cloth, because the Indians knew they could demand that exchange rate and get it.[13]

The introduction of firearms into the sea otter trade by the Americans made many Indian groups more assertive and bold once they could fight on equal footing or take what they wanted from the traders with greater chances of success. Once the Indians acquired firearms, one British observer reported, "Their former weapons, Bows, and Arrows, Spears and Clubs are now thrown aside & forgotten." He saw only bad results, noting that once the Indians traded for guns, "they turn against the donors. Few ships have been on the Coast that have not been attack'd or attempted to be attacked and in general many lives have been lost on both sides." The Indians increasingly attacked American and British ships in retaliation for ill-treatment, such as floggings for theft, as well as holding chiefs and natives for ransom aboard ship with their release gained with sea otter hides. The Indians did not care whether the same traders were involved when they attacked, thereby retaliating as a tribal responsibility in response to individual altercations for which they levied collective responsibility on the British and American traders, much in the same way Americans levied collective responsibility on tribal groups for injuries and damages caused by only a few individuals. In time, many Indians refused to trade aboard ship and instead insisted that the exchanges be conducted on land.[14]

By the late 1790s, then, the fur trade along the Northwest Coast had become ruthless and violent, particularly with Americans. Yet, while the Americans and the British offered more desirable goods than the Spanish, they primarily acted as independent entrepreneurs rather than representatives of their respective governments, and their captains often had invested in the cargo, and along with the crew, received both pay and a percentage of the voyage's proceeds. In contrast, the Spanish primarily sought political control over the Indians to ensure their territorial claims north of California. And, while the British, operating through the British East India and South Sea Companies, or the Americans operating as freelance businessmen, used any technique necessary to acquire sea otter pelts, the Spanish offered only governmental sympathy and counsel, particularly at Nootka, because the Spanish system prohibited independent fur traders from dealing with the Indians. Spain also strictly regulated trading monopolies and fixed fur prices too low to encourage the coastal trade.

As a result, by the late eighteenth century, the Indians along the Northwest Coast considered the Spaniards less of a threat than the British and Americans. Ultimately, however, Spain failed to maintain her claim to the Pacific Northwest, because she faced a far more aggressive and expansive power in the form of the Americans, and because she did not develop the intricate mission and educational system for acculturation that proved at least partially successful in California and the Southwest. Confronted with challenges to her authority and empire around the world, particularly on the European continent, Spain did not have the economic and military resources, organizational ability, or political will to claim the Pacific Northwest and keep it. Moreover, Spain's mere occupation of Nootka Sound and claims to the Pacific Northwest based on the Treaty of Tordesillas could neither hold the region nor extend its domain over the native peoples who sought trade from both Britons and Americans, and whose maritime power and economic and political aggressiveness and desire for territorial expansion could not be blocked.

The Northwest Coast, then, exceeded Spain's grasp, and it slipped through weakened fingers into the firm grasp of the British until 1800, when European affairs caused them to withdraw and permitted the United States alone to fill the trade and power vacuum along the Northwest Coast. By the time Lewis and Clark reached the Pacific Ocean at the mouth of the Columbia River in 1805, American vessels, mostly out of Boston, dominated the fur trade along the Northwest Coast. They continued to do so until the maritime fur trade peaked about 1812. In 1805, for example, more than 120 American, along with 80 British, trading ships visited the Indians along the coast, while the Spanish made only 43 contacts, largely coinciding with exploration to locate and claim ports, which could be used to block British, Russian, and American claims and settlements and which in other hands could threaten the Spanish empire to the south. Strategic geographical concerns, then, rather than trade with the Indians shaped Spanish policy.

Soon the American fur trade from ships based on glass beads, knives, copper pots, guns, powder, lead, cloth, and clothing for sea otter hides would link East Coast investors in a lucrative trade between the Atlantic and Northwest Coasts and China. The fur trade would sweep the northwest Indian peoples into a world of international business where the rewards were as high as they were volatile. This trade increasingly turned American attention to the Oregon country for settlement. It also helped create visions of opportunity and destiny that had ominous consequences for the Indian peoples of the Pacific Northwest in the decades to come, but its antecedents lay in late eighteenth century.

Mutual exploitation characterized the maritime fur trade along the Pacific Northwest Coast. Although British and American traders acquired thousands of pelts, cheaply in the traders' opinion, the Indians acquired knives, axes, chisels, guns, powder, lead, and jewelry, all of which were far more useful and valuable to them than the sea otter pelts that they so easily acquired. Although the Indians along the Northwest Coast used sea otter pelts for clothing, they could take more hides than they needed if they had sufficient reason, and the traders gave it to them. By exchanging sea otter pelts that they did not need and which, for the moment, seemed unendingly abundant, the Indians believed they received the best of the bargain from the fur traders. At the same time, because the British and American traders reaped profits ranging from $20,000 to nearly $50,000 per trip between the Northwest Coast and Macao, they believed they were the better traders, exchanging goods that they did not need for the dark, luxurious hides of the sea otter. Value, like beauty, of course, depends on the eye of the beholder. Among the maritime fur traders, such as the American William Sturgis, the most wonderful sight in the world, "excepting a beautiful woman and a lovely infant," was the full, soft, glossy, near black pelt of a sea otter. William Clark agreed; from Fort Clatsop in late February 1806, he wrote, "[I]t is the riches[t] and I think the most delicious fur in the world at least I cannot form an idea of any more so. [I]t is deep thick silkey in the extreem and strong." Sea otter skins also far exceeded the value of beaver pelts, which provided the foundation for the continental fur trade.[15]

Moreover, both Indians and whites believed they controlled the trading process. The Indians surprised Cook and the traders who came after him with their assertive demands regarding beads and jewelry, which they considered inferior in artistry and value compared to their own. Instead, they wanted metal goods, particularly iron with a cutting edge, but Cook also reported, "[B]efore we left the place, hardly a bit of brass was left in the Ship, except what was in the necessary instruments. Whole Suits of cloths were stripped of every button." Since the Indians controlled what the traders wanted, that is, sea otter pelts, they bargained from a position of strength usually on shore or in their villages, and they usually got what they wanted. A member of Cook's expedition reported, "[T]hey are very keen traders getting as much as they could for everything they had; always asking for more give them what you would."[16]

On June 25, 1786, Alexander Walker and ninety men associated with the East India Company, which sought control of the fur trade and possibly territory along the Northwest Coast, sighted Vancouver Island from the decks of the *Captain Cook* and *Experiment*. The next day they entered Nootka Sound where they stayed until July 26. Almost immediately, a group of Indians in canoes paddled out to their vessels and showed an eagerness to trade. Walker noted their shrewdness and care in the exchange process, commenting, "They would not part with anything out of their hands, before they had received the equivalent; they never forgot to examine carefully our goods." He also reported, "Nor were they contented with their own opinion alone, but handing our goods to their friends, consulted with them respecting their quality, and what they should give in return." The keen ability of the Indian traders to strike a favorable bargain impressed Walker, who reflected, "[O]ur prudence was always matched by their cunning. They were never off their guard." Moreover, the Indians always set a high price while the traders tried, often unsuccessfully, to set the exchange rate. Walker noted, "It required no small precaution and prudence to prevent the depreciation of our Currency." At the same time, the Indians at Nootka Sound attempted to monopolize the trade for themselves to later exchange goods with other tribes among whom they acted as brokers or agents. In 1799, Richard Cleveland, an American captain out of Boston, told another captain about the skillful trading practices of the Indians. Cleveland reported that "the Indians are sufficiently cunning to derive all possible advantage from competition, and will go from one vessel to another, and back again, with assertions of offers made to them, which have no foundation in truth, and showing themselves to be as well versed in the tricks of the trade as the greatest adepts."[17]

At first, the British and Americans considered most Indians honest traders, but some natives skillfully used deception and dishonesty to beguile the less-than-knowledgeable white traders who came among them. Indeed, many of the men on the trading vessels seemed so naive they deserved to be cheated. Traders who acquired flasks of fish oil sometimes discovered the product had been watered. Or, the Indians substituted an occasional land otter pelt in a pile of sea otter hides. The Indians along the Northwest Coast, of course, had a long exchange tradition among themselves. They were experienced and careful traders and as skillful as any hard-nosed Yankee. Joseph Ingraham, a Yankee shipper who sailed and traded along the Northwest Coast during the early 1790s, put it best when he said that their Indians had "a truly mercantile spirit."[18]

The arrival of other ships usually caused the value of European goods to fall and Indian furs to rise as the Indian traders used the law of supply and demand to their advantage. Many ship captains, reflecting a prejudice of their time, likened them to the best Jewish merchants, and one observed that "modern Hebrews would perhaps, have little to teach them." Whenever possible, the Indians played British, American, and Russian traders against each other to get the best prices. In turn, white traders countered the escalating prices by offering shoddy merchandise, with bribes, presents, and wine. Usually, however, the white traders bid fur prices to ruinous levels.[19]

Many of the pelts traded to whites had first been acquired from other Indians. Often traders dealt with village chiefs rather than individuals, because the Indians preferred that they dispose of communal property. The chiefs used their positions to acquire sea otter pelts in great quantities and used the goods received for gifts in potlatches, which further increased their status. Indian women also participated in the maritime fur trade by preparing hides and through direct negotiations with white traders, who often preferred to deal with them rather than their men. Sometimes, as among the Haida on the Queen Charlotte Islands, the women controlled the trading through their husbands. In 1791, for example, Joseph Ingraham, captain of the *Hope,* reported, "I have often been witness to men being abused by their wives for parting with skins before their approbation was obtained." At Nootka Sound, Alexander Walker observed that the women "managed the traffic" and were "more exorbitant in their demands than the men." William Sturgis also observed that: "Among a portion of the Indians, the management of trade is entrusted to the women. The reason given by the men was, that women could talk with white men *better* than they could and were willing to talk *more.*" Lewis and Clark also noted that the Chinook men consulted their women over trade matters and "act conformably to their opinions." Overall, native women earned reputations as keen and shrewd traders, and they played a major role in fixing the price, that is, the exchange rates of otter skins for knives, pots, and cloth.[20]

Indian women also enhanced the fur trade through prostitution, often as slaves when their owners, usually older women, forced them to provide sex to the sailors for trade goods. In 1786, Alexander Walker at Nootka Sound observed that the Indians who wanted to trade with them "gave us to understand, that for Iron, we might have their wives (or Women) explaining their meaning with many indecent actions." Chinook men also prostituted their wives and daughters and took the earnings. Chinook women, however, played an important role in the fur trade and offered sex to facilitate trade agreements. By so doing, they helped increase the wealth of their families in a society that only considered sexual intercourse wrong if it involved incest. Many Indian women, other than the slaves, no doubt thought the sailors little more than dupes because they exchanged valuable goods for nothing more than a sexual encounter.[21]

The Chinook and other native groups supported abortion and infanticide to deal with unwanted consequences of this trade. Indian women, both slave and free, paid a high price because many sailors infected them with venereal disease, particularly syphilis, which then spread to their owners and their wives and brought incredible suffering, sterility, miscarriages, stillbirths, and death. Europeans and Americans also brought smallpox, malaria, and by the 1830s, tuberculosis. In the end, disease became the only European and American cultural importation the Indians of the Pacific Northwest could not reject. After a century of contact, the Indian population had declined to approximately thirty-five thousand or at least by 80 percent, primarily due to white-introduced diseases. Otherwise, the Indians used the maritime fur trade for their own advantage.

At the same time, both white traders and Indians wantonly depleted the sea otter population. During the late 1780s, a trading ship could easily acquire 2,500 skins during a season. By 1792, traders, "well provided with cargoes," along the Northwest Coast reaped profits of at least 30 percent, while an investment of $40,000 for a ship, crew, and cargo earned more than $150,000 or a profit of 275 percent, because investors gained profits three ways—by exchanging goods for furs, marketing furs at Canton, and selling Chinese goods in Boston, with a markup of at least 100 percent. With profits such as these and with the Indians equally desirous of Euro-American goods, overhunting quickly became a serious problem, and prices at the major markets at Nootka Sound and along the Columbia River varied accordingly. With sea otters producing only one pup annually and not bearing young each year, the harvest had essentially ended the fur trade on Vancouver Island by 1795 and the maritime trade along the coast basically disappeared during the first decade of the nineteenth century. In 1810, John Jacob Astor received a report that "the furs on the Coast this Year have been very scarce." The insatiable economic needs of Indians and whites came at a high price for the sea otter population.[22]

Yet, while the Spanish wanted recognition of lands they claimed but could not hold, the British primarily preferred, in the words of Lord Shelburne in 1783, "trade to dominion," and the fur trade with the Indians contributed only a small part to the British quest for markets, commerce, and supremacy of the seas. The Americans, however, wanted land first and considered trade with the Indians the necessary means to ensure their claims by establishing a presence. As the sea otter population declined and as Britain reached the limits of its maritime influence along the Northwest Coast, the Americans prepared to reach the Pacific Northwest overland and, by trading with the Indians for inland furs, particularly beaver hides, establish a firm and incontestable claim to the region.[23]

Thomas Jefferson figuratively watched the maritime fur traders of Spain, Great Britain, and the United States from both Paris and Monticello. He had a mind for empire and a burning fear of British expansion, the latter fueled by the crown's plan to explore the interior from the Mississippi River to California, and by fur trader Alexander Mackenzie's overland journey to the Pacific to stake a claim for the North West Company operating out of Montreal. As early as November 26, 1782, Jefferson had expressed an interest in "the country between the Mississippi waters [and] the South Sea." Jefferson believed a similar expedition by Americans could stake a competitive claim to the Northwest and operate as a scientific fact-finding mission. In June 1799, when he served as vice president, Jefferson also expressed an interest in learning about the language and culture of the Indians in the Mississippi Valley. But, he noted, "Beyond that river our means fail." Jefferson, however, prepared to provide the means to explore the far reaches of the interior to the Pacific Northwest, and, after serving as president for little more than two years, on June 18, 1803, he asked Congress in a secret message for support to send an expedition to explore the Upper Mississippi Valley and the Northwest to the Pacific, even though much of that territory had been ceded to France but remained in the actual possession of Spain.[24]

Jefferson believed that an "intelligent officer, with ten or twelve chosen men . . . might explore the whole line, even to the western ocean; have conferences with the natives on the subject of commercial intercourse; get admission among them for our traders, as others are admitted; agree on convenient deposits for an interchange of articles; and return with the information acquired, in the course of two summers." By so doing, the United States could establish trade relations with the Indians, gain their friendship, lure them away from the British, and give the Americans a strong claim to the Northwest. Congress agreed and provided $2,500 "for the purpose of extending the external commerce of the United Sates," and Jefferson chose his secretary Meriwether Lewis who, in turn, asked William Clark to serve as his co-commander.[25]

Lewis's commission of June 20, 1803, instructed him to take "[l]ight articles for barter and presents among the Indians." The commission also instructed Lewis regarding the Indians to "treat them in the most friendly and conciliatory manner which their own conduct will admit; allay all jealousies as to the object of your journey; satisfy them of its innocence; make them acquainted with the position, extent, character, and peaceable and commercial dispositions of the United States; of our wish to be neighborly, friendly, and useful to them, and of our dispositions to a commercial intercourse with them; confer with them on the points most convenient as mutual emporiums, and the articles of most desirable interchange for them and us." The commission also informed Lewis: "Should you reach the Pacific ocean, inform yourself of the circumstances which may decide whether the furs of those parts may not be collected as advantageously at the head of the Missouri (convenient as is supposed to the waters of the Colorado and Oregon or Columbia) as at Nootka Sound, or any other point of that coast; and that trade be consequently conducted through the Missouri and United States more beneficially than by the circumnavigation now practised." Jefferson, then, planned to use the Lewis and Clark Expedition to gain the favor of the Indians by establishing trade that, in turn, would give the United States a claim to the Pacific Northwest. This Indian policy would benefit the Indians slightly through trade and the United States greatly by basing a bold territorial claim on peaceful relations with the Indians rather than by military power or possession.[26]

Lewis informed Clark about his instructions, and stressed "the importance to the U. States of an early friendly and intimate acquaintance with the tribes that inhabit that country, that they should be early impressed with a just idea of the rising importance of the U. States and of her friendly dispositions towards them, as also her desire to become usefull to them by furnishing them through her citizens with such articles by way of barter as may be desired by them or usefull to them." Both understood that Jefferson intended their expedition to help the United States gain control of the fur trade, block British and Canadian territorial claims, expand the China trade, and foster territorial consolidation, that is, expansion to the Northwest Coast.[27]

The Louisiana Purchase of April 30, 1803, gave Jefferson a free hand to explore the interior and Pacific Northwest, although no one precisely knew the northern boundary of the Louisiana Territory. As a result of the Louisiana Purchase, the Lewis and Clark expedition left St. Louis on May 14, 1804, laden with trade goods, such as clothing, tools, and ornaments that the northwest Indians desired, as reported by the maritime fur traders. On their way up the Missouri River, Lewis and Clark informed the Indians that Spain and France had withdrawn but the "great Chief of the Seventeen great nations of America" would meet their needs, and "from whom you can ask favours, or receive good councils, and he will take care that you shall have no just cause to regret this change; he will serve you, & not deceive you." They passed out peace medals and distributed the American flag among the tribes as they ascended the river and crossed the Rocky Mountains, telling the Indians that they came on an errand for their leader, the president of the United States, and that: "He has further commanded us to tell you that when you accept his flag and medal, you accept therewith his hand of friendship, which will never be withdrawn from your nation as long as you continue to follow the councils which he may command his chiefs to give you, and shut your ears to the councils of Bad birds," that is, the British.[28]

The Lewis and Clark expedition reached the Pacific Ocean in early November 1805, and wintered with the Clatsop near the south bank of the Columbia and a few miles from the coast. The men in the expedition disappointed the Clatsops and nearby Chinooks because they had little to trade, and did not seek sea otter hides, and the Indians were accustomed to asking high prices and getting them from the maritime traders. The men of the Corps of Discovery, as they were called, soon learned that "those people ask generally double and tribble the value of what they have to sell, and never take less than the real value of the article in such things as is calculated to do them service."[29]

Even so, the men of the expedition established working, if not good, relationships with the Clatsops, nearby Chinooks, and other tribes before their departure in late March 1806. Upon his return that summer, Lewis warned that British traders threatened the interests of the United States. If not countered, he believed the British would form the Indians in the Northwest into a "rod of iron," which they would use "to scourge our frontier at pleasure." He recommended regulating British trade with the Indians and prohibiting Americans from unrestricted hunting and trapping on Indian lands. Lewis, like Jefferson, wanted to aid the Indians as well as secure the Pacific Northwest for the United States. He hoped the United States would combine "philanthropic views towards those wretched people of America" with the means "to secure to the citizens of the United States, all those advantages, which ought of right exclusively to accrue to them, from the possession of Upper Louisiana." Prophetically, he recognized, however, "The first principle of governing the Indians is to govern the whites."[30]

While Jefferson contemplated his next move in relation to the Indians and the Louisiana Territory, maritime traders continued to visit the Northwest Coast, but firm American presence would await the establishment of a trading post near the mouth of the Columbia by John Jacob Astor's Pacific Fur Company (a subsidiary of the American Fur Company) in April 1811. As early as January 1808, Astor, a successful merchant in New York City who bought Canadian furs for sale on the London market, had proposed the creation of a global commercial network based on the Northwest fur trade. The rewards would be both personal for investors and empire for the nation. Simply put, fur and flag could be inextricably linked in the Pacific Northwest. The British could be blocked and the Indians linked to the United States by trade, both of which would give the Americans a strong claim to the region.

In 1810, Astor sent two expeditions of the newly organized Pacific Fur Company, one by sea and the other by land, to establish a base in the Pacific Northwest at the mouth of the Columbia River. The sea party arrived first, sighting land, which proved to be Cape Disappointment on the north side of the entrance to the Columbia. After scouting the area, the men of the *Tonquin*, and Astor's

8. John Jacob Astor became a fur dealer in New York City in 1793. He organized the Pacific Fur Company in 1810 as a subsidiary of his American Fur Company. Astor believed that China could become an important market for sea otter pelts. He sought financing from the federal government but only received encouragement. Soon after the return of the Lewis and Clark Expedition, Astor sent his men to the Columbia River to develop the fur trade. (Negative No. OrHi 82932. Courtesy, Oregon State Historical Society.)

partners Alexander McKay, Robert Stuart, Duncan McDougall, and David Stuart out of New York City, selected a site for their trading post and fort on Point George, a dozen miles from the mouth of the Columbia. In early April 1811, they came ashore on the south side of the Columbia in Baker's Bay across from Chinook Point. The Chinooks under the one-eyed, shrewd, and manipulative Chief Comcomly and the Clatsops gave them a friendly welcome, and the partners reciprocated, knowing as Astor had reminded them that their success and safety depended on good relations with the coastal people. Ever mindful of establishing and maintaining good relations with the Indians, Astor told his partners before they departed on September 6, 1810, "If you find them kind as I hope you will be so to them. If otherwise, act with caution and forbearance, and convince them that you come as friends."[31]

As the men went about building their quarters and post or factory, they called their site Astoria in honor or deference to their chief benefactor. They also soon discovered that Chief Comcomly used his authority to exclude other tribes and villagers from trading with them. By so doing, he controlled the flow of trade goods to and from the other tribes, set the price of exchange, and reaped

9. In 1811 an overland party of Astor's men established Fort Astoria near the mouth of the Columbia River. His traders never had adequate supplies for exchange and the British took control of the post during the War of 1812 and renamed it Fort George. Thereafter, Astor devoted his attention to the inland fur trade. This view shows Fort Astoria in 1813. (Photographer Curtis. Negative No. 63020. Courtesy, Washington State Historical Society, Tacoma.)

the profits for himself. The Chinooks traded for furs and elk hides from interior tribes, which they then sold or exchanged for Euro-American goods with the Astorians at a profit of nearly 50 percent. Other coastal tribes followed the same trading practice, and they tried to keep their sources of supply secret so the maritime traders could not circumvent them.

The Chinooks impressed the Astorians with their trading ability as the Pacific Northwest people had impressed others. Alexander Ross, a company clerk, observed that "The Chinooks are crafty and intriguing, and have probably learned the arts of cheating, flattery, and dissimulation in the course of their traffic with the coasting traders: for, on our first arrival among them, we found guns, kettles and various other articles of foreign manufacture in their possession, and they were up to all the shifts of bargaining." The Astorians also found the Chinook women as skillful in trade as their men. Ross noted, "In trade and barter the women are as actively employed as the men, and it is as common to see the wife, followed by a train of slaves, trading at the factory, as her husband."[32]

The Astorians established their post and dealt with the Chinooks and Clatsops, and they also traveled into the interior to make contacts with other Indians who would trade with them directly. With approximately one thousand Indian fighting men nearby, however, the Astorians gave as much consideration to defense as the establishment of warm trading relations. Ross reflected, "We naturally put the worst construction on so formidable an array of savages in arms." The Chinooks, however, who had a long tradition as skillful traders in fur and slaves, preferred commerce to war. Although the Astorians showed little interest in trading guns, knives, copper pots, and clothing for slaves, they eagerly sought to exchange their goods for the beaver pelts that the Chinooks acquired from other tribes.[33]

While the Astorians traded for beaver hides and explored the countryside, Astor, writing from New York City, attempted to gain government support and protection for his venture by reporting the great potential for lucrative trade with the peaceful Indians of the Pacific Northwest. Astor understood the dangers at hand with the rapidly deteriorating relations between Great Britain and the United States over the impressment of American seamen and the seizure of the nation's merchant ships and goods. When Congress declared war on Great Britain on June 18, 1812, Astor believed that not only the United States but also his trading post on the Columbia River were in great danger.

By the spring of 1812, the Astorians had traded for furs, mostly beaver, with an estimated value of approximately $10,000. Although the Astorians had standardized the exchange rate for beaver pelts, the Chinooks and Clatsops became increasingly dissatisfied with the quality of goods offered at Astoria. The British clerk Ross agreed, noting after the arrival of a supply ship in early summer 1812 that "[i]nstead of guns, we got old metal pots and gridirons; instead of trinkets, we got white cloth; and instead of blankets, molasses. In short, all the useless trash and unsaleable trumpery which had been accumulating in his [Astor's] shops and stores for half a century, were swept together to fill his Columbia ships."[34]

The shoddy goods in the storehouse at Astoria had dwindled by late 1812 and trade essentially ceased for want of merchandise for exchange. While the Astorians waited for a supply ship to replenish their stores, news arrived in late January 1813 that explained its absence—Great Britain and the United States were at war. The arrival overland of John George McTavish of the North West Company, who was determined to establish a fur trading post for the British at the mouth of the Columbia, brought the news and made a grim situation worse. By July, the supply ship still had not yet arrived and morale plummeted to a new low with one Astorian complaining of life in "this miserable country." While food and ammunition dwindled, trade with the Indians for furs declined from a flood to a trickle. Moreover, the Chinooks and Clatsops grew argumentative, belligerent, and increasingly resentful of the Astorians' presence when they could gain no benefit from it. The partners recorded that, "In fine, circumstances are against us on every hand, and nothing operates to lead us into a conclusion that we can succeed."[35]

By mid-summer 1813, Astor's venture to make a profit for himself and seize a corner of empire for his country based on the Indian trade had failed. In early July his partners, fearing a British attack, acted in accordance with an agreement with Astor that permitted the abandonment of the enterprise if the venture proved unprofitable and decided to abandon Astoria. In mid-November, they sold the property and goods of the Pacific Fur Company to the North West Company of the Canadians. The transfer of ownership, with at least some profit gained from the sale, occurred none too soon, because a British warship arrived in December and the captain took possession of the fort.

Chief Comcomly could not understand why the Americans turned their trade over to the British. To McDougall, he said, "See those few King George people [the North West Company men] who come down the river: they were poor; they have no goods, and were almost starving; yet you were afraid of them, and delivered your fort and all your goods to them; and now King George's ships are coming to carry you all off as slaves. We are not afraid of King George's people. I have got eight hundred warriors, and we will not allow them to enslave you. The Americans are our friends and allies." McDougall tried to allay Chief Comcomly's fears, but he need not have worried, because the chief, acting as a good businessman and diplomat, quickly paddled out to the British ship on arrival and pledged his friendship and aid to the English.[36]

On December 12, the British raised the Union Jack over Astoria, thereby formally taking possession, and they rechristened it Fort George. The Indians who observed the ceremony found the drama and pageantry both exciting and perplexing, and they wondered what the booming cannon from aboard ship and musketry fired by the Nor'Westers meant for them in terms of trade and relationships with a new group of white men. When those in Astor's company left aboard ship or eastward over land in early April 1814, Fort George in reality became a British post. Although the Treaty of Ghent ended the war and required the mutual return of all territory, including Fort Astoria, taken during the conflict, the Americans did not soon return to the Pacific Northwest. In August 1818, however, Captain James Biddle arrived at the mouth of the Columbia on a sloop of war and claimed the region for the United States, and two months later American and British diplomats agreed to "joint occupation" of the region, but they did not recognize the possessory rights of the Indians. The Americans would not return in force for thirty years, but when they did they based their claims to the Pacific Northwest on occupancy by a bold wave of immigrants and military power, not on trade relations with the Indian people.[37]

In retrospect, the fur trade brought temporary wealth to both Indians and whites. Euro-American goods supplemented but did not replace Indian-made wares, as well as furthered, but did not initiate, change in native society. Instead, the native people integrated European goods, such as metal pots, knives, guns, blankets, fishing line, and bread, into their daily lives. The Indian people along the Northwest Coast had been skilled traders long before the arrival of Europeans. The maritime and early continental fur traders then did not revolutionize Indian culture. At the same time, the fur trade fostered intertribal contacts and cultural borrowing and more extensive traditional practices, such as gift giving among rival chiefs at potlatches. The sea otter trade, however, brought the world and the international trading economy to the Indians of the Northwest Coast.

Some influences of the fur trade, however, proved detrimental, such as the introduction of disease, tobacco, and liquor, and it promoted slavery as ship captains purchased slaves from one group to trade to another for otter hides. The maritime trade also decimated the sea otter population. The Indian people along the Northwest Coast, however, had a comparative advantage over other native peoples who interacted with whites in frontier areas, because the Euro-Americans involved with the maritime and early continental fur trade did not stay. They came among the Indians seasonally or for a brief period and left for a variety of reasons. The Indian people for the most part took what they wanted from this contact and maintained their cultural traditions until the whites returned in great numbers to claim and settle their lands. Indeed, by the late 1840s, white settlers, who sought land rather than trade, created a hostile rather than a mutually reciprocal relationship between Indians and whites in the Pacific Northwest.

CHAPTER 5

The Trans-Appalachian Frontier

On September 3, 1783, the Treaty of Paris officially ended the war between Great Britain and the United Colonies, but it did not bring peace to the trans-Appalachian frontier, and it did not mention the Indians, who learned of it the following spring as government officials and others spread the news among the nations in the West. Beyond the mountains, white settlers now pressed incessantly for access to Indian lands, often risking their lives by crossing north of the Ohio River to take it. The government of the new nation, operating under the Articles of Confederation, wanted to gain access to those lands and keep the peace, but it struggled to institute a systematic process for the acquisition of Indian lands, and it proved woefully unable to prevent the westering frontier people from going where they would and taking what they wanted.

During the War of Independence, the national government attempted to gain control of Indian and white relations, particularly regarding the ownership and acquisition of Indian lands. Article IX of the Articles of Confederation gave Congress the "sole and exclusive right and power of regulating . . . the trade and managing all affairs with the Indians, not members of any of the states, provided that the legislative right of any state within its own limits be not infringed or violated." Unfortunately, this provision did not provide an effective governmental procedure for dealing with Indian and white land problems. Essentially, the Articles of Confederation merely continued the British precedent of recognizing the Indians' possessory right to the soil. Nevertheless, Article IX implied that Indian lands could be legally acquired through negotiations between the national government and the tribes and documented with cession treaties.[1]

Individual efforts to purchase or squat on Indians lands, however, forced the national government to clarify its authority under the articles to prevent white settlers and speculators from encroaching on Indian lands and provoking violent retribution. On September 22, 1783, Congress proclaimed that it alone had the power to prohibit and forbid "all persons from making settlements on lands inhabited or claimed by Indians, without the limits of jurisdiction of any particular state, and from purchasing or receiving any gift or cession of such lands or claims without express authority and direction of the United States in Congress assembled." Thereafter, any purchases from Indian nations or settlements on tribal lands without congressional permission were "null and void." Although this congressional proclamation clarified the power of the central government over Indian lands beyond state boundaries, it suggested that the states could deal with Indian land problems within their own borders, an impression that portended trouble for the years to come, particularly in the South.[2]

After the War of Independence, the new American government attempted to exert authority over tribal lands by treating the Indians like conquered nations, because most of the trans-Appalachian Indians had supported the British during the war. As losers in the great war for empire, white Americans expected them to pay a price for choosing the wrong side in that contest. Consequently, government Indian commissioners, who made treaties with the various Indian nations, arbitrarily drew boundary lines and took lands without compensation. Although the commissioners promised governmental protection for the newly defined Indian territory, in reality white settlers encroached on their lands with impunity, and the national government had neither the will nor the power to keep them off Indian land. Instead, the government worked to gain Indian land cessions in order to sell those lands and help pay the national debt and provide farms for soldiers who had fought during the war. In doing so the government refused to recognize the Indians' right to the soil because they, like the British, were a conquered people. The national government also operated on the premise that while the Americans were a magnanimous people, as victors they would dictate land policy to the Indians who had committed the mistake of fighting on the losing side during the Revolutionary War. This Indian land policy, however, failed from the very beginning, because the nations at whom it was directed did not agree and refused to accept the principles on which it was based.

The Indians whom the new government forced to cede lands viewed the War of Independence as no more than a continuation of the long-running, though intermittent, fighting among whites to gain control over the eastern seaboard and their own persistent struggle to keep whites off Indian lands. They had not sued for peace, and they did not consider themselves defeated. Moreover, they had no intention of ceding large tracts of land without receiving any compensation. Given this conflict over who would take and who would keep land as a matter of right, the new nation had no assurance of peace at a time when the government most needed it. The new nation could not afford an Indian war because the army was too weak and government coffers too empty to defeat the western nations individually or collectively.

By 1786, the Indian policy of the central government under the Articles of Confederation was in shambles. The western Indian nations resisted the execution of treaties that required them to cede substantial portions of their lands, and a general Indian war seemed likely. Fortunately, Henry Knox, secretary of war, foresaw the impending danger on the trans-Appalachian frontier and the implications of a major Indian war regarding the success of the new nation. Knox believed the central government had to return to the British and colonial policy of purchasing land from the Indians, instead of taking it through treaties forced on them. Accordingly, he recommended the granting of retroactive compensation for Indian lands already ceded in the Northwest as well as the purchase of future land cessions, because the Americans would surely want additional lands and the Indians needed to be kept friendly and agreeable to that possibility. Essentially, Knox believed the government had three options for shaping Indian policy on the trans-Appalachian frontier. First, it could abandon all desire for future acquisitions. Second, it could take as much land as it desired, provided that it had the required military power. Or, third, it could acquire Indian lands in a manner that would keep the peace and satisfy both parties to the negotiations. By 1786, the first two alternatives were not viable, but payment for Indian lands would keep the peace and achieve the desired end of aiding American expansion. No viable alternative existed: necessity dictated a change in Indian policy concerning the acquisition of tribal lands.

By late summer of 1787, Congress had turned away from a policy of coercion for the acquisition of Indian lands to one of conciliation and purchase. This policy, acknowledged in the Northwest Ordinance, promised the Indians that the government would not take lands without their consent. It also had an added advantage—the northern tribes on the trans-Appalachian frontier were familiar with it, because the British and the northern colonies had long used this procedure for the acquisition of Indian lands. Unstated, but clearly understood by whites, was the principle that the government would still acquire the lands that it wanted, but it would do so by negotiating cession treaties, rather than by force. Problems remained, however, because this policy was based on the assumptions that the Indians had a "right to the soil" in the trans-Appalachian region, and also that they would willingly sell their lands and that white settlers would not encroach on Indian domain prior to its sale to the federal government.[3]

With the reorganization of the central government under the Constitution in 1789, Congress held broad powers to regulate commerce and treat with the

Indians. Accordingly, in July 1790, Congress attempted to regulate the acquisition of Indian lands by passing the first Indian Intercourse Act. Congress intended this act to make the concept of acquisition by way of negotiated purchase through cession treaties a workable policy. The Intercourse Act prohibited individuals or states from acquiring Indian lands, unless those lands first passed to the federal government in a cession treaty. By so doing, the act recognized the right of Indian title by possession. Both President Washington and Secretary Knox hoped this policy would keep the peace and enable the orderly sale of Indian lands to the federal government whenever needed.

In 1793, Congress strengthened the Indian Intercourse Act when it authorized a $1,000 fine and a year in jail for individuals who attempted to purchase lands from the Indians or who settled on tribal lands. But, the federal government did not succeed in gaining the acceptance of the cession treaty as an instrument for transferring land title from the Indians until the signing of the Treaty of Greenville in August 1795. Once the federal government had the military power to demand a cession treaty and enforce its provisions, however, the cession treaty became a viable instrument of national policy for gaining access to Indian lands.

Several years later, in 1796, Congress authorized the president to use force to remove settlers from Indian lands. This protective policy remained in effect until 1802, but the federal government had no intention to guarantee the boundaries of the Indian nations in perpetuity. Rather, federal policymakers assumed that the Indian territories would be gradually pushed westward, because the Indians would willingly sell their lands and retreat as settlers advanced. The federal government did not have the resources to keep whites from encroaching on Indian lands, and the state and local governments did not have the will to strictly enforce the removal of whites from Indian territory. At best, the federal government could only make the withdrawal of the tribes and the cession of Indian lands as orderly and as peaceful as possible. As a result, federal Indian policy made clashes between the two civilizations inevitable, and the new policy proved scarcely more equitable to the Indians than it had been during the Confederation period, when lands were taken by right of conquest. Consequently, many white Americans began to adopt the attitude that the Indian problem would never be solved until all of the tribes had been moved west of the Mississippi River.

The Treaty of Paris not only ended the war with Great Britain, but it also established the Great Lakes, the Mississippi River, and the thirty-first parallel as the boundaries of the new nation. Within this vast domain, the Indian allies of Great Britain

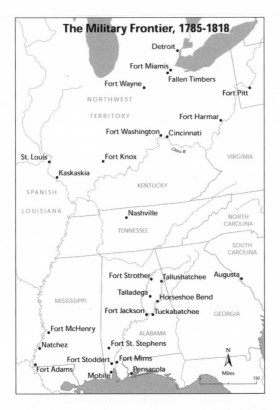

claimed, occupied, and controlled most of the trans-Appalachian backcountry. By the late 1780s, the Iroquois, Hurons, Miamis, Delawares, Shawnees, Ottawas, Ojibwas, and Potawatomies had formed a confederation in the Old Northwest. At the same time, white settlers crossed the Ohio River and defied the efforts of both the Indians and the national government to remove them. Although some of the older, compliant chiefs among the Wyandots, Delawares, Ottawas, and Ojibwas signed the Treaty of Fort McIntosh on January 21, 1785, which ceded Ohio lands south of a line from Fort Laurens to the forks of the Maumee River, the Shawnees and Miamis refused to accept it and vowed to keep their lands by force. One Shawnee chief protested government policy, saying, "God gave us this country[,] we do not understand measuring out the lands, it is all ours." Most Shawnees and the Miamis refused to take part in the cession treaty process and rejected land transfers to the government that only a few tribal members had made under duress. The Shawnees and Miamis instead demanded that the federal government and white settlers recognize their possession of lands north of the Ohio River, and they clearly indicated they intended to keep those lands by force if necessary.[4]

In December 1786, an Indian delegation representing several nations met with government officials at Detroit and reminded them that neither individual villages nor their chiefs or even nations could cede lands. Rather, they proclaimed that land cessions could only be made "by the united voice of the confederacy." Treaties that did not have the sanction of unanimous approval were, therefore, null and void. The delegates also asked Congress to "prevent your surveyors and other people from coming upon our side [of] the Ohio River." This tactic guaranteed infinite delay and protection of Indian lands because unanimity among the villages, tribes, and chiefs would be impossible to achieve. To strengthen their message, the northwestern Indians increased their attacks on white settlers both north and south of the Ohio River. The central government responded with continued efforts to intimidate them and dictate cession treaties by right of conquest.[5]

Government officials did not want war, because they could not afford it, but the government began building forts along the Ohio River to establish its presence in the Ohio Valley. In June 1789, Secretary of War Knox told President Washington that a "conciliatory system" would be the cheapest and most efficient way to deal with the Indians in order to gain land cessions. Military action, he said would mean "blood and injustice which would stain the character of the nation . . . beyond all pecuniary calculation." Still, while government officials did not want war, they did not intend to recognize the Ohio River as the boundary with the Indian nations in the northwest. Neither did the white settlers who crossed the Ohio and squatted on Indian lands. In retaliation, the Shawnees struck south of the Ohio River against settlements in Kentucky and attacked squatters who crossed the river and settled on their land.[6]

By the late 1780s, Indians and whites engaged in open but undeclared war in the Ohio country. The army did not have the strength to end it, and anything less than total defeat meant victory for the Indians. In January 1789, Arthur St. Clair, governor of the Northwest Territory, attempted to negotiate a peaceful relationship between whites and Indians in Ohio by agreeing to pay the Iroquois and several other nations for lands ceded earlier. The resulting treaties signed at Fort Harmar on January 9, 1789, reestablished the American policy of paying for Indian lands. Moreover, President Washington insisted that Congress approve the treaties just as it would any treaty negotiated with a foreign nation, thereby recognizing their independence and sovereignty. Yet, the frontier became increasingly unsafe, because the federal government still attempted to dictate policy and because white settlers pressed incessantly for Indian lands. Blue Jacket, a Shawnee leader, responded by telling an emissary sent by St. Clair to

10. In October 1790, Josiah Harmar led an expedition to the Maumee River country in present-day Ohio to strike the Shawnees and Miamis and force them to make peace. Little Turtle surprised Harmar's men and sent them fleeing back to Fort Washington. His defeat made the federal government acutely aware that the Indian nations in the Northwest Territory were a formidable foe. (Negative No. C4735. Courtesy, Indiana Historical Society.)

determine whether the northwestern Indians wanted peace or war, that he would not allow the Americans "to take away, by degrees, their lands," because they had suffered too much "pain" and too many "affronts."[7]

Confronted with Indian resistance to the loss of their lands, white settlers increasingly demanded protection by the army. Ultimately, Knox capitulated to this pressure and, in September 1790, authorized General Josiah Harmar, commander of the American forces along the Ohio, to strike north from Fort Washington (present-day Cincinnati) into the Maumee River country and destroy the Miami, Shawnee, and Delaware villages near present-day Fort Wayne, Indiana. Harmar departed with a force of nearly 1,500, men, mostly undisciplined Kentucky militia. A hundred miles north of Fort Washington, Little Turtle of the Miamis and Blue Jacket of the Shawnees set a trap. Blue Jacket later said that the 600 Indians who waited for Harmar's disorganized column were determined to prevent a "premeditated design to root us out of our land," and they believed that they were "acting in the cause of justice."[8]

Little Turtle and Blue Jacket's Indian army, consisting of Miamis, Shawnees, Delawares, and Ottawas, hit Harmar's reckless and disorganized detachments hard on October 19 and 21, near Kekionga (present-day Fort Wayne) and routed

11. In the autumn of 1791, Arthur St. Clair led a poorly trained and outfitted army to strike the Shawnees under Blue Jacket and the Miamis under Little Turtle. Like Harmar, he, too, suffered a surprise attack by an overpowering force of Shawnees, Miamis, Delawares, Wyandots, Ottawas, Ojibwas, and Potawatomies in what became the worst military defeat by the Indians in American history. (Negative No. C6290. Courtesy, Indiana Historical Society.)

his force, which reeled back to Fort Washington, leaving nearly two hundred dead in the field. Harmar attempted to save his career reporting that "our loss was heavy, but the headquarters of iniquity were broken up." He also confided in his diary that "[t]he consolation is that the men sold themselves very dear." This was not a commendable sign of success for Secretary Knox, who relieved Harmar of his command and replaced him with the experienced and arrogant Arthur St. Clair.[9]

With Harmar's defeat, the federal government implemented an Indian policy predicated on the idea that the Indians could negotiate treaties for the cession of their lands, but they could not fight to guarantee possession. The federal government also viewed the attack on Harmar as proof that the Indians beyond the Ohio River wanted war rather than peace, and it made the commitment to drive them to the bargaining table by military force rather than lead them there through diplomacy. At the same time, the Shawnees, Miamis, and other nations in the northwest became even more committed to the Ohio River as the boundary between them and the United States after Harmar's defeat, and they had no intention of compromise. They would not be moved.

On May 3, 1791, Congress responded to Harmar's defeat by authorizing the recruitment of nearly three thousand infantry and cavalry to strike the Indians north of the Ohio, and compel them to accept peace and land cessions. Two weeks later Secretary of War Knox ordered St. Clair to establish a strong and permanent military post in the heart of the Miami country and link it with a chain of posts from Fort Washington to intimidate the Indians into accepting federal authority in the Ohio country. St. Clair pledged to make "strong War" against the Miamis and Shawnees and to wreak "vengeance" and "utter destruction" on them.[10]

St. Clair did not move north from Fort Washington until mid-September, and the construction of the ordered chain of forts by his ragtag army went slowly at best. Bitter cold and snow caught him in late October near present-day Greenville, with his men suffering from fatigue, hunger, and low morale. A few days later on November 4, Little Turtle and Blue Jacket struck him hard with a thousand men, while his soldiers camped along the tail waters of the Wabash in western Ohio. While a combined force of Shawnees, Miamis, and Delawares hit St. Clair's center in the half-light of dawn, the Wyandots and Iroquois struck his right, while the Ottawas, Ojibwas, and Potawatomies pinched his left flank. St. Clair's poorly trained and unprepared army disintegrated and reeled in panic back to Fort Washington. Out of a force of approximately 1,400 men, St. Clair left 623 soldiers dead in the field and counted 258 wounded along with 24 civilians killed and 13 wounded. While St. Clair prepared his report to explain the defeat and save his career, he could not foresee that the U.S. army would never suffer a greater defeat at the hands of the Indians.

Although St. Clair's defeat can be blamed on poor planning, training, and leadership, the Indians' victory can be attributed to the opposite of those factors. Or, in the words of the turncoat Simon Girty, who participated in the attack, "The Indians were never in greater heart to meet their enemy, nor more sure of success—they [were] determined to drive them to the Ohio." While the Indians celebrated, however, Little Turtle knew better than any leader of the Indian Confederacy that British support was essential to keep the Americans at bay. He knew that after the defeats of Harmar and St. Clair, the government would organize another army to send among them. The confederacy would be able to meet the certainty of another expedition only with British guns, powder, and lead. Yet, even amidst the celebration of victory, Little Turtle worried about the commitment of the British to the Indian people.[11]

While Little Turtle worried about British commitment, Washington and Knox prepared for another expedition against the Indians in the Ohio country. Congress also doubled the military budget to $1 million and authorized the increase of the army to five thousand men. Washington also turned to Anthony Wayne to command the army in the Northwest Territory. He considered Wayne

12. In August 1794, Anthony Wayne defeated a combined force of Indians during the Battle of Fallen Timbers along the Maumee River. This defeat forced many of the Indian nations in the Northwest Territory to cede considerable lands north of the Ohio River a year later in the Treaty of Greenville. (Negative No. C6289. Courtesy, Indiana Historical Society.)

"more active and enterprising than judicious and cautious," with a reputation earned during the Revolution for tenacity, aggressiveness, and discipline. While Wayne worked to train and supply a new army and plan his attack, the Indians continued to make the northwestern trans-Appalachian frontier unsafe for settlers and the troops who occupied the isolated forts in the West.[12]

Wayne did not return to the Ohio country with a new army, called the Legion of the United States, until early May 1793. Although he planned to strike the Indians to the north quickly, a last desperate effort by the federal government to keep the peace in August delayed Wayne's departure. Commissioners Timothy Pickering, Benjamin Lincoln, and Beverly Randolph met with leaders of the Indian confederacy and the British at the mouth of the Detroit River. There, Shawnee, Miami, and Delaware leaders insisted that any treaty recognize the Ohio River as the southern boundary with the Americans. They told the commissioners, "[W]e desire you to consider[,] Brothers[,] that our only demand is the peaceable possession of a small part of our once great Country. Look back and view the lands from whence we have been driven to this spot, we can retreat no further, because the country behind hardly affords food for its present inhabitants. And we have therefore resolved, to leave our bones in this small space, to which we are now confined." Although the commissioners were prepared to negotiate a boundary north of the Ohio, they could not agree to the river as the absolute line between the Indians and the Americans because the Ohio Company had already purchased lands west of the river and had begun sales and settlement.[13]

In mid-September, Wayne received the news that the peace commissioners had failed, and although a major campaign could not be launched against the Indians in the late autumn without incurring great difficulties from the weather, he moved his five-thousand-man army north and built Fort Greenville and Fort Recovery (the site of St. Clair's defeat) where he planned to spend the winter and prepare for a spring attack. While Wayne's men built two new forts, the Indians watched them through the winter. Little Turtle and Blue Jacket and the other leaders of the confederacy expected the fight to come during the summer, and they felt great confidence that the British would honor their promise to support them with men and supplies. By late spring the Ottawas, Ojibwas, and Potawatomies had begun to arrive at an encampment along the Maumee River where they joined the Shawnees, Miamis, Delawares, and Wyandots, some six hundred strong, in preparation for war.

Wayne led the Legion out of Fort Greenville on July 26, 1794. He reached the confluence of the Maumee and Auglaize Rivers in early August, then, after building Fort Defiance to protect his rear, Wayne sent his army down the Maumee toward the British post known as Fort Miamis, where the Indians had congregated. Wayne made a final attempt to avoid a fight by sending a messenger to inform the Indian leaders that the British would not help them and that only he could make a lasting peace with them. Upon receipt of Wayne's message, the leaders of the confederacy met. Little Turtle advised compromise and peace, but the Shawnees, who contributed most the men to the confederacy's fighting force, strongly disagreed. In the council held on August 14, Little Turtle told his fellow war chiefs that "the trail has been long and bloody; it has no end. The pale faces come from where the sun rises, and they are many. They are like the leaves of the trees. When the frost comes they fall and are blown away. But when the sunshine comes again they come back more plentiful than ever before." Blue Jacket or Egushawa of the Ottawas snidely responded saying that Little Turtle only wanted to "smoke in the lodges of the Long Knives, our enemies." When he asked whether the leaders of the confederacy would make Wayne "walk in a bloody path," they agreed to war.[14]

On August 20, Wayne's legion of approximately one thousand men met an Indian force half that number in a tangled, heavily wooded area. After a sharp firefight that lasted about an hour, the Indians retreated to the protection of Fort Miamis, but the British refused to open the gates. Just as Little Turtle suspected, the British were supportive of the Indians short of war, but they did not want to renew the conflict with the United States over lands that they had already ceded. As the Indians fled downstream, the confederacy of the northwestern nations collapsed. More than a decade would pass before new Indian leaders would trust the British in another war against the Americans.

Although the Battle of Fallen Timbers proved little more than a bloody and intense skirmish, it ensured a major land cession from the confederacy. The Battle of Fallen Timbers, when coupled with the British decision to conclude a treaty with the United States and thereby resolve the lingering problem of British forts on American soil and the refusal of the British commander to allow the Indians to seek refuge in Fort Miamis, indicated the British did not want war with the Americans. This policy virtually dashed all hopes for an Indian confederacy supported by the British. As a result, during the autumn and winter, Indian delegations arrived at Fort Greenville to ask for peace. Accordingly, agreements were reached with the Wyandots, Ojibwas, Ottawas, Potawatomies, Miamis, Delawares, and Shawnees to end hostilities and exchange prisoners in preparation for a major peace council in June. The northwestern Indians, some 1,100 strong, however, did not assemble at Fort Greenville in mid-July 1795, and then took until August to negotiate an agreement. Wayne offered peace based on the cession of approximately two-thirds of Ohio and a portion of Indiana. Little Turtle spoke eloquently, but without conviction now that the British had deserted them, for the retention of their lands because it was a gift from the Great Spirit that could not be sold. In the contest for Indian lands, however, military force spoke louder than words. Little Turtle's people and the other Indians wanted peace and the annual annuities that Wayne promised them to make up for lost British support and to reward them for their new friendship with the United States as well as compensate them for the loss of considerable land.

On August 3, the Indian leaders, except Little Turtle, signed the Treaty of Greenville, in which they relinquished their lands east and south of a line that ran up the Cuyahoga River from Lake Erie, then across the portage to the Tuscarawas River and on to Fort Laurens. The Greenville treaty line then ran west to Fort Loramie and northwest to Fort Recovery, then south to the Ohio River. The treaty now ended the unavoidable conflict between the Americans

13. Born in 1768 at Piqua in present-day Ohio, Tecumseh had earned a position of leadership among the Shawnees based on his ability in war and diplomacy by the early nineteenth century. On the eve of the War of 1812, Tecumseh traveled extensively north and south of the Ohio River trying to forge an Indian confederacy to prevent further seizure of Indian lands by the United States. (Negative No. Sub. Coll. Courtesy, Indiana Historical Society.)

and the Indians on the northwestern frontier, because both claimed the same lands by force of arms. In the end, the lands in the Northwest Territory went to those who had the greatest numbers, the best weapons, and the most disciplined, organized, and supported fighting men.

By 1795, then, federal officials were well pleased with American frontier policy. The Indian confederation had been broken, Spain had conceded navigation rights on the Mississippi River and accepted the thirty-first parallel as the northern boundary of West Florida, and the British had agreed to evacuate their forts in the northwest. The obstacles to westward expansion seemed removed. The great fault of this belief, of course, was that it did not take into consideration the Indian point of view about white expansion or their beliefs about right and wrong and the necessity to protect their own interests. Moreover, while the northwestern Indian confederacy assumed the Treaty of Greenville marked a permanent boundary with the United States, government officials and white settlers considered it only a temporary line that would change when they needed more land. In the meantime, peace brought security and freedom for settlers who ventured north of the Ohio River. It would last until the Shawnee brothers Tecumseh and Tenskwatawa, known as the Prophet, organized a new Indian confederacy and gained British support to drive settlers from the northern trans-Appalachian frontier.

Indian and white relations, however, became tense once again after Thomas Jefferson assumed the presidency in 1801 and authorized William Henry Harrison, governor of the Indiana Territory, to negotiate additional treaties with the western Indian nations for land cessions. Between 1803 and 1809, Harrison pressured the Delawares, Shawnees, Potawatomies, Miamis, Eel Rivers, Weas, Kickapoos, Piankishaws, and Kaskaskias in seven treaties to sell the southern third of Indiana as well as considerable lands in Illinois, Wisconsin, and Michigan—some one hundred million acres—for white settlement. He also obtained lands from the Foxes and Sauks along the Mississippi, while the Wyandots, Ottawas, Ojibwas, Munsees, Potawatomies, Delawares, and Shawnees made other cessions north of the Greenville treaty line in Ohio. Often Harrison dictated rather than negotiated land cession treaties, and the western Indian nations became increasingly resentful of federal policy as the lands promised them in cession treaties disappeared from their control.

In Ohio and Indiana, the boundaries separating Indian and white lands were recognized by trespass rather than honor, and the Indians paid dearly for these violations. In 1801, Harrison reported that "The people of Kentucky . . . make a constant practice of crossing over the Indians lands opposite them every fall to kill deer, bear, and buffalo—the latter from being in great abundance a few years ago is now scarcely to be met with." With game depleted and their cooking pots nearly empty, many tribal groups began selling their lands to provide basic necessities. Other Indian leaders, such as Tarhe or The Crane of the Wyandots, Five Medals of the Potawatomies, Little Turtle of the Miamis, and Black Hoof of the Shawnees, accepted government programs designed to remake them into small-scale farmers.[15]

But not all. Many Shawnees, Wyandots, Potawatomies, and the western nations preferred their traditional ways, and they hoped that the British would return and offer protection from the American government and white settlers. While the grievances of the northwestern tribes over their continued loss of lands festered, the federal government continued to press for the acquisition of more land while offering token payments in annuities and government agreements to teach them to farm in the white tradition. Yet, while Jefferson believed that Indian policy was going according to plan, a Shawnee by the name of Lalawethika, the young brother of Tecumseh and later known as Tenskwatawa, or the Prophet, offered the Indians on the northwestern trans-Appalachian frontier a way to regain their traditional life.

During times of great social and economic stress, people often seek salvation

14. Lalawethika, later known as Tenskwatawa or the Prophet, was the younger brother of Tecumseh. He sought a return to native cultural and religious practices and urged his followers to give up white trade goods and whiskey and return to traditional ways as well as refuse to sell their lands. His one attempt at military resistance led to defeat by William Henry Harrison's forces at the Battle of Tippecanoe in November 1811. (Negative No. C546. Courtesy, Indiana Historical Society.)

from spiritual leaders, and the Prophet was one of many past and future leaders who offered hope for a better life through spiritual regeneration. In April 1805, Lalawethika told the Shawnees, and any other tribal members who would listen, that the Master of Life had instructed him in a dream to help his people rekindle their spiritual beliefs and rituals and save their traditional way of life. They must stop selling land, drinking whiskey, and fighting among themselves, and they should reject all things European and American, such as liquor, trade goods, and weapons. Only by spiritual renewal and unity and a return to traditional ways could the whites be prevented from overrunning Indian lands. The Prophet's call for spiritual renewal and union spread like wildfire through the Indian nations of the Old Northwest. In July 1806, Secretary of War Henry Dearborn worried about the Prophet's efforts to unify the Indian nations and he wrote, "It is excessively mortifying that our good faith should so frequently be called in question by the natives who have it in their power to make such proud comparisons in relation to good faith." Even so, it was the Prophet's brother, Tecumseh, who gained the federal government's primary attention, because he advocated political unity and military force to protect Indian lands.[16]

In 1810, Tecumseh emerged as the political leader of the Indians in the Old

Northwest, particularly among the young men eager to prove themselves in battle. Tecumseh gained this preeminent position by advocating a new Indian confederacy that would unify all of the nations from the Great Lakes to the Gulf of Mexico. Many of Tecumseh and the Prophet's followers had established a village known as Prophetstown on the Wabash at the mouth of Tippecanoe Creek, where Tecumseh informed the British in June 1808 that his brother was "endeavoring to collect the different nations to form one settlement on the Wabash . . . in order to preserve their country from all encroachments." Both Tecumseh and the Prophet now sought more secular than spiritual solutions to the problems of the northwestern Indians. They particularly wanted fixed boundaries between them and the whites as well as British aid from Canada. In the months ahead, Harrison worried that the concentration of hostile Indians at Prophetstown threatened the peace of the Indiana Territory. When he concluded a treaty with the accommodationist chiefs of the Miamis, Weas, and Delawares at Fort Wayne on September 30, 1809, in which the Indians ceded more than 2.5 million acres in present-day Indiana and Illinois, Tecumseh and the Prophet became more convinced than ever before that another military confrontation with the Americans would be necessary to guarantee the protection of Indian lands.[17]

In mid-August 1810, when Tecumseh, with seventy-five men from the war factions of the Miamis, Kickapoos, Wyandots, Potawatomies, Ottawas, and Winnebagos, met with Harrison in Vincennes to express his displeasure with the aggressive cession treaty process, he threatened Harrison and empathically stated that he would not be bound by the Treaty of Fort Wayne of 1803 even though it did not involve the cession of Shawnee lands. He told Harrison that "you have taken our lands from us and I do not see how we can remain at peace with you if you continue to do so." Harrison did not like being called a cheat and a liar, but he recognized and respected forceful leadership. After the meeting he told Secretary of War William Eustis, "Tecumseh is one of those uncommon geniuses, which spring up occasionally to produce revolutions and overturn the established order of things."[18]

On November 7, 1811, while Tecumseh traveled in the south to gain support for a new confederacy, Tenskwatawa, fearing that Prophetstown would be overrun by Harrison's 1,000-man army, led an attack on his troops who had marched from Vincennes to Prophetstown in late September to demonstrate American power and ensure the peace. The attack began at 4 A.M. with 500 to 600 men, and although Harrison's troops were unprepared, they regrouped and held their ground. After hard fighting and considerable losses on both sides, the

Indians withdrew at dawn, allowing Harrison to burn their abandoned village and claim the Battle of Tippecanoe as a "complete and decisive victory," although he lost a staggering 20 percent of his men as killed or wounded. It was, of course, neither, although Harrison had destroyed the Prophet's leadership among the Indians. Tippecanoe, however, did assert the power of the United States, but it also increased the hostility between whites and Indians on the northwestern frontier and helped ensure that another war would be necessary to determine who would control the Old Northwest for all time. It also marked the failure of the last great effort to create an Indian confederacy to keep the white settlers out of the Northwest Territory.[19]

The Treaty of Paris brought little peace and less security to the southern Indian nations, some fifty thousand Choctaws, Chickasaws, Cherokees, and Creeks, whom the Spanish particularly wanted as allies to check American expansion in the Lower Mississippi Valley. Secretary of War Knox feared unity of the southern nations, led by Creek Alexander McGillivray with Spanish support. If such an alliance developed, Knox believed it would mean war with the Creeks and necessitate the raising of a five-thousand-man army and an expenditure of $1.5 million, and he preferred negotiations to solve differences and keep the peace. In 1795, Governor General Francisco Luis Héctor, baron of Carondelet in New Orleans, reported his view on Spanish Indian policy, saying, "The sustaining of our allied tribes in the possession of their lands is . . . an indispensable object both for the conservation of Louisiana under the power of Spain, and to prevent the Americans from securing navigation of the Mississippi."[20]

In 1784, Spanish efforts to keep its Indian allies paid dividends when the major tribes, with the exception of the Cherokees, signed alliances with Spanish officials in Pensacola. The Cherokees did not participate because their lands clearly lay within the boundaries of the United States. A decade later, on October 28, 1793, Spain also signed the Treaty of Nogales at Walnut Hills in present-day Mississippi with the Creeks, Tulipists, Alabamans, Cherokees, Chickasaws, and Choctaws. In this treaty, the Indian participants agreed to an alliance of friendship with the Spanish and to consult among themselves about actions against the Americans for which Spain would reward them with an annual distribution of presents. The Spanish, moreover, did not seek Indian lands for agriculture like the white Americans. When they obtained land cessions from the Creeks, Choctaws, and Chickasaws, the Spanish did so for the purpose of constructing forts rather than distributing it to Spanish farmers. In 1790, one such cession gave Spain property on which to build Fort Nogales at present-day Vicksburg to control navigation on the Mississippi River. On June 20, 1795, the Spanish also acquired land from the Chickasaws, where they built Fort San Fernando de las Barrancas and a trading post at Chickasaw Bluffs, also to control the navigation on the Mississippi River at present-day Memphis.

The Creeks, who were the most numerous and powerful Indian nation in the South, now found themselves hard-pressed by the Americans in Georgia for their lands, by the Spanish in the Floridas and New Orleans for their loyalty, and by the British operating from Florida and Canada for their trade and friendship. Some Creeks, led by Alexander McGillivray until his death in 1793, responded to this triple threat by advocating the creation of a strong, centralized and unified nation composed of Upper and Lower Creeks. By the end of the American Revolution, McGillivray had emerged as a powerful new leader. As a mixed-blood, white officials preferred to deal with him. He was literate, experienced, and able. By 1783, McGillivray served as the chief spokesman for the Upper Creeks. Each solution to the apparent dangers posed by the Americans and the Spanish required the Creeks to overcome traditional rivalries. Creek factionalism became even more complicated because a pro-American faction, led by the Tallassee King (Hoboithle Mico), remained active for many years after the Revolution. For many Creeks, the solutions posed to solve their problems often seemed more serious than their apparent difficulties, although their problems were real enough. At the same time, the American Revolution had been an economic disaster for the Creeks. It had disrupted their deerskin trade, particularly with the British through Augusta, for guns, powder, lead, clothing, and other supplies.

The Americans, Spanish, and British, of course, wanted to use the Creeks for their own purposes, but the Spanish particularly intended to gain Creek allegiance to control the Old Southwest from the newly recovered Floridas to the Mississippi and from the Tennessee River to the Gulf. Spain, however, played a delicate diplomatic game by providing the Creeks with weapons through McGillivray and trading companies operated by Loyalist exiles at Pensacola. Spain also urged the Creeks to fight the Americans while coaxing the frontier people in Kentucky and Tennessee to join the Spanish empire. Yet, while the guns would drive the Americans away, any allegiance with the frontier people in an attempt to wrest their loyalty from the United States would alienate the Creeks. Usually, the Spanish resolved the complexities of this situation by relying on the Creeks to help ensure Spanish claims across the southern frontier.

Although the Georgians demanded that the new national government drive the

Creeks from lands that they wanted, Secretary of War Henry Knox considered the Indians "more sinned against than sinning," and he doubted that an estimated six thousand Creek fighting men could be subdued quickly. Certainly, they could not be defeated cheaply, so Knox preferred to resolve problems by negotiations. The Georgians disagreed and maintained that they had jurisdiction over the lands of the Upper Creeks on the Alabama River and of the Lower Creeks on the Chattahoochee. The Creeks, who outnumbered the Georgians, did not consider themselves dependents of the state or new American nation, and they did not intend to live under the dictation of either power. The Georgians cared not at all. They wanted Creek lands and they intended to have them and the taking of those lands, rather than their acquisition by payment and treaty, seemed the quickest way to push the Creeks out of the way. Creek leaders responded by telling the Georgians that if they wanted their land they had to "come and take it."[21]

McGillivray told the Georgians who convinced a group of pro-American Creeks to cede considerable land in the Treaty of Augusta in 1783, and who cast covetous eyes on Upper Creek lands along the Alabama River, that his people would not be "quiet Spectators" if they made another land grab. McGillivray also called on the Creek leaders who opposed the land cession to the Georgians and urged them "to take arms in our defence & repel those Invaders of our Lands, to drive them from their encroachments & fix them within their own proper limits." Several years later in 1789, in response to the pressure of Georgians, he told the Lower Creeks that "these last strides tell us they never mean to let their foot rest; our lands are our life and breath; if we part with them, we part with our blood. We must fight for them." Soon Creek war parties were striking Georgia settlements, killing settlers, and capturing slaves and livestock.[22]

The federal government attempted to end violence between the southern frontier people and the Creeks as well as negate efforts by the state of Georgia to sign land cession treaties with select groups of Indians by asserting national responsibility for Indian affairs. It did so in 1790 by entering into negotiations for a cession treaty at New York, the nation's capital. There, Washington and Knox met with a Creek delegation, led by Alexander McGillivray and other Creek leaders, who were bribed with annuities for a land cession between the Ogeechee and Oconee Rivers. The New York treaty, signed on August 7, had little practical effect, however, because some Creeks claimed that McGillivray did not speak for them, while Georgia and Spain refused to accept the transfer of lands to the United States that each still claimed. The Creeks had already lost this area to settlers, but they gained from the annual monetary annuity and trade, which the treaty provided and which the federal government hoped would lure the Creeks from British and Spanish traders.

In 1795, the federal government also established trading posts along the Georgia-Creek border, the first at Coleraine on the St. Mary's River in Georgia. There, factors or traders offered goods at cost in an effort to gain their political loyalty. With the deer population depleted, however, the Creeks had little choice but to trade acres instead of deerskins for food and clothing, and to pay debts to the traders. At the same time, the federal officials, particularly agent Benjamin Hawkins, worked to destroy Creek culture by encouraging them to adopt private property, abandon communal fields, erect fences, and abandon the matrilineal household. Little wonder that Tecumseh was well received when he visited the Creeks in 1811. William Weatherford, also known as Red Eagle, found his message of resistance to white expansion and the revitalization of Indian society inspiring. One mixed-blood Creek reported, "The whole nation was in commotion and excited . . . [T]he ferment and agitation was almost a general thing and superlatively progressing from bad to worse." Only war could come from these feelings of resentment and hope.[23]

The French Revolution caused Spain to reassess its policy with the United States, and in 1795 the crown agreed to the Pinckney treaty in which it accepted the thirty-first parallel as its northern boundary between West Florida and the United States and thereby relinquished nearly all its claims to Creek territory. Federal officials then worked hard to convince the Creeks that neither Spain nor Britain could be reliable trading partners given their concerns elsewhere, while the United States remained willing and ready to meet their needs. Accordingly, in 1796, federal commissioners signed the Treaty of Coleraine on the St. Mary's River. Here, a delegation primarily of Upper Creeks affirmed their land cessions at New York and the Americans as their new trading partners. Thereafter, federal officials capitalized on Spanish, French, and British difficulties to supply the Creeks and continued to gain land cessions through several treaties in which the federal government provided annual incomes to Creek leaders and annuities to the Creek nation. As a result, by 1806, the Upper and Lower Creeks received annuities worth $8,000 annually, much of it in the form of plows, spinning wheels, and other tools to help speed the process of civilization, while many leaders drew annual salaries of $100 or more.

The Creeks, however, understood that the Americans wanted more than peace and friendship. They wanted Creek lands. By the end of the eighteenth century, whites had settled Tennessee, which became a state in 1796, and by 1798 they occupied Natchez and had crossed the Mississippi at St. Louis. The Creeks rightfully felt encircled by an aggressive people, and they recognized that they had few alternatives to protect their lands. When Jefferson became president in 1801, he believed that intelligent and fair-minded whites and Indians should proceed with a plan whereby Indian lands would be purchased and the money used to buy agricultural and domestic tools, such as plows and looms. The Creeks would learn to practice agriculture on small tracts of land that they would retain, much in the white tradition. Henry Dearborn, Jefferson's Secretary of War, believed that if the policy of civilizing, that is, acculturating the Creeks, failed, Indian lands could be gained with a "dose of steel."[24]

Despite Dearborn's apparent willingness to use military force when dealing with the Creeks, between the end of the American Revolution and the War of 1812, the federal government made concerted efforts to keep the Creeks peaceful and friendly to the United States and to use the Creek National Council, dominated by the Muskogees, to acquire lands through cession treaties. At the same time, the Creeks who opposed this policy, notably under the leadership of the Tame King (Tallassee) and the Fat King, gave their loyalty to the Spanish operating in Pensacola. With the Creeks divided and hostilities increasing among the ethnic factions over white encroachments on their lands, the Creeks became increasingly receptive to arguments for unity to save both their lands and culture.

In the autumn of 1811, Tecumseh, the son of a Creek mother, visited the nation and spoke before the Creek council that had assembled five thousand tribal members, as well as some Choctaws and Chickasaws, at Tuckabatchee at the confluence of the Tallapoosa and Alabama Rivers. There, he urged them to unite with the other Indians from Canada to the Gulf in a religious and political union that would have the power to guarantee Indian lands and perhaps roll back white gains. In October, Tecumseh passionately and eloquently told one gathering of Creeks, "Let the white race perish. They seize your land; they corrupt your women; they trample on the bones of your dead! Back whence they came, upon a trail of blood, they must be driven! Back—aye, back to the great water whose accursed waves brought them to our shores! Burn their dwellings—destroy their stock—slay their wives and children, that [their] very breed may perish. War now! War always! War on the living! War on the dead!" Tecumseh also used ridicule to intimidate the fainthearted to accept his call for an Indian confederacy. When Big Warrior, a powerful Creek chief, hedged about giving Tecumseh his support, Tecumseh jabbed his finger in the chief's face and said, "Your blood is white. . . . You do not believe the Great spirit sent me. You shall believe it. I will leave directly and go straight to Detroit. When I get there I will stamp my foot upon the ground and shake down every house in Tookabatcha." When an earthquake destroyed the village soon after Tecumseh returned to the Ohio country, and when the British and the Americans began fighting the following spring, many Creeks saw war as their destiny.[25]

Other prophets and shamans quickly gave support to Tecumseh and urged the Creeks and other nations in the South to return to their traditional ways, reject the trader's whiskey, and fight for their lands. At the same time, the federal government began building roads into Creek country and surveying the thirty-first parallel, all of which sent a shock wave through the Creek nation, because they recognized that the Americans jeopardized their lands and that their traditional way of life teetered on the edge of oblivion. British and Spanish officials urged the Creeks to resist and promised support, more moral than practical, especially from the Spanish whose toehold of forts on Pensacola Bay was weak and impractical. Many Creeks believed only force would enable them to protect and keep their lands.

Amidst these complexities of dependence on foreigners for food and clothing, indebtedness to the traders, and the encroachment of white settlers on their lands, the Creeks also began fighting among themselves. Intratribal warfare began after a Creek war party, returning from Canada in late 1812, killed some whites near the mouth of the Ohio River. The Chickasaws believed the federal government would blame them for the deaths and demanded that the Creeks punish the killers by execution. When the Creeks carried out this punishment, however, a bloody civil war erupted between the Upper and Lower Creeks. The Upper Creeks also opposed accommodation with the Americans, while the Lower Creeks, who had greater contacts with whites, had been more amenable to acculturation.

The most hostile Creeks were known as "Red Sticks," because they painted their war clubs and arrows bright red, the color of which signified war. Many were Upper Creeks who lived in the Alabama River country in the western part of their territory. Led by Red Eagle, the son of a Scot trader and a mixed-blood mother, who owned extensive lands, slaves, and livestock, the Red Sticks accepted Tecumseh's call to arms and planned to drive the Americans from their country by striking them hard and fast. Before they could do so, however, a group of whites attacked a party of Red Sticks on July 27, 1813, at Burnt Corn Creek, less than a hundred miles north of Pensacola, but succeeded only in capturing their ammunition before the whites sought refuge in the stronghold of trader Samuel Mims, about forty miles north of Mobile. They hoped the palisades and blockhouse as well as 120 militia, commanded by Major Daniel Beasley, along with 300 whites, mixed-bloods, and friendly Indians, and perhaps an equal number of slaves, would protect them from the certainty of Creek retaliation.

The Creeks struck the poorly guarded Fort Mims in the sultry heat of noon on August 30, 1813, a thousand strong. Red Eagle, who led the attack, used the drummer's call to dinner as his signal to storm the portholes and stream through the open and undefended gates. Quickly the Indian attack became a rout and the fort a slaughter pen. Only a few whites escaped, while nearly 250 soldiers and settlers were, in the words of one contemporary, "butchered in the quickest manner, and blood and brains bespattered the whole earth. The children seized by the legs, and killed by batting their heads against the stockade. The women were scalped, and those who were pregnant were opened, while they were alive, and the embryo infants let out of the womb." Many were burned alive in their cabins. Although Red Eagle attempted to prevent these atrocities, he could not do so, but he could not help but know that the savagery inflicted by his followers at Fort Mims would be returned in kind by the whites once they learned of the attack. Indeed, the killings at Fort Mims brought the United States into the Creek civil war and gave it a broader dimension that boded ill for the Creek people. The devastating attack on Fort Mims changed the relationship of the federal government with the southern Indians. Thereafter, it sought the military defeat of the Creek people, and their removal to new lands west of the Mississippi River, not their acculturation and assimilation in the Mississippi Territory.[26]

Tennessee reacted first, rather than the federal government. When the news reached Nashville that Fort Mims had been overrun, fear spread through the settlements in western Tennessee. Although whites on the southern trans-Appalachian frontier wanted security, they also wanted revenge, and they turned to Andrew Jackson to punish if not annihilate the Creeks. Jackson, in fact, had advocated striking the Creeks in retaliation for raids against the settlements, but also to defeat them before they could "be supported by their allies the British and Spaniards." Jackson responded as militia commander to the public outcry for protection by ordering the militia to rendezvous at Fayetteville for a campaign against the Creeks. "The late attack of the Creek Indians . . . call[s] a loud for retaliatory vengeance," he said. "Those distressed citizens of that frontier . . . implore the brave Tennesseeans for aid. They must not ask in vain. . . . They are our brethren in distress and we must not await the slow and tardy orders of the General Government. Every noble feeling heart beats [in] sympathy for their sufferings and danger, and every high minded generous soldier will fly to their protection." Jackson, then, was embarking on his own Indian policy using the guise of authority from the state of Tennessee. By so doing, he forced the federal government to support a general war against the Creeks contrary to its present Indian policy of negotiation and accommodation or, at worst, applied force against selective Indians who preferred the use of violence rather than cession treaties in dealing with the United States. As fate and Jackson would have it, all of the Creeks, not just those under Red Eagle, would pay a heavy price for the attack on Fort Mims.[27]

Governor William Blount responded quickly to Jackson's call for men and asked the Tennessee legislature to support 5,000 militia, including 1,500 regulars, for three months. He also ordered Jackson to "call out[,] organize[,] rendezvous and march without delay" 2,500 militia and volunteers "to repel an approaching invasion . . . and to afford aid and relief to the suffering citizens of the Mississippi Territory." Jackson saw nothing less than opportunity handed to him by the attack on Fort Mims. He would cut a path across Tennessee to Mobile, capture Pensacola and thereby end the Creek's supply base, and while driving the Spanish from the continent, he would destroy the Creeks or at least their capacity to make war.[28]

While Jackson planned and mobilized his militia, the administration of President James Madison began plans to send four armies into Creek country for a coordinated attack in which they would scorch the earth, burn the villages, destroy the crops, and kill the Red Sticks. Amidst bureaucratic bickering about who would command the federal forces, Jackson led his men south from Fayetteville on October 10, 1813. Riding hard at a horse-killing rate of thirty-six miles per day, Jackson soon outran his supply train. Despite his eagerness to protect settlers on the southern frontier and gain military glory that could be parlayed into political gain, Jackson sent word to the peaceful Creeks that they had nothing to fear from his army of Tennesseeans. He learned that Red Eagle had threatened the Creeks who did not aid the Red Sticks, and Jackson told Chiefs Chennabee and Pathkiller to "hold out obstinately" against them. "If one hair of your head is hurt," Jackson said, "or of your family or of any who are friendly to whites, I will sacrifice a hundred lives to pay for it. Be of good heart, & tell your men they have nothing to fear."[29]

The Creeks on both sides soon learned that Jackson meant what he said. On November 3, Jackson sent his cavalry and mounted riflemen or dragoons under General John Coffee to destroy the Red Stick village of Tallushatchee about a dozen miles east of Fort Strother on the Coosa River in Alabama. Coffee's thousand-man force took the village by surprise and systematically killed every man in the village. Coffee lost only 5 men killed to the 186 Creek deaths, and he captured 84 women and children. Jackson said that Coffee "executed this order in elegant stile," and he reported to Governor Blount that "[w]e have retaliated for the destruction of Fort Mims." Davy Crockett, who participated in the attack, expressed the results less eloquently, but no less accurately, when he wrote, "[w]e now shot them like dogs."[30]

After the Tallushatchee defeat, many Creek villages sent word to Jackson that they rejected the Red Sticks and wanted peace. When Jackson learned that Red Eagle had surrounded the friendly Creek town of Talladega about thirty miles south of Fort Strother, he sent 2,000 men to break the siege and destroy the 1000-man Creek force. Jackson's men surrounded the hostile Creeks at dawn on November 9, and killed 300 while losing only 15 dead and 85 wounded before the Red Sticks broke and fled. Jackson had hoped to inflict another major defeat on the Creeks, but 700 escaped due to a "faux pas of the militia," who, along with the volunteers, after the battle wanted to go home, because they were tired, hungry, and their enlistments began to expire.[31]

While Jackson struggled to hold his army together, the Creeks killed nearly 200 militia in Georgia, the loss of which took the state out of the war. Although approximately 1,000 Creeks had been killed by the end of 1813, they had not been defeated, and Jackson was anxious to strike a killing blow, but his army began to disintegrate as the militia and volunteers returned home. When Jackson received about 800 recruits in mid-January, he led them south from Fort Strother to attack the heavily fortified Creek encampment called Tohopeka at Horseshoe Bend, a 100-acre peninsula, on the Tallapoosa River. The Red Sticks, however, struck him first on three sides in the morning light of January 22, with "quick irregular firing, from behind logs, trees, shrubbery, and whatever could afford concealment." Jackson retreated but the Red Sticks hit his men again as they crossed Enotachopco Creek, but Jackson rallied his troops and prevented a rout. As his resistance stiffened, the Creeks fell back to their stronghold, leaving approximately 200 dead to Jackson's loss of 20 killed. Jackson then returned to Fort Strother where some 5,000 reinforcements from Tennessee and the army had arrived by March.[32]

On March 14, Jackson marched his new army, some 4,000 strong from Fort Strother, toward Horseshoe Bend, where 1,000 poorly armed Creek men and some 300 women and children awaited his arrival. After leaving 1,000 men at Fort Williams to protect his rear, and encouraging his troops by promising death to anyone who fled before the enemy for want of courage, Jackson arrived before the breastworks, some five to eight feet high and running some 350 yards across

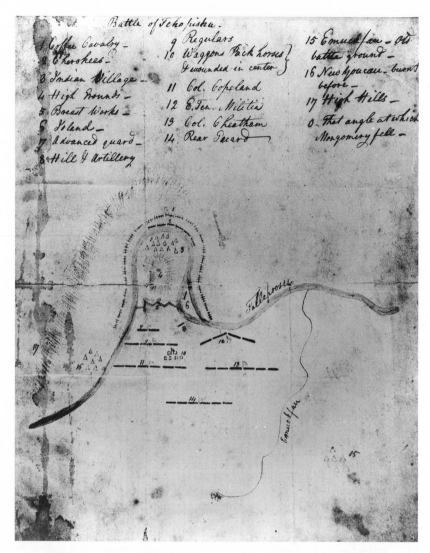

15. In March 1813, Andrew Jackson's Tennessee volunteers attacked the Creek Red
Sticks at Horseshoe Bend on the Tallapoosa River. Jackson's men savagely killed most
of the Creeks who had barricaded themselves on the peninsula. This map, dated
March 31, 1813, shows the Creek village and breastworks as well as the position of
Jackson's men, and it may have been drawn by Jackson. (Courtesy, Tennessee State
Library and Archives.)

the peninsula at Horseshoe Bend on the morning of March 27. Although his men outnumbered the Creeks by more than three to one, he was astounded at the sight of their fortification. He reported: "It is impossible to conceive a situation more eligible for defense than the one they had chosen, and the skill which they manifested in their breast work, was really astonishing." Despite the formidable defensive works, Jackson intended to pin the Creeks on the peninsula and destroy them. To do so, he sent his cavalry and Cherokee auxiliaries, dressed with white feathers and deer tails in their hair to distinguish them from the Creeks, across the river to prevent a retreat and divert Creek attention from his planned attack on the breastworks.[33]

At 10:30 A.M., Jackson attempted to batter through the fortification with his two small cannons, but could neither knock a hole in it nor blow it apart. While the Creeks taunted Jackson's men, the Cherokees crossed the river and set fire to their huts. This diversion gave Jackson the opportunity to storm the rampart. When Jackson's men reached the breastwork, the fighting became desperate, point-blank combat on both sides, but the Creeks, overwhelmed by superior numbers and weaponry, fell back. Jackson's men pursued the Creeks into the brush where the fighting became savage and hand to hand, with neither side taking prisoners. After several hours of hard fighting and with the Creeks driven into the brush for refuge, Jackson's troops spent the afternoon and evening making murder a sport, flushing the Creeks from their hiding places like rabbits from a warren, and shooting them as they ran for safety but found none, although in truth the Creeks refused to surrender, and those few who escaped did so under the cover of darkness.

Jackson considered the battle at Horseshoe Bend a great victory, although even by his standards he reported that "the *carnage* was *dreadful*," and he counted 557 Indians killed on the peninsula, with their noses cut off to ensure an accurate count, and another 350 or more dead in the river. A revised body count brought the number of Creek dead to about 900, many of whom the soldiers mutilated. In turn, Jackson lost 47 men dead and 159 wounded, plus 23 friendly Creeks and Cherokees killed and 47 wounded. Cherokee agent Return J. Meigs reported, "The Cherokee warriors have fought and bled freely, and according to their numbers have lost more men than any part of the Army." Many of the Cherokees who fought with Jackson at Horseshoe Bend would serve as leaders in the years ahead, including John Ross and Major Ridge. Jackson, however, was disappointed that Chief Red Eagle was not among the dead, and, in fact, had not been present. Even so, he had broken the power and will of the Red Sticks. The short-lived Creek

War was over. Most important, Jackson had destroyed the ability of the Creeks to make war at a time when the British prepared to land troops in the South and provide the Creeks with arms and supplies to enable them to continue their war against the United States. As a result, the Battle of Horseshoe Bend, like the Battle of the Thames to the north, proved one of the most important engagements between Indians and whites during the War of 1812. The treaty that followed would be no less important for the Creeks and white settlers on the southern trans-Appalachian frontier.[34]

After returning to Fort Williams for provisions, Jackson continued south toward an area of Creek sacred ground known as Hickory Ground, where he built a post that he called Fort Jackson on the site of the old French Fort Toulouse. Many of the chiefs, then, came into his camp and surrendered. While Jackson was pleased with their appearance, he wanted Red Eagle, who left Horseshoe Bend before the fighting started, and who, according to rumor, had fled to Pensacola. Fearing that he had missed the opportunity to capture or kill the Creek leader most responsible in Jackson's mind for the war, he was astonished when the chief walked into his camp. Red Eagle's audacity surprised Jackson. And, when he said, "I am in your power. Do with me as you please, I am a soldier. I have done the white people all the harm I could; I have fought them, and fought them bravely; if I had an army, I would yet fight, and contend to the last, but I have none; my people are all gone. I can now do no more than weep over the misfortunes of my nation," Jackson could not help but admire his courage. Jackson told him that he could have peace by settling his people north of Fort Williams where the federal government could watch over them and where they would be removed from British and Spanish influence.[35]

Red Eagle understood the situation of the Creeks as well as Jackson, and he did not want his people to suffer with a continuation of the war, which he would have pressed to the fullest if he had the strength of numbers and weapons. He told Jackson, "I have not surrendered myself thoughtlessly. Whilst there were chances of success, I never left my post, nor supplicated peace. But my people are gone, and I now ask for it for my nation, and for myself. On the miseries and misfortunes brought upon my country, I look back with deepest sorrow, and wish to avert still greater calamities. If I had been left to contend with the Georgia army, I would have raised my corn on one bank of the river, and fought them on the other; but your people have destroyed my nation. . . . Those who would still hold out, can be influenced only by a mean spirit of revenge; and to this they must not, and shall not sacrifice the last remnant of their country. You have told us where we might go, and be safe. This is a good talk, and my nation ought to listen to it. They shall listen to it."[36]

By approaching Jackson as a military equal and a soldier, both of whom had done their duty, Red Eagle dictated that Jackson treat his people fairly and mercifully rather than punitively. Jackson also knew that only Red Eagle could convince the holdouts to surrender and thereby save American lives. Although Jackson controlled the situation by destroying the Creek army, Red Eagle, by accepting peace for the Creeks as a people defeated in war but unconquered in spirit, prevented the destruction of the Creeks as a nation and people. The backcountry whites, however, did not see the subtleties of Red Eagle's surrender. They only understood that the Creeks had been defeated by military force, and they wanted more of it applied against the Indians in frontier areas. By April 18, Jackson's own mopping-up operations, together with Red Eagle's plea for the remaining Creeks in the Coosa and Tallapoosa River country to surrender, essentially brought the Creek War to an end, except for those who fled to Florida and joined the British.

With peace restored on the southern trans-Appalachian frontier, Secretary of War John Armstrong sent commissioners General Thomas Pinckney and Indian agent Benjamin Hawkins to arrange a peace treaty with the Creeks, with the only requirement being that they pay for the war. When westerners heard about these appointments they became enraged, because they considered Hawkins a friend of the Indians who would sell out white interests, particularly concerning a land cession, and the frontier whites wanted most of the land claimed by the Creeks as an indemnity for causing the war. Jackson agreed. He wanted the Creeks to cede all lands west of the Coosa and north of the Alabama Rivers to ensure their separation from the Spanish in Florida. The public outcry against Pinckney and Hawkins, who in fact negotiated a lenient treaty, achieved their dismissal and replacement by Jackson as the chief negotiator.

Jackson intended to dictate a peace treaty that would prevent the Creeks from joining the Spanish and British in Florida, destroy their power forever, and seize considerable lands for white settlers. When he arrived at Fort Jackson on July 10, 1814, to take charge of the treaty proceedings, he called for a meeting of friendly and hostile Creeks at the fort on August 1. To ensure that the Creeks understood the seriousness of the situation, he instructed Hawkins to tell them that "[d]estruction will attend a failure to comply with those orders." He also told General Coffee, "If they do not come in and submit, against the day appointed which is the first of next month, a sudden and well directed stroke may be made, that will at once reduce them to unconditional surrender." Jackson then would destroy the Creeks as a people if necessary, but he surely would take most of their lands "until at last, necessity would prompt them to industry and agriculture, as the only certain and lasting means of support." Jackson did not doubt that he had to take Creek land for their own good in order to force them to settle down and live like white farmers.[37]

On August 1, the chiefs of the Red Sticks appeared, apprehensive about what Jackson would demand of them and their people. The friendly Creek chiefs arrived, expecting a reward for their loyalty against the renegades in their nation who had caused the war. They were astounded when Jackson demanded that all Creeks, friendly as well as hostile, pay for the Creek War, which he calculated to be twenty-three million acres of land, more than half of Creek territory, essentially 60 percent of present-day Alabama and 20 percent of Georgia. By so doing, Jackson demanded a treaty that punished the Creeks and rewarded white settlers. Moreover, he required the Creeks to end all communications with the British and Spanish and permit the federal government to build roads, forts, and trading posts where it pleased.

Big Warrior and Shelocta spoke for the friendly Creeks, saying that the terms were too harsh because such a substantial loss of their homeland would destroy them as a people. Big Warrior appealed for fairness and magnanimity, saying, "The president, our father advises us to honesty and fairness, and promises that justice shall be done: I hope and trust it will be. . . . Hard is our situation, and you ought to consider it." But, he did not. Jackson, who had elevated obstinacy and self-righteousness to a fine art, replied, "[T]he part you desire to retain is that through which the intruders and mischief-makers from the lakes reached you, and urged your nation to . . . acts of violence. . . . That path must be stopped. Until this is done, your nation cannot expect happiness, nor mine security. . . . This evening must determine whether or not you are disposed to become friendly. Your rejecting the treaty will show you to be the enemies of the United States— enemies even to your self."[38]

Jackson gave the Creeks the choice between peace and war, and they had neither the men and weapons nor allies to fight. On August 9, when the moment came to sign the treaty, thirty-five chiefs made their mark; only one had been a Red Stick. Jackson had dictated a treaty that destroyed the land base of the Creek nation, but he imposed it not on his enemies but on his friends and allies who helped him win the war. His enemies, the Red Sticks, had fled to Florida. In the end, then, Jackson destroyed the Creeks not by eliminating the Red Sticks, but by taking the domain of those Creeks who were friendly to the United States. Moreover, since he considered the signatory chiefs to represent the Creek nation, the treaty obligated the hostiles to accept it at some point. The Treaty of Fort

Jackson, then, though bizarre, marked the beginning of the end for the Indians on the southern trans-Appalachian frontier. Although it did not provide for removal, it helped begin the process of taking vast tracts of Indian lands and moving the Indians to smaller allocations for their own good as well as for the benefit of white settlers. Once the process began, it could not be stopped. Indeed, the demand for total removal of the Creeks and the other southern nations would increase in the years ahead, until it became national Indian policy. Within twenty-five years, the Creeks, Chickasaws, Choctaws, and Cherokees would be gone from the southern frontier. While the southern nations now remained at peace for the remainder of the war with Great Britain out of fear of similar destruction, north of the Ohio River the Indians confronted a turning point in their relations with the white Americans.

North of the Ohio River, where Tecumseh and Tenskwatawa worked to establish a confederacy to defend Indian lands, the British strove to keep the northern nations friendly to Great Britain. By the Chesapeake crisis in 1807, the British believed that if war came with the Americans, the United States would attempt to use the Indians against them. To foil that probability, Sir James Craig, governor-in-chief of British North America, ordered his subordinates to supply the Indians with guns, powder, lead, and other provisions to keep them loyal and available in time of need. Although President James Madison told Congress in his annual message in December 1810 that the United States continued to make friends with the Indians, he and his advisors either lacked or ignored reports that the Indians north of the Ohio were becoming increasingly hostile. Tecumseh, who spoiled for a fight that would drive the Americans back across the Ohio River, had told the British at Amherstburg in Canada that his people were prepared for war.

As isolated attacks on white settlers increased, the white frontier people in Ohio, Indiana, and Illinois demanded protection by the federal government, particularly against the Shawnees. John Johnston, the Indian agent at Piqua, Ohio, however, believed after a late August meeting with the Shawnees and Wyandots that "at present there is not the smallest danger to be apprehended from the Shawanoes, Wyandotts, Delawares, or Miamies, and it is believed that many of the Puttawatomies may be considered as the true friends of the United States." Johnson's reassurance, however, did not calm the fears of the frontier people because they knew, as he must have known, that the Prophet continued to preach Indian unity and war. "What may be the result," an observer in Vincennes wrote, "God only knows."[39]

By the spring of 1812, both whites and Indians on the northwestern trans-Appalachian frontier expected war between Great Britain and the United States, and each intended to use it to solve their mutual problems of encroachment on their lands. They did not wait long. On June 18, Congress declared war against Great Britain. By mid-August, Tecumseh and his men had joined the British under General Isaac Brock to surround and force the surrender of Fort Detroit. Once General William Hull capitulated after a short bombardment and the inability of his men to break through British and Indian lines to find reinforcements, he surrendered, in part, due to a lack of will as well as to save the women and children inside the fort. Whatever the reason, white settlers north of the Ohio considered his surrender nothing less than treachery, and many began fleeing their homes for safety south of the river.

After Hull's defeat in August 1812, Madison appointed William Henry Harrison as the new commander of the Northwestern Army and ordered him to destroy the Indian confederacy and retake Fort Detroit. Harrison had a great reputation with the white frontier people, particularly after his forces defeated the Prophet at Tippecanoe the year before. In September, at his headquarters in Piqua, Harrison issued a call for volunteers by appealing to the patriotism of the whites in the northwest, saying, "The British and Indians have invaded our country." Harrison planned to gather an army at the Maumee Rapids and prepare for an attack on Fort Detroit and Fort Malden at Amherstburg. General James Winchester, whom Harrison grudgingly gave responsibility for the assignment, sent his forces north prematurely in mid-January 1813, only to be routed and captured by a 1,400-man force, half of whom were Indians, at Frenchtown (present-day Monroe, Michigan). Confronted with a second humiliating defeat in seven months, as well as flagging commitment of the War Department to the West in order to bolster forces in the East, Harrison struggled under difficult circumstances to complete the construction of Fort Meigs at the Maumee Rapids to prevent a British attack from Detroit into the Ohio country and to provide a staging ground for his own attack against the British in the spring.[40]

The British moved first. In late April, Brigadier General Henry Procter, whom one officer described as "one of the meanest looking men I ever saw," led a thousand-man British and Canadian army along with another thousand fighting men under Tecumseh against Fort Meigs. After a bloody fight and siege, the British withdrew on May 9, much to the disappointment of Tecumseh, who pressured Procter to attack again. Procter, along with Tecumseh, did so in late July, but this siege, too, failed, and the British and their Indian allies again withdrew

16. In early November 1811, followers of Tenskwatawa attacked William Henry Harrison's advancing troops near Prophetstown in present-day Indiana. After a hard-fought battle with no apparent winner, Tenskwatawa's men left the field and Harrison claimed victory for what became known as the Battle of Tippecanoe. During the War of 1812, Harrison led his army against the British and their Indian allies at Moraviantown, where, in late September 1813, during the Battle of the Thames, Tecumseh met his death. (Negative No. C5829. Courtesy, Indiana Historical Society.)

to Detroit. Although they made one last attack in the Northwest Territory on Fort Stephenson on the Sandusky River in Ohio, the war north of the Ohio River had come to an end.[41]

After Commander Oliver Hazard Perry's victory on Lake Erie, the British abandoned Detroit because they could no longer supply it by water, and they withdrew across the Thames River and away from Harrison's pursuing army. Tecumseh, however, urged attack rather than withdrawal; he considered the British retreat nothing less than a betrayal and he likened Procter to "a fat animal, that carries its tail upon its back, but when affrighted he drops it between his legs and runs off." Harrison's army caught both Procter's 800 regulars and Tecumseh's 500 men near Moraviantown, about fifty miles east of Detroit in early October 1813. Harrison's superior force of 3,000 men broke British resistance after several days of pursuit, and on October 6, when the Indians learned that Tecumseh had been killed, the opposition disintegrated. The Battle of the Thames ended not only with a victory for Harrison's army, but it also broke British power in the northwest and destroyed Tecumseh's Indian confederacy.[42]

In late February 1814, John Johnston met with leaders of the Shawnees, Wyandots, Senecas, Miamis, Potawatomies, Ottawas, and Kickapoos in Dayton for the purpose of gaining their support against the British. Johnston scolded them for joining the British and making war against the United States when they had been told to stay out of the fight. Now he told them, "As war is our trade and you cannot live quiet and take no part in it, your Father is compelled by *necessity and not choice,* to put the tomahawk in your hands. And . . . you must receive the tomahawk from my hands and when you are told you must strike. Our enemies must be your enemies. . . . If you do not, you will be considered enemies and treated as such; but if you are faithful you shall be well paid." In July, Johnston met in Greenville with delegates from the major tribes and a few Potawatomies, whom he called "very sulky." Johnston wanted their commitment to join the Americans against Great Britain, but the chiefs pledged only neutrality. Johnston refused, telling them that they could be a friend or enemy of the United States but they could not be neutral. The chiefs considered their lack of alternatives and, on July 22, 1814, signed the Treaty with the Wyandot, which obligated the Wyandots, Shawnees, Delawares, Senecas, and Miamis to join the Americans against the British and to end hostilities with the United States. Peace had now came to the northern trans-Appalachian frontier, but only after considerable suffering and loss of life by both Indians and whites.[43]

When news that the British and Americans had stopped fighting reached the trans-Appalachian frontier in the late winter of 1815, most settlers north and south of the Ohio River believed the Indian threat to the region had ended. Whites on the trans-Appalachian frontier were even happier about the treaty signed with the major Indian nations on August 31, 1815, in Detroit. There, Indian commissioners met with the Wyandots, Shawnees (including the Prophet), Delawares, Miamis, Senecas, Ojibwas, Ottawas, Potawatomies, Sauks, and Winnebagos, where "with considerable ceremony, and apparent sincerity," their leaders agreed to peace with the United States.[44]

Tecumseh and the Prophet's plans for a pan-Indian confederacy had never materialized, and the unity that they achieved had now been broken forever. Great tracts of Indian lands had been taken, and more would soon be surrendered through a host of cession treaties. Many whites in the backcountry now believed that the Indian threat east of the Mississippi River had been removed for all time. The only Indian problem that remained involved their continued presence. With the War of 1812 behind them, white Americans now began to demand the solution of that problem by removal, forced if necessary. In contrast, the Indians, whose military power had been destroyed, cast their fate with diplomacy and the rule of law to protect their interests.

CHAPTER 6

The Southern Nations

The Treaty of Ghent brought peace to the trans-Appalachian frontier and with it the demand by whites that the tribes be moved, either peacefully or forcibly, west of the Mississippi River. Thomas Jefferson had first posed this idea for dealing with the Indian nations in the backcountry by exchanging their domain for federal lands across the great river. There, they would be beyond the corrupting influence of whiskey peddlers, cheating traders, and aggressive, land-grabbing squatters. West of the Mississippi the Indians would have time to learn agricultural practices in the white tradition as well as gain a rudimentary education, particularly knowledge of English, both skills that would enable them to support themselves and make their way in the white world. In time, with beneficent support from the federal government, the trans-Appalachian Indian people would become assimilated and acculturated into white American society. In 1803, the Louisiana Purchase provided the extensive lands to make removal feasible.

The War of 1812 dashed the thoughts of both friends and enemies of the Indians regarding the formulation and implementation of a removal policy. When the war ended, however, the idea reemerged in the minds of many government officials, friends, and potential settlers. In January 1817, the Senate Committee on Public Lands urged the exchange of lands. President James Monroe also favored removal, and he told a sympathetic and supportive Andrew Jackson that "The hunter or savage state requires a greater extent of territory to sustain it, than is compatible with the progress and just claims of civilized life, and must yield to it." He told Congress much the same thing in his annual message in December. Monroe's successor John Quincy Adams also favored removal, but he did not believe the southern tribes could be compelled to move against their will because of federal treaty obligations. Adams contended that only negotiation would legally achieve the desired goal. During his administration, Congress continued to talk about removal, but neither the House nor the Senate could agree on a policy and appropriate funds to implement it.[1]

By the early 1820s, government officials, such as Monroe, Jackson, and Secretary of War John C. Calhoun, advocated removal of the Indians for their own good, because white intruders wantonly settled on Indian lands with no intent to pay for them or move. No one needed the southern Indians anymore. The fur and deerskin traders had vanished with the game on which both depended, and the army no longer sought the Indians as allies. Consequently, in January 1824, Calhoun told a delegation in Washington to be mindful of "the discontent of Georgia and the pressure of her citizens." They had much to worry about, because the State of Georgia forced action rather than thoughtful reflection among those charged with implementing and executing Indian policy. On April 24, 1802, Georgia had ceded its western lands to the United States, and the federal government agreed to extinguish Indian land claims within the state and give those lands to Georgia. By 1824, however, Georgia had tired of waiting for the federal government to terminate the land claims of the Indians who inhabited the northwestern portion of the state. Georgia wanted title to those lands and the Creeks and Cherokees removed, and the governor talked of extending state control over those lands in violation of federal treaty commitments to the tribes. Congress debated removal in the months ahead but failed to act.[2]

In 1829, Andrew Jackson succeeded Adams as president, and he too believed that the Indians could not claim land just because they hunted over it. Nor did he believe that Congress should negotiate with the Indian nations as it did with France, England, or Spain. Jackson thought it absurd to deal with the Indian tribal groups as though they were independent nations. Instead, he contended that the Indians should be treated like other subjects of the United States regarding law. Accordingly, Jackson argued that Congress should legislate policy rather than negotiate treaties that required approval of the Senate. Jackson, however, did not advocate the theft of Indian lands. Rather, he argued that Congress should define Indian boundaries and occupy their lands, provided the government compensated them fairly when exercising the right of eminent domain. Jackson also adamantly believed that Indians could not live independently, that is, subject to tribal laws, on their own lands within a state. If they were not willing to live subject to the laws of a state, they had no alternative but to move west of the Mississippi where the government could provide them title to new lands in perpetuity that were not colored by the political jurisdiction of any state. Only in this way could the nation grow with peace. By favoring removal, Jackson demonstrated his commitment to states' rights and limited federal power as well as nationalism and federally directed territorial expansion for purposes of both land and security.

Jackson's election to the presidency, however, heartened and embolden the Georgia legislature, and soon after the presidential election in 1828, it began extending state authority over Creek and Cherokee lands, with the intent of adding all Indian lands to state jurisdiction by June 1, 1830. The Creeks and Cherokees protested, but Jackson gave no quarter. In his annual message on December 8, 1829, he told Congress that some Indians had "lately attempted to erect an independent government within the limits of Georgia and Alabama." But, he contended, the Constitution prohibited the creation of an independent government or state within a state. The Indians, he argued, had only the possessory right to the soil, that is, the mere right of occupancy not ownership. Consequently, these Indian nations could not claim territorial sovereignty, and the tribal members could either submit to the authority of the state or remove beyond the Mississippi. Jackson, of course, wanted to avoid a confrontation with Georgia over states' rights that conceivably might require the use of troops to guarantee federal power and authority, but he also genuinely believed removal would serve the best interests of the southern Indian nations. Others who considered themselves friends of the Indians also supported removal so the Indians could be educated, Christianized and thereby "civilized," far from the corrupting influence of white society.[3]

In 1829, Thomas L. McKinney, a humanitarian who had considerable knowledge of Indian culture and who had served as head of the Bureau of Indian Affairs during the Adams administration, agreed with Jackson. McKinney contended: "Seeing as I do the condition of these people, and that they are bordering on destruction; I would, were I empowered, take them *firmly* but *kindly* by the hand, and tell them they must go; and I would do this, on the same principle that I would take my own children by the hand, firmly, but kindly and lead them from a district of Country in which the plague was raging." Jackson also expressed this paternalistic view, which he too believed was both benevolent and right.[4]

Congress agreed with Jackson, and on February 2, 1830, the House and the Senate introduced removal bills. The Senate Committee on Indian Affairs spoke for all who supported this policy when it urged removal of the Indians west of the Mississippi "where they can be secured against the intrusion of any other people; where, under the protection of the United States, and with their *aid,* they can pursue their plan of civilization, and, ere long, be in the peaceable enjoyment of a civil government of their own choice, and where Christian and philanthropist can have ample scope for their labors of love and benevolence." Ultimately, in late May, Congress approved the Indian Removal Bill after bitter argument on both humanitarian and political grounds. It authorized the president to select lands west of the Mississippi River, "not included in any state or organized territory," for the relocation of the trans-Appalachian tribes. These lands would be exchanged for Indian lands east of the Mississippi, and Indian title to these new lands would be guaranteed "forever." The tribes that emigrated would be supported with food, clothing, and shelter for one year to help them adjust to their new location, and Congress appropriated a half million dollars for that work. Jackson signed the Removal Act on May 28, 1830. Quickly, he developed the procedure for removal that he hoped to achieve as speedily, economically, and humanely as possible. Unfortunately for the Indians, speed and economy superceded humanitarianism in the execution of the removal policy.[5]

The Choctaws in Mississippi were the first to go. They occupied the central and southern portions of Mississippi where in May 1818 Secretary of War John C. Calhoun began his efforts to gain their removal. Calhoun picked the Choctaws because they had a highly developed economy, much in the white tradition, and he believed they would be best able to make the transition to a new life beyond the Mississippi. The Choctaws were also the closest major tribe to the new Indian Territory and supposedly their removal would cause fewer logistical problems. Federal commissioners, including Andrew Jackson, who were sent to treat with the Choctaws, however, received a rebuff when, on August 12, 1819, Pushmataha, a major leader, told them: "We wish to remain here . . . and do not wish to be transplanted to another soil." In response, Jackson favored using force to remove them and to abandon the cession treaty process as both unnecessary and a waste of time, but Monroe and Calhoun favored moderation and continued negotiation.[6]

Unfortunately for the Choctaws and the other southern nations, the frontier people would not give the commissioners time to pursue an honorable Indian policy that sought removal of the tribes. Consequently, Calhoun sent Jackson back to the Choctaws as chief negotiator in October 1820, where he urged them to emigrate beyond the Mississippi River for their own good by exchanging approximately five million acres, or one-third of their lands in Mississippi, for thirteen million acres of new land in Arkansas and Indian Territory. Although Pushmataha believed those new lands were "exceedingly poor and sterile," and "tractless, sandy deserts," he knew that white intruders would soon overrun Choctaw lands and ruin their way of life, and thus he urged acceptance of the treaty. If they did not sign, Jackson promised to abandon them to their fate. Given no satisfactory alternative, the Choctaws signed the Treaty of Doak's Stand on October 18, 1820. The Choctaws,

17. Pushmataha, one of the major Choctaw chiefs, rejected Tecumseh's arguments to join an Indian confederacy and the British against the United States. He urged the Choctaws to look to the future rather than to the past and recognize that good relations with the Americans were prudent and necessary. During the Creek War, Pushmataha offered the military power of the Choctaws to the federal government. Until his death in 1825, however, Pushmataha resisted removal and spoke eloquently for his people. (Courtesy, Mississippi Department of Archives and History.)

however, refused to emigrate, in part because the treaty permitted them to live on the remainder of their tribal land, where they remained when Congress passed the Removal Act in May 1830.[7]

Under the Removal Act, the Jackson administration began negotiations to move the Choctaws west of the Mississippi River and gain the remainder of their lands. Secretary of War John Eaton and General John Coffee warned the Choctaws that the federal government could not protect them and guarantee the tribal integrity of their lands despite treaty commitments. Moreover, they would come under the jurisdiction of Mississippi if they did not emigrate. If they agreed to removal, however, they would be able to maintain their tribal identity and existence. Eaton also told the Choctaws that if they did not sign a removal treaty, federal troops would invade their homeland within twenty days. He also told them that they could no more resist than "for a baby to expect to overcome a giant."[8]

On January 19, 1830, Mississippi responded to Jackson's position by extending state law "over the persons and property of the Indian residents within its limits." Any Indian who failed to comply would be subject to a fine of $1,000 and a year in prison. The Choctaw leaders knew that Mississippi could not compel them to obey, but they also understood that extralegal violence by whites would be the result, all to the detriment of their people.[9]

Greenwood Leflore, a mixed-blood leader of the Choctaws, who called himself "chief of the Choctaw Nation," although he served as only one of three district leaders, connived for sole tribal leadership. The full-blood leaders, Mushulatubbe and Nittucachee (also Nitakichi or Natticache), however, deposed Leflore and blocked his ambition to consolidate Choctaw leadership in himself, particularly regarding negotiations with federal officials for removal, because he wanted to use the crisis to enhance his own political power and wealth. Leflore also recognized the problems that the extension of state power over Indian lands posed for his people, and he convinced the other Choctaw leaders to meet with federal commissioners at Dancing Rabbit Creek in Noxubee County, Mississippi, in mid-September 1830. Federal officials met this opportunity with great excitement and anticipation because the negotiation of a removal treaty with the Choctaws would be the test case for Jackson's Indian removal policy. Ultimately, Leflore, Nittucachee, and Mushulatubbe agreed to removal after the commissioners promised them each four sections of land, while some fifty selected favorites also received from one to two sections as bribes to support the treaty. Intimidated by threats of violence and seduced with bribes, the Choctaws clearly understood their choices, and they did not consider either of them good.[10]

Even so, other Choctaws led by Peter Pitchlynn rejected the federal offer of money and support, because they were displeased with those lands. Essentially, the mixed-bloods favored removal and the full-bloods, who composed the majority, opposed it, and some even threatened to kill the chiefs who succumbed to bribery and signed the treaty. Secretary of War Eaton, however, told them they could accept the treaty or be subjected to almost immediate military force. Given this choice on September 28, Choctaw leaders signed the Treaty of Dancing Rabbit Creek, but only after considerable argument and division within the tribe, in part because the federal government refused to recognize as chiefs anyone except those who signed the treaty. Secretary of War Eaton, however, warned the Choctaws to "[k]eep at peace and be happy." When hostile Choctaws confronted Leflore for signing the treaty, he shrewdly asked, "Which is worse, for a great government to offer a bribe or for a poor Indian to take one?"[11]

The Treaty of Dancing Rabbit Creek, ratified and proclaimed on February 24, 1831, symbolized the achievement of Jefferson's desire to move the eastern Indian nations west of the Mississippi River. In the treaty, the Choctaws agreed to cede all of their lands east of the Mississippi for lands west of the river. In turn, the commissioners pledged that "The Government and people of the United

18. Greenwood Leflore, a mixed-blood, called himself the chief of the Choctaw nation. He helped negotiate the Treaty of Dancing Rabbit Creek in 1830, which led to the removal of his people to Indian Territory. Leflore accepted a government bribe for his cooperation, although he denied it and argued that the Choctaws would have a better life in the West. (Courtesy, Mississippi Department of Archives and History.)

States are hereby obliged to secure to the said Choctaw Nation of Red People the jurisdiction and government of all the persons and property that may be within their limits west, so that no Territory or State shall ever have a right to pass laws for the government of the Choctaw Nation of Red People and their descendants; and that no part of their land granted them shall ever be embraced in any Territory or State." The federal government also agreed to protect the Choctaws "on the same principle that the citizens of the United States are protected," and it agreed to spend $20,000 for twenty years in addition to previous treaty annuity pledges as well as provide and support schools for twenty years.[12]

Jackson hoped the Treaty of Dancing Rabbit Creek would serve as the model for the removal of other tribal groups east of the Mississippi because it recognized Indian property and political rights and offered support once they reached their new lands. While Jackson and those who supported removal basked in the success of what they hoped would be a model treaty providing the foundation for a policy to solve the Indian problem, the Choctaws accepted it with resignation. Chief David Folsom wrote, "Our doom is sealed. There is no other course for us but to turn our faces to our new homes toward the setting sun." Chief Folsom had good reason for pessimism, because the removal did not go well, presumably because the federal government had never done anything like this before, and officials did not know what to do or expect.[13]

The army scheduled the first group of Choctaws to leave Mississippi in three groups between 1831 and 1833, with the first departing in the autumn of 1831. Civilians contracted to provide provisions along the route west, but they soon argued with the commissary officers about organization, supply, prices, and payment. Quickly, the carefully planned process began to break down, in part due to government economizing and crooked contractors who received their positions by submitting the lowest bid and who took federal funds but did not provide adequate food and services. Inordinate delays prolonged departure until winter gripped the land, causing extreme hardship and want along the route.

Alexis de Tocqueville, the French traveler and observer of American life, stood on the east bank of the Mississippi at Memphis that year in the dead of winter and watched the Choctaws cross over. The ground was frozen and snow covered and great rafts of ice floated downriver. He later wrote, "The Indians brought their families with them; there were among them the wounded, the sick, newborn babies, and old men on the point of death. They had neither tents nor wagons, but only some provisions and weapons. I saw them embark to cross the great river, and the sight will never fade from my memory. Neither sob nor complaint rose from that silent assembly. Their afflictions were of long standing, and they felt them to be irremediable."[14]

The Choctaws were a people without alternatives. If they had hope at all, it was to safely cross the river, reach their new lands, and live until spring. The War Department evaluated the fiasco of the Choctaw removal, terminated its civilian supply agents, and took control of the operation. The second and third stages of Choctaw removal went more smoothly, but not without hardship. By 1833, as many as fifteen thousand Choctaws had been resettled in Indian Territory, but approximately half that number remained in Mississippi, where they lived under state authority and where they were soon swindled out of most of their individual land allotments. The Creeks were next, but they did not go willingly.

In 1814, the Creeks had lost considerable lands in Georgia and Alabama in the Treaty of Fort Jackson. They made other land cessions in 1818 and 1821, convinced that the annual annuities were more important than land that held no game, particularly for the Lower Creeks who lived closer to white settlements. About

19. William McIntosh, the son of a Loyalist officer and a Creek mother, helped negotiate a land sale in 1805 that gained the attention of federal authorities. McIntosh had prominent relations on both sides of his family, and he could speak and write English. His followers aided Andrew Jackson during the Creek War, and McIntosh was the most well-known Creek in the United States. He moved easily between the Indian and white worlds. In 1825, he lost his life for negotiating a great Creek land cession in Georgia and Alabama known as the Treaty of Indian Springs. (*M'Intosh. A Creek Chief.* From *History of the Indian Tribes of North America.* Accession No. 1985.66153, 324. Courtesy, Smithsonian American Art Museum.)

1818, the Creek territory extended from the Flint River on the east to the Coosa River on the west, a ten-million-acre tract divided by the Chattahoochee. After 1821, neither the Upper nor Lower Creeks intended to cede more land, and the National Council adopted a law that defined Creek territory and provided the death penalty for anyone who sold or otherwise cede it to whites. The Council, however, suspended the law in 1821 because it needed money and the land cession that year provided it, but they did not negotiate an exchange of lands until the Treaty of Indian Springs in 1825.

William McIntosh, speaker of the National Council and a leader of the pro-removal faction, negotiated the Treaty of Indian Springs despite Creek law that mandated the execution of any chief who committed the tribe to an unauthorized land cession. McIntosh also had the responsibility for implementing the death penalty provision without exception in case of a land sale. Some Creeks thought he should have been executed for the 1821 cession, particularly because they believed federal commissioners had bribed him to support the cession treaty.

McIntosh worked hard to restore his reputation, even stating in August 1824 that "Any man who should offer to sell the first bit of land as large as that between his feet should die by the law." At the same time, the Monroe administration planned to acquire as much Creek land as possible. The Creeks knew, however, that they were a weak people who could only contest with the federal and state governments with their wits and by using diplomacy, law, and a plea for justice. Accordingly, on October 24, 1824, several headmen, including Big Warrior, Little Prince, and Hopie Hadjo, drafted a document for the federal commissioners who pursued a cession treaty. In it they professed the weakness of the Creek nation, saying that they "earnestly admonish our white brethren not to take advantage of our weak and unlearned situation; but treat us with tenderness and justice." They could no longer fight but they could argue and contend with words where their rifles would have spoken for them in the past.[15]

As a result, when federal commissioners Duncan G. Campbell and James Meriwether opened negotiations on December 7, 1824, for a land cession treaty that would require the nation to move west of the Mississippi River, the Creeks balked. McIntosh, however, secretly negotiated a land cession with the commissioners after accepting a bribe of $15,000 "for his trouble." McIntosh would not sign the treaty, however, because he feared execution, and he, along with his supporters, petitioned President Monroe for protection, arguing that the Upper Creeks could not sensibly agree to negotiate a treaty because they were engaged in a civil war. McIntosh claimed that the National Council had been co-opted by Big Warrior, who led the hostile Red Sticks. More important, several Lower Creek towns authorized McIntosh to cede their Georgia lands if they could not gain fee-simple title for their people from the state. In turn, the commissioners argued that McIntosh spoke for the majority of Creeks.[16]

Negotiations among Campbell, Meriwether, and McIntosh resulted in the Treaty of Indian Springs, signed on February 12, 1825. In it, the Creeks ceded all of their lands in Georgia and the northern two-thirds of their territory in Alabama. Before McIntosh betrayed his people, Opothle Yoholo, a Creek leader, interrupted the proceedings and told McIntosh: "My friend, you are about to sell our country; I now warn you of your danger." McIntosh may have worried, but he believed the federal government could protect him while the "emigrating party" moved beyond the Mississippi where he would assert his authority as leader of the legitimate Creeks.[17]

Creek agent John Crowell complained to Secretary of War John C. Calhoun that McIntosh did not speak for all Creek people and that with few exceptions those who signed the treaty were either "chiefs of low grade, or not chiefs at all." Big Warrior complained as well, arguing that Creek lands could not be sold and that the $200,000 promised McIntosh and his followers in the treaty comprised half the amount designated to compensate the tribe for the improvements they would leave behind and pay removal expenses. Although the Creek National Council removed him from office, it did not plan his execution for treason until it received word in mid-March that the Senate had approved the treaty.[18]

The National Council, then, moved quickly. On the night of April 30, Menawa, an Upper Creek council chief, led a force of nearly 150 men, all whose land had been lost in the treaty, to McIntosh's plantation on the Chattahoochee River. There under the authorization of the Creek Council, they set fire to his house and riddled his body with bullets when the flames drove him outside. McIntosh had bargained away his nation for monetary and political gain. He had falsely represented the Creek people and violated tribal law, for which the nation demanded his life. If the Creeks could not receive justice from the federal government, they could dispense it on their own terms.

They could not, however, keep intruders off their lands. With more than half the Creek people living on ceded lands, they feared for their safety if they stayed, but they had no place to go. While they worried, the National Council worked to overturn the treaty, arguing as Opothle Yoholo, who emerged as the leader of the nation after Big Warrior's death in March, that "The treaty was made by fraud, by thieves, by walkers in the night." Over the months that followed McIntosh's death, President Adams began to sympathize with the National Council, but no one, except the Creeks, believed the treaty could be overturned, because no precedent existed for such action once the Senate ratified it. General Edmund P. Gaines, however, acting on behalf of the federal government, informed the Creeks that the Treaty of Indian Springs would be revoked if they agreed to cede their Georgia lands in exchange for an equal acreage west of the Mississippi River, plus $400,000. Otherwise, the Treaty of Indian Springs would stand. Gaines told the National Council, "The President and myself did not cause your distress; you must therefore aid us in our efforts to relieve you."[19]

Faced with accepting either a bad bargain or a worse one, the Creeks agreed, but the negotiation of a new treaty took until January 1826, when they signed the document known as the Treaty of Washington, which required them to withdraw to the area of the present-day Georgia-Alabama line. Adams then told the Senate that the Creeks refused to be bound by the Treaty of Indian Springs. As a result, the government had two options. It could "resort to measures of war," or "attempt the adjustment" of Creek concerns with a "new compact." Adams favored the second alternative, contending that "The nature of our institutions and . . . the sentiments of justice and humanity which the occasion requires for measures of peace" dictated acceptance of a new treaty. The Senate agreed and ratified the Treaty of Washington on April 22, 1826, after adjusting the boundary a bit more. Significantly, the treaty gave back and guaranteed the tribal integrity of the remaining Creek lands in Alabama and nullified the Treaty of Indian Springs. The Creeks had accomplished what no Indian nation had ever done or would do again—achieve the annulment of a ratified treaty.[20]

Even so, by the end of 1827, the Creeks controlled only five million acres in Alabama. There, in the homeland of the Upper Creeks the Lower Creeks took refuge. Disparate in language and tradition, the Creeks were bound together by the National Council, which was controlled by the conservative Upper Creeks as the Lower Creeks lost influence when their towns broke up due to the loss of their land. The National Council alone gave them identity as an organized nation, and it was this identity that the Alabamians, like the Georgians, wanted removed from their midst. Accordingly, during the two years following January 1827, the Alabama legislature extended state jurisdiction over all Creek territory, but the Adams administration made no effort to challenge the state even though the Creek lands had previously been federal not state domain. The legislature worked intensively with threats and bribes to convince the Creeks to emigrate.

Jackson, soon after his inauguration, told the Creeks, "My white children in Alabama have extended their law over your country. If you remain in it, you must be subject to that law." If they moved beyond the Mississippi, however, Jackson assured them that they could have both land and peace "as long as the grass grows or the water runs, in peace and plenty." He did not, however, offer to guarantee their lands and protect them in Alabama. The Creek National Council protested Alabama's legal and physical harassments and questioned how the Treaty of Washington, which "the Government of the United States guaranteed to the Creek Nation forever all the lands we now hold," could be "broken by whim or caprice of any State Legislature."[21]

Early in 1830, the National Council, led by Opothle Yoholo, who traveled to Washington, appealed to both Jackson and Congress for enforcement of their treaty rights from Alabama's infringement. "We beg permission to be left, where your treaties have left us, in the enjoyment of rights as a separate people, and to be treated as unoffending, peaceable inhabitants of our own, and not a borrowed country." Jackson could make no headway among men of such intransigence, so he targeted the Lower Creeks who were more willing to emigrate. Using the time-honored technique of divide and conquer, the administration persuaded a group of Lower Creeks, led by Eneah Micco and Tuskeneah of Cusseta, to strip Opothle Yoholo of his power to represent the Creek nation in Washington. Based

20. Opothle Yoholo, chief and speaker for the Upper Creek Towns, refused to sign the Treaty of Indian Springs that McIntosh negotiated. He pledged that McIntosh's "blood should wash out the memory" of that treaty, and he warned McIntosh that he would be killed for betraying the Creeks and ceding their lands. (*Opothle Yoholo. A Creek Chief.* From *History of the Indian Tribes of North America.* Accession No. 1985.66.153, 316. Courtesy, Smithsonian American Art Museum.)

on that action the administration refused to deal with the Upper Creeks while it pressed the Lower Creeks hard about the benefits of removal, especially the avoidance of Alabama law and confrontation with white intruders.[22]

By 1831, hunger due to depleted game and smallpox aided the government's arguments for removal. And, on January 7, 1831, Eneah Micco, principal chief of the Lower Creeks, sent a delegation to Washington. There, they pleaded for protection from white intruders who settled on their lands and murdered their people. When Opothle Yoholo led another delegation to Washington in December, they again met an obstinate refusal by the new secretary of defense, Lewis Cass, to guarantee their lands and protect them. Disheartened and worn down to the point of surrender, the Creeks now recognized the necessity and inevitability of their relocation to Indian Territory, and they contemplated removal, which they proposed in March 1832. In the treaty that followed, the Creeks agreed to sell all tribal lands east of the Mississippi River. The federal government, in turn, agreed to allot these lands on the basis of 640 acres to the chiefs and 320 acres to heads of households. The federal government also pledged to keep intruders off the allotted lands and pay for removal when the Creeks were ready to emigrate. The allotted lands could be sold or the Creeks could remain on them and receive title after five years, but they would live under state law. If they chose to sell and emigrate, the federal government also agreed to finance their removal and support them for one year in Indian Territory.

The treaty signed by the Creeks and Secretary of War Cass in Washington on March 24, 1832, known as the Treaty of Cusseta, then, technically was not a removal treaty, although it provided lands in the west and an annuity of $210,000 over twenty years, federal payment of removal costs, and support for one year on their new lands, among other considerations. The federal government did not take Creek lands but permitted the nation to keep 2.1 of their 5.2 million acres. The government, however, expected the Creeks to sell those lands and move west, because the treaty ended the existence of the Creek nation east of the Mississippi River. Thereafter, the Creeks could only exist as a people if they reconstituted their nation west of the Mississippi. They had little alternative, then, but to place their faith in the federal government whom they no longer believed could be trusted. They also believed that removal was the "worst evil" that could befall them. They were correct on both counts.[23]

Although the federal government had pledged to remove intruders from Creek domain until they could dispose of it by sale, squatters and land speculators quickly used fraud and overt theft to take tribal lands. Whites, whom one observer reported as "some of the most lawless and uncouth men I have ever seen," also began to kill Creeks, who retaliated in kind. As the violence escalated, the Creeks begged the federal government for protection, but to no avail. On December 20, 1832, a Creek council at Wetumpka notified the secretary of war that: "We are without friends and surrounded by enemies. Our only alternative is protection from the United States. This is promised in the treaty; we claim it as a right."[24]

While the Creeks waited for aid and protection, whites took advantage of their naiveté about land values, which one observer called "helpless ignorance," and the Creeks soon began losing their allotments through sales, leases, and mortgage indebtedness. In 1835, white land speculators and intruders made land "stealing ... the order of the day." The government attempted to defuse the anger of the Creeks by pressing for immediate removal, but they refused. Many Creeks, fearing violence and forced removal, fled to Cherokee lands in Alabama and Georgia where they sought refuge. The Georgians were not amused and sent the militia to evict them from Cherokee lands that the legislature had claimed as its own.[25]

In 1836, the Georgia militia attacked the Creeks, who retaliated by striking at white settlers. Secretary of War Cass moved quickly to end the violence by ordering

General Winfield Scott and several thousand federal troops to stop the killing and forcibly send the Creeks "immediately to their country west of the Mississippi." When General Thomas Jesup, leading a contingent of Alabama militia, captured Eneah Micco, the principal chief of the Lower Creeks who opposed removal, the "Creek War of 1836" came to an end. Opothle Yoholo, principal chief of the Upper Creeks, now argued convincingly that the Creeks could only prevent starvation as well as the wanton killing of his people by emigrating. On July 2, some 2,500 Creeks, the first of five major groups, many in handcuffs and chains and under armed guard, left Fort Mitchell for boats on the Alabama River that took them to Mobile, then by ship to New Orleans for further transport up the Mississippi and Arkansas Rivers to Indian Territory. By the end of the year, more than 14,600 Creeks had been forcibly removed without provision for adequate food, clothing, shelter, or transportation. On Christmas Day, 1836, one observer at Little Rock reported their appalling misery: "Many of them, not being able to endure this unexampled state of human suffering, die, and are thrown by the side of the road, and are covered only with brush ... where they remain until devoured by wolves." Without the protection of the federal government, lacking a politically united tribal government, and wanting a strong military presence, their fate was sealed. The Alabamans, like the Georgians, wanted Indian lands, not Creeks as farmers and neighbors, so they took it.[26]

In 1837, Chief Eufaula, one of the last Creeks to depart, addressed the Alabama legislature and said, "In these lands of Alabama, which have belonged to my forefathers, and where our bones lie buried, I see that the Indian fires are going out—they must soon be extinguished." Indeed, the fires of the Indian people were going out across the South, never to be rekindled again. In Mississippi and northwestern Alabama the Chickasaws watched with little hope.[27]

The Chickasaws, who confronted the same problems as the Cherokees and Creeks, found white settlers on their lands and stood helpless when the State of Mississippi extended its authority over their territory. By the end of the War of 1812, the Chickasaws had endured considerable pressure from the federal government for land cessions, and they had become adept at taking money, gifts, and their own good time while listening to the commissioners who thought they were negotiating with them. In 1818, Commissioner Isaac Shelby complained that "the Indians have been very litigious and slow in the decisions; the business which might have been done in two or three days, it has taken twenty days to effect." The federal government ultimately countered these delays by withholding annuity payments to force the Chickasaws to negotiate in good faith, that is, cede their lands. This tactic proved successful, and, on October 19, 1818, the Chickasaws ceded their lands north of the Tennessee River for $20,000 per year over fifteen years. Only their claim to approximately 496,000 acres in northeastern Mississippi and northwestern Alabama remained. Here, they raised cotton with slave labor along with cattle and hogs, all of which they sold at market to purchase the "necessaries and luxuries of life."[28]

By the mid-1820s, the Chickasaws numbered approximately four thousand. Politically, they were divided not by allegiance to nation-states as in the past, such as France, Great Britain, Spain, and the United States, but rather by degree of Indian blood. On the eve of the Indian Removal Act, the mixed-bloods, who comprised about one-fourth of the nation, dominated the tribe. Led by Levi Colbert, they did so by shrewdly maneuvering through tribal institutions. In 1824, the council divided the nation into four judicial districts and adopted a legal code. White settlers in Mississippi and Alabama cared naught, however, about the high state of Chickasaw civilization compared to their own, and between 1819 and 1830, both states enacted a series of laws that incorporated the Chickasaw under state authority. The mixed-bloods, however, who had established prosperous farms, plantations, and businesses, refused to accept that jurisdiction or move.

In 1824, Colbert informed Secretary of War Calhoun that the Chickasaws would "sell no more land, despite pressure of the State of Mississippi." The federal government responded by periodically sending agents to press them for removal and to take advantage of any breaks in the ranks of Chickasaw unanimity. In 1826, federal commissioners urged removal and admonished the Chickasaws to stop "throwing obstacles in the way." Colbert responded by telling them, "We never had a thought of exchanging our land for any other, as we think that we would not find a country that would suit us as well as this we now occupy, it being the land of our forefathers." So far as coming under the jurisdiction of the United States if they remained, Colbert said that since they were not "enlightened," they could not consent to submit to federal authority, all of which infuriated the commissioners. The commissioners blamed their failure to achieve a removal treaty on the mixed-bloods whom they reported had been "enlightened by education and otherwise."[29]

In 1827, Thomas L. McKinney, Commissioner of Indian Affairs, who had considerable knowledge of Indian society and culture, began to pursue a less threatening and demanding approach to gain a removal treaty by appealing to the mixed-bloods based on their business interests and desire to protect their people. He spoke with Colbert about the "collision with state sovereignty, and states rights" and the inability of the federal government to protect the Chickasaws. McKinney urged Colbert and the other leaders to at least seriously consider removal for their own benefit, and he was both surprised and relieved when they agreed to look at promised new lands. A delegation departed in October 1828, but returned unimpressed and reported, "We cannot consent to remove to a country destitute of a single corresponding feature of the one in which we at present reside."[30]

The Chickasaws, however, could not maintain their tactic of delay after Mississippi and Alabama adopted laws dissolving tribal governments in 1829 and 1830, which provided fines and imprisonment for tribal leaders who maintained their offices and duties. Moreover, the Indian Removal Act of 1830 established a unified federal policy to pursue removal immediately. Unable to force the Chickasaws to negotiate, Jackson used state action to achieve his goal. Accordingly, he refused to help the Chickasaws and instead told them they could only preserve their national identity by moving beyond the Mississippi River. Jackson's response convinced Colbert and the other Chickasaw leaders that their past delaying tactics would no longer work. They had been given a choice of losing their tribal identity or moving, and they decided to preserve their culture. Federal agents now pressed hard for a removal treaty and denied annuity payments, obligated under previous agreements, to speed the process.

As a result, on October 20, 1832, the Chickasaws signed a treaty at Pontotoc Creek in which they ceded all tribal lands east of the Mississippi River. In this treaty, signed in the council house at Pontotoc Creek, the commissioners recorded that the Chickasaws, "[b]eing ignorant of the language and laws of the white man, they cannot understand or obey them. Rather than submit to this great evil, they prefer to seek a home in the West, where they may live and be governed by their own laws." In reality, the Chickasaws agreed to emigrate because the mixed-blood leaders clearly understood the problems and dangers before them, and once they had been convinced that they would be settled on adequate lands west of the Mississippi, they agreed to emigrate. Removal was delayed, however, because the Chickasaws had difficulty locating lands in Indian Territory that suited them and because of an outbreak of cholera. Finally, on January 17, 1837, in the Treaty of Doaksville, the Chickasaws agreed to settle on Choctaw lands that they purchased for $530,000. The Chickasaws began emigrating in June. At Memphis, one observer watched a group load onto steamboats for transport down the Mississippi and up the Arkansas to Fort Coffee.

He wrote, "I do not think that I have ever been a witness of so remarkable a scene as was formed by this immense column of moving Indians. . . . The women also very decently clothed like white women, in calico gowns—but much tidier and better put on than common white people—& how beautifully they managed their horses, how proud & calm & erect, they sat in full gallop." And, he reflected, "Much money could not compensate for the loss of what I have seen."[31]

In all, the Chickasaws ceded 6.4 million acres and received $3.3 million for their tribal fund. By the end of the year most of the 4,914 Chickasaws and their 1,156 slaves had relocated in Indian Territory, where they confronted hostile Kickapoos, Shawnees, Kiowas, and Comanches as well as smallpox, dysentery, malnutrition, and hunger due to poor federal planning and corrupt contractors. Small groups, however, continued to emigrate every year until 1850.

The removal of the Cherokees created the most controversial episode of Jacksonian-era Indian policy. They became the symbol of removal, and they too did not go willingly and without a fight. By 1816, some two thousand Cherokees had already migrated to Arkansas, where they established prosperous farms and where they were joined by others during the next few years as the federal government negotiated land cession treaties. In 1828, these Cherokees ceded their Arkansas lands for some seven million acres in the Indian Territory, where upon settlement, they became known as the Old Settlers or Cherokees West. By 1836, approximately six thousand Cherokees occupied lands in Indian Territory where they had become relatively prosperous farmers. Most of these Cherokees were full-bloods who accepted their fate and saw better prospects west of the Mississippi than east of the river.

But not all. By the mid-1820s, the Cherokees practiced small-scale agriculture in the white tradition; many owned slaves who worked their fields of cotton and corn; they sent their children to English-language schools; published their own newspaper, the *Cherokee Phoenix;* and Christian missionaries spread the gospel among them. In 1820, the Cherokees established a republican form of government modeled after the United States. It included an elected representative council with an upper and a lower house as well as a council president. Nearly two years later, the Cherokees established a supreme court to hear appeals from eight district courts. The centralization of Cherokee government reduced the importance of the towns and individuals in the decision-making process. It also meant that the federal government had fewer leaders to deal with concerning the decision for removal. Most leaders now were mixed-bloods with education, land, and wealth, such as John Ross, a principal chief and, in 1818, the first president of the National

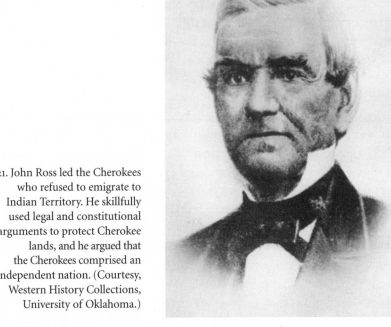

21. John Ross led the Cherokees who refused to emigrate to Indian Territory. He skillfully used legal and constitutional arguments to protect Cherokee lands, and he argued that the Cherokees comprised an independent nation. (Courtesy, Western History Collections, University of Oklahoma.)

Committee. Ross owned a plantation, worked by 19 slaves at the head of the Coosa River in Georgia. Similarly, Lewis Ross, a merchant, owned 40 slaves, while John Martin, chief justice of the Cherokee Supreme Court, owned 69 slaves in 1835. Joseph Vann used his 110 slaves to work three hundred acres and to help operate his mill, ferry, and tavern. These men with Cherokee blood were not "common Indians," but they formed a ruling class based on wealth, education, talent, and ambition.[32]

The mixed-blood cadre of the Cherokee leaders, who had some education, substantial lands, and considerable ambition, created a new group in Cherokee society. They did not divide the nation by race but rather by different social values more akin to white than Cherokee society. Most important, these new leaders had the ability and will to meet whites head to head and mind to mind. When Georgia officials tried to intimidate them as they had the Creeks concerning payment for slaves that had escaped to Cherokee territory during the American Revolution, the Cherokee leaders urged them to read the Treaty of Tellico of 1798 that absolved them of that responsibility. When federal commissioners threatened to take Cherokee lands by right of discovery and conquest, the Cherokees asked them why the United States had purchased Indian land and made treaties on many occasions, if they did not own it. By 1820, both state and federal officials, then, had learned the Cherokees would use treaties and the law to protect their interests. Treaties that federal officials believed enabled them to run roughshod over the Indians would be used against them time and again by the Cherokees.

In October 1822, the newly reconstructed Cherokee government met and passed a resolution "declaring unanimously . . . to hold no treaties with any Commissioners of the United States to make any cessions of lands, being resolved not to dispose of even one foot of ground." John Ross signed this document and sent it to Return J. Meigs, Cherokee agent, who considered it a "rash resolution." Nearly two years later, Ross again reminded President Monroe, Secretary of War John C. Calhoun, Secretary of State John Quincy Adams, and the House and Senate of the rule of law when the government pressed hard for removal. On April 15, he sent a letter to Congress saying, "We appeal to the magnanimity of the American Congress for justice, and the protection of the rights, liberties, and lives, of the Cherokee people. We claim it from the United States, by the strongest obligations, which imposes it upon them by treaties; and we expect it from them under that *memorable* declaration, 'that all men are created equal.'"[33]

By 1827, Ross, who had led many delegations to Washington to forestall removal negotiations and keep Georgia and her intruders at bay, ranked second in influence only to Chief Charles Hicks, who in many ways ran the nation as proxy for the ageing Path Killer, principal chief of the Cherokee nation. Davis S. Beatrice, a missionary among the Cherokees, observed: "Mr. Ross is rising highly in the opinion of the nation. He is not in point of influence inferior to any except Mr. Hicks. These men walk hand in hand in the Nations' Councils and are the hope of the Nation." When Path Killer and Hicks died in 1827, Ross became the second principal chief behind William Hicks, son of Charles, pending the election of a new principal chief by the General Council in 1828 as provided by the new constitution. When the General Council voted, Ross won handily over Hicks. He also became a member of a newly appointed committee to represent the Cherokees in Washington. Ross had a reputation for skillful use of the English language, both written and spoken, as well as shrewdness and mental toughness and an unwavering commitment to serving the Cherokee nation even though he was more white than Indian. Federal and state officials considered him a major roadblock to their removal plans, in part because Ross apparently could not be bribed like some other Indian leaders.[34]

By now Ross had gained the most political experience of any Cherokee. He had met with Monroe, Adams, Calhoun, and Jackson on his trips to Washington. Ross had learned much about negotiating and diplomatic maneuvering, and he intended to use his experience to preserve and protect the territorial integrity of the Cherokees and their existence as a people. Ross now led approximately sixteen thousand of the seventeen thousand Cherokees in the South. He would soon find need to practice all of his diplomatic and political skills.

Moreover, on July 26, 1827, the Cherokee Nation adopted a constitution in which the members proclaimed their independence and sovereignty and jurisdiction over their territory. The Georgia legislature reacted quickly, calling the Cherokee constitution a "presumptuous document," and, on December 27, began plans to incorporate Cherokee lands under the authority of the state. Once under state jurisdiction, Georgia could divide, apportion, sell, and tax those lands. If the Cherokee could not purchase those lands or pay their taxes, they would necessarily, and Georgians hoped inevitably, forfeit their property and either leave the state, become tenants, or find some other way to make a living. In the meantime, the state would have revenues from both land sales and taxes.[35]

In the summer of 1830, after passage of the Removal Act, Jackson told the Cherokees that he did not intend to prevent Georgia from extending its authority over Cherokee lands. Ross would not be intimidated, and responded, "[T]he territory of the Cherokees is not within the jurisdiction of Georgia, but within the sole and exclusive jurisdiction of the Cherokee nation." In July, the General Council convened at Ross's calling and authorized him to begin legal proceedings to determine the sovereignty of the disputed lands. Ross told the Council, "[I]n the appearance of impossibilities, there is still hope."[36]

Like Ross, most Cherokees refused to emigrate. As a people, they ranked first among the so-called Five Civilized Tribes as the most acculturated if not assimilated Indian people. They reacted quickly to the Removal Act, striking back with legal and constitutional maneuvering to protect their lands and prevent forced removal west of the Mississippi River. The Cherokee took their case to the Supreme Court where they asked for an injunction to stop Georgia from taking their lands in violation of their treaty rights with the federal government. They also contended that they were a sovereign nation and therefore beyond the reach of Georgia law.

On March 18, 1831, Chief Justice John Marshall delivered the court's opinion in the case of *Cherokee Nation v. Georgia.* Marshall held firmly for the Indian cause by ruling that the Cherokees possessed their land until they chose to alienate it voluntarily, and they could only cede land to the federal government. In the meantime, the Indians had the right of self-government, and the federal government had the obligation to protect them because they were "domestic dependent nations." A year later, Marshall also ruled in the case of *Worcester v. Georgia* that Georgia law did not extend over Cherokee territory and that the Cherokee Nation was a distinct, independent political community that could keep whites off its lands. It also held that the federal government had the responsibility to preserve and protect those lands. This decision gave encouragement to a group of mixed-blood leaders to resist federal removal policy, and neither Jackson nor the War Department could budge them short of military force.[37]

Jackson did not agree with Marshall's decisions and chose not to enforce them. He knew that they ran contrary to public opinion, and that armed force would be required to protect Indians on lands that state governments and squatters considered their own. Jackson was far too astute a politician to authorize white soldiers to shoot white settlers to protect Indian lands. As a result, white intrusions on Cherokee lands increased and violence grew, due to Jackson's response and Georgia's impatience. Ross, in turn, jockeyed for delay in the hope that Henry Clay would win the presidential election in November 1832 and listen to the Cherokees. Ross also asked Jackson how he could protect the Cherokees in the West if he could not do so in Georgia. The reelection of Jackson, however, caused a growing crack in Cherokee unity that soon split open.

John Walker, a Ross opponent, contacted Hugh Montgomery, the tribal agent, and told him that he would lead a delegation to Washington to discuss removal. Major Ridge, John Ridge, and Elias Boudinot, among others, also expressed dissatisfaction with Ross's leadership and attempts to maintain tribal unity, even advocating stifling dissent by preventing the discussion of removal in the *Cherokee Phoenix*. In contrast, the Ridge faction believed, for reasons of both private gain and patriotism, that the Cherokees could endure as a nation only with removal. Factionalism increased among the Cherokees during the next two years with the followers of Ridge favoring removal, while the majority of the tribe supported Ross and the maintenance of their homeland.

Ultimately, a Cherokee faction led by Ridge, who had fought with Jackson against the Creeks at Horseshoe Bend, agreed to accept removal on the grounds that it would preserve the Cherokee nation, colored, in part, by their desire to use the treaty negotiations to gain control of tribal politics and garner rewards of money and land from federal and state governments for cooperating. Quickly, they became known as the "National party" or "Treaty party." Jackson believed that these middle-class Cherokees were the real Cherokees who spoke for the

22. Major Ridge led the Cherokee faction that favored removal. Many of these Cherokees had fought with Jackson at Horseshoe Bend. They became known as the Treaty party and bitterly contested with Ross's anti-treaty Cherokees for power. Like William McIntosh, Major Ridge lost his life for signing the Treaty of New Echota, which provided for the removal of the Cherokees. (Courtesy, Western History Collections, University of Oklahoma.)

Nation and he intended to deal only with them over matters of land cession and removal. By 1832, as a result of these developments, a pro-treaty party emerged, led by Ridge, his son John, and Elias Boudinot. The Ridge faction met bitter opposition from the "anti-treaty party" Cherokees, led by the elected principal chief Ross. Ross wanted to prevent removal or hold out as long as possible to increase the federal ante for removal and to keep the nation unified.[38]

When the Ross faction refused to enter into treaty negotiations, the federal government turned to the Ridge faction and its commissioners signed a removal treaty at New Echota, Georgia, on December 29, 1835. The Senate approved the treaty by one vote on May 18, 1836, and the president signed it five days later. Jackson considered the Treaty of New Echota binding on the entire Cherokee nation. Ross and the anti-treaty party Cherokees adamantly rejected the Treaty of New Echota claiming that "the instrument entered into at New Echota, purporting to be a treaty, is deceptive to the world, and a fraud upon the Cherokee people." In fact, the Treaty of New Echota was a swindle of the Cherokee nation. Ridge and his followers had not been authorized to negotiate or approve it, and neither Ross nor any other elected Cherokee official ever signed it. The Treaty of New Echota was nothing less than an illegal act perpetrated on the Cherokees by the federal government and a renegade faction. Everyone involved, including President Jackson, knew that without the sanction of the Cherokee people, it was a fraud.[39]

The Treaty of New Echota called for the cession of all Cherokee lands east of the Mississippi River and payment of $5 million to satisfy tribal claims against the federal government. It also permitted the Cherokees a two-year grace period to plan their move beyond the Mississippi. The Treaty party soon emigrated and like the Old Settlers established small-scale farms in Indian Territory where they restored their economic prosperity. The Ross faction, however, still refused to abide by the treaty and emigrate. In April 1838, Ross made one of many appeals to Congress and public opinion to prevent their removal by throwing his faction at the mercy of the government. "It is true," he professed, "we are a feeble people; and, as regards physical power, we are in the hands of the United States; but we have not forfeited our rights, and if we fail to transmit to our sons the freedom we have derived from our fathers, it must not only be by an act of suicide, it must not be with our own consent." With the deadline for removal set at May 23, Ross's desperate plea fell on deaf ears. By now Ross realized that the power of the federal government and Jackson and Martin Van Buren's intransigence had defeated his efforts to maintain Cherokee territorial integrity. The future offered only despair and hardship.[40]

By the spring, Van Buren, newly elected and inaugurated as president, had lost patience because only two thousand Cherokees had emigrated, and some fifteen thousand remained. Consequently, the War Department ordered General Winfield Scott to take command of some seven thousand troops already in Cherokee territory and remove the Indians by the deadline. Scott told the Cherokee chiefs that while he hoped to avoid bloodshed, he would use force if necessary and destroy them if they did not assemble at designated stockades in preparation for removal. Scott declared, "My orders from Washington require that the collection of the Indians for emigration shall go on; and it shall." Van Buren would only agree to increase the money promised the Cherokees in the Treaty of New Echota and to permit them to conduct their removal.[41]

The end had come for the Cherokee people east of the Mississippi. During the spring and summer of 1838, the military brutally gathered the Cherokee at the assembly points for departure. By June 16, 1838, one observer noted, "The Cherokees are nearly all prisoners. They have been dragged from their houses, and encamped at forts and military posts, all over the [Cherokee] nation. In Georgia, especially, multitudes were allowed not time to take any thing with them except the clothes they had on." But, he wrote, more was involved than the theft of land: "Well-furnished

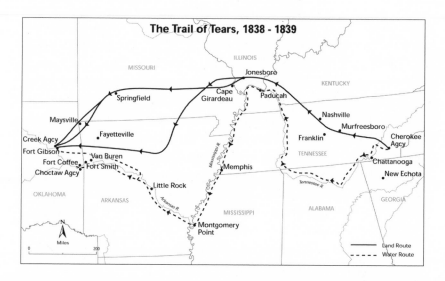

The Trail of Tears, 1838 - 1839

houses were left a prey to plunderers, who, like hungry wolves, follow in the trail of their captors. These wretches rifle the houses and strip the helpless, unoffending owners of all they have on earth." Women as well as men experienced the degradation of forced removal from their homes. He observed, "Females who have been habituated to comforts and comparative affluence are driven on foot before the bayonets of brutal men. Their feelings are mortified by the blasphemous vociferations of these heartless creatures. It is a painful sight." One minister wrote that the Cherokees were confined in twenty-three stockades and that they did not have adequate food, clothing, shelter, or sanitation. They were, he wrote, "prisoners, without a crime to justify the act." Years later one Georgia soldier reflected, "I fought through the civil war and have seen men shot to pieces and slaughtered by thousands, but the Cherokee removal was the cruelest work I ever knew."[42]

Although Scott sent some Cherokees west in June, the great migration did not begin until the autumn due to oppressive heat and drought. Finally, in late September and early October some thirteen thousand Cherokees, under the leadership of John Ross, began heading in their wagons north and west for the Mississippi at Memphis. Other parties followed, some organized in Alabama and Tennessee. Before the removal of the Cherokees had been completed, approximately four thousand had died due to exposure when winter came early and hard as well as from dysentery and starvation. Their suffering became etched deep and black in American memory as the Trail of Tears.

Jackson never doubted his judgment on Indian removal. In his farewell address on March 4, 1837 he said, "The States which had so long been retarded in their improvements by the Indian tribes residing in the midst of them are at length relieved from the evil." Yet, just as important, he contended, "this unhappy race—the original dwellers in our land—are now placed in a situation where we may well hope that they will share in the blessings of civilization and be saved from that degradation and destruction to which they were rapidly hastening while they remained in the States." Moreover, Jackson observed, "while the safety and comfort of our own citizens have been greatly promoted by their removal, the philanthropist will rejoice that the remnant of that ill-fated race has been at length placed beyond the reach of injury or oppression, and that the paternal care of the General Government will hereafter watch over them and protect them." Martin Van Buren, who followed him to the presidency and who oversaw the Cherokee removal, agreed.[43]

Despite the harshness and inhumanity of the Indian removal policy, however, Jackson and his supporters cannot be blamed for maliciousness. Between 1830 and 1835, when the War Department negotiated the removal treaties with the Choctaws, Creeks, Chickasaws, and Cherokees, Jackson merely implemented the mechanics of a policy that traced back to Thomas Jefferson. Neither Jackson nor his supporters on the removal issue advocated extermination. Rather, they believed that both whites and Indians would be best served by separation. They argued that assimilation and acculturation required considerable time, both whites and Indians resisted that process, and neither assimilation nor acculturation had worked yet. Consequently, removal seemed not only the best policy for dealing with Indians whose lands white farmers coveted but also the only policy to prevent violence and federal and state jurisdictional disputes.

Jackson never questioned the correctness of the removal policy, in part because his options were few and unsatisfactory. At the same time, assimilation and acculturation never took precedence over removal as the ultimate policy goal, but each justified it. As a result, from the administrations of Jefferson to Van Buren, the federal government pursued an Indian policy characterized by both cruelty and good intentions. Above all, however, it was an Indian policy of paradox because it championed isolation and segregation to achieve assimilation and acculturation. Simply put, most white Americans agreed that the removal of the southern Indians had been necessary not only to acquire their lands with minimal bloodshed but also to save them.

Given Indian-white relations during the two decades following the War of

1812, no one should be surprised that the southern nations were forced to move west of the Mississippi River, but rather that they prevented that removal for so long. In the end, the rule of law failed to protect the Indians, and in the case of the Cherokees, Andrew Jackson wantonly ignored it and instead used a fraudulently devised treaty to give the cosmetic veneer of legitimacy to his removal policy. After reason and will had failed to gain removal of the southern Indians, Jackson used fraud to achieve his goal, that is, he used immoral or at least unethical means to achieve what he believed to be a moral end—the removal of the Indian people for their own good. With neither adequate military force nor the law behind them, the Cherokees, like the Choctaws, Chickasaws, and Creeks, could not resist the certainty of military force if they refused to emigrate. They were a defeated people who blew west before a strong federal wind.

CHAPTER 7

The Black Hawk War

The Treaty of Ghent officially concluded the War of 1812, but the Indians on the trans-Appalachian frontier were not part of the peace negotiations. Although the Americans had supported the war to end Indian hostilities in the West, and while the conflict destroyed the ability of the Indian nations to make war against the United States, many western nations had not agreed to peace. Some bands still marshaled enough strength to make western settlement worrisome, if not hazardous. Article IX of the treaty, however, provided that the United States would make peace with the Indian nations and restore "all the possessions, rights, and privileges" that they enjoyed before the war. Accordingly, on March 11, 1815, President James Madison appointed three commissioners to inform the Indians in the Mississippi River valley that Great Britain and the United States had made peace and to invite them to sign treaties of peace and friendship.[1]

Working from St. Louis, the commissioners arranged a grand council a few miles to the north at Portage de Sioux where, between July 1815 and October 1818, they signed thirteen treaties, all promising "perpetual peace and friendship," and confirmed previous treaties. Similar treaties with the other tribes followed during the next three years. At the same time, the federal government planned to establish forts in the Upper Mississippi River valley and Great Lakes region to assert its newly won power and control over the Indians. Moving quickly in 1816, the War Department reoccupied Fort Dearborn at present-day Chicago and built Fort Howard at Green Bay and Fort Crawford at the mouth of the Wisconsin River. Two years later, the army established Fort Atkinson on the Missouri at present-day Council Bluffs, and, in 1819, Fort Snelling at the mouth of the Minnesota River. These and other posts would help the government prevent British trade with the Indians from Canada. If the British violated the Treaty of Ghent—which prohibited them from trading with the Indians—the posts would, in the words of Secretary of War John C. Calhoun, "put in our hand the power to correct the evil," and ensure American domination of the fur trade.[2]

White settlers north of the Ohio River between the Appalachians and the Mississippi Valley appreciated the efforts of the War Department to ensure their safety, but they believed the removal of the tribes merited as much attention as military force in the shaping of Indian policy. Indeed, north of the Ohio River, settlers new and old wanted the Indians removed for reasons of security and greed, and they soon found that these northern Indians could be pushed aside more easily than the southern nations. Indeed, the Indians north of the Ohio had far less unity and control over their lands than the nations to the south. Indian land claims north of the Ohio River lacked the relatively well-defined boundaries of the southern tribes. Tribal claims often overlapped, and the federal government easily used Indian disagreements over territory to its own advantage. In addition, more Indian nations occupied lands north of the Ohio River than to the south, and these tribes often divided into scattered bands with no political unity. Some northern nations also frequently moved their villages across the Midwest, and this custom weakened their claim to lands based on possession or control for a long time. White settlers, of course, only wanted agricultural lands that the Indians claimed. They showed little interest in the forests of Michigan and Wisconsin, and the northern woods remained a refuge for some tribal groups, such as the Ojibwas, Menominees, and Ottawas, because they lived on lands poorly suited for agriculture. In addition, they had close ties to the British, and federal officials preferred not to press for the removal of these nations at any cost, and instead largely chose to ignore them.

In many respects the Indian Removal Act did not change the relationship between the northern Indian nations and the federal government, because both had entered into cession treaties for a long time. Usually these treaties permitted the signatory Indians to remain in a smaller land area and hunt on the ceded lands until survey and sale. As a result, by 1830, most of the Indians in Ohio, Indiana, and Illinois had ceded their lands, many had moved west, and the few who remained lived on concentrated enclaves or reserves where they subsisted on annuities and rudimentary agriculture. The creation of tribal reserves within the states and territories in the Old Northwest, where the federal government would remake the Indians in the white man's image by teaching them to farm, became federal policy in 1817. On September 29, the Treaty with the Wyandot confined this once powerful people to reservation lands in northwestern Ohio where they would remain for a quarter century while other treaties nibbled away at their lands before ultimately sending them west of the Mississippi River in 1842. In many cases, however, the Indians demanded the right to remain on a tribal reserve, maintain their traditional cultural practices, and forestall removal to a strange new land.

In Ohio, for example, the Quakers and Methodists made some progress in their efforts to assimilate and acculturate the Shawnees and Wyandots by teaching them white agricultural practices and Christianity. The pressure of white settlers for Wyandot lands, however, denied missionaries and government officials sufficient time to teach their charges agriculture in the white tradition. Moreover, when the Methodist missionaries attacked the traditional feasts, dances, and ceremonial practices of the Wyandots, they created animosity. The Wyandots particularly did not understand why a book called the Bible, which contained stories of distant lands and peoples long ago, should apply to them. Still caught in the middle ground between Indian and white cultures, Mononcue, a Wyandot chief, felt that ambivalence when he said, "I have some notion of giving up some of my Indian customs; but I cannot agree to quit painting my face. This would be wrong, and it would jeopard[ize] my health." Bloody Eyes also rejected a Methodist minister's preaching about the sins of dancing and feasting. "I do not believe the Great Spirit," he said, "will punish his red children for dancing [and] feasting. . . . Yet I cannot say that he will not punish white people for doing these things; for to me it looks quite possible that the Great Spirit has forbidden these things among whites, because they are naturally wicked, quarrelsome and contentious; for it is a truth they cannot deny, that they cannot have a dance, a feast, or any public amusement, but some will get drunk, quarrel, fight, or do something wrong." In contrast, he observed, "[W]e have our public amusements in peace, and goodwill to each other, and part in the same manner. Now, where is the great evil you see[?]" At best the missionaries could expect only selective acculturation, and most whites believed even that achievement would be a waste of time, because the Indians did not intensively use their lands for agriculture, and, therefore, had no reasonable claim to keep it in denial of white ambitions. Armed with both political and military power, while confronting an opposition that had neither, they pressed hard for removal of the Indians from the Old Northwest.[3]

The relatively level and fertile lands of the Old Northwest, then, lured tens of thousands of settlers after the War of 1812, and they pressured their territorial and state representatives to support removal of the Indians at nearly any cost. In January 1829, the Indiana legislature spoke for most whites in the region when it urged Congress to remove the Indians from within its boundaries because their presence tended to "materially impede a system of internal improvements essential to the prosperity of our citizens, and in a degree jeopardizes the peace and tranquility of our frontier, which it is our right and duty to secure." In Indiana, legislators argued that the Indians occupied vast lands, but lived on federal annuities and not by productive agriculture. Moreover, if the Indians remained in Indiana, they would continue to "retard the settlement, the revenue, and the prosperity of the State."[4]

In 1831, Indian Commissioner James B. Gardiner negotiated removal treaties with the Senecas, Shawnees, and Ottawas in Ohio. The Wyandots, however, refused to go after they received an unfavorable report about the western lands assigned to them. As a result, Gardiner could only persuade them to cede 16,000 acres in northwestern Ohio where they retained a "Grand Reserve" of some 146,000 acres near Upper Sandusky, which they shared with a few Senecas and Shawnees. The treaty that Gardiner signed with the Wyandots on January 19, 1832, promised payment of $1.25 per acre for the ceded lands, and he believed the Wyandots would soon sell their remaining lands, because in Gardiner's words, they had "become fully convinced that, whilst they remain in their present situation in the State of Ohio, in the vicinity of a white population which is continually increasing and crowding around them, they cannot prosper and be happy, and the morals of many of their people will be daily becoming more and more vitiated." With this view in mind as well as because of the obstinacy of the Wyandots, Gardiner provided that the Wyandots "may, as they think proper, remove to Canada, or to the Huron River in Michigan, where they own a reservation of land, or to any place they may obtain a right or privilege from other Indians to go." In the meantime, the federal government would wait and see.[5]

Between 1815 and 1825, white settlers rapidly moved into the prairie region of Indiana and Illinois, and they did not hesitate to squat on Indian lands, particularly those claimed by the Potawatomies. Many of the Potawatomie bands, particularly those under the leadership of chiefs Metea and Moran, continued their friendship with the British. To counter this potential threat, the federal government reestablished an agency at Chicago and created new agencies to aid communications and the distribution of annuities at Green Bay and Prairie du Chien as well as a subagency at Peoria. In addition to constructed posts at Chicago, Green Bay, and Prairie du Chien, it built Fort Armstrong on Rock Island in the Mississippi River to help deter potential hostilities.

Yet, the carrot-and-stick approach with the establishment of agencies and forts complicated the problem of dealing with the Indians in a systematic manner based on the use of bribes and force. The new agencies and posts, for example, helped divide the Potawatomies politically and made the application of a single treaty difficult, if not impossible. At the time, however, tribal divisions enabled federal agents to isolate and gain specific lands in the absence of substantial Indian unity. At the Potawatomie agency and subagencies, for example, government agents treated a few Potawatomie leaders as though they spoke for the entire tribe as principal chiefs. By paying tribal annuities at only one or two villages, the other bands necessarily traveled far to receive their allotted portion, or they did not get their share of the annuities. Factionalism and bickering among the Potawatomies soon prevailed, and the federal government used tribal division to negotiate cession treaties that gained Potawatomie lands in Michigan and Indiana. When Indian commissioners met with approximately three thousand Potawatomies, led by Metea, at Chicago in August 1821 for the purpose of acquiring all of its tribal lands in Michigan, however, they met with obstinacy. Metea argued that the federal government wanted too much and complained that "the plowshare is driven through our tents before we have time to carry out our goods and seek other habitation."[6]

Indian Commissioner Lewis Cass, however, countered with the offer to give the Potawatomies enough whiskey "to make every man, woman, and child drunk," if only they would agree to the cession treaty. He also refused to distribute trade goods or whiskey until they signed the cession treaty. Metea spoke eloquently for his people, but other leaders who wanted the annuities and whiskey more than they coveted their lands prevailed and signed the cession treaty. Although the treaty reserved a number of small tracts for individual Potawatomies, the recipients tended to be mixed-bloods with some education who had connived to gain those lands for their own personal gain. By the late-1820s, federal commissioners attempted to work with the mixed-bloods, rather than the full-bloods who preferred to follow a traditional lifestyle based on hunting and subsistence agriculture. By the Removal Act, most of the old Potawatomie leaders had died or lost influence, and the mixed-bloods now spoke for many bands. Moreover, the influence of the mixed-bloods increased because they controlled the flow of government annuities and gifts and served as negotiators for the village bands. As a result, by 1830 the Potawatomies had ceded many tracts, and the federal government focused its efforts to remove the Prairie Potawatomies who lived in western Indiana and eastern Illinois. Before they could achieve that goal, however, the worst violence of the removal era broke out, and it became known as the Black Hawk War.[7]

Within a year of signing the peace treaty dictated by William Clark in St. Louis on May 13, 1816, which ended hostilities between the federal government and the Sauks and Mesquakies, the Rock River Sauks in the Illinois Territory had

23. The Sauks and Mesquakies or Foxes lived near the mouth of the Rock River in present-day Illinois. They considered the Sioux to the north and west their traditional enemies, and despite efforts of the federal government to keep the peace among both groups, culture rather than law usually prevailed, making the Upper Mississippi country dangerous well into the 1830s. (Karl Bodmer, *Saukie and Fox Indians,* engraving. Courtesy, State Historical Society of Missouri, Columbia.)

become increasingly hostile and reluctant to vacate lands that they previously ceded for settlement in northwestern Illinois. This earlier Treaty with the Sauk and Foxes, signed on November 3, 1804, in St. Louis, had ceded fifty million acres of Sauk and Mesquakie or Fox lands that covered the eastern third of Missouri and the area between the Wisconsin River to the north and the Fox and Illinois Rivers on the east and south, and the Mississippi River on the west. Saukenuk, the principal Sauk village with approximately five hundred families, extended three miles on either side of the mouth of the Rock River. As the years passed the Sauks and Mesquakies, the federal government, and white settlers argued about the validity of the treaty. The Sauks and Mesquakies considered it invalid because the Indians who signed it had no authority to do so from their tribal councils. The Indians also contested the cession treaty boundaries, while whites challenged the right of the Indians to use ceded lands until the government surveyed and offered it for sale. The federal government did not force the Sauks to move, however, and they became increasingly belligerent in demanding their right to the Rock River country. The Winnebagos and Potawatomies gave the Sauks sympathy and support, and many frontier people began to fear another Indian war.[8]

The great migration of whites to Missouri after the war had made life worse for the tribes. As settlers encroached on Indian lands, the game became scarce, and other treaties forced many tribes to live closer together than ever before. The Sauks and Mesquakies who lived along the Missouri and Rock Rivers now began to range far to the north and west in search of deer and buffalo. By doing so, however, they crossed onto Sioux lands, and bloody confrontations became common as these traditional enemies struck and retaliated against each other. At St. Louis, Clark pleaded with the Sauks and Mesquakies to resolve their disputes with the Sioux and other nations short of war, but such a policy violated tribal culture and the chiefs could not restrain their young men bent on revenge and war. To make matters worse, federal officials never completely understood intertribal relations and problems, and Indian leaders often thought government agents meddled where they did not belong. When the War Department built Fort Armstrong on Rock Island across from Saukenuk in 1816, the Sauks were particularly offended. A year later, they began refusing to sign receipts for annuities to ensure they would not be cheated out of more land by a paper document they could not read.

During the early 1820s, Sauk, Mesquakie, Winnebago, and Sioux war parties continued to raid and take scalps, and the Sauks and Mesquakies even struck south to the Missouri and fought with the Osages, Otos, and Ioways. Indian commissioner William Clark threatened the Sauks and Mesquakies with war if they did not stop their raids against the Sioux and other tribes, but Secretary of War John C. Calhoun would only permit him to withhold presents and annuities if they did not behave. Clark, however, succeeded in cultivating the friendship of Keokuk, a Sauk leader, who spoke for the peaceful bands of the tribe. Black Hawk, his rival, said that Keokuk had a "smooth tongue" and credited him for being a "great speaker." But Keokuk could never gain the confidence of Black Hawk, who yearned for British aid that would help him keep Sauk lands east of the Mississippi from the ever-westering white settlers.[9]

To make matters worse, the Sauks and Mesquakies now strongly disputed the boundary lines between tribal lands and the United States. In 1821, they claimed that their southern boundary began at the mouth of the Des Moines River, while the northern line ran west from the mouth of the Two Rivers opposite Prairie de Chien. In July 1824, Keokuk traveled with a delegation and Clark to Washington, D.C., and told Secretary of War Calhoun that they claimed this land by right of conquest. With whites infringing on Sauk and Mesquakie lands, the Indians demanded both restraint and restitution. Specifically, Keokuk and other leaders urged the federal government to hold a grand peace council with the Upper Mississippi River tribes in order to clearly define and establish tribal boundaries and promote peace.

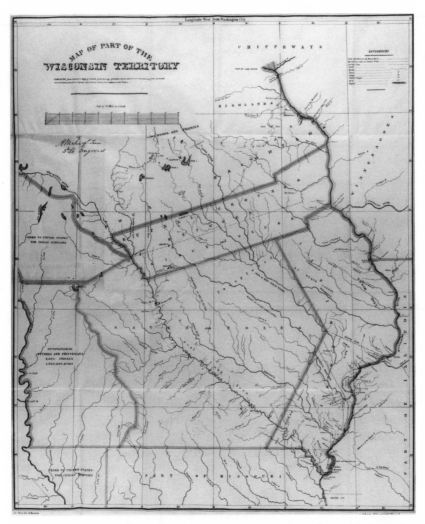

24. In the Treaties of Prairie du Chien in 1825 and 1830, the Sioux along with the Sauks and Mesquakies agreed to respect a 40-mile-wide area called the Neutral Ground, where each tribe could hunt without fear of attack. In 1832, William Clark sent Nathan Boone to survey the center line and mark it with posts so hunting parties could see the line where they were not to cross, thereby keeping the Sioux to the north and the Sauks and Mesquakies to the south. (Author's Collection.)

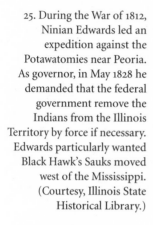

25. During the War of 1812, Ninian Edwards led an expedition against the Potawatomies near Peoria. As governor, in May 1828 he demanded that the federal government remove the Indians from the Illinois Territory by force if necessary. Edwards particularly wanted Black Hawk's Sauks moved west of the Mississippi. (Courtesy, Illinois State Historical Library.)

By 1825, federal officials believed Sauk and Mesquakie raids against the Sioux would trigger a general Indian War that would ruin the fur trade and endanger white settlers. They, too, believed a meeting with the tribes in the Upper Mississippi River valley was necessary. Congress agreed and authorized James Barbour, who succeeded Calhoun as secretary of war, and Lewis Cass, governor of the Michigan Territory, to join Clark at Prairie du Chien for a treaty council in August 1825, where they would make peace with the Sauks, Mesquakies, Ioways, Ojibwas, Winnebagos, Ottawas, Menominees, Potawatomies, and Sioux. When Clark opened the council on August 5, he suggested that fixed boundaries be established between the hunting grounds of the tribes, which, if honored, would keep peace among them. The Sauks and Mesquakies, however, did not trust the Sioux; Keokuk, who usually spoke with reason concerning Indian and white relations, shook his lance at the Sioux delegation when Clark tried to discuss the subject of a mutually recognized boundary across which neither would cross. Clark and the other officials could clearly see that "he wanted but an opportunity to make their blood flow like water."[10]

Still, Clark remained persuasive, and on August 19 the tribes agreed to sign a

26. Black Hawk led the Sauks who opposed removal. He did not recognize land cession treaties signed by others, because they did not speak for him. Black Hawk hoped his resistance to removal would help the cause of an Indian confederacy and convince the British to provide support. The result was the near destruction of all his followers in needless fighting that became known as the Black Hawk War. (Courtesy, State Historical Society of Iowa, Des Moines.)

peace treaty that essentially set tribal boundaries and proclaimed peace among them. Articles 1 and 13 of this Treaty with the Sioux or Treaty of Prairie du Chien contained the most important provisions for the tribes. Article 1 provided, "There shall be a firm and perpetual peace between the Sioux and the Chippewas; between the Sioux and the confederated tribes or Sacs and Foxes; and between the Ioways and the Sioux." Article 13 said, "It is understood by all the tribes, parties, hereto, that no tribe shall hunt within the acknowledged limits of any other without their assent." After considerable speech making, smoking of the peace pipe, and feasting, the council broke up. Both Indian and white leaders wondered how long the peace would last. Few believed that it had been established for all time.[11]

To Black Hawk, the Treaty of Prairie du Chien did not apply to him because he had not attended the peace council, and he did not agree with the settlement. Now sixty years of age, he intended to live as he had in the past, hunting the same lands and striking his traditional enemies. In May 1827, Black Hawk planned to send a war party against the Sioux, and Thomas Forsyth, the Sioux agent at Rock Island, reported to William Clark that an Indian war seemed a certainty. "The Chiefs, Braves and women of the Sauk Nation of Indians residing near the mouth of the Rocky River have (alternately) done everything in their power to dissuade the Black Hawk from going to war, but all to no effect," he wrote. But, he had informed Black Hawk that he would send him to St. Louis in irons for life imprisonment if he made war. Forsyth, however, believed Black Hawk would go to war because "nothing but death will prevent him."[12]

Although Black Hawk backed down, he refused to leave his homeland in the Rock River area. By 1828, the Sauks and Mesquakies had lived on lands ceded with the treaty of 1804 for a generation, and many saw no need to give up those lands now despite Governor Ninian Edwards's call for the army to remove all the Indians from the lands ceded in Illinois. Edwards particularly wanted the Rock River Sauks moved beyond the Mississippi River. In May 1828, however, when the Sauk and Mesquakie agent met with the band chiefs who resided near the Rock River and suggested that they move west of the Mississippi, he met with quick rejection. The chiefs told Forsyth that "they had never sold the land higher up the Mississippi River than the mouth of the Rocky River—that they would not move from the land where the bones of their ancestors lay, and that they would defend themselves against any power that might be sent to drive them from their present villages." Governor Edwards then proposed to take matters into his own hands. On May 25, 1828, he wrote to Indian Commissioner William Clark that unless the War Department acted quickly, "those Indians will be removed, and that very promptly." Secretary of War Peter B. Porter tried to calm the governor by assuring him that all Indians, except for a few Kickapoos, would be removed from the Illinois Territory by May 25, 1829. He did not, however, take the intransigence of Black Hawk and his followers into his calculations.[13]

If Black Hawk's unwillingness to abide by the treaty with the Sauk and Foxes threatened the peace in theory, a raid against the Sioux by half-blood Mesquakie Chief Morgan in 1828 destroyed it in reality, along with white encroachment on Sauk lands, all of which made the Treaty of Prairie du Chien of 1825 a dead letter. When a Sioux war party killed a Sauk chief and his wife in retaliation, the three-year-old peace collapsed. During the spring of 1829, while the Sauks and Mesquakies eagerly went about the business of making war against their traditional Sioux enemies along the Upper Mississippi River valley, white squatters made major intrusions on Sauk lands, plowing their fields, stealing their property, assaulting their people, and tearing down their lodges. Even Black Hawk lost his home to an aggressive white squatter. As a result, in late May, Black Hawk's followers told Forsyth "very fiercely" that "the land was theirs, that they never

27. Keokuk, a Sauk leader, opposed Black Hawk and supported removal and accommodation with the federal government. After the Black Hawk War, Keokuk emerged as the leader of the Sauks and Mesquakies, and the federal government designated him their principal chief although he did not come from a ruling clan. Keokuk argued that present-day Iowa belonged to his people by right of conquest. (Courtesy, Iowa State Historical Society, Des Moines.)

sold the land, that this land contained the bones of their ancestors and would not give it up, that they had defended it against all your power during the late war, and would again defend it as long as they existed." The peaceful Sauk and Mesquakie chiefs, who had already moved to the mouth of the Iowa River on the west bank of the Mississippi, had asked Keokuk to remain in Saukenuk "to keep things in order if possible." Acting in that position, Keokuk told the agent that "the Sauks who spoke did not know what they were saying" and that it was only "Black Hawk with a few others . . . who are making all the fuss."[14]

By the summer of 1829, white encroachment on Indian hunting lands forced the Sauks and Mesquakies to invade Sioux territory in search of game, and mutual attacks and reprisals became common. War parties roamed the Upper Mississippi River country with impunity, and they did not always discriminate between friends and foes. By the onset of winter, the white traders, who contributed to the problem of tribal disintegration by exchanging whiskey for pelts and skins, predicted a general Indian war. At the same time, the Rock River Sauks scuffled with whites, tearing down their fences and buildings and often received beatings in return. By the time Congress passed the Removal Act, Black Hawk believed the Sauks could survive only by retaining Saukenuk, while Keokuk argued they could remain a people only by moving west of the Mississippi. Black Hawk, however, rejected Keokuk's position and called him a "coward, and no brave" to abandon his village to strangers. The Sauk tribal council, however, hoped to avoid armed conflict over Saukenuk by authorizing Keokuk to persuade Black Hawk's followers to remain west of the Mississippi after their winter hunt in 1830. Keokuk did not welcome the task or expect much success among those who followed Black Hawk, and he said, "If any Indians did attempt to return to reside at Rocky River next spring, they must take their chance."[15]

In March 1830, Clark met with a Sauk and Mesquakie delegation at St. Louis, and reminded them that they had ceded the territory north of the Rock River in the treaty of 1804. Clark also told the chiefs that they could best live in peace with the whites if they moved west of the Mississippi River and sold their lands along the Fever River where important deposits of lead had been discovered and where miners were staking their claims. Keokuk, however, disagreed. Speaking for the delegation, he told Clark that the peace was threatened because the boundary line between the Sauks and Mesquakies and their enemy the Sioux did not prevent the Sioux from attacking his people. He also said that the Sauks were upset because the federal government had purchased land from the Kansa Indians that rightfully belonged to them. Since Clark could not prevent the Sioux from striking the Sauks and Mesquakies or return their lands, the conference broke up and the danger of war remained, although Clark attempted to buy their friendship with additional gifts to "cover the dead" killed by Sioux war parties.[16]

On July 15, 1830, U.S. Indian Commissioners William Clark and Colonel Willoughby Morgan, commander at Fort Crawford, met with tribes from the Upper Mississippi River valley at Prairie du Chien. There, aided by lavish gifts, the commissioners reached a peace agreement, known as the Treaty with the Sauk and Foxes, which also included the Ioways, Winnebagos, Omahas, Otos, Menominees, and Sioux. According to the treaty, each nation agreed to keep the peace and cede a large area between the Missouri and Mississippi Rivers to the United States. Specifically, the Sioux, Sauks, and Mesquakies ceded a tract of land twenty miles wide on each side of a line that ran from the mouth of the Upper Iowa River on the Mississippi to the upper forks of the Des Moines River, a line that had been established by the treaty of 1825. The forty-mile-wide strip extended about two hundred miles southwest, and it became known as the "Neutral Ground" for the purpose of effectively preventing further tribal wars. In this treaty, Clark pledged that the federal government would provide each tribe with as much as $3,000 worth of goods annually for ten years and to send them blacksmiths, teachers, and farm implements to help them transform their way of life from hunting to farming. With clearly defined and mapped boundaries, Clark believed that the animosity, tension, and violence could be reduced to an inconsequential minimum, if not eliminated entirely. In October 1830, the Dakota Sioux also approved this agreement at a council in St. Louis.[17]

Clark intended to survey the cession boundary of the Neutral Ground as soon as possible. He had not considered, however, Black Hawk's opinion about the cession nor informed him that Sauk lands north of the Rock River would be opened for sale and settlement. When Black Hawk learned about the latter plan, he adamantly refused to abandon tribal lands, and the governor of the Illinois Territory and the Sauk agent alike began to threaten military action to force the Rock River Sauks to vacate their homes and move west of the Mississippi. These threats did not intimidate Black Hawk, but Keokuk believed that war against the army would be suicidal, and he counseled peace and accommodation. Black Hawk later reflected, "We were a divided people," but he had a "sacred reverence" for Sauk lands east of the Mississippi and north of the Rock River, and he did not intend to give up that area without a fight. By the autumn of 1830, Black Hawk worked to establish an Indian confederacy that would stop white encroachment on tribal lands, and he hoped for British support from Canada.[18]

When spring came, Black Hawk's band crossed over the Mississippi after its winter hunt on the prairies to the west, and settlers fled to the safety of Fort Armstrong or back to central Illinois. Governor John Reynolds responded by asking the Illinois General Assembly to call out the militia to drive the Indians from the territory. In May 1831, when the legislators balked, preferring help from the federal government, Reynolds called for several hundred militiamen to remove the Indians "dead or alive." When Clark learned about Reynolds's plan, he sent General Edmund P. Gaines, commander of the Western Department of the Army, along with troops from St. Louis to Fort Armstrong. Gaines had a reputation for irascibility and toughness, and he quickly arranged a meeting with Black Hawk, Keokuk, and other Sauk and Mesquakie chiefs at Fort Armstrong on Rock Island in early June. When they met, both Black Hawk and Gaines were in foul moods, and neither intended to back down. Gaines told Black Hawk that his people had agreed to cede lands north of the Rock River and that they must now move west of the Mississippi. Black Hawk responded that the Sauks intended to stay and "lay their bones with those of their ancestors." Gaines then threatened to remove them by force, but the old Sauk chief replied, "Black Hawk is satisfied with the lands the Great Spirit has given him. Why then should he leave them?" He also spoke of his ancestors, saying, "They have left their bones in our fields, and there I will remain and leave my bones with theirs." With that exchange, the conference broke up. Although Keokuk counseled patience, war seemed closer than ever before.[19]

Gaines now decided to remove the Sauks and Mesquakies by force, but he waited for the arrival of 1,400 militia that Governor Reynolds had called out. These men, Reynolds wrote, possessed "all the qualities except discipline, that were necessary in any army." From the time of their muster, the Illinois militiamen proved difficult to control, and they "entertained rather an excess of *Indian ill-will,* so that it required much gentle persuasion to restrain them from killing, indiscriminately, all the Indians they met." For the moment, however, a military confrontation was avoided, because Keokuk convinced Black Hawk to talk once again with Gaines.[20]

On June 30, 1831, Gaines presented Black Hawk with a document that he called "Articles of Agreement and Capitulation." It called for Black Hawk and his band to submit to Keokuk's authority, move west of the Mississippi, and end all communication with the British. In return, the federal government would guarantee Sauk lands west of the river and their right to hunt on the Neutral Ground. After the articles had been translated, Gaines invited Black Hawk to sign the document along with the other chiefs in attendance. Angry and humiliated, Black Hawk knew that he did not have an alternative, he faced overwhelming military force, and his people needed corn for the coming winter because white settlers had ruined their planting and harvest seasons. Reluctantly, he stepped forward before the hushed delegates and drew "a large, bold cross with a force which rendered *that* pen forever unfit for further use." Later he said, "I touched the goose quill to this treaty, and was determined to live in peace." Gaines then promised to provide the Sauks with the equivalent amount of corn that they would have harvested from their fields that autumn, an action that caused the frontier people, who clearly preferred the forced removal and even the bloodshed of the Sauks, to dub the agreement the "corn treaty." Still, most Sauks and Mesquakies as well as white settlers and militiamen were pleased that the confrontation had ended peacefully. The militia then went home and the Sauks prepared for their winter hunt.[21]

By the end of July 1831, however, the agreement unraveled after Sauk and Mesquakie war parties struck the Sioux and Menominees in retaliation for past attacks, and the Sioux and Menominees planned retribution. When the government contractors failed to deliver the corn that Gaines had promised, some Sauks attempted to return to Saukenuk to harvest their corn, but whites shot at them. By the autumn of 1831, intertribal and white relations had not changed in the Upper Mississippi River valley. Hatred, violence, and revenge remained the operating principles for both Indians and whites.

Keokuk tried to explain the attacks by the Sauks and Mesquakies as mere retribution that the Sioux and Menominees richly deserved. Besides, neither he nor Black Hawk nor the other chiefs could control their young men. He argued that the problems between tribal groups should be solved by the Indians themselves. Since the whites seemed to be constantly fighting, the Sauks and Mesquakies believed that they should be free to settle their own affairs in the time-honored and traditional way of war. When federal officials demanded that the Sauks and Mesquakies who had committed several murders against the Menominees be turned over for punishment, many peaceful Sauks and Mesquakies cast their fate with Black Hawk. Soon, thereafter, Black Hawk received a report that the British would help him resist the pressure of the United States and that the Potawatomies, Ojibwas, Ottawas, Winnebagos, and Kickapoos had agreed to join the Sauks in any fight against the Americans. If Black Hawk failed, the informant reported, his confederation could retreat to Canada and live in peace.

As the autumn of 1831 faded into winter, the Sauks remained west of the Mississippi, and government officials and white settlers expected that they would remain there with the arrival of spring. But not Black Hawk. He had signed the Articles of Agreement under compulsion, and he continued to communicate with the British operating out of Canada for which his followers became known as the British Band. He also counseled the formation of a confederacy with the tribes in the Upper Mississippi River valley and Great Lakes regions. With the death of chiefs Bad Thunder of the Sauks, Morgan of the Mesquakies, and Namoett of the Ioways, who favored removal, a younger group of leaders emerged who supported resistance. Napope, a young Sauk chief, openly advocated killing Clark, agent Forsyth, and the interpreter, trader, and commanding officer at Fort Armstrong. He and White Cloud, the Winnebago, pro-British Prophet, also created unreasonable expectations of British aid in case of renewed war. Keokuk, however, told Black Hawk that he had been imposed upon by "liars" and to keep the peace. Black Hawk by now despised Keokuk, and he believed the Americans only understood force or at least a strong show of unity. Black Hawk also believed that he had an obligation to uphold Sauk honor and protect his people.[22]

Accordingly, on April 5, 1832, Black Hawk crossed to the east side of the Mississippi below Rock Island with some five hundred mounted fighting men in a band of approximately a thousand, including about one hundred Kickapoos, and another hundred of White Cloud's Winnebagos and a few Mesquakies, with the intent to reclaim Saukenuk and Sauk lands. At the same time, the Sioux and Menominees prepared to attack the Sauks and Mesquakies to gain revenge for their losses during the past autumn. As a result, from Jefferson Barracks in St. Louis to Fort Crawford at Prairie du Chien, the officers and officials of the War Department expected nothing less than a new Indian war.

On April 8, Brigadier General Henry Atkinson, who had relieved General Gaines as commander of the Western Department, and 220 soldiers boarded the steamboats *Enterprise* and *Chieftain* at Jefferson Barracks for a trip upriver to prevent Black Hawk from crossing the Mississippi and to drive him back if he attempted to reoccupy Saukenuk. Three days later Atkinson received word near the mouth of the Des Moines River that Black Hawk had already crossed the Mississippi and his people had camped two miles below Fort Armstrong. In response, Atkinson held a conference with Keokuk and the other friendly Sauk and Mesquakie chiefs on April 13 and told them that Black Hawk's band "can be as easily crushed as a piece of dirt—If they do not recross the river measures will soon be taken to compel them." Atkinson said that until Black Hawk and his people crossed west over the Mississippi River, he would "treat them like dogs."[23]

Keokuk and the other chiefs were taken aback by Atkinson's threats because they knew he could deliver on his promise, and they asked for time to think about the situation. When the chiefs met again on April 19, Black Hawk already had departed up the Rock River toward refuge in the Winnebago and Potawatomie villages, and, in a fit of anger, Atkinson told Keokuk that "if Black Hawk's band strikes one white man in a short time they will cease to exist." Keokuk again counseled patience and sent messengers after Black Hawk asking him to return, but Black Hawk merely reported that he was prepared to die within twenty days. On May 24, General Atkinson sent Black Hawk a letter demanding that he recross the Mississippi. In it he said, "It is not too late to do what is right—and what is right do at once." Atkinson also told him, "Some foolish people have told you that the British will assist you—do not believe it— you will find when it is too late that it is not true."[24]

Governor Reynolds also believed that the time had arrived to stop Black Hawk's Sauks once and for all, and he mobilized 2,600 militia to aid Atkinson. One observer noted, "They were a hard-looking set of men, unkempt and unshaved." He did not need to add that they yearned to kill Indians and that the authority of their officers meant little to them. Even so, Atkinson planned to use the militia and the regulars at his command to sweep up both banks of the Rock River, catch Black Hawk's band, and defeat it. The general had great confidence, and on June 15 wrote, "I cannot fail to put an end in a short time to the perplexed state of Indian hostilities in this quarter."[25]

By late June, Atkinson had not yet caught Black Hawk and the militia under his command grew tired and began to go home. While his army unraveled, Atkinson wrote that as long as Black Hawk's band could "subsist on roots and fish taken from the swamps and lakes," the army could never defeat his people. Atkinson, however, gave too much credit to the Sauks' ability to live off the land and the intent of the Winnebagos and Potawatomies to befriend them. As Black Hawk's band fled from the soldiers, they lived on roots and bark because they could not fish or hunt in the best areas, and his would-be allies pleaded insufficient corn supplies to aid them. By early July, starvation became another enemy of the Sauks. Black Hawk now realized that he could only save his people from entrapment and starvation by fleeing west to the Wisconsin River and descend it to the Mississippi, then cross over, and either link with Keokuk's band or flee to the Great Plains. Before Black Hawk could move his people far from their camp near present-day Hustisford, Wisconsin, however, a band of Winnebagos reported his location. Major Henry Dodge's troops were the nearest, but they did not make contact with Black Hawk's band until they reached the area of Four Lakes, near present-day Madison, on July 21. Then, a running fight began that lasted all day. When darkness fell about seventy Sauks had been killed. Dodge had lost only one man.[26]

While Dodge rested his men, Black Hawk moved his band across the Wisconsin River under the cover of darkness. When dawn came Dodge decided not to pursue until he could replenish his supplies, and he did not cross the river until July 28, after Atkinson joined him with more soldiers. On August 1, the army finally made contact with Black Hawk and his five hundred remaining Sauks when they reached the Mississippi north of the Bad Axe River. When the steamboat *Warrior*, which had been patrolling the river, withdrew for fuel, many Sauks crossed the Mississippi during the night while Black Hawk prepared to take the remainder of his band over the next morning. Atkinson's force, however, struck Black Hawk's camp during the early morning of August 2. Less of a battle than a massacre, the fighting lasted about eight hours, with the muddy waters of the Mississippi tinged red along the east bank from the blood of the Sauks killed as they tried to swim the river. The action was one-sided, with at least 150 Sauks killed, including 68 by the Sioux, at the behest of federal officials, who struck them after they crossed to the west bank, to Atkinson's loss of seven men. Although

Black Hawk escaped and fled northeast into Winnebago territory, where he would be captured a few days later, the Black Hawk War had ended on the killing fields at the mouth of the Bad Axe River.

Although Governor Reynolds and most white settlers near the Mississippi River considered Black Hawk's band a war party that had invaded Illinois and deserved to be destroyed to ensure the safety of the frontier settlements, the Indians viewed the Black Hawk War differently. Many Sauk and Mesquakie chiefs and leaders, such as Keokuk, regarded it as a foolish and disastrous mistake by a chronic malcontent and his followers. For Keokuk and the other leaders, Black Hawk not only embarrassed them but also ruined their considerable efforts over the years to maintain peace with the whites while systematically and peacefully exchanging eastern for western lands. Black Hawk, however, saw the confrontation from a third, legalistic viewpoint. He believed previous treaties entitled the Sauks and Mesquakies to reside in the Rock River area. Consequently, he and his band merely exercised their legal right to return to and live on their own lands without infringement by whites. In the end, Black Hawk caused the deaths of most of his band and many white soldiers who died of cholera. The Black Hawk War also seriously diminished the diplomatic bargaining power of the Sauks and Mesquakies who thereafter became more the recipients of federal policy than actors who helped shape it.

After the wanton and needless destruction of Black Hawk's band, the federal government pressed hard to gain the removal of the northern Indian nations. On September 10, 1832, General Scott and Governor Reynolds ordered the Winnebagos to meet for the purpose of making a land cession to pay for their role in the Black Hawk War. The Winnebagos complained that only a few of their young men had been responsible for aiding Black Hawk, but they could only acquiesce when, on September 14, Scott and Reynolds dictated a treaty in which they ceded all of their lands south and east of the Wisconsin River in Wisconsin and Illinois for a strip of land west of the Mississippi in present-day Iowa. After the quick disposal of the Winnebagos, Scott and Reynolds turned to the Sauks and Mesquakies for retribution and reparation in the form of a large land cession. Scott and Reynolds ordered the leaders of both tribes to meet with them on the west bank of the Mississippi across from Fort Armstrong on September 19. There, like the Creeks nearly twenty years before, all of the people of both nations were forced to pay for the transgressions of a few. Although Black Hawk's band did not represent the majority of the Sauk and Mesquakie people, either in number or sentiment, the government used his attempt to live east of the Mississippi River as an excuse not only to remove both nations but also to take additional lands from them west of the Mississippi. Keokuk understood that the Sauks and Mesquakies had no bargaining power, but he spoke eloquently for a just treaty because the majority of both tribes had refused to follow Black Hawk. Reynolds and Scott tried to recognize his efforts to keep all but Black Hawk's followers west of the Mississippi by designating him head chief of all the Sauks and Mesquakies, an honor that neither he nor his people wanted. In the end, on September 21, Keokuk and the other Sauk and Mesquakie leaders signed the Treaty of Fort Armstrong, which soon became known as the Black Hawk Purchase, because it required the Sauks and Mesquakies to cede all Sauk lands east of the Mississippi River as well as most of their lands in Iowa, some six million acres along the river. The tribes in return received a small reservation along the Iowa River and an annual annuity of $20,000 for thirty years, or put differently, $600,000 for six million of the richest acres on the North American continent.

With this land cession and removal of the Sauks and Mesquakies to their reservation by June 1, 1833, under the terms of the Treaty of Fort Armstrong, federal officials believed the Indian threat to the Missouri and Upper Mississippi River valleys had finally ended. Even so, many tribes continued to claim lands across the Midwest. Although they did not pose a threat to the safety of whites, state officials, land speculators, and settlers wanted them removed and access to their lands. Among the Indian nations in the Midwest, the Potawatomies were particularly vulnerable, especially the prairie bands in Illinois and Indiana, because they showed little interest in agriculture, and whites saw their unused lands as nothing less than a waste that reaffirmed the right and necessity of white settlement and cultivation. By the mid-1830s, whites who cast a covetous eye on Potawatomie lands were aided by the tribe, which by now had fragmented into clans and villages separated by vast distances across the Midwest. Each village chief, with government encouragement, considered himself independent and the speaker for his people. Consequently, the Potawatomies could not act with unity. The inability of the Potawatomies to easily reach consensus in relation to federal policy helped delay their loss of territory and removal, but it also aided government officials who worked to keep them divided and weak in order to gain their lands.

In 1833 the federal government responded to white pressures for Potawatomie land by calling those bands living in northern Illinois and Wisconsin, along with several incorporated bands of Ojibwas and Ottawas collectively known as the United Bands, to meet at Chicago to discuss a cession treaty. The government wanted them to cede some five million acres or nearly eight thousand square miles in northern Illinois, Wisconsin, and Michigan. When George B. Porter, governor of the Michigan Territory and chief Indian commissioner charged with negotiation of a cession treaty, began the talks on September 14, he told them that their Great Father in Washington had heard their complaints about white settlers who took their lands, and he had come to help them. "Your Great Father is an old man, but before he dies and is buried with his fathers, he wants to see all his red children made happy and removed far beyond the evils which now surround them. He rejoiced when he heard that you wanted to sell your lands." The Mississippi River would give them the protection they needed from white encroachment.[27]

After deliberation, the Indians responded through their spokesman by the name of Aptakisic (Half Day), a chief from the Fox River area, who told Porter and the other commissioners that they were pleased that the Great Father cared about them. The Potawatomies, however, were tough diplomats who had learned to deal with whites by negotiating more than thirty treaties with the Americans and a half dozen with the British before 1833. They knew how to get the best results in difficult circumstances. They were also more conservative and less divided than the Potawatomie bands in Michigan and Indiana, and in the autumn of 1833, the six thousand Potawatomies in the United Bands intended to secure the best possible bargain. Porter and the other commissioners were no doubt surprised when the Potawatomies flatly refused their offer. Aptakisic expressed surprise that the federal government had heard that they wanted to sell their lands. "When our Great Father heard that we wanted to sell our lands and remove from our country," he said, "your red children are afraid that he opened his ears to a bad bird—All your red children were not together, and did not consent that such word should be sent to our Great Father." He also told the commissioners that they would never move until they saw their promised lands. In the meantime, they wanted their annuities, after which they intended to go home.[28]

The United Bands of the Potawatomies knew that the federal government would take whatever lands that it wanted, but also that they had the diplomatic skills to stretch the negotiating process to gain as high a price for their lands and as many concessions as possible, particularly the receipt of the annuities and the whiskey that the traders brought with them to the rendezvous. While they drank and ate the government's provisions, they professed confusion about the exact locations of the lands that the commissioners wanted to purchase. Finally, on September 26, Porter, who had lost his patience, demanded that the Indians sign

28. Shabbona, an Ottawa, married a Potawatomie, and became a chief among his wife's people. He led the Potawatomies that fought with Tenskwatawa's Indian force at Prophetstown and at the Battle of the Thames. After the Black Hawk War, Shabbona led a large group of Potawatomies from Illinois to Missouri for resettlement. (Courtesy, Chicago Historical Society.)

the treaty that he waved before them. Realizing that they could hold out no longer, and with the advice of mixed-blood leaders, such as Sauganash, known as Billy Caldwell, and Chechebinquey or Alexander Robinson, seventy-seven Indian leaders from Wisconsin, Illinois, and Michigan signed the cession treaty in which they exchanged about five million acres for a similar area west of the Mississippi in the Iowa Territory and Missouri. Annuities for twenty years, the payment of debts to traders, gifts or bribes to certain leaders, and the federal payment of removal costs formed the heart of the treaty. The Indians would also move as soon as possible.

The Senate, however, did not ratify the treaty until February 21, 1835, because it took time to resolve the claims of traders and the demand of Missouri's senators that the Indians be kept in Iowa. In the meantime, the Potawatomies did as they pleased. After 1833, some 1,200 Potawatomies in Wisconsin and Michigan simply shifted their villages northward away from white pressures for their lands, and some 2,500 moved to Canada contrary to federal policy. Between 1833 and 1852, when the last substantial group of Potawatomies arrived in Kansas, most of the bands totaling approximately 9,000 pure-bloods moved west on their own and without military escort.

Ultimately, the federal government forced most of the other Potawatomies in the Midwest, especially the prairie bands in eastern Illinois and Indiana, to move by denying them their annuities in the form of food, livestock, and money unless they collected it at designated locations west of the Mississippi River. As a result of coercion, by 1840, most of the Prairie Potawatomies were ready to move west. The army, however, provided a military escort for the removal of a recalcitrant village under the leadership of Menominee in Indiana. The soldiers accompanied them as far at Peru, Illinois, and the waiting steamboats because, as Major Robert Forsyth, who commanded the village removal, put it, "not 20 of the 439 Indians moved willingly." By the late 1840s, then, most of the Potawatomies had left the Old Northwest. Many who made the removal journey suffered hardship, disease, and ill-treatment similar to that experienced by the southern nations, largely due to poor planning, incompetent white leadership, and dishonest contractors, particularly during the forced removals to Iowa and Kansas between 1835 and 1840.[29]

After the Treaty of Chicago, the federal government chipped away at the land base of the other Indian nations in the Old Northwest. By 1839, only the Wyandot remained on a small reservation in Ohio, and they had no political power to resist the loss of their lands. Confronted with insurmountable white demands for their reservations, the Wyandots signed a treaty on March 17, 1842, in which they terminated their title to 109,000 acres in exchange for 148,000 acres west of the Mississippi. Once known as the "Iroquois of the West," who fought with a ferocity that few tribes challenged, when they trekked from north-western Ohio to the waiting steamboats at Cincinnati in the July heat, they were a dispossessed and "melancholy" people with little hope.[30]

Anti-Indian sentiment and canal fever in Indiana after the Black Hawk War also pressed government officials to demand the cession of Miami lands. Although the federal government negotiated land cessions, but not removal, in 1834 and 1838, the Miamis refused to move until 1840. During the negotiations leading to the treaty at the Forks of the Wabash, signed on November 6, 1838, however, the Miamis revealed an astute awareness of cultural change. In Article 6, they insisted that only tribal members could share the annuities or the land. Whites or mixed-bloods, who lived among them or married into the tribe, could become Miamis only by adoption approved by the tribal council. The Miami leaders designed this provision to prevent the granting of allotments or reserves to mixed-bloods whose allegiance often resided in the white camp and who often sold those lands. The treaty also prohibited tribal members from contracting individual debts that would enable traders to attach liens against tribal lands and annuities. Until now traders had elevated fraud to a fine art to swindle Indians of all nations out of their lands and annuities through treaty provisions that guaranteed payment of their claims.

In 1840, for reasons that remain unclear, four chiefs—Richardville, Godroy, Lafontaine, and Meshingomesia—supported by other Miami leaders, signed a new treaty at the forks of the Wabash on November 28. Although the treaty provided for the removal of about half the tribe, it exempted most of the chiefs and their families as well as the mixed-bloods. Those privileged to remain received money and land grants, but the treaty essentially opened the Miamis' country to white settlement in Indiana. The Miamis agreed to leave Indiana within five years and resettle on five hundred thousand acres along the Maries des Cygnes in present-day Kansas. The federal government agreed to pay emigration expenses and support the tribe in their new home for twelve months. Despite the relative beneficence of the treaty, it aided only the elite members of the tribe who had the political and economic connections to gain exemption from removal.

The Miamis who had fallen into considerable debt to traders and who had been unable to ensure lands of their own necessarily turned over their share of the tribal annuities to their creditors and moved west, but not before they had delayed their removal as long as possible. Indeed, the chiefs, while ensuring their own prosperity, comfort, and residence, while abandoning any traditional reverence for tribal property, did not anticipate that their followers, whom they pledged to emigrate, would refuse to leave Indiana. Many did refuse, however, and in 1845, Secretary of War William Wilkins informed the Miamis that they could no longer avoid removal. Even so, the delay continued because all the Miamis' debts had not been paid and the Indians refused to assemble for removal. In 1846, the government forced the issue by letting a removal contract, which provided for payment of their debts and warned them that further annuity payments would be made only at their new reserve. The arrival of a small contingent of troops from Cincinnati at Peru in September ultimately convinced the Miamis that they could no longer delay removal and, amidst mass confusion, their emigration began in early October. Approximately three hundred Miamis left Indiana via boats on the Wabash and Erie Canal bound for Cincinnati where they loaded onto steamboats that eventually deposited them at present-day Kansas City for travel overland to their reservation farther west. A smaller group arrived in 1847. The Miamis who stayed soon found that despite their allotted lands, assimilation and acculturation proved impossible because whites refused to accept them as equals. They descended into a netherworld where they were neither Indian nor white. The Miamis who emigrated suffered little hardship compared to earlier removals of the Indian nations, but like many of their predecessors their reserve on the Maries des Cygnes would not be their last.

After the War of 1812, whites north as well as south of the Ohio River wanted Indian land, and they had the power to take it, paid for of course, but taken nonetheless, because the Indians seldom offered to sell it without coercion. The more desirable tribal lands became, the stronger the argument to save the Indians by removal. Where the Indians occupied lands that whites did not deem immediately essential for settlement, such as the forests of the Menominees and the Ojibwas in Wisconsin and Minnesota, they did not confront strong government pressure to leave. These Indians occupied the fringe of white society that largely ignored and forgot them. The Indian nations forced to move beyond the Mississippi, however, struggled to begin life anew and preserve their culture on another frontier where other Indian peoples increasingly resented not only their presence but also the whites who drove them west.

CHAPTER 8

The Great Plains

The end of the Black Hawk War and the removal of the eastern nations west of the Mississippi River required a reassessment of Indian policy. The new arrivals in the trans-Mississippi country, particularly those relocated to Indian Territory in present-day Oklahoma, settled on government-assigned lands that other Indian nations claimed for their home and hunting grounds. As a result, the federal government necessarily confronted the dual task of protecting the newly removed nations while reaching accommodations with the plains tribes to keep the peace, both in relation to the Indian immigrants and white traders and travelers. At the same time, federal authorities knew little about the plains tribes, particularly in the southern Great Plains, other than their reputation for war since contact with the Spanish in the early eighteenth century. In order to extend federal authority over the Great Plains, most of which the government claimed but did not occupy, the War Department intended to send a strong contingent of soldiers into the region to fly the flag, intimidate the Indians with periodic shows of force, and coerce them to keep the peace. To do so, federal officials first looked to the Southwest, where lucrative trade beaconed from Santa Fe, in contrast to the northern plains where the Sioux, Blackfeet, and other tribes offered limited trade possibilities.

Indeed, while Fort Snelling established in 1819 provided the Sioux of the Upper Mississippi with a needed and welcomed trading post as well as created a neutral ground for U.S. Indian commissioners to meet in council with chiefs from the Sioux bands, Ojibwas, Winnebagos, and Menominees, and while the post indicated to the Indians the intent of their Great Father to care for them, no such fort or relationship developed in the Upper Missouri and Yellowstone country. At the same time, the Lakotas consolidated their power in the northern Great Plains by reaching agreements with the Cheyennes and Arapahos over hunting grounds, pushed the Pawnees south of the Platte, and coerced other tribes into obeying their will. The U.S. Army did not have the resources to push them back nor did the government have the need or will to do so, because settlers were not yet pressing for the acquisition of Lakota lands.

The Prairie and Plains Frontier, 1820-1846

Moreover, with the supply of furs rapidly declining during the 1820s, and with no major trading potential for exploitation in the Northwest other than the fur trade, which essentially ended by 1840, traders looked to the Southwest to make their mark. And, by developing trade with Santa Fe and Taos, they necessarily made contact with Indian nations that, in turn, required the federal government to develop a policy for dealing with the plains tribes.

Moreover, in the early autumn of 1821, the need for a strong military presence on the Great Plains emerged when William Becknell left Franklin, Missouri, bound for Comanche country with trade goods tied to a pack train of mules. Becknell ended up in Santa Fe where he sold, among other things, cloth for $3 per yard. The residents of Santa Fe, isolated far to the north of Mexican

29. The Osages were the most powerful Indian nation in the prairie-plains transition area by the turn of the nineteenth century. In 1804, Thomas Jefferson called them the "greatest nation" south of the Missouri to the Red River. The Osages competed with the Comanches for buffalo between the Arkansas and Red Rivers. The Comanches respected the Osages and considered them the only enemy that they feared. (From George Catlin, *North American Indians.*)

supply centers, hungered for everyday goods and luxuries of all kinds. Upon his return in late January 1822, word spread quickly about the lucrative market in Santa Fe and the profits that could be earned there. The only problems that gave traders momentary pause were the approximately eight hundred miles across the southern plains and the potentially hostile Comanche, Kiowa, and Wichita Indians, among others, who claimed the region as their home and who might make the journey hazardous if not impossible. Upon reflection, however, the traders preferred to risk their lives for the silver that could be earned in Santa Fe, but they also sought federal protection to lessen their risks. As commerce with Santa Fe increased during the 1820s, one trader urged Congress and the War Department to keep it in the largest economic, political, and military perspective possible. He believe that Indian attacks on traders along the Santa Fe Trail should be considered not merely a "private injury, but a *public wrong,* a *national insult,* and one which will bring down upon the heads of the guilty, the strong arm of national power."[1]

The Comanches proved as anxious to trade with the Americans as they were with them. In 1822, Thomas James and his party of traders made contact with a Comanche village on the upper reaches of the North Fork of the Canadian River.

James reported that these Comanches "united in requesting me to encourage my countrymen to visit them with goods and trade with them. Trade with the Spaniards they said was unprofitable; they had nothing to give them for their horses." The Southwestern Indian trade also proved lucrative for white entrepreneurs. A year later James bragged that he purchased a bison robe for "one plug of tobacco, a knife and a few strings of beads, in all worth but little more than a dime," and he could sell these hides for at least $5 each on any American market. Josiah Gregg, an early trader on the Santa Fe Trail, reported that the Comanches charged from $10 to $20 worth of trade goods for mules, but he considered the exchange favorable considering the demand for these animals by teamsters and emigrants in Missouri. The declining fur trade to the north could not return comparable profits, and it required greater capital investment to supply posts, traders, and Indians. In the Southwest, both Indians and traders considered their exchanges profitable and desirable. The Comanches complained, however, that the Americans traded guns, lead, and powder to the Osages, who were their traditional enemies. One chief informed James that "this is wrong, very wrong.... [T]ell our Great Father ... to protect us and send his people out to trade with us."[2]

Federal authorities wanted to provide protection to traders and travelers along the Santa Fe Trail, but insufficient men and resources prevented the requisite construction of a line of posts from the Missouri River to the Arkansas, which served as the northern boundary of Mexico, and from which Mexican soldiers would necessarily need to guarantee their safety on the Santa Fe. Ultimately, the federal government decided to build a chain of forts on the edge of the Great Plains extending from Minnesota to Indian Territory. Fort Smith in Arkansas, completed in 1822, became the first post in that scheme, while Fort Snelling, designated in 1825, became the northernmost post in this plan for the white defense of the frontier. Fort Leavenworth, occupied in 1827, served as the command center for executing Indian policy on the plains.

By the late 1820s, while federal officials worked to complete a corridor of forts and an all-weather road linking them to facilitate rapid communication and the movement of troops along the edge of the plains, traders on the Santa Fe Trail began experiencing Indian attacks, primarily designed as horse-stealing raids. By September 1828, however, two traders had been killed, probably by Kiowas or Comanches, the latter of whom had also driven off nearly a thousand horses and mules from freighters near the great bend of the Arkansas River. In response, the Missouri legislature asked Congress to protect the Santa Fe trade, arguing that the Indians "are restrained by nothing but *force*." The army responded in June 1829 by providing traders with occasional infantry escorts as far as the Arkansas River, a portion of which served as the international boundary with Mexico. Infantry, however, proved no match for the best horsemen on the Great Plains. One officer reported that "It was a humiliating condition to be surrounded by these rascally Indians, who by means of their horses, could tantalize us with the hope of battle, and elude our efforts; who could annoy us by preventing all individual incursions for hunting, etc., and could insult us with impunity."[3]

As a result, in November 1829, Secretary of War John Eaton asked Congress to provide funds for mounted troops to protect traders and settlers who ventured onto the Great Plains. Quarter Master Thomas S. Jesup agreed and likened the need for mounted troops on the plains to the necessity of providing naval vessels on the high seas to protect American interests. In early April 1830, Jesup wrote to Representative A. H. Sevier that "without a mounted force on the frontier south of the Missouri, the Indian, confident in the capacity of his horse to bear him beyond the reach of pursuit, despises our power, chooses his point of attack, and often commits the outrages to which he is prompted either by a spirit-of-revenge or a love of plunder in the immediate vicinity of our troops; and the impunity of the first act invariably leads to new aggressions."[4]

Congress delayed, however, and ultimately failed to provide a force of mounted soldiers to patrol the Santa Fe Trail and the fringes of the Great Plains where settlers would soon reside. As intertribal warfare increased between the Sauks and Foxes with the Sioux in the Upper Mississippi River valley, along with hostile confrontation between Kiowas and Comanches and traders along the Santa Fe Trail, the War Department continued to press Congress for a mounted force. In early February 1832, Secretary of War Lewis Cass told the Senate: "It is quite time that the United States should interpose, efficaciously, to put a stop as well to the depredations of the Indians against our own citizens, as to their hostilities among themselves." If Congress would not authorize such a force, Cass believed hostilities among Indians as well as between Indians and whites would soon increase, particularly as the eastern tribes migrated west of the Mississippi as provided by the removal treaties. Cass particularly used the newly arriving eastern tribes to justify mounted troops on the plains, arguing, "We shall be bound by every principle of duty to protect them; and as they will be placed in juxtaposition with the savage tribes of the plains, unless we restrain the latter, a perpetual border warfare will be the consequence." Cass had reason to worry because the Comanches and Wichitas soon attacked Cherokee hunters who ventured into their territory, while the Osages sent a 300-man war party against their old enemy the Kiowas south of the Arkansas. The Osage raid resulted in the destruction of an entire Kiowa village, near present-day Fort Sill, Oklahoma, and an act of atrocity that left more than 150 dead with their heads cut off. The raid became known as the Cut Throat Massacre of 1833.[5]

Although Congress preferred economy rather than increased expenditures for the army, it could not ignore the inability of infantry soldiers to guard travelers over the Santa Fe Trail. As a result, the War Department decided to use the battalion of six hundred mounted rangers that Congress authorized in mid-June 1832 for the Black Hawk War to guard the western frontier. In late September 1833, Colonel Henry Dodge, commander of the rangers, sent three companies from Fort Armstrong and Jefferson Barracks near St. Louis to Fort Gibson, Indian Territory. There, they would help separate immigrant and native Indians, keep the peace, and aid the treaty-making process with the tribes on the southern Great Plains. The War Department had built Fort Gibson in 1824 to help administer the removal process. Located near the convergence of the Arkansas, Verdigris, and Grand Rivers, Fort Gibson became known as a hardship post plagued by malaria and a host of other diseases, which gained it the reputation as the charnel house of the army.[6]

Despite the rough and raw circumstances bred from insufficient supplies of food and inadequate clothing that made army life as much a challenge as a service, the War Department intended to implement federal Indian policy from Fort Gibson. Accordingly, in the spring of 1833, Brigadier General Matthew Arbuckle, post commander, planned to send two companies of infantry and three companies of rangers up the Blue and Washita Rivers to find the chiefs of the Comanche and Wichita villages and convince them to come to Fort Gibson for a peace council. Arbuckle wanted the infantry and rangers as well as the soldiers at Fort Gibson to impress the Indians with the power of the United States and to gain their assurances that they would not attack the immigrant eastern nations or traders traveling over the Santa Fe Trail. Although the expedition left Fort Gibson in early May, it failed to find any Indians who wanted to talk peace, and the expedition returned exhausted and humiliated from the capture of a soldier by an unidentified band of Indians, rather than triumphant from intimidating potentially hostile tribes to keep the peace. More important, in March 1833, Congress authorized the creation of a regiment of mounted soldiers called dragoons and the disbandment of the temporary, volunteer ranger companies that the army considered too expensive and undisciplined for cost-effective and reliable service. Military officials believed dragoons would enable the structuring of a disciplined, mobile command to execute Indian policy on the Great Plains.

The War Department intended the regiment of dragoons to reflect a national commitment to the defense of the frontier. Secretary of War Cass contended: "It is deemed indispensable to the peace and security of the frontiers that a respectable force should be displayed in that quarter, and that the wandering and restless tribes who roam through it should be impressed with the power of the United States by the exhibition of a corps so well qualified to excite their respect. The Indians are beyond the reach of a mere infantry force. Without stationary residences, and possessing an abundant supply of horses, and with habits admirably adapted to their use, they can be held in check only by a similar force, and by its occasional display among them." Cass also argued that the eastern tribes needed protection from the plains Indians as well as white settlers, but peace and security could "only be fulfilled by repressing and punishing every attempt to disturb the general tranquility." By so doing, Cass believed, "there is reason to hope that the display of this force will itself render unnecessary its hostile employment. The more barbarous tribes will perceive that their own safety is closely connected with the permanent establishment of pacific relations both with the United States and with the other Indians."[7]

The recruits mustered, outfitted, and drilled in their dragoon companies at Jefferson Barracks during the autumn of 1833 and when their officers judged them ready for service they left for Fort Gibson, where they prepared for another expedition deep into Indian Territory. Colonel Henry M. Dodge, who commanded the dragoons, accompanied by General Henry Leavenworth, who assumed command of Fort Gibson in May 1834, would lead the expedition about 250 miles west to the Pawnee Pict (Wichita), Kiowa, and Comanche villages located somewhere along the Red River. These tribes had not yet signed peace treaties with the federal government and their nomadic lifestyle made them difficult for the army and Indian commissioners to find for the purpose of calling a council. In keeping with his earlier belief, Secretary of War Cass wanted the dragoons to ride deep into the southern Great Plains to impress these tribes with the power of the United States. In so doing, he thought, the army would intimidate them into keeping the peace and convince them to refrain from attacking white traders and trappers who might venture into the region. They would do what the infantry could not do. The dragoons would serve as a mobile police force and fly the flag in the vast and sprawling frontier.

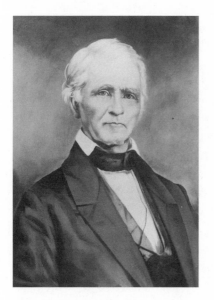

30. In 1834, Colonel Henry Dodge led a
dragoon expedition into present-day
western Oklahoma to meet with the
Comanches and Wichitas, impress them
with the military power of the United
States, and invite them to sign a peace
treaty. Dodge had orders to gain their
promise to refrain from attacking
emigrant Indians involved with the
removal process as well as travelers over
the Santa Fe Trail. His expedition led to
a treaty in 1835 in which the Comanches
and Wichitas pledged perpetual peace and
friendship with the United States, but the
agreement did not last. (Courtesy, State
Historical Society of Iowa, Des Moines.)

The expedition got off to a late start. Not until June 15, when the summer
heat already bore down oppressively on men, horses, and the buffalo grass, did
the dragoons head west. When the bugler called the dragoons to horse, eight
companies, totaling about five hundred dragoons, assembled in the morning
sun on the parade ground at Fort Gibson. Both officers and enlisted men were
restless and anxious to begin a great adventure. When Dodge gave the order to
march, the column wheeled and moved away from the post and crossed the
Arkansas near the mouth of the Neosho River. The cavalcade was an imposing
sight with the company horses—bays, sorrels, blacks, whites—all forming a long
line of two columns. The drawn-out calls from the officers carried over the land,
and the creak of the baggage wagons accompanied the men and horses as the
expedition moved west under a blinding sun. George Catlin, who went along,
observed that the column strung out for more than a mile, and from a hilltop it
looked like a "huge black snake, gracefully gliding over a rich carpet of green."
He wrote, "I started this morning with the dragoons for the Pawnee country,
but God only knows where that is." Dodge, Leavenworth, and the other officers
and dragoons did not know either.[8]

The expedition included not only Leavenworth, Dodge, and Stephen Watts
Kearny, but also First Lieutenant Jefferson Davis and Count Beyrick, a German
botanist from the University of Berlin whom the War Department had authorized to accompany the dragoons to conduct scientific research. Four bands of

31. In 1834, when Colonel Henry Dodge's dragoons reached a Comanche village somewhere in present-day western Oklahoma, they were met by a line of mounted warriors. George Catlin, who accompanied the expedition, wrote that the Comanches rode like "well-disciplined Cavalry." After sitting on their horses and watching each other for an hour, a Comanche leader rode forward and invited them to his village. (From George Catlin, *North American Indians.*)

Indians, including eleven Osages, eight Cherokees, six Delawares, and seven Senecas, also traveled along to serve as guides, hunters, interpreters, and representatives of their people. A fifteen-year-old Kiowa girl, who had been captured by the Osages in 1833, and an eighteen-year-old Wichita woman, who had been taken prisoner by the Osages several years earlier, also accompanied the expedition to be returned to their tribes as a sign of goodwill by the United States.

The dragoons saw their first Comanches on July 14, when they discovered a band of thirty riders watching them from a distance as the expedition approached a village of about two hundred conical skin lodges with approximately four hundred inhabitants. Before the dragoons reached the village, a hundred mounted Comanches rode out to meet them, but they showed neither fear nor hostility. The dragoons noticed that the Comanches rode with such skill that every movement flowed with ease. Each carried a lance, bow, quiver, and buffalo-hide shield, and they rode good horses. The Comanches also carried themselves proudly and acted with boldness and confidence as they escorted the horse soldiers to

32. George Catlin recorded the dragoon expedition of 1834 with pen and brush. When the dragoons spotted a Comanche war party, Dodge sent a rider forward with a white flag. The Comanche's leader responded by approaching the dragoons with a piece of white buffalo hide dangling from his lance, and both parties professed peace. (From George Catlin, *North American Indians.*)

their village, where Lieutenant T. B. Wheelock found the women "good looking" with short-cut hair. There, the men rested and traded blankets and knives for fresh mounts. Catlin noted that the Comanche children and dogs were afraid of the dragoons, while the village in general treated them "with as much curiosity as if we had come from the moon." The principal village leaders were absent, however, and after several days rest, Dodge convinced a Comanche to lead the expedition to the Wichita camp.[9]

By mid-July, depleted rations and little game threatened starvation for the dragoons, while the shoes of the horses began to wear out and their mounts "suffered very much" from sore hooves. Lieutenant Wheelock recorded that the men had become "very improvident." Still, Dodge pressed forward and reached the Wichita village of approximately two hundred grass lodges on July 21. He felt relieved when the Wichitas offered food and seemed peaceful. While the dragoons rested and regained their strength, Comanche, Kiowa, and Waco bands arrived at the Wichita village to meet with Dodge in a grand council. With the

33. In July 1834, Colonel Henry Dodge's dragoons reached a Comanche village where George Catlin reported that the soldiers frightened the children and dogs and the Comanches treated them "with as much curiosity as if we had come from the moon." (From George Catlin, *North American Indians.*)

chiefs present, Dodge told them, "We are the first American officers who have ever come to see the Pawnees [Wichitas]. We meet you as friends, not as enemies, to make peace with you, to shake hands with you. The great American captain is at peace with all the white men in the world; he wishes to be at peace with all the red men in the world; we have been sent here to view this country, and to invite you to go to Washington, where the great American chief lives, to make a treaty with him, that you may learn how he wishes to send among you traders, who will bring you guns and blankets, and everything that you want." The chiefs listened intently, but they were not convinced that a great white leader far away wanted peace and a council with them, even though they wanted trade. When the council broke up, one dragoon wrote in his diary that "suspicion reigned in the bosom of all."[10]

During the days that followed, Dodge successfully exchanged the Wichita girl who had accompanied the expedition for two boys that the Comanches held, although the black boy did not want to return with Dodge for a probable reunion with his master. Even though Dodge learned that the ranger captured the previous year had been killed, his relations with the chiefs gave him hope that he could gain their pledge for peace and friendship. When Dodge reconvened the council, he told the chiefs that the president of the United States wanted to make a peace treaty with them and to exchange all prisoners. "Peace cannot be made with all the tribes," he said, "till a large white paper be written and signed by the President and the hands of the chiefs. Will your chiefs go with me now to see the American President?" Dodge then promised many presents, but the chiefs still showed skepticism, and they did not want to return to Fort Gibson with him to make a treaty. Chief We-ter-ra-shah-ro, however, came forward and told Dodge, "We wish to make peace with the Osages; we have been long at war with them; we wish to see the lands of the Creeks and Cherokees also, to shake hands with them all." This acknowledgment broke the impasse, and leaders of the Osages, Cherokees, and Delawares who had accompanied the expedition stepped forward and testified that they lived with the whites in peace and friendship and that they had nothing to fear from each other. Monpisha, an Osage, also told the Wichitas, "Your buffalo will be gone in a few years. Your great father, the President will give you cattle, and teach you how to live without buffalo." With these speeches of encouragement, the chiefs decided to select some men who would accompany Dodge to Fort Gibson and learn more about the wishes of the white leaders.[11]

Before the expedition returned to Fort Gibson, however, Dodge returned the Kiowa girl brought with them to her parents and held a council with the chiefs of this nation who were present. Dodge told them, "Kiowa chiefs! I herewith present to you your relation; receive her as the best evidence of the sincere friendship of the Americans." Then, the chiefs and officers smoked the peace pipe and pledged lasting friendship, and the council drew to a close. Only a few Kiowas, however, agreed to accompany Dodge back to Fort Gibson on a return march that proved as grueling as the trek to the Wichita village. By the time the first contingent of the straggling expedition returned to Fort Gibson on August 15, more than a hundred men had died, and more would not recover from the ordeal. Lieutenant Wheelock, however, reported that the Kiowas who had joined them suffered not at all from the heat and scanty supplies of food and water. "Our friends from the prairie are in good health," he wrote, "and are apparently contented."[12]

In retrospect, the dragoon expedition of 1834 proved an unmitigated disaster. It had been poorly planned and desperately executed, and the army had only the deaths of a hundred men to show for it. Many of the dragoons no doubt wondered whether they had accomplished anything. Certainly, the War Department questioned the organization and leadership of the expedition, and critics charged that it had left Fort Gibson six weeks too late. As a result, the campaign was carried out during the hottest part of the year. In the minds of most officers in the War Department and among the dragoons, the expedition had been a disaster from the beginning. While many dragoons doubted the value of the campaign, they became convinced of its folly when they learned that the Indians, who had accompanied them back to Fort Gibson, had no intention of going to Washington to meet the president of the United States. As a result, Dodge, in an attempt to salvage something of consequence from the disastrous expedition, hurriedly arranged a grand council with the Kiowas, Comanches, and Wichitas who had returned with him and the nearby Cherokees, Osages, Choctaws, Creeks, and Senecas.

When some 150 Indian delegates assembled at noon on September 1, 1834, Dodge and Major Francis W. Armstrong, acting superintendent of Indian affairs for the Western Territory, again professed the peaceful intentions of the United States, and they gave the Indians medals and flags as symbols of friendship. They also told the Indians that traders wanted to visit their villages and cross their lands to Santa Fe. They would come in peace and both whites and Indians would profit from this trade. Dodge believed that he had laid the foundation for a lasting peace with the tribes of the southern Great Plains with the expedition and conference, but not everyone agreed. George Catlin contended that the summer expedition had been a "most disastrous campaign." Others took a wait-and-see attitude toward the results of the expedition and the proceedings that followed.[13]

Dodge, however, did not have the authority to hold a peace conference and negotiate a treaty at Fort Gibson, but he could offer peace and friendship until formal proceedings could be organized the next year. Still, the conference at Fort Gibson provided the first official contact between federal officials and the tribes of the southern Great Plains. It also began the process of negotiation that opened the Indian Territory to occupation by more than one hundred thousand members of the Cherokee, Creek, Chickasaw, Choctaw, and Seminole nations, as well as others. In addition, the conference laid the groundwork for providing safe passage for white travelers through the area. Yet, while Dodge believed the expedition and conference would soon lead to a "permanent peace" with these tribes, and although Secretary of War Cass reported that "the efforts to introduce amicable relations were successful," considerable hostility and fighting would take place in the future between whites and Indians in the region. Still, the summer expedition of 1834 and the September conference at Fort Gibson initiated the efforts of the federal government to make peace with the nomadic tribes of the southern Great Plains.[14]

Although many officers and government officials believed that the dragoon expedition of 1834 accomplished little, in reality it made the council at Fort Gibson possible. There, the Comanches and Osages agreed to keep the peace among themselves. Thereafter, they became trading partners with the Comanches exchanging horses stolen in Texas and Mexico for goods that the Osages acquired from white trading posts on the frontier. Neither the Comanches nor the Osages ever broke this treaty. Moreover, the meeting at Fort Gibson enabled government emissaries to make the initial contacts that led to a major conference the next year. Accordingly, in August, chiefs from the Comanches, Wichitas, Cherokees, Creeks, Choctaws, Osages, Senecas, Quapaws, and other associated bands met with commissioners Governor Montfort Stokes of North Carolina, Brigadier General Arbuckle, and Francis W. Armstrong, acting superintendent of Indian affairs for the Western Territory, at Camp Holmes on the South Fork of the Canadian River near present-day Purcell, Oklahoma, to discuss peace, travel through Indian country, indemnities, hunting grounds, and relations with Mexico.

On August 24, 1835, they reached an agreement, formally known as the Treaty with the Comanche, Wichita, and Associated Bands, in which each party pledged "perpetual peace and friendship," and that past injuries and grievances against each other would be "mutually forgiven and forever forgot." More to the point, the commissioners included an emphatic provision about which there could be no compromise. It held that citizens of the United States were "freely permitted to pass and repass through their settlements or hunting ground without molestation or injury on their way to any of the provinces of the Republic of Mexico, or returning therefrom," and that the tribes would pay for any injuries and thefts that occurred in violation of this provision. The tribal chiefs also agreed that "all of the nations present" had "free permission to hunt and trap in the Great Prairie west of the Cross Timber, to the western limits of the United States." Furthermore, to prevent intertribal war from the north, the Comanches and Wichitas also agreed that any nations residing south of the Missouri River and west of the State of Missouri would be treated with "kindness and friendship," if they were found on the hunting grounds of the signatory tribes.[15]

Last, in an effort to maintain friendly relations with Mexico, the commissioners received a pledge from the Comanches and Wichitas that they would not interrupt the friendly relations of the United States with Mexico. Then, the commissioners and chiefs signed the treaty and Indians received presents as symbols of goodwill by the United States. By the winter of 1835, however, some Comanches had torn up their copy of the treaty because the promised trade goods proved insufficient, and they regretted opening their territory to the eastern tribes. The Comanches, Wichitas, and Tawakonis did not observe the treaty of 1835, and they raided south across the Red River whenever they saw opportunity to strike the Texans who had driven them from their villages and lands. During the summer of 1837, however, epidemic disease struck the Wichita villages, crop failure brought severe hunger, and Pawnee raiders further weakened the bands, all of which brought an end to Wichita forays south of the Red River, although they still considered Texans their enemies.

On May 26, 1837, Montfort Stokes and Colonel A. P. Chouteau negotiated a similar treaty of "peace and friendship" with the Kiowas along with several bands of Kiowa Apaches and Tawakonis. This treaty specifically required the Kiowas to maintain peace with Texas, an important provision because the tribes of the southern Great Plains considered Texans different from Americans. The Americans they believed talked peace, provided traders, and recognized their rights, even though the federal government claimed sovereignty over Kiowa lands. In contrast, the Texans claimed all lands in the republic and demanded that the tribes move without the use of a cession treaty whenever those lands were needed or desired by settlers. Both Americans and Anglo-Texans, of course, expected the Indians to retreat before white settlement, but for the moment, the Americans talked about accommodation and then used force, while the Texans resorted to force immediately and then discussed peace. Simply put, the Americans followed a policy of accommodation and removal, while the Texans pursued a policy of extinction.[16]

These treaties, however, helped make the Santa Fe Trail relatively safe for travelers, although the absence of serious danger stemmed more from the lack of heavy pressure by whites for Indian lands and serious depletion of the buffalo. Even so, the army continued to provide an escort for travelers and traders over the Santa Fe Trail until the summer of 1839, after which it abandoned that service until 1843. The army, however, made other forays similar to the Dodge expedition into the central plains for the purpose of flying the flag, impressing tribes with the power of the United States, and seeking assurances of peace and friendship for travelers and traders who might venture onto their lands. During the summer of 1835, Dodge led an expedition from Fort Leavenworth to the

Rocky Mountains and met with the Otos, Omahas, Pawnees, Arapahos, and Cheyennes as well as the Arikaras, Gros Ventres, and Blackfeet. On July 5, Captain Lemuel Ford reported a council with the Arikaras during which Dodge told them to stop stealing from other tribes and to let white traders pass through their country. If they did not stop their killing and robbing, they would be "destroyed," and in Ford's words Dodge "advised them to change their course." The Arikaras pledged that any whites who came among them would have "no cause of complaint and that they would be treated well." Dodge also held a council with the Cheyennes and Arapahos at Bent's Fort where he talked peace and made every effort to impress them with the power of the United States exemplified by his three companies of disciplined and well-armed dragoons.[17]

Reflecting on the overall success of the expedition, Lieutenant Gaines Pease Kingsbury reported that the Indians were "already impressed with a high opinion of the United States, and it will not be difficult for the Government in a short time, to exert a controlling influence over them." Upon completion of this 1,600-mile march back along the Santa Fe Trail, Kingsbury reported that the command had "visited all the Indians between the Arkansas and Platte, as far west as the mountains, had made peace with several tribes, and established friendly relations with them all." General Edward P. Gaines considered the expedition a successful execution of Indian policy, and he believed it had impressed the various tribes with the "*justice, magnanimity, humanity,* and *power* of our Government and Country." For their part, the Indians whom Dodge had contacted, like those he met a year earlier to the south, accepted the dragoons cautiously, and, while professing peace and friendship as the best diplomatic option at the moment, privately took a wait-and-see approach to what the presence of soldiers in their country meant.[18]

In 1843, however, immigrants began making their way along the Platte River bound for the Oregon country, and periodic thefts and injuries began to occur among Indians and whites. As a result, in 1844, the army sent a detachment of dragoons from Fort Leavenworth commanded by Major Clifton Wharton to meet with the offending tribes and threaten them with force if they did not keep the peace. Wharton first met with the Pawnees along the Platte to impress them and any other tribe with the "power of the U.S. Government to punish them for aggressions" and "to urge upon them the policy of peace among themselves & their neighbors, and to endeavor to effect a reconciliation between the Pawnees and the Sioux, between whom a most ferocious war has been carried on for many years." With this purpose in mind and after some difficulty, Wharton's detachment found the Pawnees in the Platte Valley and convened a council on August 30.[19]

Wharton quickly got to the point, telling the assembled chiefs and other leaders that their troubles with the Sioux and Kanzas resulted from the propensity of all to steal horses. Showing a flagrant ignorance of Plains Indian culture, Wharton told them, "This practice which so often causes the hatchet to be raised between the Red men should be checked, and when horses are stolen from your neighbors by your young men they should be returned to their owners with a friendly talk." The result would be "promoting kind feelings instead of hostile ones." The Pawnees were amazed and amused with Wharton's advice, and both parties quickly put it aside for a more important matter when Wharton told them, "A great many of your Great Father's white children are now going to the big water which lies beyond the Stony mountains. He expects that when you meet such of his children and others you will treat them kindly and afford them aid, if they require it, and that you will act in like manner to his children who may pass down the river which now flows at our feet" He also reminded them that in 1833 they had agreed to move north of the Platte, and he insisted that they now fulfill that pledge.[20]

Char-a-cha-ush or Cunning Chief, the principal leader of the Grand Pawnees, disagreed and rose his feet to say, "My great father said I was good in giving him this land. I did not hear my Great father say I must move. . . . We see nothing on the other side of the river which our Great father promised. He said he would give me cows and horses, but, as yet none are there. . . . These lands are as much mine as my Great Father's." Cunning Chief admitted that horses had been stolen but not from whites, yet traders provided the Sioux with guns, lead, and powder, which they used to attack the Pawnees, and he wanted guns to fight back. Wharton responded by telling Cunning Chief that the Pawnees had stolen horses from whites and that they were as free as the Sioux to purchase guns from white traders, and closed the council. Before Wharton's column departed, however, he fired his two howitzers for "edification, and as a manifestation of our power." Before Wharton returned to Fort Leavenworth, however, he met with the Otos, Omahas, Potawatomies, Sauks and Foxes, and other Pawnee bands, and urged them to keep the peace with whites and among themselves. Often, as among the Otos, the chiefs listened politely and then reminded Wharton that the federal government had taken their lands but failed to keep treaty promises. As a result, they were hungry, poorly clothed, and without weapons to help feed and defend themselves, and that government farmers and blacksmiths had not

34. In 1845, Stephen Watts Kearny led an expedition to Fort Laramie where he urged the Sioux to keep the peace with the other nations of the central and northern Great Plains and to let white travelers pass safely on the Platte River Road or Oregon Trail. A year later he led the Army of the West to Santa Fe. (Courtesy, State Historical Society of Iowa, Des Moines.)

yet arrived to help them begin a new life. Wharton countered by reminding them of certain military punishment if they harmed whites, and the chiefs professed that they could not control their young men.[21]

A year later, Colonel Stephen Watts Kearny led five companies of the First Dragoons along the Oregon Trail to the fur trading post of Fort Laramie near South Pass and then turned south to Bent's Fort before returning to Fort Leavenworth via the Santa Fe Trail. Kearny had the responsibility to provide protection to travelers on both trails, serve as a viable symbol of military power, and indicate the willingness of the United States to enforce its Indian policy in the region. In June 1845, Fort Laramie was still four years away from becoming a military post, but it served as a middle ground on the frontier where Indians and whites alike sought advantage. Captain Philip St. George Cooke, who accompanied the expedition, reported that "The Fort swarmed with women and children, whose language—like their complexions—is various and mixed—Indian, French, English, and Spanish." Cooke was amazed with the swarm of humanity at the fort. "Here," he wrote, "barbarism and a traditional or half civilization meet on neutral ground . . . represented chiefly by females . . . while the male representatives of civilization have the orthodox, although questionable aids of alcohol and gunpowder, avarice, lying and lust."[22]

At Fort Laramie, Kearny sent messengers to invite the Sioux to come in for a council. On June 16 approximately 1,220 Oglala and Brulé heard Kearny tell them: "I am opening a road for the white people, & your great father directs that his red children shall not attempt to close it up—there are many white men coming on this road moving to the other side of the mountains—they take with them women, children & cattle—they all go to lay their bones there & never to return— you must not disturb them in their persons or molest their property—should you do so, your Great father would be angry with you, & cause you to be punished." Kearny also told them, "Your Great father is the friend of his Red children, & as long as they behave themselves properly will continue to be so." A chief by the name of Bull's Tail replied that his people would follow Kearny's advice. Then, the soldiers distributed some presents, fired their howitzers, and headed south toward Bent's Fort to return to Fort Leavenworth.[23]

Kearny, upon arrival back at Fort Leavenworth in late August, believed his expedition had been a success and that similar forays into Indian country "would serve to keep the Indians perfectly quiet, reminding them of (as this one proved) the facility with which our dragoons can march through any part of their country, & that there is no place they can go but the dragoons can follow." President James K. Polk agreed, and in his annual message to Congress on December 2, 1845, reported that "The exhibition of this military force among the Indian tribes in those distant regions and the councils held with them by the commanders of the expeditions, it is believed, will have a salutary influence in restraining them from hostilities among themselves and maintaining friendly relations between them and the United States." Although Dodge, Wharton, and Kearny, among others, believed their expeditions designed to fly the flag and make the military presence of the United States known to the Indians on the Great Plains would keep the peace, many bands were less than certain and viewed the American presence in the form of soldiers, traders, and emigrants with apprehension. At the same time, many of the newly settled eastern nations, such as the Chickasaws, feared their new neighbors, particularly the Comanches and Kiowas, and refused to settle on their lands until the federal government could protect them.[24]

Indeed, the Chickasaw District, allocated in the central and western part of the Choctaw nation in Indian Territory, bordered the homeland of the Comanches and Kiowas, who resented their presence and competition for the buffalo. A band of Kickapoos from the Old Northwest also used the Washita Valley as their route to the south and west for trade and to strike the Anglo-Texans, who, in turn, often retaliated across the Red River and struck the Chickasaws, exercising the axiom that vengeance could be gained against any and all Indians, peaceful or not. As a result, in 1839 Chickasaw leaders asked for federal protection, saying, "We are placed entirely on the frontier and surrounded by various bands of hostile Indians . . . and we wish to know of our Great Father if he will not have some of his men placed at some suitable situation in our District to protect the lives and property, both of which are at the mercy of these roving bands." Ultimately, in the summer of 1841, the War Department responded by authorizing Colonel Zachary Taylor to construct Fort Washita near the mouth of that river in the Chickasaw District to protect these and other immigrant Indians from the tribes of the southern plains. Two years later in September 1843, the Chickasaws joined with the Caddos, Tawakonis, and Keechis to meet with a Texas delegation at Bird's Fort to negotiate a peace treaty. There, the government of Texas agreed to protect the tribes from renegade raids by Texans and to regulate trade south of the Red River. Thereafter, the immigrant tribes gained increased security and peace. By the beginning of the Mexican War, however, the best that could be said about Indian and white relations on the Great Plains was that time would ultimately tell whether the future held much promise for mutual understanding and peace.[25]

South of the Red River in Texas, the Comanches along with the Kiowas and other allies remained the focus for those who made Indian policy in Mexico and later the Republic of Texas. In late December 1819, on the eve of Mexican independence, Juan Antonio Padilla, a government official in San Antonio, urged the governor of Texas to send a "respectable and well-organized campaign" against the Comanches and Lipanes who had "occasioned so many evils in the province during these last years." He believed only force would bring peace and advocated that these tribes "should be followed until they are exterminated or forced to an inviolable and lasting peace." Padilla also requested that "there be established a line of *presidios* to guard this frontier extending from the old *presidio* of San Sabá to that of Nacogdoches . . . another at San Xavier, another on the Brazos, another on the Tortuga, another on the Trinity, and the last at Nacogdoches on the frontier of the United States." These presidios would require two thousand soldiers with "full pay and other necessary supplies in order to attract to the settlement all kinds of people useful in these lands." Two years later, Mexican independence made this request a moot point, with military forces divided and funds insufficient for Spain to conduct both a war and a forceful Indian policy.[26]

With the collapse of Spanish military power and the inability of Mexico to assert authority over the tribes in its northern territory, the Comanches resumed raiding south across the Rio Grande from their villages in present-day Kansas,

Colorado, Oklahoma, and Texas. They ran off cattle and horses with nonchalant skill and audacity to earn traditional recognition for bravery and, thereby, gain glory, status, and wealth. The Comanches stole horses from Mexican settlers and garrisons for trade to the Pawnees for guns, which the latter nation acquired through an elaborate trade network that extended into Canada. Or, they traded horses for guns and other goods with Stephen F. Austin's colony, which became a lucrative business for both groups. The Comanches proved so skillful at stealing horses that cynical Mexicans, who had no faith in the ability of the government to protect life and property, claimed that these Indians did not completely devastate northern Mexico because they would ruin their source for horses. During the horse raids, however, they often killed settlers, travelers, and miners, and affirmed, if anyone had ever doubted, that the southern plains belonged to them more than to the Mexicans or anyone else. In 1833, a traveler in San Antonio reported that "not a man ventures into his field, or to a distance of a quarter of a mile to procure wood, without taking his gun along," while Loredo's population reportedly declined because of illness caused by "bullets, lances, and arrows of the barbarous Comanches." During the years when the Comanches did not raid in Texas, settlers who occupied farms, ranches, and villages remained in a constant state of apprehension.[27]

Anglo-American traders tipped the balance of power away from Mexico on the northern frontier by trading weapons for horses, a policy that Mexican officials prohibited. In 1830, one Mexican reported that before the arrival of the Americans, the Indians "did not have firearms except a small number of old muskets which they received as gifts from the Spaniards, with a very small supply of powder that hardly served them because of its bad quality." After 1821, however, American traders arrived with guns, "very exquisite powder," and whiskey, in search of suppliers of good horses that would bring high prices east of the Mississippi River on markets from Louisiana to Illinois. The Comanches, Wichitas, and Apaches wanted these goods, and Mexican settlements and presidios had large and fine horse herds that grazed peacefully, seemingly for the taking. By the mid-1820s, Indian raiding for horses and mules for the firearms trade had become so serious that the Mexican government asked the United States to stop the "[t]raders of blood who put instruments of death in the hands of those barbarians." And, in 1830, one Mexican official questioned whether the Americans intended "to use savage Indians to menace defenseless Mexicans in order to force them to abandon their lands or . . . request the protection of the United States Government." By the mid-1830s, traders from Arkansas and

Missouri had established posts on the north bank of the Red River, which, in part, separated the United States from Mexico. There, in 1835, one trader reportedly told the Comanches, Wacos, and Tawakonis "to go to the interior and kill Mexicans and bring their horses and mules to him and he would give them a fair price." By the late 1830s, American traders gave each other considerable competition for the horses and mules that the Comanches brought from Mexico. Moreover, the weapons and ammunition that American traders offered in Santa Fe soon found their way into the hands of a host of Indian people as far west as Arizona.[28]

While Mexican officials complained about American traders, they attempted, at least theoretically, to treat the Indians as citizens as provided by the Constitution of 1824. In 1835, President Santa Anna, when questioned about the rights of the hostile Indians, contended that they "are Mexicans, because they were born and live in the Republic. . . . The state of barbarity in which they are raised prevents them for knowing their universal obligations, and those that belong to them as Mexicans." Santa Anna urged his presidio commanders to treat the rebellious nations with "kindness and consideration." In reality, many commanders responded to Indian raids with force while civil authorities often attempted to tax or treat them like foreign nations. Others advocated a return to the Spanish policy of luring the Indians into peaceful relations through trade rather than forcing peace and conformity with a mailed fist. Indeed, as early as 1821, some government officials argued that "It is necessary to abandon all ideas of conquest," based on the premise that "commerce and friendship" always proved cheaper than war. But, neither government officials nor the Mexican people could reach agreement about crafting an Indian policy based on peace or war, although they did give more emphasis to the former than to the latter between 1821 and 1846, in part because Mexican settlers in Texas and New Mexico made money through the Indian trade. At the same time, American traders gave the Indians options and decreased their dependency on Mexico, which, in turn, forced the government to use military force in attempts to control or punish the tribes.[29]

In 1821, the government of the newly declared Republic of Mexico also attempted to deal with the Indians in Texas by establishing colonies of Americans to form a buffer between the new republic and the hostile tribes, such as the Comanches, Kiowas, and Wichitas, as well as the aggressive and ever-westering Americans, some of whom had already settled illegally near Nacogdoches and on the south bank of the Red River. As a result, in December 1821, Stephen F. Austin established a colony on lands granted to his father, Moses Austin, earlier that year. The Mexican government affirmed the transfer of the grant from father to son in April 1823, and by late summer he had settled some three hundred families between the Colorado and Lower Brazos Rivers. A decade later, nearly eight thousand Americans had settled in Austin's colony, which lay only about one hundred miles south of the Wichita bands known as the Wacos and Tawakonis, but it was far enough from the Comanche villages for relative safety from raiders. For these Wichita bands, Austin's colony offered an inviting target where they could take horses and livestock at their pleasure for sale to American traders north of the Red River. Unfortunately for the Wichitas and Comanches, who soon struck these settlers as well, the Americans had a far different view of property rights and punishment for transgressions than the Spanish or Mexicans. Where the Spanish had tolerated occasional thefts of horses and cattle and provided periodic gifts to the tribes to maintain peaceful relations, the Americans in Texas considered private property sacrosanct. Moreover, most of Austin's colonists came from the South where they had considerable experience driving Indians before them and taking their land, legally or illegally. In Texas, they had no intention of ignoring the theft of their livestock for the greater good of peace and security. They would protect their land, horses, and cattle by force, and they would give little thought to the consequences.

At first, Mexico and the Anglo-Americans attempted to negotiate peace treaties with the tribes on the eastern fringe of the southern plains. In 1823, several Comanche chiefs signed a treaty of peace and friendship with Mexican emissaries in which Mexico agreed to establish trading posts for the tribes in Texas. In turn, the Comanche leaders, for example, promised to control their young men, maintain a representative in San Antonio, and send a dozen young men every four years to boarding schools in Mexico. But, Mexico did not fulfill its promise to provide trading posts, and by 1825, the Comanches increased their raids in Texas. Still, until the early 1830s, Comanche chiefs, such as Little Bear, Isazona, and Yncoray, periodically returned horses that their people had taken from the Tawakoni, Mexican, and Anglo-Texan villages and settlements. By October 2, 1835, when Anglo-Texans and Mexicans fought the first battle of the Texas Revolution, Mexican-Comanche relations had deteriorated due to isolated skirmishes initiated by both sides.

In addition to the Wichitas and Comanches, the Texans confronted a rapidly increasing population of Indians who had emigrated from the east, usually pushed west by force following the War of 1812. By the early 1820s, hundreds of Choctaws, Kickapoos, Delawares, Shawnees, and Cherokees had established villages from the Red River above Nacogdoches, an area known as Lost Prairie, to the south and along the headwaters of the Sabine and Angelina Rivers. Austin worked to enlist the support of the immigrant Indians, who wanted land of their own guaranteed by the Mexican government, against the hostile Wichitas and Comanches to the north and west who considered the southern Great Plains their own by right of conquest and occupancy. By the spring of 1824, Austin also believed he had impressed the Indians in the vicinity of his colony with the willingness of the Americans to make war to protect their lives and property. Accordingly, he reported to the governor of Texas that "the Indians are now beginning to fear us."[30]

Austin's confidence in his militia and Indian auxiliaries to force the Wichitas and Comanches to respect Anglo-Texan property and keep the peace proved premature when bands from both tribes raided San Antonio and his colony at will during the summer of 1825. Neither Mexico nor Austin commanded sufficient military force to prevent these raids, which involved more loss of horses, mules, and cattle than lives. Consequently, in the spring of 1826 when Richard Fields, a mixed-blood Cherokee war chief, offered to help patrol the frontier, that is, the unsettled area between the Comanches and the Anglo-Texans, and to prevent the Wichitas and Caddos from attacking the peaceful Indian nations in order to gain the favor of Mexico for both land and trade, Austin saw an opportunity. He asked Fields to gather Delawares and Shawnees along with his Cherokees and join his militia for an attack on the Wichita villages located along the Colorado and Brazos Rivers. Austin told the Cherokees this raid would be "the means of securing you land in the country for as many of your Nation as wish to remove here." Although Austin's proposed alliance and attack did not materialize due to unfavorable weather, both the Texans and eastern Indians were prepared to join the other to ensure their own claims for Mexican lands against those of the western Indian nations.[31]

During the late 1820s, Wichita raiders struck Austin's colony, San Antonio, and La Bahía with impunity for horses and mules. Occasionally, they killed teamsters and settlers, and the Texans and Mexicans shot at them whenever possible. Early in 1829, a Waco raiding party also stole a large number of horses from a Cherokee village. The Cherokees retaliated by striking a Waco village in April and killed fifty-five of this Wichita band. By the summer of 1830, attacks by Mexicans, Anglo-Americans, and immigrant Indians had severely weakened the Wacos and Tawakonis, but Mexican troops could not catch and decisively defeat them. As a result, Antonio Elosúa, military commander of Texas, refused to accept any overtures for peace by the Wichitas. His chief commander, Colonel

José Francisco Ruíz, agreed, and believed that the Wichitas would accept peace only after the army made them "taste the bitter cup of war."[32]

Despite the intention of the Mexican government to force the Wichitas to accept peace and leave the new settlers and older residents alone, the Wichitas continued to raid at will. As a result, in July 1831, Ruíz offered to pay six pesos for each Tawakoni scalp as well as a reward for the return of branded livestock. Continued pressure by the Mexican army made their villages increasingly unsafe while an outbreak of smallpox in 1831 encouraged the Wichitas to retreat northwest toward the upper Red, Trinity, and Brazos Rivers, where they essentially had relocated by late 1835. Thereafter, they refocused their economy from stealing horses for trade to acquiring needed goods from the Pawnees to the north for buffalo hides. It was into one of these Wichita villages that Colonel Henry Dodge rode in the summer of 1834 to seek peace between the Wichitas and Comanches and the eastern tribes that the government intended to move into the area between the Red and Canadian Rivers during the removal process. Although the Wichitas, then, temporarily reached accommodation with the Mexicans and Anglo-Americans by the mid-1830s, relocated far beyond the settlements, and gave up raiding for horses, mules, and cattle, the Comanches continued to see the Mexican and Anglo-American settlements in Texas as bountiful opportunities for glory and wealth.

While the Wichitas raided settlements in Texas before withdrawing to the northwest beyond the reach of reprisal from both the Mexican army and Austin's militia, most Anglo and Mexican settlements lay east of a line running from San Antonio to the forks of the Trinity River near present-day Dallas. The greatest pressure from Anglo-Texans on Indian lands came along the Brazos, Colorado, and Guadalupe Rivers in the south-central region of the newly declared Republic of Texas, an area commonly claimed by the Comanche. Confrontations over land became inevitable. Texas declared independence from Mexico on March 2, 1836, and the situation worsened when the legislature approved, over President Sam Houston's veto, all "Indian lands" for white settlement. Soon surveyors, speculators, and farmers left the settled areas and moved into the open country that served as a buffer zone between the Comanche villages and buffalo range and the Anglo settlements to the east. Houston knew this legislative action would provoke war with the Comanches and that he did not have the power to force a peace. Consequently, he attempted to prevent inevitable confrontation by refusing to build forts and garrison Comanche territory to ensure the sovereignty of Texas. The Comanches did not oppose peace with the Texans, provided a firm and mutually recognizable boundary existed between them, a guarantee that only Houston was prepared to extend. Instead, companies of volunteers, whom the Texans called rangers, patrolled the western borderland between the Anglo settlements and the Comanche villages, with the intent of driving away any Indians encountered by force. Until the mid-1830s, however, the Comanches remained relatively peaceful.[33]

As early as January 1833, Houston met with several chiefs in San Antonio, where he found them "well disposed" to negotiating a treaty with the United States. Houston reported that these Comanches had "a high regard for the Americans while they cherish the most supreme contempt for the Mexicans." The meeting, however, did not result in a treaty with the Texans because neither party had the power to make one. Three years later, however, the peaceful relations between Texas and the Comanches deteriorated rapidly. In September 1836, David G. Burnet, president of the Republic of Texas, sent Alexander LeGrand to negotiate a peace treaty and thereby neutralize a potential enemy, while the Texans spent their efforts winning independence from Mexico. Somewhere in Comanche Territory, LeGrand met with a chief, possibly Esacony. The meeting did not go well. LeGrand reported that "so long as he saw the gradual approach of whites and their habitations to the hunting grounds of the Comanches, so long he would believe to be true what the Mexicans had told him, viz., that the ultimate intention of the white man was to deprive them of their country; and so long would he continue to be the enemy of whites."[34]

Houston, however, believed the Comanches could be enlisted as auxiliaries because the Spanish and Mexicans had long been their enemies. Accordingly, in December 1836, he sent a message to the Comanche chiefs saying, "Your enemies and ours are the same. I send you my friends to talk to you—to give presents and to make peace with you and your people. . . . You have many things to trade and swap with us. You need many things that we can let you have cheaper than you have ever been able to get from the Mexicans. You can let us have horses, mules and buffalo robes in change for our paints, tobacco, blankets and other things which will make you happy. . . . I wish to have a smooth path, that shall lead from your camp to my house, that we can meet each other and that it shall never become bloody." Unfortunately for both parties, nothing came from this effort.[35]

The Comanches rightfully felt threatened by the ever-advancing Texans, and they wanted a clear boundary line that neither people would cross. Since Texas did not recognize any Indian right to the soil and claimed the entire state, they would not accept the Comanches' claim to all lands west of a line running from the Gulf to the Red River through San Antonio. When General Albert Sidney

Johnston, commander for the Texas Army, and two other commissioners met with several chiefs in April 1838 at San Antonio to negotiate a peace treaty while carefully avoiding the question of a boundary line, one chief by the name of Esawacany favored peace, but not with the Mexicans. He also told Johnston that his offered trading posts scared away the buffalo and that the Comanches met their needs by trading with the Wichitas who lived north of the Red River and by raiding into Mexico. Johnston considered the meeting a success and told Esawacany that "if they were better acquainted with the white people, they might like them better," oblivious to the century-old contacts between the Spanish and Comanches. Then, he distributed presents and the council ended with the Comanches "well pleased."[36]

In May, the Comanches again met with Houston in the town that bore his name and again insisted on a boundary line between them. Although Houston would not agree to a line, he convinced these Comanches to accept the Treaty of Peace and Amity, which they signed on May 29, 1838. This treaty pledged mutual peace and friendship but obligated the Comanches to restore stolen property and punish offenders. In turn, Texas would send licensed traders among them so that they would not be "cheated by bad Men." This treaty, of course, did not bind other Comanches and the Texans quickly ignored their obligation to treat them fairly or peacefully. Mutual killing escalated and, by the end of 1838, the relations between the Texans and Comanches had deteriorated to a state of war rather than having built to a common peace.[37]

By late 1838, the Comanches raided Anglo settlements with such impunity that Indian policy became a major issue in the presidential election of Texas. Houston's policy of accommodation had proved so unsuccessful that Mirabeau Buonaparte Lamar, the tough-talking, Indian-hating hero of San Jacinto, easily won the election on September 3. Lamar advocated an Indian policy of war for extermination or removal from Texas. He also told the Texas Congress that Mexico had never ceded lands to the Indians nor granted them civil rights and the Indians occupied Texas lands "against the public wish, and at the sacrifice of the public tranquility." In addition, Lamar contended that Houston's policy of peace and accommodation had failed, and he advocated a policy for "the prosecution of an exterminating war on [Indian] warriors; which will admit no compromise and have no termination except in their tribal extinction or tribal expulsion." Lamar, however, did not advocate extermination as long as the Indians accepted peace, which meant refraining from attacking Anglo settlements for livestock and captives and agreeing to forfeit the lands desired by Texas and to live on only those lands given to them. If they did not, Lamar wanted to drive them from the republic.[38]

Lamar's Indian policy was based on steel and lead. It was clear and unequivocal. The Indians, particularly the Comanches, could have peace or war. If they chose the latter they would either cease to exist as a people or be driven from their homeland never to return. The Congress of Texas agreed and, in 1839, appropriated a million dollars to finance a war against the Indians, and some two thousand men volunteered for service. At the same time, Albert Sidney Johnston, already an experienced soldier and Lamar's secretary of war, recruited allies among the enemies of the Comanches, such as the Tonkawas and Lipan Apaches, for scouts and as auxiliaries to help find and destroy the Comanches. The Tonkawas and Lipan Apaches hated their ancestral enemies, the Comanches, more than they feared the Texans on whom they depended for both land and survival.

At the same time, Mexico changed its Indian policy from supporting Anglo settlements for the creation of a buffer between the plains tribes and its northern settlements to persuading the immigrant tribes, such as the Cherokees and Kickapoos, to form a shield along the Sabine River to protect what land it still claimed if not held, in Texas. This action gave the Texans the excuse to drive the Cherokees from rich lands on which they had squatted and which whites coveted. But, the Texans did not stop with their brutal attack on the poorly armed and largely accommodating Cherokee people. By late July 1839, an army of volunteers had burned the villages and destroyed the cornfields of all Cherokees, Shawnees, Delawares, Creeks, Caddos, and Seminoles in Texas. The Indians who escaped death fled northward beyond the Red River. When the summer ended, most of the Indians in the eastern half of Texas had been killed or forced to flee the republic, a policy that opened thousands of square miles for occupation by white settlers.

In the western half of Texas, however, the situation was far different. There, the Comanches organized and struck the outlying white settlements, and the Texas rangers could neither catch nor decisively defeat them. West of a line running north from San Antonio, then, the Comanches did as they pleased, until the rangers adopted the .44 caliber revolver early in 1840. This easily loaded weapon gave the rangers the firepower needed to make successful expeditions into Comanche country and forgo fighting from defensive positions, where they could reload their single shot weapons in relative safety, and instead take their attack directly into Comanche ranks. The Texas rangers now became deadly Indian hunters, and the Comanches began to seek peace.

By 1840, Mirabeau Lamar also was ready to negotiate a peace treaty with the

Comanches, many of whom favored accommodation. Lamar first sought the return of all white captives as an expression of good faith by the Comanches. General Johnston also told W. S. Fisher, his messenger to the Comanche bands, that they could have peace only by accepting the sovereignty of Texas to "dictate" where they could live, and "that their own happiness depends on their good or bad conduct towards our citizens: that their remaining within such limits as may be prescribed, and an entire abstinence from acts of hostility or annoyance to the inhabitants of the frontier, are the only conditions for the privilege of occupancy that the government believes it is at this time necessary to impose: that the observance of these conditions will secure to them the peace they profess to seek." The Comanches also had to understand that "our citizens have a right to occupy any vacant lands of the Government, and that they must not be interfered with by the Comanche. To prevent any further difficulty between our people and theirs, they must be made clearly to understand that they are prohibited from entering our settlements." Lamar, however, did not care whether the Comanches continued to raid south of the Rio Grand because Texas was still at war with Mexico.[39]

Crossing the cultural divide on a bridge built of mutual self-interest, however, proved impossible as long as neither party had been decisively defeated. The Texans, like their American counterparts east of the Mississippi River, did not consider the Comanches an autonomous, independent people, but rather interlopers who trespassed on Texas soil, where they were subject to the law of Texas, particularly concerning the theft or destruction of property or the seizing of hostages for adoption into the tribe. In contrast, the Comanches considered the Texans an enemy who took tribal lands and elevated the loss of a few horses for the purposes of gaining glory, status, and enhancing trade as meriting retaliation to the point of war to annihilation. The Comanches also contended that Lamar's conditions for peace were nothing less than a dictate, but they believed the Texans wanted peace so badly that they would pay a great deal for it and their white captives, whom they considered the spoils of war.

As a result, in January 1840 a group of Comanches rode into San Antonio under a white flag and told Colonel H. W. Karnes that they would exchange their white prisoners for peace. Karnes passed the information to Johnston, Lamar's secretary of war. Lamar responded by sending word to the southern Comanche bands or division, known as the Penatekas, that he was prepared to negotiate at San Antonio. Lamar wanted peace but on his own terms, which meant that the Comanches and other Indians would leave white settlers alone and defer lands to those settlers whenever the Texans demanded. Lamar also wanted the white prisoners at all costs. When twelve chiefs and "principle men," led by Muguara or Spirit Talker, and an entourage of more than fifty men, women, and children arrived on March 19, they were prepared to bargain for the release of their captives one by one and thereby receive a handsome return in the form of guns, ammunition, and trade goods. But, they walked into a trap because the Texans planned to hold them hostage until all captives had been returned. To do so, however, the Texans had to violate the rules of a truce for council purposes. When Colonel William G. Cooke, the senior officer, informed Muguara that they were "prisoners and would be kept as hostages for the safety of our people" until all of the white prisoners had been returned, pandemonium broke out in the room as the chiefs rushed for the door. One chief stabbed a soldier as he tried to escape, and the soldiers responded by firing a volley into the chiefs, an act that wounded whites as well as Indians. Other soldiers then began firing on the Comanches outside who tried to flee but were soon hunted down in the streets and either killed or captured; no one escaped. When the massacred ended, thirty-five Comanches, including the chiefs, women, and children, had been killed, and another twenty-seven, mostly women and children, seized as hostages. Seven whites had died and ten had been seriously wounded in what quickly became known as the Council House Fight.[40]

The commissioners released the wife of one of the dead chiefs the next day so that she could return to the villages with the news that the Comanche prisoners would be killed unless the white captives were set free. More important to the Comanches was the news that the Texans had violated a truce, an act inconceivable in Comanche culture. Many white captives were soon killed in retaliation. With these deaths, both Indian and white, peace between the Comanches and Texans passed from a dream to an impossibility. At the same time, culture prevented the Texans from killing their Comanche hostages if the white captives were not returned, and culture prevented the Comanches from returning all of their captives because no chief controlled all of the bands and some whites who had been captured as children were now more Comanche than Anglo and did not want to return to white society. Eventually, a few captives on both sides were exchanged and many Comanches were permitted to escape while others were given to residents in San Antonio for servants, but they, too, soon fled back to their people. By late summer 1840, the Comanches had retreated northwest to the high plains, far beyond the white settlements. The Texans hoped the Comanches had been intimidated to keep the peace, but the Penateka bands planned a deadly retaliation.

The Penatekas did so by meeting with other Comanche bands as well as the Cheyennes and Kiowas near Bent's Fort in April 1840. The Comanches, Kiowas, and Kiowa Apaches needed guns and ammunition, which they could not easily acquire in Texas or from the New Mexicans. Consequently, they made peace with the Cheyennes and Arapahos to protect their northern flank and to gain access to those supplies at Bent's Fort on the Arkansas. Yet the other Comanche bands, while sympathetic to the losses of the Penatekas, were unwilling to join them in a new war against the Texans. The northern bands of the Yampahreekuk and Kuhtsoo-ehkuh were more interested in peacemaking and trade with the Cheyennes and Arapahos. Other bands were scattered and remote, and they did not feel the need to retaliate for wrongs that had been done to others. Even so, a new leader of the Penatekas by the name of Potsanoquahip or Buffalo Hump emerged, and by late July 1840, had assembled a strong body of Comanches to strike the Texans. This force of more than four hundred well-mounted fighting men quietly passed San Antonio in the dead of night on August 4, headed for the towns, farms, and ranches lying between the Colorado and Guadalupe Rivers. Before their trail was discovered, the Comanches had attacked the village of Victoria, killed fifteen residents, set houses afire, driven off more than two thousand horses and mules, and swept toward the coast, burning more houses and barns, killing settlers, and driving off livestock. In doing so, the Comanches gained the satisfaction of levying retribution for the Council House massacre.

Yet, these Comanche warriors soon became too successful. Their horse and mule herds became unwieldy, and their loads of booty, ammunition, cloth, clothing, pots and pans, and iron barrel hoops for crafting into arrowheads became cumbersome after striking Linnville on the Gulf Coast. After ransacking the town and turning northwest for the safety of the high plains the Comanches moved too slowly. Instead of splitting into small bands and fleeing quickly and without rest until they reached the safety of the high plains, the Comanches became greedy and unwilling to leave their spoils behind. As a result, a large force of Texas rangers, volunteers, and soldiers under the command of Brigadier General Felix Huston caught up with them in an area of open country called Big Prairie near Plum Creek, which ran into the San Marcos River.

The Comanches were strung out and unprepared for the surprise attack from the Texans, who charged among them, scattering horses and mules and shooting them down. Less a battle than a rout, the fighting strung out for fifteen miles as the Comanches fled north and west, with vicious brutality on both sides as Comanches killed many of their captives and as the Texans shot women and children who could not run fast enough or who fell wounded. When the fighting ended, the Texans counted eighty dead Comanches to the loss of only one of their own. The Texans then divided the booty, horses, and mules that the Comanches had taken from other Texans and went home. Lamar, however, was not satisfied with this punishment, and he sent Colonel John H. Moore with ninety rangers and twelve Lipan Apache scouts into Comanche country in September to levy more retribution. When this punitive expedition returned to Austin in November, driving some five hundred horses along with it, Moore reported the killing of some 130 Comanche men, women, and children while losing only one Texan. All of the dead had been killed in a night attack on a Penateka village. Moore's men did not take prisoners of either sex or any age. The Texans believed only unmitigated violence such as this would ensure peace, either by destroying or forcing the "red niggers" to flee the republic.[41]

By the end of 1840, then, brute force had driven the Comanches from central Texas. The leadership of the Penatekas, the largest division of the nation, had essentially been destroyed at the Council House in San Antonio, while Buffalo Hump had led his people to disaster at Plum Creek and Moore had inflicted further devastation on the upper reaches of the Colorado River. Confronted with persistent, ruthless force, the Comanches moved north of the Red River during the autumn of 1840. In truth, the Comanches invited much of this misery on themselves. Although the Texans claimed Comanche territory, they had not yet moved onto Comanche lands. Rather, the Comanches struck the settlements far to the east of their villages for horses, mules, and other spoils just as they had struck Spanish and Mexican settlements for more than a century. But now, they confronted an enemy that had not only the will but the means, that is, deadly force to enforce their own cultural code concerning property rights and captives, and the Texans did not believe as the Spanish that slight transgressions could be overlooked to ensure peace, trade, and mutual prosperity. With the Comanches gone, the Texans quickly moved across the Sabine and onto the fringes of the southern Great Plains.

In September 1841, Houston returned to the presidency. He continued to advocate peace through trade with the Indians, and thereby to make the tribes dependent on the Texans. He sharply rejected Lamar's Indian policy, telling the Texas Congress, "The hope of obtaining peace by means of war has hitherto proven utterly fallacious." Houston wanted to bring the tribes together in a great council for the purpose of making a lasting peace. The Comanches refused to attend, and remained in a foul mood north of the Red River. They could neither understand how the Texans could claim land they did not occupy nor why Houston as their leader could not recognize a boundary between his people and the Comanches and keep the Texans from infringing on their territory. The Comanche leader, Mopechucope, later told Houston that central and western Texas was "Comanche Country and ever has been," ignoring, of course, that his people had taken it from the Apaches and Tonkawas not many years earlier, but reflecting the Comanches' own sense of manifest destiny.[42]

In 1843, Houston sent agents to a Comanche chief by the name of Pahayuko to urge him to meet with J. C. Eldredge, superintendent of Indian affairs, to talk peace. Eldredge made contact in July and told Pahayuko: "The chief Houston is not the same who was Chief in Texas when your people were slain," in reference to the Council House fight. He also told the Comanche, "Houston . . . has sent me with two others to you having in our hands this white flag, an emblem of peace . . . and these presents—they are not the offerings of fear but the gifts of friendship—as such you will receive them for no more will be given until a firm treaty of peace is made." Pahayuko professed his willingness for peace and pledged to meet Eldredge again in December when he would have the chiefs of the other bands with him. That meeting, however, never occurred, and Houston sent out messengers again in 1844 to urge the Comanches to come in for a council. This meeting took place in early October along Tehuacana Creek where Pahayuko pledged friendship and promised to stop raiding south of the Red River and agreed to return white captives. In turn, Houston agreed to give the Comanches gifts at annual meetings and to provide trading posts to meet their needs. The Comanches, however, still insisted on a line of separation, but Houston would not support a territorial demarcation, since Texas claimed all the lands held by the Comanches. Still, on October 9, Houston signed a treaty with the Comanches in which both sides agreed that "The tomahawk shall be buried." Houston promised that Texas would not permit "bad men" to enter Comanche hunting grounds. If the Comanches found such men, they were to take them to an agent without harm. The Comanches also promised not to make a treaty with any nation at war with Texas as well as pledged not to steal horses or other property. Licensed trading houses at Bird's Fort, near present-day Fort Worth, at Comanche Peak west of the Brazos in present-day Hood County, and at San Sabá would provide the Comanches with guns, powder, and lead. Blacksmiths, mechanics, and schoolteachers would be sent to teach them English and Christianity, along with farmers who would show them how to cultivate the soil and raise corn. The treaty also called for an annual council where the chiefs would receive gifts and other presents "as the President from time to time [should] deem proper."[43]

On January 24, 1845, when the Texas Senate ratified the treaty with the Comanches, it became one of the few agreements ever approved between Texas and the Indians, even though the Texas government could not prevent white settlers from moving onto Comanche lands and even though not all Comanche bands accepted the treaty. At the same time, the Comanches continued to raid across the Rio Grande for horses just as they had for generations to gain wealth and status, and levy vengeance, and they struck isolated settlements in Texas as they came and went, attacks that the Texans called "murder raids." Neither the Texans nor the Comanches were willing to restructure their worldview to alter the treatment of the other. War and violence and land, each perceived differently by both whites and Comanches, meant that culture continued to determine their relationship, just as it had elsewhere on the North American continent since the French and Indian War.[44]

In November 1845, Texas commissioners again met with twelve Comanche chiefs at Tehuacana Creek to reaffirm the peace, but they could do nothing about the persistence of the Comanches to steal horses from Anglo and Mexican communities, some located south of the Rio Grande. At Bent's Fort, the Comanches could sell or trade all the horses that they could supply, and whites who had lost horses to raiders often bought mounts from traders who dealt with the Comanches. Moreover, the Comanches depended on raiding to increase their horse herds rather than by breeding, that is, by natural increase. Furthermore, when white traders north of the Red River and Arkansas exchanged guns for horses they essentially sent an army against Mexico, a matter that Texas did not oppose. After the revolution, Mexico did not have sufficient funds to continue Spain's policy of relatively generous trade with the Comanches, who then took their buffalo robes and tongues, deerskins, horses, and mules north to traders, both white and Indian, across the Red River.

While the Texans sought peace with the Comanches, in September 1844, Charles H. Raymond, speaking for the Legation of Texas in Washington, D.C., informed Secretary of State Anson Jones that "there is reason to apprehend an attack upon our frontiers by any of the various tribes of Indians upon and adjacent to the boundary line of Texas and the United States through the instigation of emissaries of the Mexican Government." To deal with this problem, Raymond requested that "United States troops be stationed within our limits for the purpose of restraining these Indians." He did not need to mention that American troops would help Texas prevent an attack by the Mexican army and aid annexation.

When the U.S. Congress passed a bill admitting Texas to the Union, the federal government permitted the Lone Star State to retain its public lands, thereby precluding the extension of American Indian policy based on the creation of reserves and the cession treaty process. When President James K. Polk signed the final document admitting Texas to statehood on December 29, 1845, the Indian affairs of Texas passed to the federal government, but peace did not come with annexation for either Texas or the Comanches.[45]

By the beginning of the Mexican War in 1846, the Comanches were crossing the Red River with increasing frequency to trade at the government-sponsored posts as well as to follow the buffalo, often dangerously close to white settlements. As a result, horses and cattle disappeared, isolated settlers were killed and their buildings burned, in part because of Comanche culture but also because they proved unforgiving for the violence that the Texans had inflicted against them. No one, either Indian or white, could foresee that American Indian policy, extended to Texas, would keep the Comanches at war for another thirty years.

CHAPTER 9

The Far West

In the Far West, officials of the newly independent Mexico at first attempted to follow Spanish Indian policy reflected in Rubís's Report of 1768, the *Regulations of 1772,* and the *Instructions of 1786,* the latter of which particularly emphasized both military strength and friendship as the basis for an Indian policy built on the premise that a bad peace was better than a good war. Such policy, as in the past, would be administered with the flexible use of trade, gifts, and diplomacy rather than constant brute, military force to keep the peace. Accordingly, in 1821, a government report held that "It is necessary to abandon all ideas of conquest," because war proved unacceptably expensive compared to "commerce and friendship."[1]

Although the Mexican Constitution of 1824 did not specifically mention Indians, legislation soon recognized Indians as Mexicans with the same rights and responsibilities. Some efforts were made to abolish the use of the word "Indian" on private and public documents. The Chamber of Deputies, however, was divided over the matter of Indian equality. Liberals attempted to ignore them politically, while blaming the Spanish for causing problems of poverty among the Indians. They also believed that by abolishing racial class distinctions, the worst features of Spanish paternalism could be rectified. In contrast, the Conservatives and Catholic Church advocated a return to the colonial mission system, which sought a slow, but forced, acculturation and assimilation into Mexican society.[2]

As a result, confusion reigned, particularly in the northern regions of Mexico where settlers and soldiers wanted to use force to keep the Indians, especially the Comanches and Apaches, not only subdued but militarily impotent. Consequently, in 1835, the commanding general in Chihuahua asked the secretary of war about the manner in which he should treat the Indians under his jurisdiction who raided and otherwise made war against the republic. "Should they," he asked, "be considered as children of the great Mexican family, or as enemies to be driven beyond the boundaries of the state?" President Santa Anna responded by telling the general that the Indians were Mexicans by birth and residence and urged humane treatment and aid to help them learn to live peacefully under the rule

35. The Comanches proved the most formidable Indian people for the Spanish, Mexicans, and Anglo-Americans in present-day Texas and New Mexico. The Comanches developed a far-ranging trade network in which they exchanged horses, guns, and other goods among themselves and other nations, particularly to the north. They considered the Apaches their enemy and everyone who encountered them considered the Comanches skilled raiders. (From George Catlin, *North American Indians.*

of Mexican law. If that failed, however, Santa Anna would authorize the use of force to subdue them.[3]

In New Mexico, Arizona, and California, Mexican officials saw their Indian policy severely tested, particularly by the Comanches and Apaches in the Southwest, between independence in 1821 and war with the United States in 1846. Although Mexico technically attempted to deal with the Indians as subjects who had equal rights under the law, in reality it treated the Indians as enemies who only understood military force, primarily because tribes such as the Comanches and Apaches continued to raid deep into Mexican territory. The Comanches, however, riding south from the west Texas plains, left settlers, soldiers, and traders alone in New Mexico, possibly because little could be gained from them in contrast to the large horse herds that waited for the taking in the northern states of Coahuila, Nuevo León, Tamaulipas, Chihuahua, and Durango. By 1825, the Comanches used the eastern plains of New Mexico as a highway to strike Mexico, particularly Chihuahua. The Comanches, in the words of American trader Josiah Gregg, "cultivated peace" with the New Mexicans in order to maintain "amicable intercourse and traffic" to ensure that they would not interfere with their raids to the south. At the same time, the New Mexicans always seemed more fearful of the Cheyennes who struck settlements from the north rather than the Comanches who passed through on their way to Chihuahua, where they stole horses "in great masses."[4]

Conflicting needs and political jurisdictions made a mockery of Mexican Indian policy. In 1841, for example, General Mariano Arista in Chihuahua ordered Governor Manuel Armijo of New Mexico to join a campaign against the Comanches who raided his province at will. Armijo, however, refused, responding that "to declare war on the Comanches would bring complete ruin to the Department." New Mexico had relatively good relations with the Comanches, and a joint campaign would shatter the peace and bring retaliation and war. Moreover, Armijo had his scant military at war with the Navajos, and New Mexico could not fight two formidable enemies on separate fronts at the same time. Mexicans, however, did not particularly blame the New Mexicans for their problems with the Comanches, but rather the "ingrates from Texas" whom they believed encouraged the Comanches to raid below the Rio Grande. At best, New Mexico would warn officials in Chihuahua about impending Comanche attacks, but it would not attempt to prevent those raids to the south. By making no effort to halt Comanche raids to the south and by offering trade, New Mexico gained peace, but this Indian policy also earned the displeasure of government officials in Chihuahua who refused to send much aid when New Mexico needed help against the Apaches, Navajos, and Utes.[5]

Apache bands also raided southward from eastern Arizona, western New Mexico, and southwestern Texas. By the 1830s, the Apaches, whom one editor in Chihuahua called "venomous serpents," struck northern Mexico with such deadly consistency that one observer reported that they "would long before this have destroyed every sheep in the country, but that they prefer leaving a few behind for breeding purposes, in order that the Mexican shepherds may raise them new supplies." Indeed, raiding remained a way of life for the Apaches while the rewards in livestock proved essential to their economy and the scalps taken met cultural needs for bravery and status. As a result, in Arizona, Mexican settlers gave up and moved southward to safety. While Apache raiders drove settlers from their farms and ranches in Sonora, one settler reported that between 1821 and 1835, "over 5,000 citizens or friendly Indians . . . have been sacrificed to the ferocity of those barbarians."[6]

In early September 1835, Mexican officials in Sonora attempted to deal with the Apache raids from the north by enacting a bounty system for scalps. This legislation did not denote a new policy. Rather, it merely reflected a desperate return to Spanish policy that provided for the buying of Indian heads, scalps, and ears. This bounty law guaranteed one hundred pesos, or about $100 in current U.S. money, for the scalp of each Apache male, and it permitted bounty or Indian hunters to keep any booty or livestock that they took from their victims. On July 29, 1837, government officials in Chihuahua were so impressed by the results of this aspect of Sonora's Indian policy that they adopted a similar "plan of war."[7]

In Chihuahua, funds for the bounty came from subscription among the citizenry, and the payout brought $100 for the scalp of a male over fourteen years of age, while female scalps brought half as much. The scalps of children of either sex younger than fourteen years old brought the equivalent of $25 in pesos. With prices such as these and the Panic of 1837 creating severe financial distress in the United States, a few Americans saw opportunity in the Southwest where considerable money could be earned in this gruesome business. More important, Chihuahua's officials "wished to establish a permanent company for hunting Indians and making the activity lucrative in order that it may be effective." City councils inspected and verified the authenticity of the scalps and gave the bounty hunters warrants redeemable for cash at the state treasuries, but the national government never gave these bounty laws official sanction.[8]

James "Santiago" Kirker, a Scots-Irishman, best provided the services that Mexican officials in Sonora and Chihuahua wanted. In 1838, he began plying his trade as a scalp hunter. Kirker used the technique of ambush to surprise entire villages with help from his "volunteer corps" of twenty-three Delawares, Shawnees, and white American helpers, otherwise known as the Old Apache Company. Whether Kirker used cannon loaded with scrap iron, which made cutting, deadly shrapnel when fired at close range, as did James Johnson of Kentucky, remains unknown. But, Kirker achieved such great success that, in 1839, Governor José María de Irigoyen de la O of Chihuahua offered him a lucrative contract that would not only make Kirker wealthy but also, the governor hoped, solve the Indian problem in northern Mexico for all time. Governor Irigoyen persuaded a group known as the War Society, a patriotic organization of wealthy citizens, to provide $100,000 to pay for a major campaign against the Indians. The primary use of this money would be to buy Indian scalps. Irigoyen offered the job to Kirker, and he eagerly accepted it.[9]

Governor Irigoyen paid Kirker $5,000 in advance to begin the operation. Irigoyen authorized Kirker to hire two hundred men at the rate of $1 per day. This army of scalp hunters would also divide half of the horses, mules, and other spoils taken during the process. Kirker's group proved more effective and

36. James "Santiago" Kirker became the most infamous scalp hunter employed by the Mexicans to eliminate the Apaches or force them to make peace. Kirker often killed and scalped peaceful Indians as well as Mexicans because authorities could not determine whether a scalp came from an Apache. Indian hunters like Kirker were known to scalp their own men who had been killed while pursuing and fighting Apaches to increase their income. (Courtesy, Edward E. Ayer Collection, The Newberry Library, Chicago.)

efficient than the Old Apache Company, although it included many of the same men, in part because it was larger and composed of well-armed Indian hunters from the United States. On September 4, 1839, this group attacked an Apache party that had been raiding for horses near Taos and killed forty and "fleeced" them. The bounty program, however, brought recrimination from both civilian and military authorities alike, in part because it proved expensive. As a result, in December 1839, the government of Chihuahua changed Kirker's contract so that he would be paid a bounty for scalps rather than a flat fee for ridding the state of Apaches. Essentially, Chihuahuans wanted to pay Kirker for performance based on a piece rate that they considered the most cost-effective means of financing this war on the Apaches. When Kirker stopped his scalp-hunting raids in the spring, the Comanches and Apaches renewed their attacks on Chihuahua, and the government reinitiated the bounty system in late July 1840. This time the bounties would only be paid for the entire body of an Indian with the head and ears or a head with ears to ensure that the Indian hunters no longer killed and scalped innocent Mexicans.[10]

The scalp bounty system proved comparatively unproductive. Apache and Comanche raiders rode at will against Mexican ranches and settlements. As a result, early in 1841, Chihuahuan Governor Francisco García Conde, once again, sought

Kirker's aid. Kirker's new contract, paying an estimated $5 per scalp, also provided for the payment of $2.50 for all Indian horses and mules taken and let him keep one half of the booty. By the end of 1841, Kirker and his men reportedly had earned $37,000 for some fifteen thousand horses and mules that they drove into Chihuahua City. The number of scalps that Kirker took that year remains unknown, but one contemporary reported that he had been "very successful," although rumors circulated that he did not discriminate between Mexicans and peaceful or hostile Indians and collected "counterfeit scalps."[11]

Scalp hunters such as Kirker had no noticeable effect on Apache and Comanche raiders. Consequently, in 1843, Governor José Mariano Monterde of Chihuahua negotiated treaties with the Mimbreños, Chiricahuas, Gileños, and Mescaleros in which he promised trade goods if they would make war against the Comanches rather than the Mexicans, but these desperate efforts had little effect on Apache raiding. Even so, by July 1844, Kirker's continued success killing Apaches convinced Governor Miguel Zubirle of Durango to adopt a similar bounty system, which paid ten pesos for the head or scalp of an Indian. In 1845, Don Angel Trías, Chihuahua's new governor, renewed the scalp bounty system and contracted to pay Kirker $50 per scalp. Soon Kirker, with the aid of 150 men, brought in 182 scalps and collected $9,100. When the Mexican War began, Kirker still plied his trade and on July 7, 1846, scalped 149 Apaches near Galeana, and collected his bounty money in Chihuahua City. By the end of 1846, Kirker had taken 487 Apache scalps, but Apache attacks into present-day northern Mexico continued unabated, even though Kirker was only one of many scalp hunters, a business that included Comanches, Kickapoos, Delawares, and runaway slaves. Although the scalp-hunting Indian policy of the northern Mexican states provided lucrative monetary rewards, it proved a grisly, risky business with considerable occupational hazards. Moreover, the Mexican policy of buying scalps to force a peace merely escalated the already high level of violence in the Southwest, where, by the beginning of the Mexican War, it had become a feature of daily life.

The Indian policy of the Mexican states, however, must be kept in the proper context. The citizens of Chihuahua, for example, welcomed Kirker and praised his success. The killing of Apaches for money was not a moral issue to them but rather a matter of necessity for their own security. In May 1850, the congress of Chihuahua assessed its past policy of paying Kirker to kill Apaches, and the representatives concluded that it had been successful because it enabled the state "to make war upon the barbarous tribes by itself independently of the central government." Moreover, public opinion had "appeared pronouncedly in favor of the plan." Chihuahuans had not considered the scalp bounty policy "unconstitutional, barbarous ... inhumane ... indecorous" or "inefficient." And, Chihuahua's congress contended that the people believed Kirker and his "alien mercenaries . . . had borne their arms against the Indians without scandal or harm to the honor of the country." Kirker and his men, the government concluded, had been "well received generally and had produced good results." Even so, the scalp bounty policy did not end the attacks by the Apaches, and it proved that war alone would not force them to make peace.[12]

The Navajos also proved troublesome for New Mexico. Between 1818 and 1846, they devastated New Mexico's economy by running off livestock, taking grain, corn, and other crops, and seizing settlers for ransom, sale, or trade to other tribes. In 1836, Governor Albino Pérez blamed New Mexico's "critical circumstances" on "the ferocious war that the Navajos made upon it." During the governorship of Manuel Armijo from 1837 to 1843, New Mexico sent four expeditions against the Navajos, the most significant of which resulted in a treaty signed at Jemez on July 15, 1839, in which both parties agreed to restore peace and trade. The treaty also provided that "in order to carry out the good faith which animates the agreeing parties, the Navajo chieftains have agreed to surrender our captives, which are in their nation . . . and have agreed also [that] those of their own remain among us as a just reprisal, acquired through honorable war." The Navajos also agreed to abide by Mexican law in the case of murder, which meant hanging, while New Mexicans agreed to pay the family thirty sheep if they killed a Navajo. In addition, the treaty required the Navajo to report pending attacks by other tribes. By September, however, the treaty had unraveled and Armijo sent two expeditions that killed thirty-three Navajos and seized a considerable number of horses, sheep, and containers of grain. Another expedition resulted in a sharp fight near Canyon de Chelly on November 20, but the soldiers withdrew without a clear sense of victory. These expeditions, however, encouraged the Navajos to seek peace and end the attacks that the New Mexicans sent against them. As a result, on March 10, 1841, several thousand headmen and a hundred followers met with officials in Santo Domingo and signed a treaty with provisions similar to the treaty negotiated at Jemez, although it now required Mexico to pay five hundred sheep to the family of a Navajo murdered by a New Mexican, a clear indication that this problem persisted between these two civilizations. Thereafter, the Navajos and New Mexico enjoyed a guarded peace until the Navajos began raiding in 1844 in retaliation for the continuing New Mexican practice of capturing their children for slaves. By the time the Mexican War began, Governor Armijo believed that "the war with the Navajos is slowly consuming the Department, reducing to very obvious misery the District of the Southwest." There, New Mexico and Navajo relations remained when the war began, all to the advantage of American forces under Brigadier General Stephen Watts Kearny, soon to lead the Army of the West toward Santa Fe.[13]

In 1840, to make matters worse, a party of Utes sold some captive Arapaho slaves to New Mexicans. Several Arapaho chiefs appealed to Charles Bent to ask Governor Armijo to release them for the payment of one horse for each Arapaho. Armijo refused, despite Bent's warning that he invited war with the Arapahos and Cheyennes, whom he called "the most formidable warriors of the North." Armijo declined to return the captives because he believed such action would convince the Arapahos that the Mexicans feared them and any return would cause the Utes to attack New Mexicans for spite. In April 1841, Bent reported that a party of Arapahos arrived at Bent's Fort with "8 Spanish scalps," which apparently satisfied their need for retribution, but which also indicated Armijo's inability to protect his people.[14]

The Utes also periodically raided New Mexico from the north, and their enmity became total on September 5, 1844, after more than one hundred fighting men rode into Santa Fe and demanded reparations for the deaths of ten tribal members whom Mexican authorities accidentally killed while campaigning against the Navajos. The Utes demanded "two small children and two small boys," all captive Utes, as well as ten horses, bridles, and serapes, for which they would "forget all their sorrows and remain peaceful for ever." Governor Mariano Martínez did not understand the Ute cultural concept of reciprocity, that is, the payment of captives or gifts for the loss of a life rather than the extraction of a comparable number of lives to cover their dead. Martínez gave the Utes and their six chiefs food and tobacco, but they rejected these gifts and demanded their price. When Martínez ordered the chiefs out of his office to "calm themselves," he reported that the six chiefs "broke into the most intolerable, inhumane insults . . . and beat me on the chest for which reason I gave them a push toward the door." At this point a fight broke out between the chiefs, several of their followers, and the soldiers. The Indians fled, but troops and citizens fired on them and killed and wounded a number, whom they left in the streets for more than a week. In his self-serving report of the incident, Martínez wrote, "Under these circumstances, the guard of honor and various citizens, seeing the resistance and effrontery of the enemy and his hostile action, commenced a fight ending in eight deaths, in spite of everything I could do to stop this tragedy." Governor Martínez did not have enough soldiers, guns, funds, and supplies, however, to end Ute attacks, in part because revolutionary troubles in Mexico prevented such aid. Thereafter, the Utes levied full-scale war against the New Mexicans and drove many settlers from their homes in the northern part of the territory.[15]

Mexican officials attempted to lessen the threat of Indian attacks by prohibiting traders to exchange guns for Indian goods, and proclaiming that any American caught trading guns, powder, and lead, particularly to the Apaches, would be executed. No one paid any attention to this warning, and American traders conducted a thriving business, exchanging guns for horses at their posts north of the Arkansas River and along the front range of the Rocky Mountains, all within easy reach of the Indian nations in New Mexico. As a result, by the Mexican War one official reported that "the lot of the Indians around New Mexico has improved at the time that ours has worsened." Throughout the Mexican period from 1821 to 1846, then, relations between the government and the tribes to the north remained hostile. The Indians checked settlement, and in some areas, forced settlers to retreat. Yet, Mexico invited much ill will from the Indians. New Mexicans continually seized Indian men, women, and children for sale in Santa Fe, where after the appropriate breaking or training, they entered the households of the wealthy residents for domestic service. To the west, Mexicans continue to trade with the Pimas for Yuma and Apache captives whom they used for servants. At the same time, the rapid immigration of whites from the United States into northern Mexico changed trading relationships and upset the balance of power between the tribes and the settlers, while Mexico failed to maintain alliances with the tribes or to provide a military force capable of handling Indians attacks on its property and people. Without question so far as Mexico was concerned, the Indians, particularly the Comanches and Apaches, determined relations with the settlers in New Mexico, Arizona, and the states south of the Rio Grande and, by so doing, forced Mexico to craft a reactionary and an ineffective Indian policy.[16]

Santa Anna's threat ultimately to use force proved hollow. The presidios that Spain had used to keep the peace by making them trade centers and places of communication as well as forts that established a military presence among potential enemies, fell into disarray, primarily because the government could not afford to garrison them correctly. In 1826, reorganization of the army command system placed the commanding officers away from the posts, and no commanding officer was ever stationed on present-day U.S. soil. As a result, for some time the ranking officer at Santa Fe could not pursue or attack Indian raiders until he received permission from the commanding general in Chihuahua who was responsible for that military district. Mexico also failed to provide sufficient funds to recruit, train, and station soldiers at the presidios. On paper, for example, Tubac had been designated a garrison of eighty-eight men but less than a dozen soldiers occupied the post, which soon fell into disrepair. Similarly, in New Mexico, which was authorized to have three presidial companies with ninety soldiers each, had only one garrison as late as 1836. When the Mexican War began, Governor Martínez believed that peace would come to New Mexico only when the Indians lost interest in raiding, because his paper army and militia could not force an end to hostilities. Indeed, with only 107 soldiers garrisoned at the main presidio of Santa Fe and only 34 militiamen under arms, they could do little to regulate the behavior, either trade or military, of an estimated 6,000 Apaches, 12,000 Comanches, 7,000 Navajos, and 4,500 Utes, among others, or nearly 30,000 hostile Indians in all. When the soldiers were assigned to Santa Fe, Taos, and other posts in New Mexico, they were spread so thin as to be nearly worthless.

Mexico also could not recruit a sufficient number of soldiers to provide for the defense of the frontier, and few soldiers received adequate pay, food, clothing, and equipment, making them soldiers in name only and preventing them from doing their jobs with high morale and effectiveness. The soldiers' task was difficult under peaceful conditions, but when confronted with the hostile Comanches and Apaches, it proved impossible. Between October 1827 and April 1828, Indians, for example, had stolen some three hundred horses from the presidio at Santa Fe, during frequent raids that the soldiers could not prevent. Moreover, without mounts, the presidial soldiers could not launch offensive campaigns or even pursue the Indians when raids occurred, particularly since the Comanches and Apaches rode better horses.

By the eve of the Mexican War, then, the Comanches, Apaches, Navajos, and Utes essentially controlled Mexico's frontier in New Mexico and Arizona. Diplomacy, trade, gifts, and strong presidios no longer served as essential principles of Indian policy, because the government had not committed the resources to make them work. Although Mexican Indian policy, particularly in New Mexico, during the governorship of Armijo attempted to follow Spanish policy, Indian relations on the borderlands were far more difficult and hostile than during the days of Galvéz. Armijo and other leaders never had adequate financial or military support to use the carrot-and-stick approach to gain peaceful relations with the Indians. With access to guns and ammunition from American

traders to the north and with no economic reasons to keep the peace with
Mexico, the Comanches, Apaches, Navajos, and Utes among other Indian nations
in the present-day Southwest made raiding and war a profitable way of life,
particularly because Mexico did not have the ability to retaliate, let alone force
the hostile bands to keep the peace.

After the rebellion in 1844 that ended Santa Anna's dictatorship, the appointment
of new governors followed, and, on February 14, 1845, Alejo García Conde,
Secretary of War, proposed a new defensive system for northern Mexico. Conde
recommended an outer defense in the form of a line of posts extending from
Matamoros on the Rio Grande to El Paso to the Pacific Ocean. These posts would
be fashioned much like Roman military colonies, with both soldiers and
families. Behind this line, Conde proposed an inner defense system, which
involved a similar line of posts across Chihuahua, Durango, and Coahuila. The
Mexican Congress did not approve this plan to establish military colonies on
the northern frontier until December 4, and war with the United States in the spring
delayed commitment to Conde's plan until 1849. Moreover, in September 1845,
when Mexicans learned about the plans of the United States to admit Texas to
the Union, both Comanches and Apaches also heard the news and increased
their raids to take advantage of Mexico's even weaker position. By November, the
citizens of Chihuahua, Coahuila, Durango, and Zacatecas were more concerned
about the Comanche raiders, who had taken most of their horses and mules so
that few were left to pull artillery and supply trains, than an invasion by the
army of the United States. And, in late November, General Francisco García
Conde took four hundred troops who were watching for the Americans at the
Rio Grande to search for Apaches who raided to the west. When the United
States declared war on Mexico on May 13, 1846, Comanches and Apaches raided
at will in northern Mexico. One commander complained that "public security
has disappeared," while another observer wrote to the commanding general in
Chihuahua that "an absolute lack of disposable force, no less than of usable
arms, munitions of war, and other necessary resources is the reason that those
Indian evils are not checked."[17]

By 1846, then, many Mexican officials, civil and military, treated the Indians
as hostile nations that required the use of force to make them abide by Mexican
wishes for them to acculturate and assimilate into society. But this policy failed.
By the Mexican War, the Apache sweep southward had become so common and
dangerous that one member of the Chihuahua legislature reported that "we travel
along the roads . . . at their whim; we cultivate the land where they wish and in

the amount that they wish; we use sparingly things they have left to us until the moment that it strikes their appetite to take them for themselves." By 1846, Mexico served as a well-stocked larder where goods, in the form of livestock, could be taken for trade to the Americans who came among them or lured them to their posts on the fringe of Mexican territory. Relations between New Mexico and the Utes remained hostile, and Governor Martínez held the opinion that the Indians had "neither honor, decency, nor conscience, and only consider . . . superior those who are the bravest and the most skillful to kill—their enemies as well as others." During the course of the war, the American army provided more protection against Apache and Comanche raids for horses and captives than Mexican officials who attempted to provide security with a ragtag military and a bounty-hunting system. Moreover, Mexico, like the United States, occasionally signed peace treaties with the Indians, and, by so doing, recognized them not as Mexican citizens equal under the law but rather as independent nations.[18]

In California, the Indian nations did not pose a major threat to Mexican settlement. Compared to the raiding by the Comanches and Apaches from New Mexico and Arizona into northern Mexico, the California Indians remained relatively peaceful. The problems that Mexican officials confronted primarily concerned the relationships between the missions and the Indians regarding both past and current policies intended to achieve acculturation and assimilation. At the heart of the problem lay the threat of Russian and American encroachments, which, in turn, stimulated government authorities to press for rapid settlement to give Mexico a better claim to Upper California. Government officials also considered the mission Indians more an underclass than citizens, and they did not agree with the Franciscan fathers that the Indians would return to their former way of life or be enslaved by white Mexicans if they were released from the missions and permitted to do as they pleased.

After gaining independence, liberal Mexican officials wanted to release the Indians from the control of the missions, give them land, and train them to support themselves, and, by so doing, contribute to a strong economy, acculturation, and assimilation. This sense of Indian policy emerged from the egalitarian and humanitarian spirit that developed among officials as a result of the revolution. On another level, this policy reflected the new liberalism that emerged in the late eighteenth century in Europe and the United States, which valued individual rights and rewards to individuals for their labor, in contrast to missions, which were considered communal societies.

At the same time, many Californians wanted access to mission lands and Indian labor. Moreover, for a decade after the revolution, Mexico could not send adequate financial support to the missions, which were controlled by Spanish priests and who naturally had little sympathy for the new regime. In order to meet their needs, military and civilian authorities levied the missions for food and labor, which the Indians supplied.

At the same time, the Indians who lived under the control of the missions remained plagued with sickness and disease. In 1826, Captain F. W. Beechey, a British naval officer, reported, "Sickness in general prevails to an incredible extent in all the missions, and . . . the proportion of deaths appears to be increasing." A decade later Alexander Forbes, a Scots merchant, wrote that many mission Indians died from "fevers, dysenteries, and other acute diseases." He also observed that "Syphilis prevails to a frightful extent, being almost universal not only among the Indians but the Creoles and the Spaniards: it produces frightful ravages among the [Indians] and they refuse all treatment of it even when this is accessible to them, which is not always the case." Forbes contended that "These circumstances, with the natural tendency which all the Indian race have to diminish in numbers in a state of civilization, much more in a state of bondage, make the loss of life very great in the missions."[19]

Despite diseases that weakened and killed the mission Indians, the friars expected their charges to work. During the revolution, Spain could not support the missions with men, supplies, and money for both protection and sustenance, and the friars kept the missions economically viable and the presidios fed by selling hides and tallow to American and English shippers and raising grain crops, all with the use of Indian labor for herding, butchering, tanning, planting, and harvesting. Although their labor—tilling fields, harvesting crops, and tending livestock—was not terribly strenuous or difficult, it remained forced, that is, unfree labor. The priests believed they needed to maintain that system or the missions would not be self-supporting or the presidios maintained. In 1826, Father Francisco González de Ibarra observed, "It seems to me that no other person in the nation has shouldered so much of the burden of supporting the government as the Indians have done in supporting this province, . . . and if a person spends all his time working for the common good and if everybody lives on his work and one asks how he should be rewarded for this [the answer would be] in a way beyond calculation. But this is the situation the Indian is in, for he has ceased to eat and clothe himself so that the province might subsist, and it could not continue in any other way." At that same time, another priest asked, "Where would California be without the Indians? Nothing, absolutely nothing."[20]

Although the Franciscans recognized the dependence of the missions, the military, and even the colonists on Indian labor, they did not favor freeing their charges because the Indians were now too far removed from their own cultural past. The missions had become their homes, not tribal villages. If the Indians were freed, that is, allowed to come and go and do as they pleased, the Franciscan argued, they would become idle, lazy like the white Mexicans, or, in time, revert to their old ways. In 1824, Luis Argüello, acting governor of California, disagreed, saying the Indians were being kept in a "state akin to that of slavery." The priests, however, argued that they needed the Indians to work at the missions because the military placed such demand on them for food and labor. Moreover, the Franciscans believed the Indians would remain perpetual children and unable to advance economically or socially beyond their status at the missions. One priest expressed this sentiment when he reported, "No matter how old they are, California Indians are always children." As late as 1830, another priest reported that the mission Indians "are almost without exception and during their whole life like school children, who if left to themselves will quite certainly not profit thereby." Given the fact that the Indians in central Mexico had not been acculturated and assimilated into society after nearly three hundred years of occupation, colonization, and state making, few priests believed that after little more than fifty years since the founding of the first settlement of San Diego that the California Indians could be acculturated and assimilated and freed from mission control. This general belief by the clergy that the Indians were incapable of adopting Spanish or Mexican cultural practices and thereby becoming civilized reflected paternalism at best and racism at worst.[21]

This paternalistic and racist policy for dealing with the Indians could have remained unchanged except that Mexico needed California to be settled and developed economically to foil any grab for territory by the Russians and Americans. In order to encourage great numbers of Mexicans to settle in California, extensive lands had to be available, and the best lands for such settlement purposes were controlled by the missions. Indian policy needed redirection. As a result, on July 17, 1824, the Mexican government created the Commission on the Development of the Californias and charged it to "consider and suggest to the Supreme Government the most necessary measures for promoting the progress of culture and civilization of the territories of Upper and Lower California." This commission met until June 1837 and issued a number of reports that formed the basis for a new Indian policy. The commission particularly disagreed with the assessment of the California Indians by the mission priests, saying, "[I]t must be very difficult for those whose minds are entirely preoccupied with European civilization to form any impartial idea of the character and so-called government of a people who have no knowledge of the division and ownership of land." The commission also contended that the Indians would be more valuable to the new nation if they were not forced to live the spartan life of the priests and compelled to work. Rather, if freed they could be "attracted to social and civil life more efficiently by means of trade and friendly relations." The commission believed that the mission system, with its forced labor and monastic lifestyle imposed on the Indians, was not only inefficient but also anti-republican, because the missions still used the military to capture runaway Indians to ensure their salvation and to keep them at the missions.[22]

When Governor José María Echeandía arrived in Upper California in October 1825, he carried orders to secularize the missions, that is, place the priests under the control of the state and to grant qualified Indians their own lands. Accordingly, in July 1826, Echeandía permitted mission Indians who had been Christians for a minimum of fifteen years and who were married or adults to leave the missions if they could demonstrate that they could support themselves. The priests and other conservatives opposed this policy and expected this plan to fail. Soon they were reporting evidence of Echeandía's folly. One observer noted that the Indians did not know how to use their freedom properly, and who now "finding themselves their own masters, indulged freely in all those excesses which it had been the endeavor of their tutors to repress, and that many, having gambled away their clothes, implements, and even their land, were compelled to beg or to plunder in order to support life." Moreover, "[t]hey at length became so obnoxious to the peaceable inhabitants, that the padres were requested to take some of them back to the missions, while others who had been guilty of misdemeanors were loaded with shackles and put to hard work." Some of these Indians were "employed transporting enormous stones to the beach to improve the landing place." In 1830, Father Narciso Durán agreed and reported, "It is in evidence that these emancipated neophytes pass the greater part of their life in indolence and drunkenness." Continued revolutionary troubles in Mexico, however, prevented further development of the new Indian policy or the settlement of white Mexicans in Upper California. When José Figueroa became governor of Upper California in 1833, approximately 17,000 Indians lived under the control of the missions while some 81,000 resided beyond the reach of the fathers and the military. Only approximately 6,000 whites lived in Upper California, and they had done little to expand the economy.[23]

Father Durán, who supervised the priests at the missions, reported that Indian policy failed under Echeandía because white settlers duped the freed Indians into servitude. "All in reality are slaves or servants of white men who know well the manner of securing their services by binding them a whole year for an advanced trifle," he wrote. The new government in Mexico under President Santa Anna did not care whether whites abused the Indians or that the Indians exchanged one kind of servitude for another. Rather, Santa Anna wanted California settled by as many people as possible to give Mexico greater territorial claim to the region. Accordingly, on August 17, 1833, the Chamber of Deputies passed a law that provided for the immediate secularization of the missions, that is, transferring control of the mission lands and livestock from the friars to civil authorities and the colonization of California by the allotment of mission lands to the Indians and settlers.[24]

Governor Figueroa did not believe that freeing the Indians from the missions met their best interests. He asked how could "the Indian, still ignorant, poor, and half wild be absolutely and identically equal in the exercise of political rights with other citizens[?]. . . . According to these principles we should strike out from our laws that regulate the powers of parents over children or that provide for the dominance of husband over wife in marriage or those that discuss guardianship and tutelage of minors, fools, the insane, wastrels and several others. Carried to such an extreme, legal equality would unhinge society." But, he followed his orders and issued instructions for the "emancipation" of the mission Indians. Those Indians who had been Christians for twelve years and who were married, who knew how to till the soil or practice a trade, and who had an "application to work" could receive their freedom. The governor would determine the emancipation rate for each mission and give the Indians property carved from mission lands. Indians who did not ply a trade or become successful farmers faced a return to the missions.[25]

No substantive action occurred, however, until the spring of 1834 when California's new governor, José María Híjar, arrived with the authority to take control of all mission property, develop it into towns, and distribute the land among the neophytes, that is, the baptized Indians. Heads of households and males over the age of twenty-one would receive thirty-three acres. Half of the livestock, tools, and seeds also would be apportioned, but all surplus land and livestock would be the responsibility of a newly appointed administrator of the missions. The government, however, retained the right to force the Indians to work on undistributed fields and vineyards, and they could not sell their allotted lands. Many mission Indians now took advantage of their freedom and left the missions or refused to work their lands, and thereby invited mistreatment by the new civil authorities at the missions.

While officials in Mexico City wanted immediate reform that involved the emancipation of the Indians from the missions to make Upper California self-sufficient so that it would no longer drain resources from the national government as well as foil potential Russian and American incursions, others charged with implementing such policies disagreed with the very premises on which they were based. Ultimately, since government officials and church leaders alike in California did not know how to make the mission Indians into landowning farmers and equal participants in Upper California's Mexican society, they chose to reject these concepts and worked against their implementation. For their part, after secularization had been completed in 1836, many Indians left the missions and took jobs on nearby ranches and farms where their lives remained little changed from the their lives in the missions. Others stayed on mission lands until they were divided and granted to Mexican immigrants and California residents, many of whom were politically influential. Most mission Indians soon lost the land allotted to them because of indebtedness and creditors who took their lands in payment for bills. In 1842, one mission Indian told a visitor that "the Fathers cannot protect us, and those in power rob us." He asked, "Would we be blamed if we defend ourselves, and returned to our tribes in the Tulares, taking with us all the livestock that could be led away?"[26]

The increased reliance of the military on the missions for food and laborers while the Mexicans worked to decrease the power of the priests gave the mission Indians the opportunity to shape daily affairs. In 1824, Indian leaders at Santa Barbara, Santa Inés, and La Purísima led uprisings. In 1827 at Mission San José, alcaldes convinced four hundred Indians to flee. Although the soldiers suppressed these rebellions and punished the leaders, these insurgencies indicated the increasing power of Indian leaders at the missions while the authority of the priests waned because they could not prevent such rebellions. As the Indian population at the missions changed due to death, disease, disaffection, and flight, new leaders emerged through the election process that the Franciscans often could not control. Indian politics at the missions now became a matter linked to, but also separate from the Mexican system of governance, and gave legitimacy to the exercise of increased Indian authority. After secularization of the missions,

Indian officials continued to lead the nearby communities that survived the collapse of the mission system.

Although the Indian nations in California did not pose the threat to Mexican farms, ranches, and communities that the Comanches, Apaches, Navajos, and Utes in New Mexico and Arizona did, many tribes raided with increasing boldness for horses to trade to Americans farther east. During the 1830s, nonmission Indians swept down from the Sierra Mountains and from the Central Valley to raid coastal settlements. By the mid-1830s, Indians who had fled the missions often joined with the so-called wild or free Indians in the interior to steal horses and cattle from the missions and ranches for food and sale. In 1836, one observer noted, "They plunder farms of the colonists for horses, which they eat in preference to beef, though horned cattle are more abundant." By 1842, Indian raids had intensified to such an extent that another contemporary reported that they had become "a symptomatic course of savage depredation." He also noted that with the constant "pilferings" of cattle and horses, "the two races live in a state of warfare, that knows no truce. The Indian makes a regular business of stealing horses, that he may ride the tame ones and eat such as are wild."[27]

Although the governor and others advocated building more forts in the interior as another line of defense for the coastal missions and ranches, revolutionary problems in Mexico and Texas prevented the commitment of men and resources to suppress Indian raiding and, in fact, made it easier because the Indians took advantage of Mexico's weak military position in California. As a result, the raiding increased and, in 1846, one observer reported, "Some few farms are being vacated by the Californians from fear of further depredations of the wild Indians, who yearly steal thousands of horses even out of the enclosed yards near their dwelling houses." The theft of livestock occurred weekly and little could be done about it. Although these Indian raiders killed few settlers, they forced the abandonment of many ranches and the population of San Diego dropped precipitously from 520 in 1830 to approximately 150 a decade later as residents left in fear for their property and lives. In California, Mexican officials also reported that the Navajos stole cattle near Los Angeles in 1840. At the same time, the Utes exercised a disciplined aggressiveness to raid ranches for horses but not to the extent that they ruined their source of supply. One Ute leader by the name of Walkara led a raiding party that stole 1,200 horses and mules from Mission San Luis Obispo in 1840. By 1846, a contemporary reported, "[T]he Indians are losing all fear of the inhabitants and with their arrows have shot several of them during the years 1845 and 1846." Little more than a month after the beginning of the Mexican War, another contemporary wrote from San Francisco: "The Indians are inveterate horse thieves, and during six days in May, while I was making an excursion of three hundred miles on horseback, they stole over *four thousand horses* from the farms I visited, or the immediate neighborhood." The Californians responded by organizing pursuit parties and indiscriminately killing nearby villagers. One contemporary succinctly noted the relationship between the Indians and the Californians, saying, "[T]he Indian makes a regular business of stealing horses. . . . In his turn, the Californian treats the savage, whenever he finds him very much like a wild beast of prey, shooting him down, even in the absence of specific charge, as a common pest and a public enemy." The military usually waited until the raids caused such a public demand for retaliation that an expedition had to be sent to the interior to punish any Indians that the soldiers could find.[28]

The raids in California differed from those in the Southwest because the Indians only sought horses. Although they occasionally killed whites, that was not their goal. Rather, horse stealing had an economic value because the Spanish had introduced a new element in the food supply and enabled them to extend their traditional cultural practice of hunting. In this sense, then, the horse brought change but only within the existing cultural system. When bloodshed occurred, it was usually inflicted by the Californians on the Indians. Most of the Indian attacks came from the San Joaquín Valley, where the Church had been unable to establish missions among the Yokuts and Miwoks, the latter under the leadership of Estanislao. One new American immigrant reported, "They are known as the Horse Thief Indians, and live chiefly on horseflesh; they have been raiding the ranches even to the very coast, driving away horses by the hundreds into the mountains to eat."[29]

The Mexicans could blame themselves for the Indian attacks that became more common after independence. Until the secularization of the missions in the 1830s, the Mexicans, for example, continued the Spanish policy of sending military expeditions into the interior to capture and return runaway Indians to the missions for religious training as well as punishment. After control of the missions passed from the Church to the state, settlers increasingly moved inland from the coast and seized Indian lands. Similarly, during the 1830s, American traders traveled throughout California looking for horses and mules, and they did not care whether they got them from Mexicans or Indians or where the latter got their livestock. As a result, in 1831, Governor Manuel Victoria observed, "[T]he interior valleys are being overrun by foreigners, who come in great numbers to corrupt the gentiles, and to steal." José de Figueroa, who followed Victoria as governor, prohibited trade with the "heathen Indians," and sent presidio soldiers to patrol for illegal traders and hostile Indians. Although the raids diminished, the demand for horses and mules for sale to American traders operating either illegally in California or at posts farther east, such as Bent's Fort, proved too lucrative to ignore, and after Figueroa's death in 1837, the patrolling ceased and raiding resumed. Moreover, the Indians of the interior increasingly adopted Mexican culture, particularly the use of horses, and became effective mounted fighters who also appropriated horses for their own status and personal gain. Government officials could only respond with occasional retaliatory raids and talk about building more defensive positions rather than launch deep offensive moves into the interior. After 1846, the Americans would solve the Indian problem in California by essentially eliminating them.[30]

Epilogue

Although reciprocity and respect sometimes characterized Indian and white relations on the frontiers of the North American continent during the late eighteenth and early nineteenth centuries, in general the Europeans and Anglo-Americans either treated the Indians as enemies or developed paternalistic polices that relegated them to the status of inferior civilizations. The Europeans and Americans claimed sovereignty over the land and worked to dispossess the Indians by concentrating them in controlled areas, much like reservations, near the presidios and missions by the Spanish, or removing them to a vast, isolated area west of the Mississippi River in the case of the Americans. Spanish, British, Mexicans, and Americans all treated the Indians as foreign nations by negotiating treaties. The Americans particularly treated the Indians as inferiors and commonly referred to them as children and the president as their Great Father, who as any father would take care of his children. Both Spanish and American policymakers used religion as a method to break down Indian cultural values and help achieve acculturation and assimilation. The American constitutional requirements for the separation of church and state, however, prevented replication of the Spanish presidio-mission system for destroying Indian culture. In contrast to the Spanish, however, American culture really did not welcome assimilation and acculturation, nor could the Americans use the Indians as slaves or as near serfs as did the Spanish. Although federal policymakers talked about the importance of each and devised policy to achieve it, the Americans did not want and would not accept the mass acculturation and assimilation of the Indians, because of racial and cultural prejudices. Ultimately, as the Cherokees discovered, the most acculturated and assimilated Indians really had no place, and, indeed, were unwanted in white American society, and they were pushed away. Moreover, for the Indians in general, the United States did not have a recognizable underclass where they could be relegated. The Indians simply did not fit anywhere in the American class structure, and rather than deal with the problem, the Americans chose to remove it.

Although the European nations and Americans officially determined Indian policy, on the local level Spanish governors and military commanders often devised

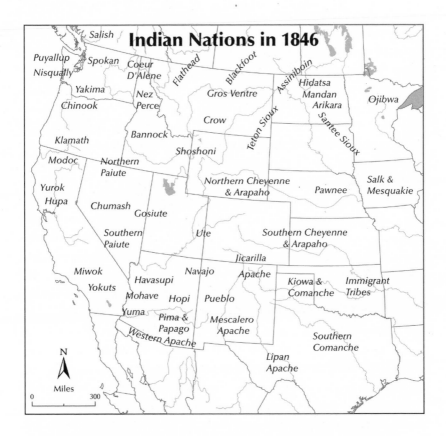

Indian Nations in 1846

their own relationships with nearby Indian nations. Similarly, the states, particularly
the southern states, illegally shaped American Indian policy, if only by causing
the federal government to react to state-initiated directives. Both Europeans and
Americans tried to give system and order to their dealings with the Indians by
intervening in tribal politics and often designating chiefs who would speak for all,
or at least many of their people. For the Americans, the Indians simply practiced
too much democracy, and, in the case of the Comanches, seemed entirely anarchistic.
The Europeans and Americans also used gifts and bribes to achieve their goals.
This latter flagrant violation of Indian culture proved divisive, problematic, and
ultimately successful. Indian cultures used gift giving to create and strengthen
friendships, but the British, French, Spanish, and Americans who also employed
that technique, used gifts in expectation of reciprocity that involved more than
the maintenance of friendly relations. Gifts meant obligations imposed on those
who received them. For the Europeans and Americans, gift giving was not done
for reasons of status and hospitality.

Moreover, while the British had introduced the treaty-making process, the Americans developed the cession treaty councils into a fine art. These councils had their required ceremonies and usually ended with scripted conclusions—lands forfeited, annuities promised, and guarantees made. For the Americans, however, the law proved malleable. Guaranteed and protected lands with precise boundaries, drawn by the Americans, incessantly melted away because the government could not control its people who saw Indian lands there for the taking. Yet many of the Indian nations also seized lands from other tribes, although none held their territory from time immemorial. Rather, they did so because of force, and kept it by power. The white Americans, however, grew far more rapidly in population, demanded Indian lands in great quantity, and moved into the frontier areas more quickly than policymakers predicted. They did not halt at the Appalachians, and they did not stop at the Mississippi River, nor pause for long when they reached the Great Plains. Moreover, American treaty negotiators seldom gave much attention to Indian wishes, and they operated from the premise that the question was not whether the Indians would be removed, but how and when they would be moved and confined to their own reserves.

At the same time, neither whites nor Indians ever exercised complete control of their own people. The federal government could not keep whites off Indian lands, and the chiefs could not prevent their young men from making war despite a tribal consensus against it. Thus, neither the Indians nor whites could guarantee treaties. Moreover, both Indians and whites usually remained unwilling to compromise until they had no alternative. In addition, neither Indians nor whites had a monopoly on morality and virtue. Each people had their own cultural standards, and each levied incredible violence and brutality on the other without shame or mercy. Yet, each group had its advocates for peace. Still, while the Europeans and Americans often talked in terms of protection and action in the best interests of the Indians, the Indians sought neither until they had lost the ability to take care of themselves or the hope of ever doing so again. Invariably, the Americans asked the tribes to give up their cultural life, such as raiding and stealing horses, while offering only an alien lifestyle in return, the Indian nations of the southern United States being the exception because they already lived like most white farmers. In their case, they were offered the opportunity to continue their lifestyle and improve on it far removed from the corrupting influences of white civilization.

By 1846, the great American sweep across half the continent marked the near completion of the expansion of Europe in terms of population, economics, politics, and technology—in a word, power—that began in the late fifteenth century. It would continue with the mass migration to the Far West after the acquisition of the Oregon Territory in June 1846 and the discovery of gold in California two years later. Even so, by 1846, the Comanches, Cheyennes, and Sioux still controlled the Great Plains, while the Apaches in the Southwest remained an undefeated people. The acquisition, that is, closure of those Indian frontiers would not be an easily achieved certainty. By the late 1840s, many civilians who influenced or made Indian policy also had begun to divide among themselves because some increasingly distrusted the military as the best agent for enforcing their directives. At the same time, disease, not the army, in the form of cholera, measles, and smallpox, remained the greatest danger to the Indians on the frontier.

Difficult days lay ahead. Cultural contacts that had involved negotiations, both formal and informal, gave way to territorial conquest achieved by violence that escalated to total war before the nineteenth century ended. The frontier as an inclusive, intercultural borderland gave way to subjugation by the Americans who absorbed those frontiers into their national boundaries and made the previous frontiers exclusive regions for their own use and determination.

By the end of the Mexican War, the United States had become a continental nation by extending its western border to the Pacific Ocean. At mid-century, approximately 360,000 Indians lived west of the Mississippi River, while more than 20 million people comprised the United States. In 1860, on the eve of the Civil War, 1.4 million Americans would live in the trans-Mississippi West. By the time of the massacre at Wounded Knee in 1890, 8.5 million people would make the West their home, four railroads would cross the continent, and the Indian frontier as an intercultural borderland or middle ground would cease to exist.

Between the Mexican War and Wounded Knee, the federal government would develop, if not perfect, the reservation system and force the tribes onto those reserves where officials and missionaries could continue their efforts to remake the Indians in the white man's image of small-scale farmers. This transition would be made with incredible violence, such as that which occurred at Sand Creek in 1864, at the Washita in 1868, and at Little Big Horn in 1876. During that time, American Indian policy would be based on good intentions but executed with force of arms. It would achieve not acculturation and assimilation of the Indians into white American society but rather cultural disintegration and dispossession on a scale never before experienced by either whites or Indians on the frontiers.

Ironically, in California, only the Church would save them, physically and culturally. Physically it would save Indians because it gave them some protection from violence intended to annihilate them. Culturally it would save them because the Church enabled the Indians to show the veneer of assimilation and acculturation behind which they continued to practice their own religious and cultural traditions. For the vast majority of the Indians in the trans-Mississippi West following the Mexican American War, the future brought cataclysmic change to their lives, with forced relocation, compulsion to leave their old ways and adopt new ones, the near extinction of the buffalo, and the seizure of their lands, all backed by military force. Nearly a century would pass before cultural rejuvenation began to lift the Indians from oblivion.

In the final analysis, self-interest determined Indian, European, and American interactions on the frontiers of the North American continent. Put simply, the Spanish wanted peace and trade with the Indians in the Southwest, but domination in California, where, comparatively speaking, the tribes were less warlike and easier to control. The Mexicans followed suit in both areas. But, in New Mexico between the Texas Revolution of 1835 and the beginning of the Mexican War, the government proved incapable of providing a military defense against hostile Indians, maintaining peace, or developing a successful Indian policy. In contrast, the British sought loyalty as cheaply as possible so that they could send the Indians against the Americans in time of need. The Americans demanded land and the tribes removed from their midst, either peacefully or by force. For their part, the Indians sought trade, peace, and guarantees of their lands. Sometimes that interaction was peaceful; often it proved violent, but those relationships were always complex and driven by both motive and ulterior motive in the minds of both Indians and whites on the frontiers of the North American continent.

Chronology

1763 February, Treaty of Paris
May, Pontiac's Confederacy attacks Detroit
June, Indians given smallpox-infected blankets at Fort Pitt
October, Henry Bouquet leads expedition to Tuscarawas River valley
Proclamation of 1763
Comanches push Apaches from southern Great Plains

1764 April, Sugar Act passed
British divide Florida at Chattahoochee River

1765 March, Stamp Act passed
May, Congress of Pensacola (British and Creeks)
October, Stamp Act Congress convenes
Creeks and Choctaws at war until 1771

1766 March, Marqués de Rubí begins inspection tour

1767 March, Stamp Act repealed
June–July, Townshend Acts passed

1768 January, Spanish receive a report about a Russian landing on the Pacific Coast
April, Marqués de Rubí submits inspection report that recommends a change
in Indian policy
September, British troops arrive in Boston
October/November, Treaty of Fort Stanwix (Iroquois cede lands south of
the Ohio River)

1769 April, Spanish arrive in San Diego Bay and establish a presidio
Spanish begin mission system in California
Spanish establish a presidio at Monterey

1770 March, Boston Massacre

1771 August, Spain makes contact with Quechans near Yuma Crossing

1772 September, *Royal Regulations*

1774 January, Anza leads expedition from Tubac to California
March–June, Coercive Acts passed
July, Juan José Pérez Hernández sights Pacific Northwest Coast and reaches
Queen Charlotte Islands
October, Lord Dunmore's War

Battle of Point Pleasant
Treaty of Camp Charlotte (Shawnees accept Treaty of Fort Stanwix, which
    ceded their lands south of the Ohio River)
Fifty thousand whites west of Appalachians

1775   April, Battles of Lexington and Concord
    July, Bruno de Hezeta and Francisco de Bodega y Quadra trade with Indians
       along present-day Washington coast
    Captain James Cook leaves Plymouth, England, for Pacific Northwest Coast
    Continental Congress seeks peace with northern Indian nations
    November, Ipai attack mission at San Diego
    Great Plains Indians using horses

1776   July, Declaration of Independence
    Spanish establish a presidio at San Francisco

1777   May–June, Mobile council among British, Chickasaws, Choctaws, and Creeks

1778   March, Captain James Cook reaches Pacific Northwest Coast at Cape Flattery
       and Nootka Sound
    June, France enters American Revolution against Great Britain
    September, Delawares sign peace treaty at Fort Pitt
    Americans John Kendrick and Robert Gray arrive at Nootka Sound

1779   June, Spain enters American Revolution against Great Britain
    August–September, Spanish send Juan Bautista de Anza against the Comanches
    September, Anza's soldiers kill Cuerno Verde
    Spanish seize Baton Rouge and Natchez

1780   Summer, extensive Comanche raids in Texas
    August, George Rogers Clark leads a raid against the Shawnees north of
       the Ohio River
    September, Creeks and British foil an American attack on Augusta

1781   March, Articles of Confederation proclaimed, which gives Congress authority
       for Indian affairs beyond the states
    May, Spanish capture Pensacola
    July, Quechans attack Spanish at Yuma Crossing

1782   September, Shawnees maintain control of Ohio River valley
    November, Jefferson expresses interest in trans-Mississippi West
    Spanish establish a presidio at Santa Barbara

1783   August, Spain ends war with Quechans
    September, Treaty of Paris
    November, Pro-American Chickasaws make peace with the Americans
    Treaty of Augusta (Creeks and Georgia)

1784 Official publication of Cook's voyages to the Pacific Northwest Coast
Russians found first settlement in the Pacific Northwest on Kodiak Island
June, Pro-Spanish Chickasaws sign peace treaty with Spain
Major southern tribes, except Cherokees, sign treaties of alliance with Spanish

1785 January, Treaty with the Wyandot (Fort McIntosh; Wyandots, Delawares,
Ojibwas, and Ottawas acknowledge protection of the United States,
boundaries, and reserves)
February, western Comanches and Utes agree to peace
March, Confederation Congress authorizes commissioners to negotiate peace
treaties with Indians
September, American fur traders arrive along Pacific Northwest Coast
Autumn, eastern Comanches make peace with Texas
British send ships to Pacific Northwest for sea otter trade
Land Ordinance of 1785

1786 February–March, western Comanches make peace with Spanish in New Mexico
June, Treaty of Hopewell (Cherokees acknowledge protection of the United States
and boundaries)
Instructions of 1786

1787 Summer, Congress begins a policy of conciliation and negotiation with the Indians
May–September, Constitutional Convention meets in Philadelphia
July, Northwest Ordinance passed
November, Spanish, Comanches, and Pueblos attack Apaches in New Mexico

1788 Constitution ratified, giving federal government sole authority for Indian policy

1789 January, Treaty with the Wyandot and treaty with the Six Nations (Fort Harmar;
regulate trade and establish boundaries north of the Ohio River)
George Washington elected president
Spanish seize British ships at Nootka Sound
French Revolution begins

1790 July, Congress passes first Intercourse Act to regulate Indian trade and
land purchases
October, Nootka Convention (Spain agrees to return captured ships and cede
land to the British at Nootka Sound)
Miamis, Shawnees, Delawares, and Ottawas route Harmar's force near
present-day Fort Wayne, Indiana

1791 November, Little Turtle and Blue Jacket defeat Arthur St. Clair's army in
present-day northwestern Ohio

1792 George Washington reelected president

1793 February, Creek leader Alexander McGillivray dies
May, Anthony Wayne arrives at Fort Washington with the Legion of the
United States

October, Spain signs Treaty of Nogales with Creeks, Choctaws, Chickasaws,
    Cherokees, and other southern nations

1794   August, Anthony Wayne defeats Indians during the Battle of Fallen Timbers

1795   October, Pinckney treaty signed with Spain
        August, Treaty of Greenville (establishes peace with northern nations
            and provides land cession)

1796   June, Treaty with the Creeks (Coleraine; establishes boundary and approves
            military and trading posts in Creek country)
        John Adams elected president

1800   Thomas Jefferson elected president
        Spanish, British, Russian, and American ships explore Pacific Northwest Coast
        Americans begin expansion into the interior southeast

1802   Georgia pressures federal government for Indian lands

1803   April, Louisiana Purchase
        June, Jefferson asks Congress for funds to support expedition to Pacific Northwest

1804   May, Lewis and Clark expedition leaves St. Louis
        November, Treaty with the Sauk and Foxes (Mesquakies) cedes Indian lands
            east of Mississippi River
        Thomas Jefferson reelected president

1805   April, Lalawethika or Tenskwatawa (the Prophet) emerges as a spiritual
            Shawnee leader
        November, Lewis and Clark reach Columbia River and Pacific Ocean and
            winter at Fort Clatsop near Pacific Coast

1807   June, Chesapeake Crisis

1808   James Madison elected president

1809   September, Treaty of Fort Wayne (Miamis, Delawares, and Weas make
            a major land cession)

1810   Tecumseh emerges as a political leader among the Shawnees and northern nations
        September, Mexican War of Independence begins

1811   April, John Jacob Astor's Pacific Fur Company establishes Fort Astoria on
            the Columbia River
        Autumn, Tecumseh travels to South to gain support for an Indian confederacy

1812   June, Congress declares war on Great Britain
August, General William Hull surrenders Detroit to British, Tecumseh present
President James Madison appoints William Henry Harrison commander
    of the Northwest Army
James Madison reelected president
Maritime fur trade peaks

1813   May, British and Indians attack Fort Meigs
July, Battle with Creeks at Burnt Corn Creek
August, Creeks attack Fort Mims
October, Tecumseh killed near Moraviantown, Canada
November, Andrew Jackson's force destroys Tallushatchee
Pacific Fur Company sells out to North West Company
December, British flag raised over Fort Astoria, which is renamed Fort George

1814   March, Andrew Jackson attacks Creeks at Horseshoe Bend
April, Red Eagle surrenders
July, Treaty with the Wyandot (Wyandots, Delawares, Shawnees, Senecas,
    and Miamis agree to peace)
August, Andrew Jackson dictates peace to Creeks in Treaty of Fort Jackson
San Antonio nearly abandoned due to Mexican War of Independence
December, Treaty of Ghent

1815   March, President James Madison appoints a commission to make peace with
    the Indians
August, remaining northwest Indians agree to peace with the United States

1816   May, Sauks and Foxes sign peace treaty
July, Fort Dearborn (Chicago) rebuilt and reoccupied
James Monroe elected president

1817   September, Treaty with the Wyandot (Wyandots, Potawatomies, Ottawas, and
Ojibwas cede lands)

1818   August, Americans reclaim Fort Astoria

1820   January, Mississippi extends state jurisdiction over Choctaw lands
October, Treaty of Doak's Stand (Choctaws ceded lands)
Autumn, Choctaw removal begins
James Monroe reelected president
Cherokees establish a republican form of government

1821   July, Mexico becomes independent
August, Potawatomies sign land-cession treaty at Chicago
November, William Becknell reaches Santa Fe
December, Stephen F. Austin establishes a colony in Texas
Mexico plans to establish colonies of U.S. citizens as a buffer between Indians
    and major towns of the republic

1822   Americans open trade with the Comanches

1824   February, Pomponio executed
        John Quincy Adams elected president
        Mexican Constitution designates that Indians are citizens
        Indian uprisings in California

1825   February, Treaty with the Creeks (Indians Springs; Creeks cede lands in
            Georgia and Alabama)
        April, William McIntosh executed for negotiating Treaty of Indian Springs
        August, Treaty with the Sioux (Prairie du Chien; Sioux, Ojibwas, Sauks,
            Foxes, Ioways, Winnebagos, Ottawas, Menominees, and Potawatomies
            agree to mutual peace)
        Potawatomies begin moving west of Mississippi River
        Comanches increase raids in Texas and northern Mexico

1826   January, Treaty of Washington (readjusts Creek boundary and nullifies Treaty
            of Indian Springs)
        July, Secularization of California missions begins
        Comanches increase raiding in Texas and Mexico

1827   July, Cherokees adopt a constitution

1828   May, Governor Ninian Edwards of Illinois demands removal of all Indians
            from the territory
        Andrew Jackson elected president
        Georgia plans to extend state authority over Indian lands by June 1, 1830

1829   Andrew Jackson supports Georgia and Alabama in their intent to seize
            Indian lands
        Alabama dissolves Chickasaw tribal government
        Sioux attack Sauk and Mesquakies (Foxes) who raid Sioux in Upper
            Mississippi River valley

1830   February, Indian removal bill introduced in Congress
        May, Jackson signs Indian Removal Act
        July, Treaty with the Sauk and Foxes (land cession)
        September, Treaty of Dancing Rabbit Creek (Choctaws agree to peace and
            land cession)
        Apache attacks increase into Mexico from Arizona, New Mexico, and Texas
        Wichitas raid at will in Texas

1831   March, *Cherokee Nation v. Georgia*
        June, General Edmund P. Gaines demands Black Hawk's capitulation
        Autumn, Choctaw removal begins

1832 January, Treaty with the Wyandots (land cession)
March, *Worcester v. Georgia*
Treaty with the Creeks (Cusseta; major land cession)
April, Black Hawk's band crosses to east side of Mississippi River
General Henry Atkinson pursues Black Hawk
June, Congress authorizes mounted troops to protect Santa Fe Trail
August, Black Hawk's band annihilated at Bad Axe River
September, Treaty with the Sauk and Foxes (Fort Armstrong; establishes
    peace and provides a land cession)
October, Treaty at Pontotoc Creek (Chickasaws cede tribal lands east
    of Mississippi River)
Andrew Jackson reelected president

1833 May, dragoon expedition in Indian Territory
August, secularization of California missions renewed
September–October, Treaty with the Chippewas (Chicago; Chippewas [Ojibwas],
    Ottawas, and United Bands of the Potawatomies agree to land cession
    and removal)
Cut Throat Massacre (Osages attack Kiowas)

1834
June, Colonel Henry M. Dodge leads dragoon expedition to the Wichitas,
    Kiowas, and Comanches
September, Council at Fort Gibson with southern Great Plains and
    immigrant tribes

1835 Summer, dragoon expedition along Platte River
August, Treaty with the Comanche, Wichita, and Associated Bands (provides
    for peace and friendship)
September, Sonora offers bounty for Apache scalps
October, Texas and Mexico fight first battle of Texas War of Independence
December, Pro-removal Cherokees sign Treaty of New Echota (provides
    for removal)
American traders well established north of Arkansas River and trading south
    with the Comanches
Comanches increase raiding in Texas
Apaches increase raiding into northern Mexico

1836 March, Texas declares independence from Mexico and acquires all Indians
    lands by legislation
July, Creek removal begins
September, Texas seeks peace with Comanches
Martin Van Buren elected president
Navajos make war on New Mexico
Creek War

1837   January, Treaty of Doaksville (Chickasaws agree to settle on Choctaw land)
      May, Treaty with the Kiowas, Apaches, and Tawakonis (establishes peace and trade)
      June, Chickasaw removal begins
      July, Chihuahua offers a bounty for Apache scalps

1838   May, Texas signs Treaty of Peace and Amity with several Comanche bands
      September, Cherokee removal begins
      November, Treaty with the Miami (Forks of the Wabash; provides land cession)
      Texas and Comanches in a state of war
      James Kirker begins work as a scalp hunter

1839   July, Treaty of Jemez establishes peace between Navajos and New Mexico

1840   March, Council House fight in San Antonio
      August, Comanches retaliate for Council House Fight
      November, Treaty with the Miami (Forks of the Wabash; provides for land cession)
      William Henry Harrison elected president
      Most Prairie Potawatomies now west of Mississippi River

1841   March, Treaty of Santo Domingo; Navajos and New Mexico agree to peace
      Wichitas, Caddos, Shawnees, and Delawares make peace in Texas

1842   March, Treaty with the Wyandots (last land cession for Wyandots in Ohio
        and Michigan)
      Indian raids increase in California's Central Valley

1843   September, Chickasaws, Caddos, Tawakonis, and Keechis sign peace treaty with Texas
      Oregon-bound immigrants begin trek west along Platte River
      Chihuahua attempts to send Apaches against the Comanches

1844   July, Durango offers a bounty for Apache scalps
      Summer, Dragoon expedition along Platte River
      September, Utes fight in Santa Fe
      October, Texas signs peace treaty with Comanches
      James K. Polk elected president

1845   Summer, Dragoon Expedition along Oregon Trail (Platte)
      December, Texas annexed
      Comanche and Apache raids increase into Mexico

1846   May, Mexican War begins with congressional declaration
      September, Comanches continue raiding in Texas
      Apaches raiding into northern Mexico
      Central Valley in California subject to frequent Indians raids
      Comanches, Kiowas, Cheyennes, and Sioux control Great Plains
      Comanches and Apaches control Southwest
      October, Miamis begin removal

Notes

Chapter 1

1. C. S. Weslager, *The Delaware Indians: A History* (Rutgers: Rutgers University Press, 1972), 210.

2. Arrell M. Gibson, *The Chickasaws* (Norman: University of Oklahoma Press, 1971), 7; Samuel Cole Williams, ed., *Adair's History of the American Indians* (Johnson City, Tenn.: Watauga Press, 1930), 7.

3. Michael A. McConnell, *A Country Between: The Upper Ohio Valley and Its Peoples, 1724–1774* (Lincoln: University of Nebraska Press, 1992), 181; Francis Jennings, "The Indians' Revolution," in *The American Revolution: Explorations in the History of American Radicalism*, ed. Alfred F. Young (DeKalb: Northern Illinois University Press, 1976), 334.

4. Eric Hinderaker, *Elusive Empires: Constructing Colonialism in the Ohio Valley, 1673–1800* (Cambridge: Cambridge University Press, 1997), 154; Paul E. Kopperman, "The Captives Return: Bouquet's Victory," *Timeline* 7 (April–May 1990): 2; Nicholas B. Wainwright, ed., "George Croghan's Journal, 1759–1763," *Pennsylvania Magazine of History and Biography* 71 (July 1946–47): 438.

5. Richard White, *The Middle Ground: Indians, Empires, and Republics in the Great Lakes Region, 1650–1815* (Cambridge: Cambridge University Press, 1991), 285; McConnell, *A Country Between*, 182.

6. McConnell, *A Country Between*, 186.

7. Bernard Knollenberg, "General Amherst and Germ Warfare," *Mississippi Valley Historical Review* 1 (June 1954): 492; Albert T. Volwiler, ed., "William Trent's Journal at Fort Pitt, 1763," *Mississippi Valley Historical Review* [Cedar Rapids] 11 (December 1924): 400.

8. Knollenberg, "General Amherst and Germ Warfare," 493.

9. Paul K. Adams, "Colonel Henry Bouquet's Ohio Expedition in 1764," *Pennsylvania History* 40 (April 1973): 143.

10. McConnell, *A Country Between*, 203.

11. R. Douglas Hurt, *The Ohio Frontier: Crucible of the Old Northwest, 1720–1830* (Bloomington: Indiana University Press, 1996), 55.

12. Ibid.

13. Woody Holton, *Forced Founders: Indians, Debtors, Slaves, & the Making of the American Revolution in Virginia* (Chapel Hill: University of North Carolina Press, Published for the Omohundro Institute of Early American History and Culture, Williamsburg, Virginia, 1999), 7.

14. Hurt, *The Ohio Frontier*, 55; White, *The Middle Ground*, 340.

15. McConnell, *A Country Between*, 245.

16. Ibid., 248.

17. Ibid., 255–56; Gregory Evans Dowd, *A Spiritual Resistance: The North American Indian Struggle for Unity, 1745–1815* (Baltimore: Johns Hopkins University Press, 1992), 43.

18. Alexander C. Flick, ed., *The Papers of Sir William Johnson* (Albany: University of the State of New York, 1951), 7:652.

19. McConnell, *A Country Between*, 259.

20. White, *The Middle Ground,* 340.

21. Hurt, *The Ohio Frontier,* 56.

22. Ibid., 60; Reuben Gold Thwaites, *Documentary History of Dunmore's War, 1774* (1905; reprint, Harrisonburg, Va.: C. J. Carrier, Co., 1974), 386.

23. McConnell, *A Country Between,* 275.

24. Hurt, *The Ohio Frontier,* 61.

25. James H. O'Donnell, III, *Southern Indians in the American Revolution* (Knoxville: University of Tennessee Press, 1973), 22, 23.

26. Hurt, *The Ohio Frontier,* 63.

27. Reuben Gold Thwaites and Louise Phelps Kellogg, *Frontier Defense on the Upper Ohio, 1777–1778* (Madison: Wisconsin Historical Society, 1912), 241.

28. Louise Phelps Kellogg, *Frontier Advance on the Upper Ohio Frontier, 1778–1779* (Madison: State Historical Society of Wisconsin, 1916), 22; Colin G. Calloway, "The Continuing Revolution in Indian Country," in *Native Americans and the Early Republic,* eds. Frederick E. Hoxie, Ronald Hoffman, and Peter J. Albert (Charlottesville: University of Virginia Press, Published for the United States Capitol Historical Society, 1999), 4.

29. Thwaites and Kellogg, *Frontier Defense on the Upper Ohio,* 242; Charles J. Kappler, ed., *Indian Affairs: Laws and Treaties* (Washington, D.C.: Government Printing Office, 1904), 2:3–4.

30. David H. Corkran, *The Creek Frontier, 1540–1783* (Norman: University of Oklahoma Press, 1967), 278.

31. Colin G. Calloway, *The American Revolution in Indian Country: Crisis and Diversity in Native American Communities* (Cambridge: Cambridge University Press, 1995), 213, 216, 217.

32. Ibid., 219.

33. O'Donnell, *Southern Indians in the American Revolution,* 30.

34. J. Russell Snapp, *John Stuart and the Struggle for Empire on the Southern Frontier* (Baton Rouge: Louisiana State University Press, 1966), 197, 205.

35. James Alton James, ed., *George Rogers Clark Papers, 1771–1781* (Springfield: Illinois Historical Society, 1926), 3:261.

36. Calloway, *The American Revolution in Indian Country,* 226.

37. Ibid., 227.

38. Colin G. Calloway, "Suspicion and Self-Interest: The British-Indian Alliance and the Peace of Paris," *Historian* 48 (November 1985): 49, 51, 52.

39. Calloway, *The American Revolution in Indian Country,* 174.

40. Grace Steel Woodward, *The Cherokees* (Norman: University of Oklahoma Press, 1963), 102.

41. John Walton Caughey, *McGillivray of the Creeks* (Norman: University of Oklahoma Press, 1959), 91.

42. Kappler, *Indian Affairs,* 2: 14–16.

43. Calloway, *The American Revolution in Indian Country,* 174.

Chapter 2

1. John Francis Bannon, *The Spanish Borderlands Frontier, 1513–1821* (1970; reprint, Albuquerque: University of New Mexico Press, 1997), 169.

2. Pekka Hämäläinen, "The Western Comanche Trade Center: Rethinking the Plains Indian Trade System," *Western Historical Quarterly* 29 (winter 1998): 496, 498.

3. Gary Clayton Anderson, *The Indian Southwest, 1580–1830: Ethnogenesis and Reinvention* (Norman: University of Oklahoma Press, 1999), 227.

4. David J. Weber, *The Spanish Frontier in North America* (New Haven, Conn.: Yale University Press, 1992), 188.

5. Marc Simmons, trans. and ed., *Indian and Mission Affairs in New Mexico, 1773 By Pedro Fermin de Mendinueta, Governor of New Mexico, 1767–1778* (Santa Fe, N.Mex.: Stagecoach Press, 1965), 19, 20.

6. Ibid., 19.

7. Weber, *The Spanish Frontier in North America*, 191.

8. Lawrence Kinnaird, *The Frontiers of New Spain: Nicholas de Lafora's Description, 1766–1768* (Berkeley, Calif.: Quivira Society, 1958), 24, 79, 91.

9. Ibid., 215, 216.

10. Ibid., 151.

11. Ibid., 185, 186.

12. Ibid., 44; Max L. Moorhead, *The Presidio: Bastion of the Spanish Borderlands* (Norman: University of Oklahoma Press, 1975), 58.

13. Sidney B. Brinckerhoff and Odie B. Faulk, *Lancers for the King; A Study of the New Frontier Military System of Northern New Spain, With a Translation of the Royal Regulations of 1772* (Phoenix: Arizona Historical Foundation, 1965), 49, 61; Kinnaird, *The Frontiers of New Spain*, 216.

14. Weber, *The Spanish Frontier in North America*, 220.

15. Kinnaird, *The Frontiers of New Spain*, 40; Bannon, *The Spanish Borderlands Frontier*, 180; Brinckerhoff, *Lancers for the King*, 6; Mary Lu Moore and Delmar L. Beene, trans. and eds., "The Interior Provinces of New Spain: The Report of Hugo O'Conor, January 30, 1776," *Arizona and the West* 13 (autumn 1971): 267.

16. John L. Kessell, *Friars, Soldiers, and Reformers: Hispanic Arizona and the Sonora Mission Frontier, 1767–1856* (Tucson: University of Arizona Press, 1976), 267.

17. Weber, *The Spanish Frontier in North America*, 224; David M. Vigness, "Don Hugo Oconor and New Spain's Northwestern Frontier, 1764–1776," *Journal of the West* 6 (January 1967): 37.

18. Alfred Barnaby Thomas, *Teodoro de Croix and the Northern Frontier of New Spain, 1776–1783* (Norman: University of Oklahoma Press, 1968), 24, 77.

19. Weber, *The Spanish Frontier in North America*, 228, 229; Jack August, "Balance-of-Power Diplomacy in New Mexico: Governor Fernando de la Concha and the Indian Policy of Conciliation," *New Mexico Historical Review* 56 (April 1981): 144.

20. Sidney B. Brinckerhoff, "The Last Years of Spanish Arizona, 1786–1821," *Arizona and the West* 9 (spring 1967): 10; Weber, *The Spanish Frontier in North America*, 229.

21. Thomas, *Teodoro de Croix and the Northern Frontier of New Spain*, 66; Elizabeth A. H. John, *Storms Brewed in Other Men's Worlds: The Confrontation of Indians, Spanish, and French in the Southwest, 1540–1795* (Norman: University of Oklahoma Press, 1996), 589.

22. Thomas, *Teodoro de Croix and the Northern Frontier of New Spain*, 74, 77.

23. Catherine Price, "The Comanche Threat to Texas and New Mexico in the Eighteenth Century and the Development of Spanish Indian Policy," *Journal of the West* 24 (April 1985): 43; Ronald J. Benes, "Anza and Concha in New Mexico, 1787–1793: A Study in New Colonial Techniques," *Journal of the West* 4 (January 1965): 65.

24. Odie Faulk, "Spanish-Comanche Relations and the Treaty of 1785," *Texana* 2 (spring 1964): 50–51.

25. Frank D. Reeve, "Navaho-Spanish Diplomacy, 1770–1790," *New Mexico Historical Review* 35 (July 1960): 219.

26. Weber, *The Spanish Frontier in North America,* 233; Benes, "Anza and Concha in New Mexico," 72.

27. Odie B. Faulk, "The Comanche Invasion of Texas, 1743–1836," *Great Plains Journal* 9 (1969): 36, 37.

Chapter 3

1. Charles Edward Chapman, *A History of California: The Spanish Period* (New York: Macmillan Co., 1921), 217–18.

2. David J. Weber, *The Spanish Frontier in North America* (New Haven, Conn.: Yale University Press, 1992), 239.

3. Ibid., 94.

4. Ibid., 243, 244.

5. Edith Buckland Webb, *Indian Life at the Old Missions* (Lincoln: University of Nebraska Press, 1952), 9.

6. James H. Rawls, *Indians of California: The Changing Image* (Norman: University of Oklahoma Press, 1984), 16.

7. Ibid., 35.

8. George Harwood Phillips, *Indians and Intruders in Central California, 1769–1849* (Norman: University of Oklahoma Press, 1993), 44.

9. Edward D. Castillo, "Neophyte Resistance and Accommodation in the Missions of California," in *The Spanish Military History of the United States* (San Antonio: National Parks Service, 1993), 66; S. F. Cook, *The Conflict Between the California Indians and White Civilization: I* (Berkeley: University of California Press, 1943), 125.

10. Weber, *The Spanish Frontier in North America,* 263.

11. Rawls, *Indians of California,* 39.

12. Sherburne F. Cook, *The Population of the California Indians, 1769–1970* (Berkeley: University of California Press, 1976), 22.

13. Edward D. Castillo, "The Native Response to the Colonization of Alta California," in *Columbian Consequences,* vol. 1, ed. David Hurst Thomas (Washington, D.C.: Smithsonian Institution Press, 1989), 382.

14. George Harwood Phillips, *Chiefs and Challengers: Indian Resistance and Cooperation in Southern California* (Berkeley: University of California Press, 1975), 31.

15. Weber, *The Spanish Frontier in North America,* 115; Castillo, "The Native Response to the Colonization of Alta California," 384; Robert H. Jackson and Edward Castillo, *Indians, Franciscans, and Spanish Colonization: The Impact of the Mission System on California Indians* (Albuquerque: University of New Mexico Press, 1995), 290., 74–75.

16. Castillo, "The Native Response to the Colonization of Alta California," 385.

17. Steven W. Hackel, "The Staff of Leadership: Indian Authority in the Missions of Alta California," *William and Mary Quarterly* 54 (April 1997): 361, 362.

18. Jackson and Castillo, *Indians, Franciscans, and Spanish Colonization,* 38.

19. Mark Santiago, *Massacre at the Yuma Crossing: Spanish Relations with the Quechans, 1779–1782* (Tucson: University of Arizona Press, 1998), 21.

20. Ibid., 28

21. Ibid., 33, 36, 38.

22. Ibid., 70, 81.

23. Ibid., 87, 88; Jack D. Forbes, *Warriors of the Colorado: The Yumas of the Quechan Nation and Their Neighbors* (Norman: University of Oklahoma Press, 1965), 189.

24. Santiago, *Massacre at the Yuma Crossing,* 94, 98, 104.

25. Ibid., 117.

26. Ibid., 130, 131.

27. Ibid., 140.

28. Phillips, *Indians and Intruders in Central California,* 54.

29. Ibid., 60, 61.

30. C. Alan Hutchison, *Frontier Settlement in Mexican California: The Híjar-Padrés Colony, and Its Origins, 1769–1835* (New Haven, Conn.: Yale University Press, 1969), 61, 74–75, 89.

31. Rawls, *Indians of California,* 42.

Chapter 4

1. Warren L. Cook, *Flood Tide of Empire: Spain and the Pacific Northwest, 1543–1819* (New Haven, Conn.: Yale University Press, 1973), 55, 57–58.

2. Derek Pethick, *First Approaches to the North-West Coast* (Vancouver, B.C., Canada: J. J. Douglas, Ltd., 1976), 40.

3. Herbert K. Beals, trans., *Juan Pérez on the Northwest Coast: Six Documents of His Expedition in 1774* (Portland: Oregon Historical Society Press, 1989), 77.

4. James R. Gibson, *Otter Skins, Boston Ships, and China Goods: The Maritime Fur Trade of the Northwest Coast, 1785–1841* (Seattle: University of Washington Press, 1992), 4.

5. James R. Ronda, *Lewis and Clark Among the Indians* (Lincoln: University of Nebraska Press, 1984), 170; Alexander Ross, *Adventures of the First Settlers on the Columbia River* (1849; reprint, Chicago: R. R. Donnelley & Sons, 1923), 128.

6. Cook, *Flood Tide of Empire,* 78.

7. Barry M. Gough, *The Northwest Coast: British Navigation, Trade, and Discoveries to 1812* (Vancouver, B.C., Canada: University of British Columbia Press, 1992), 39.

8. Ibid., 58–59.

9. Pethick, *First Approaches to the North-West Coast,* 76.

10. Cook, *Flood Tide of Empire,* 109.

11. Ibid., 329–30.

12. Ibid., 330.

13. Ibid., 340–41; Gibson, *Otter Skins, Boston Ships, and China Goods,* 30.

14. Cook, *Flood Tide of Empire,* 341.

15. Gough, *The Northwest Coast,* 57; Bernard DeVoto, ed., *The Journals of Lewis and Clark* (Boston: Houghton Mifflin Co., 1953), 326.

16. Gough, *The Northwest Coast,* 57; Robin Fisher, *Contact and Conflict: Indian-European Relations in British Columbia, 1774–1890* (Vancouver, B.C., Canada: University of British Columbia Press, 1977), 4–5.

17. Robin Fisher and J. M. Bumsted, eds., *Alexander Walker, An Account of a Voyage to the North West Coast of America, in 1785 & 1786* (Seattle: University of Washington Press, 1982), 40, 43.

18. James P. Ronda, *Astoria & Empire* (Lincoln: University of Nebraska Press, 1990), 340.

19. Gibson, *Otter Skins, Boston Ships, and China Goods,* 120.

20. Ibid., 115; Fisher and Bumsted, *Alexander Walker,* 47.

21. Fisher and Bumsted, *Alexander Walker,* 42.

22. Gibson, *Otter Skins, Boston Ships, and China Goods,* 176; Kenneth Wiggins Porter, *John Jacob Astor: Businessman* (Cambridge: Harvard University Press, 1931), 1:449.

23. Gough, *The Northwest Coast,* 198.

24. Robert H. Ruby and John A. Brown, *The Chinook Indians: Traders of the Lower Columbia River* (Norman: University of Oklahoma Press, 1976), 92; H. A. Washington, *The Writings of Thomas Jefferson* (Washington, D.C.: Taylor & Maury, 1853), 1:323; Frank E. Ross, "The Early Fur Trade of the Great Northwest," *Oregon Historical Quarterly* 39 (March 1938–December 1938): 391.

25. Ross, "The Early Fur Trade of the Great Northwest," 391, 392.

26. Nicholas Biddle, ed., *The Journals of the Expedition Under the Commands of Capts. Lewis and Clark to the Sources of the Missouri, Thence Across the Rocky Mountains and Down the River Columbia to the Pacific Ocean, Performed During the Years 1804–5 By Order of the Government of the United States* (New York: Heritage Press, 1962), xx, xxii–xxiii.

27. Donald Jackson, ed., *Letters of the Lewis and Clark Expedition With Related Documents, 1783–1854* (Urbana: University of Illinois Press, 1978), 1:59.

28. Ibid., 203–8.

29. Ronda, *Lewis and Clark among the Indians,* 190.

30. Francis Paul Prucha, *The Great Father: The United States Government and the American Indians* (Lincoln: University of Nebraska Press, 1986), 1:74–75.

31. Ronda, *Astoria & Empire,* 101.

32. Ross, *Adventures of the First Settlers on the Columbia River,* 88, 92.

33. Ibid., 82.

34. Ibid., 154.

35. Wayne R. Kime, "Alfred Seton's Journal: A Source for Irving's Tonquin Disaster Account," *Oregon Historical Quarterly* 71 (December 1970): 313; T. C. Elliott, "Sale of Astoria, 1813," *Oregon Historical Quarterly* 33 (March 1932): 45.

36. Ross, *Adventures of the First Settlers on the Columbia River,* 256.

37. Ruby and Brown, *The Chinook Indians,* 163.

Chapter 5

1. "The Articles of Confederation," in *Documents of American History,* ed. Henry Steel Commager (New York: Appleton-Century-Crofts, 1963), 1:114.

2. Charles C. Royce, "Indian Land Cessions in the United States," *Eighteenth Annual Report of the Bureau of American Ethnology to the Secretary of the Smithsonian Institution, 1896–'97,* pt. 2 (Washington, D.C.: Government Printing Office, 1899), 533.

3. Reginald Horsman, *Expansion and American Indian Policy, 1783–1812* (East Lansing: Michigan State University Press, 1967), 44.

4. Ibid., 22.

5. *American State Papers: Indian Affairs* (Washington, D.C.: Government Printing Office, 1834), 1:8–9.

6. Ibid., 1:12–14.

7. Andrew R. L. Cayton, *Frontier Indiana* (Bloomington: Indiana University Press, 1996), 143.

8. R. Douglas Hurt, *The Ohio Frontier: Crucible of the Old Northwest, 1720–1830* (Bloomington: Indiana University Press, 1996), 107.

9. Francis Paul Prucha, *Sword of the Republic: The United States Army on the Frontier, 1783–1846* (New York: Macmillan, 1969), 18.

10. Cayton, *Frontier Indiana*, 154.

11. Hurt, *The Ohio Frontier*, 114.

12. Allan R. Millett, "Caesar and the Conquest of the Northwest Ohio Territory: The Wayne Campaign, 1792–95," *Timeline* 14 (May–June 1997): 9.

13. Hurt, *The Ohio Frontier*, 124.

14. Ibid., 133.

15. R. David Edmunds, "Tecumseh's Native Allies: Warriors Who Fought for the Crown," in *War on the Great Lakes: Essays Commemorating the 175th Anniversary of the Battle of Lake Erie*, eds. William Jeffrey Welsh and David Curtis Skaggs (Kent, Ohio: Kent State University Press, 1991), 56.

16. Horsman, *Expansion and American Indian Policy*, 153.

17. Cayton, *Frontier Indiana*, 209–10.

18. Ibid., 218; Allan R. Millett, "Caesar and the Conquest of the Northwest Territory: The Harrison Campaign, 1811," *Timeline* 14 (July–August 1997): 10.

19. Prucha, *The Sword of the Republic*, 42.

20. Jack D. L. Holmes, "Spanish Policy toward the Southern Indians in the 1790s," in *Four Centuries of Southern Indians*, ed. Charles M. Hudson (Athens: University of Georgia Press, 1975), 66.

21. J. Leitch Wright, Jr., *Creeks & Seminoles: The Destruction and Regeneration of the Muscogulge People* (Lincoln: University of Nebraska Press, 1986), 133, 137.

22. John Walton Caughey, *McGillivray of the Creeks* (Norman: University of Oklahoma Press, 1938), 104; Kathryn E. Holland Braund, *Deerskins & Duffels: The Creek Indian Trade with Anglo-America, 1685–1815* (Lincoln: University of Nebraska Press, 1993), 175.

23. Braund, *Deerskins & Duffles*, 186.

24. Wright, *Creeks & Seminoles*, 146.

25. Ibid.; H. S. Halbert and T. H. Bell, *The Creek War of 1813 and 1814* ([Tuscaloosa]: University of Alabama Press, 1969), 79–80.

26. Robert V. Remini, *Andrew Jackson and the Course of American Empire, 1767–1821* (New York: Harper & Row, 1977), 190.

27. Ibid.

28. Ibid., 191.

29. Ibid., 193.

30. Ibid.; Davy Crockett, *Life of David Crockett: The Original Humorist and Irrepressible Backwoodsman* (Philadelphia: Porter & Coates, 1865), 75.

31. Remini, *Andrew Jackson and the Course of American Empire*, 197.

32. Ibid., 207.

33. Ibid., 214.

34. Ibid., 215; Stanley W. Hoig, *The Cherokees and Their Chiefs: In the Wake of Empire* (Fayetteville: University of Arkansas Press, 1998), 118.

35. Remini, *Andrew Jackson and the Course of American Empire*, 218.

36. Ibid., 218–19.

37. Ibid., 226.

38. Ibid., 228, 229.

39. Hurt, *The Ohio Frontier*, 325.

40. Ibid., 332.

41. Allan R. Millett, "Caesar and the Conquest of the Northwest Territory: The Second Harrison Campaign, 1813," *Timeline* 14 (October 1997): 9.

42. Ibid., 17.

43. Hurt, *The Ohio Frontier,* 342.

44. Ibid., 343.

Chapter 6

1. John Spencer Bassett, *Correspondence of Andrew Jackson* (Washington, D.C.: Carnegie Institution, 1927), 2:331–32.

2. *American State Papers: Indian Affairs* (Washington, D.C.: Government Printing Office, 1834), 2:473–74.

3. Fred L. Israel, ed., *The State of the Union Messages of the Presidents, 1790–1966* (New York: Chelsea House, 1967), 1:308–10.

4. Paul Francis Prucha, *The Great Father: The United States Government and the American Indians* (Lincoln: University of Nebraska Press, 1984), 1:199.

5. Ibid., 201; Theda Perdue and Michael D. Green, eds., *The Cherokee Removal: A Brief History with Documents* (Boston: St. Martin's Press, Bedford Books, 1995), 116.

6. Arthur H. DeRosier, Jr., *The Removal of the Choctaw Indians* (Knoxville: University of Tennessee Press, 1970), 51.

7. Ibid., 66.

8. William C. Davis, *A Way Through the Wilderness: The Natchez Trace and Civilization of the Southern Frontier* (New York: HarperCollins, 1995), 302.

9. DeRosier, *The Removal of the Choctaw Indians,* 104.

10. Grant Foreman, *Indian Removal: The Emigration of the Five Civilized Tribes of Indians* (Norman: University of Oklahoma Press, 1932), 24.

11. Ronald N. Satz, *American Indian Policy in the Jacksonian Era* (Lincoln: University of Nebraska Press, 1975), 71; Davis, *A Way Through the Wilderness,* 302.

12. Charles J. Kappler, ed., *Indian Affairs: Laws and Treaties* (Washington, D.C.: Government Printing Office, 1904), 2:311.

13. DeRosier, *The Removal of the Choctaw Indians,* 128.

14. Alexis de Tocqueville, *Democracy in America* (Garden City, N.Y.: Doubleday & Co., 1969), 324.

15. Michael D. Green, *The Politics of Indian Removal: Creek Government and Society in Crisis* (Lincoln: University of Nebraska Press, 1982), 76; *Niles Weekly Register* 27 (December 4, 1824): 222–23.

16. Green, *The Politics of Indian Removal,* 82.

17. Ibid., 88.

18. Ibid., 90.

19. Ibid., 109, 117.

20. James D. Richardson, ed., *Messages and Papers of the Presidents* (Washington, D.C.: Bureau of National Literature and Art, 1908), 2:325.

21. Green, *The Politics of Indian Removal,* 156, 157.

22. Ibid., 160.

23. Ibid., 173.

24. Ibid., 176; Foreman, *Indian Removal,* 115.

25. Foreman, *Indian Removal,* 121; Kenneth L. Valliere, "The Creek War of 1836, A Military History," *Chronicles of Oklahoma* 57 (winter 1979–80): 464.

26. *American State Papers: Military Affairs* (Washington, D.C.: Government Printing Office, 1861), 6:622–23; Foreman, *Indian Removal,* 177.

27. Davis, *A Way Through the Wilderness,* 303.

28. Arrell M. Gibson, *The Chickasaws* (Norman: University of Oklahoma Press, 1971), 102.

29. Ibid., 145; *American State Papers: Indian Affairs,* 2:718–27, 709.

30. Gibson, *The Chickasaws,* 150, 153.

31. Kappler, *Indian Affairs,* 2:356; John E. Parsons, ed., "Letters of the Chickasaws Removal of 1837," *New York Historical Society Quarterly* 37 (July 1953): 280, 282.

32. Theda Perdue, "The Conflict Within: Cherokee and Removal," in *Cherokee Removal: Before and After,* ed. William L. Anderson (Athens: University of Georgia Press, 1991), 63.

33. Annie Heloise Abel, "The Cherokee Negotiations of 1822–1823," *Smith College Studies in History* 1 (July 1916): 205; Gary E. Moulton, ed., *The Papers of Chief John Ross: Cherokee Chief* (Norman: University of Oklahoma Press, 1985), 1:78.

34. Gary E. Moulton, *John Ross: Cherokee Chief* (Athens: University of Georgia Press, 1978), 31.

35. Prucha, *The Great Father,* 1:189.

36. Moulton, *The Papers of John Ross,* 1:194.

37. *Cherokee Nation v. Georgia,* 5 Peters 1 (1831), 302.

38. Satz, *American Indian Policy in the Jacksonian Era,* 99.

39. Prucha, *The Great Father,* 1:237.

40. Ibid., 238.

41. Moulton, *John Ross,* 124.

42. Foreman, *Indian Removal,* 288–89; Satz, *American Indian Policy in the Jacksonian Era,* 101.

43. Richardson, *Messages and Papers of the Presidents,* 3:294.

Chapter 7

1. Paul Francis Prucha, *The Great Father: The United States Government and the American Indians* (Lincoln: University of Nebraska Press, 1984), 1:81.

2. Charles J. Kappler, ed., *Indian Affairs: Laws and Treaties* (Washington, D.C.: 1904), 2:110–23; *American State Papers: Military Affairs* (Washington, D.C.: Government Printing Office, 1864), 2:33–34.

3. R. Douglas Hurt, *The Ohio Frontier: Crucible of the Old Northwest, 1720–1830* (Bloomington: Indiana University Press, 1996), 365–66.

4. Prucha, *The Great Father,* 1:245.

5. Hurt, *The Ohio Frontier,* 1; Prucha, *The Great Father,* 1:248; Kappler, *Indian Affairs,* 2:339–40.

6. R. David Edmunds, *The Potawatomies: Keepers of the Fire* (Norman: University of Oklahoma Press, 1978), 220.

7. Ibid., 221.

8. Kappler, *Indian Affairs,* 2:74.

9. Roger L. Nicholas, *Black Hawk and the Warrior's Path* (Arlington Heights, Ill.: Harlan Davidson, Inc., 1992), 69. Here, I follow my earlier discussion of the Black Hawk War in R. Douglas Hurt, *Nathan Boone and the American Frontier* (Columbia: University of Missouri Press, 1998), 120–28, 132–38.

10. William T. Hagan, *The Sac and Fox Indians* (Norman: University of Oklahoma Press, 1958), 98.

11. Kappler, *Indian Affairs,* 2:250, 253.

12. Anthony F. C. Wallace, *Prelude to Disaster: The Course of Indian-White Relations Which Led to the Black Hawk War of 1812* (Springfield: Illinois State Historical Society, 1970), 25, 26.

13. Ibid., 27; E. B. Washburne, ed., *The Edwards Papers,* Chicago: Historical Society's Collection (Chicago: Fergus Printing Co., 1884), 3:338.

14. Wallace, *Prelude to Disaster,* 30–31.

15. Nicholas, *Black Hawk and the Warrior's Path,* 85, 88.

16. Ibid., 93.

17. Kappler, *Indian Affairs,* 2:305; Jacob Van der Zee, "The Neutral Ground," *Iowa Journal of History and Politics* 13 (July 1915): 312.

18. Hagan, *The Sac and Fox Indians,* 124.

19. Nicholas, *Black Hawk and the Warrior's Path,* 96, 97.

20. Hagan, *The Sac and Fox Indians,* 131.

21. Ibid., 132–33.

22. Nicholas, *Black Hawk and the Warrior's Path,* 110.

23. Roger L. Nicholas, ed., "The Black Hawk War: Another View," *Annals of Iowa* 36 (winter 1963): 528–29.

24. Ibid., 529; Wallace, *Prelude to Disaster,* 48.

25. Otis E. Young, "The Mounted Ranger Battalion, 1832–1833," *Mississippi Valley Historical Review* 41 (December 1954): 455–56.

26. Hagan, *The Sac and Fox Indians,* 174.

27. Anselm J. Gerwing, "The Chicago Treaty of 1833," *Journal of the Illinois State Historical Society* 57 (summer 1964): 125.

28. Ibid.

29. Edmunds, *The Potawatomies,* 271.

30. Hurt, *The Ohio Frontier,* 2.

Chapter 8

1. Henry H. Goldman, "A Survey of Escorts of the Santa Fe Trail Trade, 1829–1843," *Journal of the West* 5 (October 1966): 505.

2. Thomas James, *Three Years Among the Indians and Mexicans* (1846; reprint, Lincoln: University of Nebraska Press, 1984), 244, 253–54.

3. Ray Allen Billington, *The Far Western Frontier, 1830–1860* (New York: Harper & Row, 1956), 37, 38.

4. *American State Papers: Military Affairs,* 4:371.

5. Francis Paul Prucha, *The Sword of the Republic: The United States Army on the Frontier, 1783–1846* (Lincoln: University of Nebraska Press, 1969), 240.

6. Grant Foreman, *Fort Gibson: A Brief History* (Norman: University of Oklahoma Press, 1936), 20. Here, I follow R. Douglas Hurt, *Nathan Boone and the American Frontier* (Columbia: University of Missouri Press, 1998), 140–71.

7. *American State Papers: Military Affairs,* 6:169–70.

8. Louis Pelzer, *Marches of the Dragoons in the Mississippi Valley* (Iowa City: State Historical Society of Iowa, 1917), 35.

9. George H. Shirk, "Peace on the Plains," *Chronicles of Oklahoma* 28 (spring 1930): 18.

10. Pelzer, *Marches of the Dragoons,* 40; [Albert Miller Lea], "A Journal of Marches by the First United States Dragoons, 1834–1835," *Iowa Journal of History and Politics* 7 (July 1909): 356.

11. Pelzer, *Marches of the Dragoons,* 42, 43.

12. Ibid., 45.

13. Ibid., 48.

14. *American State Papers: Military Affairs,* 5:358.

15. Charles J. Kappler, ed. *Indian Affairs: Laws and Treaties* (Washington, D.C.: Government Printing Office, 1904): 2:435–36.

16. Ibid., 489.

17. Louis Pelzer, "Captain Ford's Journal of an Expedition to the Rocky Mountains," *Mississippi Valley Historical Review* 12 (March 1926): 559.

18. Prucha, *Sword of the Republic,* 374.

19. C. Wharton, "The Expedition of Major Clifton Wharton in 1844," *Collections of the Kansas State Historical Society* 16 (1925): 273.

20. Ibid., 284.

21. Ibid., 284–85.

22. Hamilton Gardner, "Captain Philip St. George Cooke and the March of the 1st Dragoons to the Rocky Mountains in 1845," *Colorado Magazine* 30 (October 1953): 259.

23. Ibid., 264–65.

24. Ibid., 266; James D. Richardson, ed., *A Compilation of the Messages and Papers of the Presidents, 1789–1897* (Washington, D.C.: Government Printing Office, 1897), 4:411.

25. Arrell M. Gibson, *The Chickasaws* (Norman: University of Oklahoma Press, 1971), 189.

26. Mattie Austin Hatcher, trans., "Texas in 1820," *Southwestern Historical Quarterly* 23 (July 1919): 62–63.

27. David J. Weber, *The Mexican Frontier, 1821–1846: The American Southwest Under Mexico* (Albuquerque: University of New Mexico Press, 1982), 89.

28. Ibid., 95, 97.

29. Ibid., 103, 104.

30. F. Todd Smith, *The Wichita Indians: Traders of Texas and the Southern Great Plains, 1540–1845* (College Station: Texas A & M University Press, 2000), 118.

31. Ibid., 120.

32. Ibid., 125.

33. T. R. Fehrenbach, *The Comanches: The Destruction of a People* (1974; reprint, New York: Da Capo, 1994), 305.

34. Thomas Kavanagh, *Comanche Political History: An Ethnohistorical Perspective, 1706–1875* (Lincoln: University of Nebraska Press, 1996), 236, 243.

35. Ibid., 251.

36. William Preston Johnston, *The Life of General Albert Sidney Johnston, Embracing His Services in the Armies of the United States, the Republic of Texas, and the Confederate States* (New York: Appleton, 1878), 89.

37. Dorman H. Winfrey and James M. Day, eds., *The Indian Papers of Texas and the Southwest* (Austin, Tex.: Pemberton Press, 1959–66), 1:50, 51.

38. H. Allen Anderson, "The Delaware and Shawnee Indians and the Republic of Texas, 1820–1845," *Southwestern Historical Quarterly* 94 (October 1990): 243; Smith, *The Wichita Indians,* 145.

39. Winfrey and Day, *eds., The Indian Papers of Texas and the Southwest,* 1:105.

40. Kavanagh, *Comanche Political History,* 263.

41. Stanley Noyes, *Los Comanches: The Horse People, 1741–1845* (Albuquerque: University of New Mexico Press, 1993), 289.

42. Smith, *The Wichita Indians,* 146; Winfrey and Day, eds., *The Indian Papers of Texas and the Southwest,* 2:8.

43. Kavanagh, *Comanche Political History,* 271, 272; Winfrey and Day, *eds., The Indian Papers of Texas and the Southwest,* 1:268–69; 2: 114–19.

44. Fehrenbach, *The Comanches,* 359.

45. "Texas Diplomatic Correspondence," Annual Report of the American Historical Association, 1908, Vol. 2, Part 1 (Washington, D.C.: Government Printing Office, 1911), 313.

Chapter 9

1. David J. Weber, *The Mexican Frontier, 1826–1846: The American Southwest Under Mexico* (Albuquerque: University of New Mexico Press, 1982), 104.

2. David Tyler, "Mexican Indian Policy in New Mexico," *New Mexico Historical Review* 55 (April 1980): 104.

3. Weber, *The Mexican Frontier,* 103.

4. Josiah Gregg, *Commerce of the Prairies,* ed. Max Moorhead (Norman: University of Oklahoma Press, 1954), 314; Ralph A. Smith, "Indians in American-Mexican Relations Before the War of 1846," *Hispanic American Historical Review* 43 (February 1963): 35.

5. Weber, *The Mexican Frontier,* 115; Tyler, "Mexican Indian Policy in New Mexico," 112.

6. Smith, "Indians in American-Mexican Relations Before the War of 1846," 41; Weber, *The Mexican Frontier,* 87, 89.

7. Ralph A. Smith, *Borderlander: The Life of James Kirker, 1793–1852* (Norman: University of Oklahoma Press, 1999), 71; Smith, "Indians in American-Mexican Relations Before the War of 1846," 101.

8. Smith, *Borderlander,* 71.

9. Ralph A. Smith, "The Scalp Hunter in the Borderlands, 1835–1850," *Arizona and the West* 6 (spring 1964): 5.

10. Ibid., 7.

11. Ralph A. Smith, "Mexican and Anglo-Saxon Traffic in Scalps, Slaves, and Livestock, 1835–1841," *Western Texas Historical Association Yearbook* 36 (1940): 114.

12. Smith, *Borderlander,* 117.

13. Weber, *The Mexican Frontier,* 92; Frank McNitt, *Navajo Wars: Military Campaigns, Slave Raids and Reprisals* (Albuquerque: University of New Mexico Press, 1972), 80, 90.

14. Charles L. Kenner, *A History of New Mexico-Plains Indian Relations* (Norman: University of Oklahoma Press, 1969), 76.

15. Ward Alan Minge, "Mexican Independence Day and a Ute Tragedy in Santa Fe, 1844," in *The Changing Ways of Southwestern Indians: A Historic Perspective,* ed. Albert H. Schroeder (Glorieta, N. Mex.: Rio Grande Press, 1973), 109, 110, 112.

16. Weber, *The Mexican Frontier,* 100.

17. Smith, "Indians in American-Mexican Relations Before the War of 1846," 61.

18. Ibid., 62; Charles R. McClure, "Neither Effective nor Financed: The Difficulties of Indian Defense in New Mexico, 1837–1846," *Military History of Texas and the Southwest* 10 (1972): 90.

19. C. Alan Hutchinson, "The Mexican Government and the Mission Indians of Upper California, 1821–1835," *Americas* 21 (April 1965): 337.

20. Ibid., 338.

21. Ibid., 339, 341, 342.

22. Ibid., 343, 344.

23. Ibid., 347.

24. Ibid., 350.

25. Ibid., 349, 360–61.

26. George Harwood Phillips, *Chiefs and Challengers: Indian Resistance and Cooperation in Southwestern California* (Berkeley: University of California Press, 1975), 40.

27. Sylvia M. Broadbent, "Conflict at Monterey: Indian Horse Raiding, 1820–1850," *Journal of California Anthropology* 1 (1974): 89, 90.

28. Ibid., 90, 95.

29. Ibid., 96.

30. Weber, *The Mexican Frontier,* 101; S. F. Cook, "Expeditions to the Interior of California: Central Valley, 1820–1840," *Anthropology Records* 20 (February 1962): 188.

Bibliography

Abing, Kevin. "A Holy Battleground: Methodist, Baptist and Quaker Missionaries Among the Shawnee Indians, 1830–1844." *Kansas History* 21 (summer 1998): 118–37.

Adelman, Jeremy, and Stephen Aron. "From Borderlands to Borders: Empires, Nation-States, and the Peoples in Between in North American History." *American Historical Review* 104 (June 1999): 813–41.

Agnew, Brad. "The Dodge-Leavenworth Expedition of 1834." *Chronicles of Oklahoma* 53 (fall 1975): 376–96.

American State Papers. 38 vols. Washington, D.C.: Government Printing Office, 1832–1861.

Anderson, Fred. *Crucible of War: The Seven Years' War and the Fate of Empire in British North America, 1754–1766.* New York: Alfred A. Knopf, 2000.

Anderson, Gary Cayton. *Kinsmen of Another Kind: Dakota-White Relations in the Upper Mississippi Valley, 1650–1862.* Lincoln: University of Nebraska Press, 1984.

———. *The Indian Southwest, 1580–1830: Ethnogenesis and Reinvention.* Norman: University of Oklahoma Press, 1999.

Anderson, H. Allen. "The Delaware and Shawnee Indians and the Republic of Texas, 1820–1845." *Southwestern Historical Quarterly* 94 (October 1990): 231–60.

Anderson, William L., ed. *Cherokee Removal: Before and After.* Athens: University of Georgia Press, 1991.

Anson, Bert. *The Miami.* Norman: University of Oklahoma Press, 1970.

August, Jack. "Balance-of-Power Diplomacy in New Mexico: Governor Fernando de la Concha and the Indian Policy of Conciliation." *New Mexico Historical Review* 2 (April 1981): 141–60.

Bannon, John Francis, ed. *Bolton and the Spanish Borderlands.* Norman: University of Oklahoma Press, 1964.

———. *The Spanish Borderlands Frontier, 1513–1821.* Albuquerque: University of New Mexico Press, 1974.

Barnard, Susan K., and Grace M. Schwartzman. "Tecumseh and the Creek Indian War of 1813–1814 in North Georgia." *Georgia Historical Quarterly* 82 (fall 1998): 489–506.

Bassett, John Spencer. *Correspondence of Andrew Jackson.* 7 vols. Washington, D.C.: Carnegie Institution, 1926–1935.

Beers, Henry Putney. *The Western Military Frontier, 1815–1846.* Philadelphia: Porcupine Press, 1975.

Benes, Ronald J. "Anza and Concha in New Mexico, 1787–1793: A Study in New Colonial Techniques." *Journal of the West* 4 (January 1965): 63–76.

Benn, Carl. *The Iroquois in the War of 1812.* Toronto: University of Toronto Press, 1998.

Berlandier, Jean Louis. *The Indians of Texas in 1830.* Edited by John C. Ewers. Translated by Patricia Reading Leclercq. Washington, D.C.: Smithsonian Institution Press, 1969.

Betty, Gerald. "Comanche Society, 1706–1850." Ph.D. diss., Arizona State University, 1999.

Billington, Ray Allen. *The Far Western Frontier, 1830–1860.* New York: Harper & Row, 1956.

Bossu, Jean-Bernard. *Travels in the Interior of North America, 1751–1762.* Norman: University of Oklahoma Press, 1962.

Boyd, Robert. *The Coming of the Spirit of Pestilence: Introduced Infectious Diseases and Population Decline among Northwest Coast Indians, 1774–1874.* Seattle: University of Washington Press, 1999.

Braund, Kathryn E. Holland. *Deerskins & Duffels: The Creek Indian Trade with Anglo-America, 1685–1815.* Lincoln: University of Nebraska Press, 1993.

Brinckerhoff, Sidney B., and Odie B. Faulk. *Lancers for the King: A Study of the Frontier Military System of Northern New Spain, With a Translation of the Royal Regulations of 1772.* Phoenix: Arizona Historical Foundation, 1965.

———. "The Last Years of Spanish Arizona, 1786–1821." *Arizona and the West* 9 (spring 1967): 5–20.

Broadbent, Sylvia M. "Conflict at Monterey: Indian Horse Raiding, 1820–1850." *Journal of California Anthropology* 1 (1974): 86–101.

Burrus, Ernest J. "Rivera y Moncada, Explorer and Military Commander of Both Californias, in the Light of His Diary and Other Contemporary Documents." *Hispanic American Historical Review* 50 (November 1970): 682–92.

Burson, Caroline Maude. *The Stewardship of Don Esteban Miró, 1782–1792.* New Orleans: American Printing Company, 1940.

Calloway, Colin G. "Suspicion and Self-Interest: The British-Indian Alliance and the Peace of Paris." *Historian* 48 (November 1985): 41–60.

———. "Simon Girty: Interpreter and Intermediary." In *Being and Becoming Indian: Biographical Studies of North American Frontiers*, edited by James A. Clifton, 38–58. Chicago: Dorsey Press, 1989.

———. *The American Revolution in Indian Country: Crisis and Diversity in Native American Communities.* Cambridge: Cambridge University Press, 1995.

Campbell, Janis Elaine. "The Social and Demographic Effect of Creek Removal, 1832–1860." Ph.D. diss., University of Oklahoma, 1997.

Carlson, Paul H. *The Plains Indians.* College Station: Texas A & M University Press, 1998.

Carter, Clarence Edwin, ed. *The Territorial Papers of the United States.* 28 vols. Washington, D.C.: Government Printing Office, 1934–1975.

Carter, Harvey Lewis. *The Life and Times of Little Turtle: First Sagamore of the Wabash.* Urbana: University of Illinois Press, 1987.

Castillo, Edward D. "The Native Response to the Colonization of Alta California." In *Archaeological and Historical Perspectives on the Spanish Borderlands West*, edited by David Hurst Thomas, 377–94. Washington, D.C.: Smithsonian Institution Press, 1989.

———. "Neophyte Resistance and Accommodation in the Missions of California." *Spanish Military Heritage of the United States* (1993): 60–75.

Caughey, John Walton. *McGillivray of the Creeks.* Norman: University of Oklahoma Press, 1959.

Cave, Alfred A. "The Delaware Prophet Neolin: A Reappraisal." *Ethnohistory* 46 (spring 1999): 265–90.

Cayton, Andrew R. L. *Frontier Indiana.* Bloomington: Indiana University Press, 1996.

Cayton, Andrew R. L., and Fredrika J. Teute, eds. *Contact Points: American Frontiers from the Mohawk Valley to the Mississippi, 1750–1830.* Chapel Hill: University of North Carolina Press in association with Omohundro Institute of Early American History and Culture, Williamsburg, Virginia, the Newberry Library, Chicago, and the Historic New Orleans Collection, 1998.

Chapman, Charles Edward. *The Founding of Spanish California: The Northwestern Expansion of New Spain, 1687–1783*. New York: Macmillan, 1916.

———. *A History of California: The Spanish Period*. New York: Macmillan, 1923.

Clark, Thomas D., and John D. W. Guice. *Frontiers in Conflict: The Old Southwest, 1795–1830*. Albuquerque: University of New Mexico Press, 1989.

Clemmons, Linda Marie. "Satisfied to Walk in the Ways of Their Fathers: Dakotas and Protestant Missionaries, 1835–1862." Ph.D. diss., University of Illinois at Urbana-Champaign, 1998.

Clifton, James A. "Chicago, September 14, 1833: The Last Great Indian Treaty in the Old Northwest." *Chicago History* 9 (summer 1980): 86–97.

———. *The Prairie People: Continuity and Change in Potawatomi Indian Culture, 1665–1965*. Iowa City: University of Iowa Press, 1998.

Coker, William S., and Thomas D. Watson. *Indian Traders of the Southeastern Borderlands: Paton, Leslie & Company, 1783–1847*. Pensacola: University of West Florida Press, 1986.

Coley, C. J. "Creek Treaties, 1790–1832." *Alabama Review* 11 (July 1958): 163–76.

Connelley, William E. "A Journal of the Santa Fe Trail." Parts 1 and 2. *Mississippi Valley Historical Review* 12 (June 1925): 72–98; 12 (September 1925): 227–55.

Cook, S. F. *The Conflict Between the California Indians and White Civilization*. 4 vols. Berkeley: University of California Press, 1943.

———. "Expeditions to the Interior of California: Central Valley, 1820–1840." *Anthropological Records*, 20, no. 5 (February 1962): 151–213.

Cook, Sherburne F. *The Population of the California Indians, 1769–1970*. Berkeley: University of California Press, 1976.

Corkran, David H. *The Creek Frontier, 1540–1783*. Norman: University of Oklahoma Press, 1967.

Cutter, Donald C. *California in 1792: A Spanish Naval Visit*. Norman: University of Oklahoma Press, 1990.

Daniel, James M., ed. and trans. "Diary of Pedro José de la Fuente, Captain of the Presidio of El Paso del Norte, August–December, 1765." *Southwestern Historical Quarterly* 83 (January 1980): 259–73.

Danziger, Edmund Jefferson, Jr. *The Chippewas of Lake Superior*. Norman: University of Oklahoma Press, 1978.

Davis, Carl L., and LeRoy H. Fisher. "Dragoon Life in Indian Territory, 1833–1846." *Chronicles of Oklahoma* 48 (spring 1970): 2–24.

Davis, James E. *Frontier Illinois*. Bloomington: Indiana University Press, 1998.

Davis, William C. *A Way Through the Wilderness: The Natchez Trace and the Civilization of the Southern Frontier*. New York: HarperCollins, 1995.

Debo, Angie. *The Road to Disappearance: A History of the Creek Indians*. Norman: University of Oklahoma Press, 1941.

———. *The Rise and Fall of the Choctaw Republic*. Norman: University of Oklahoma Press, 1961.

Deloria, Vine, Jr., and Raymond J. DeMallie, eds. *Documents of American Indian Diplomacy: Treaties, Agreements, and Conventions, 1775–1979*. 2 vols. Norman: University of Oklahoma Press, 1999.

DeRosier, Arthur H., Jr. *The Removal of the Choctaw Indians*. Knoxville: University of Tennessee Press, 1970.

"Diary of a Visit of Inspection of the Texas Missions Made by Fray Gaspar José de Solis in the Year 1767–68." Translated by Margaret Kenney Kress. *Southwestern Historical Quarterly* 35 (July 1931): 28–76.

Din, Gilbert C. *Francisco Bouligny: A Bourbon Soldier in Spanish Florida.* Baton Rouge: Louisiana State University Press, 1993.

Donald, Leland. *Aboriginal Slavery on the Northwest Coast of North America.* Berkeley: University of California Press, 1997.

Dowd, Gregory Evans. *A Spirited Resistance: The North American Indian Struggle for Unity, 1745–1815.* Baltimore: Johns Hopkins University Press, 1992.

Drozier, Edward P. *The Pueblo Indians of North America.* Prospect Heights, Ill.: Waveland Press, Inc., 1983.

Drucker, Philip. *Culture of the North Pacific Coast.* San Francisco: Chandler Pub. Co., 1965.

Dunmore, John. *The Journal of Jean-François de Galaup de la Pérouse, 1785–1788.* 2 vols. London: Hakluyt Society, 1994.

Dutton, Bertha P. *American Indians of the Southwest.* Albuquerque: University of New Mexico Press, 1983.

Edmunds, R. David. *The Potawatomies: Keepers of the Fire.* Norman: University of Oklahoma Press, 1978.

———. *American Indian Leaders: Studies in Diversity.* Lincoln: University of Nebraska Press, 1980.

———. *The Shawnee Prophet.* Lincoln: University of Nebraska Press, 1983.

———. *Tecumseh and the Quest for Indian Leadership.* Boston: Little, Brown and Company, 1984.

———. "'Evil Men Who Add to Our Difficulties': Shawnees, Quakers, and William Wells, 1807–1808." *American Indian Culture and Research Journal* 14, no. 4 (1990): 1–14.

Eid, Leroy V. "'National' War Among Indians of Northeastern North America." *Canadian Review of American Studies* 16 (summer 1985): 125–54.

———. "'A Kind of Running Fight': Indian Battlefield Tactics in the Late Eighteenth Century." *Western Pennsylvania Historical Magazine* 71 (April 1988): 147–71.

Elliott, T. C. "Sale of Astoria, 1813." *Oregon Historical Quarterly* 33 (March 1932): 43–50.

Everett, Dianna. *The Texas Cherokees: A People Between Two Fires, 1819–1840.* Norman: University of Oklahoma Press, 1990.

Faulk, Odie B. *The Last Years of Spanish Texas, 1778–1821.* The Hague, Netherlands: Mouton & Co., 1964.

———. "Spanish-Comanche Relations and the Treaty of 1785." *Texana* 2 (spring 1964): 44–53.

———. "The Comanche Invasion of Texas, 1743–1836." *Journal of the Great Plains* 9 (fall 1969): 10–50.

Fehrenbach, T. R. *The Comanches: The Destruction of a People.* 1974. Reprint, New York: Da Capo, 1994.

Fisher, Robert L. "The Treaties of Portage Des Sioux." *Mississippi Valley Historical Review* 19 (March 1933): 495–508.

Fisher, Robin. *Contact and Conflict: Indian-European Relations in British Columbia, 1774–1890.* Vancouver, B.C., Canada: University of British Columbia Press, 1977.

Fisher, Robin, and J. M. Bumsted, eds. *An Account of a Voyage to the North West Coast of America in 1785 & 1786.* Seattle: University of Washington Press, 1982.

Flick, Alexander C., ed. *The Papers of Sir William Johnson*. 14 vols. Albany: University of the State of New York, 1921–1965.

Flores, Dan L., ed. *Journal of an Indian Trader: Anthony Glass and the Texas Trading Frontier, 1790–1810*. College Station: Texas A & M University Press, 1985.

Forbes, Jack D. *Warriors of the Colorado: The Yumas of the Quechan Nation and Their Neighbors*. Norman: University of Oklahoma Press, 1965.

———. *Native Americans of California and Nevada*. Healdsburg, Calif.: Naturegraph Publishers, 1969.

Foreman, Grant. *Pioneering Days in the Early Southwest*. Cleveland: Arthur H. Clark, Co., 1926.

———. *Indian Removal: The Emigration of the Five Civilized Tribes of Indians*. Norman: University of Oklahoma Press, 1932.

———. *Advancing the Frontier, 1830–1860*. Norman: University of Oklahoma Press, 1933.

———. *Fort Gibson: A Brief History*. Norman: University of Oklahoma Press, 1936.

Franchère, Gabriel. *Adventure at Astoria, 1810–1814*. Norman: University of Oklahoma Press, 1967.

———. *A Voyage to the Northwest Coast of America*. New York: Citadel Press, 1968.

Franklin, W. Neil. "Pennsylvania-Virginia Rivalry for the Indian Trade of the Ohio Valley." *Mississippi Valley Historical Review* 20 (March 1934): 463–80.

Franks, Kenny A. *Stand Watie and the Agony of the Cherokee Nation*. Memphis, Tenn.: Memphis State University Press, 1979.

Fuller, George W. *The Indian Empire of the Pacific Northwest, A History*. Denver: H. G. Linderman, 1928.

Galvin, John, ed. and trans. *A Record of Travels in Arizona and California, 1775–1776 by Fr. Francisco Garces*. San Francisco: John Howell Books, 1967.

Gardner, Hamilton. "Captain Philip St. George Cook and the March of the 1st Dragoons to the Rocky Mountains in 1845." *Colorado Magazine* 30 (October 1953): 246–69.

Geiger, Maynard, ed. and trans. "Fray Antonio Ripoll's Description of the Chumash Revolt at Santa Barbara in 1824." *Southern California Quarterly* 52 (fall 1970): 345–64.

Gelo, Daniel J. "'Comanche Land and Ever Has Been': A Native Geography of the Nineteenth-Century Comancheria." *Southwestern Historical Quarterly* 103 (spring 2000): 273–307.

Gerwin, Anselm J. "The Chicago Indian Treaty of 1833." *Journal of the Illinois Historical Society* 57 (summer 1964): 117–42.

Gibson, Arrell M. *The Chickasaws*. Norman: University of Oklahoma Press, 1971.

Gibson, James R. *Otter Skins, Boston Ships, and China Goods: The Maritime Fur Trade of the Northwest Coast, 1785–1841*. Seattle: University of Washington Press, 1992.

Godsey, Roy. "The Osage War, 1837." *Missouri Historical Review* 20 (October 1925): 96–100.

Goldman, Henry L. "A Survey of Federal Escorts of the Santa Fe Trade, 1829–1843." *Journal of the West* 5 (October 1966): 504–16.

Gough, Barry M. *The Northwest Coast: British Navigation, Trade, and Discoveries to 1812*. Vancouver, B.C., Canada: University of British Columbia Press, 1992.

Green, Michael D. *The Politics of Indian Removal: Creek Government and Society in Crisis*. Lincoln: University of Nebraska Press, 1982.

Griffen, William B. "Apache Indians and the Northern Mexican Peace Establishments." In *Southwestern Culture History: Collected Papers in Honor of Albert H. Schroeder*, edited by Charles H. Lange, 183–95. Santa Fe: Ancient City Press in association with Archaeological Society of New Mexico, 1985.

Gunther, Erna. *Indian Life on the Northwest Coast of North America As Seen by the Early Explorers and Fur Traders During the Last Decades of the Eighteenth Century.* Chicago: University of Chicago Press, 1972.

Gutiérrez, Ramón A. *When Jesus Came, the Corn Mothers Went Away: Marriage, Sexuality, and Power in New Mexico, 1500–1846.* Stanford: Stanford University Press, 1991.

Hackel, Steven W. "The Staff of Leadership: Indian Authority in the Missions of Alta California." *William and Mary Quarterly* 54 (April 1997): 345–76.

Hafen, LeRoy R., and Ann W. Hafen. *Old Spanish Trail: Santa Fé to Los Angeles.* Glendale, Calif.: Arthur H. Clark Co., 1954.

Hagan, William T. *The Sac and Fox Indians.* Norman: University of Oklahoma Press, 1958.

Halbert, H. S., and T. H. Ball. *The Creek War of 1813 and 1814.* [Tuscaloosa]: University of Alabama Press, 1969.

Hall, G. Emlen, and David J. Weber. "Mexican Liberals and the Pueblo Indians, 1821–1829." *New Mexico Historical Review* 59 (January 1984): 5–32.

Hämäläinen, Pekka. "The Western Comanche Trade Center: Rethinking the Plains Indian Trade System." *Western Historical Quarterly* 29 (winter 1998): 485–514.

Harmon, Alexandra. *Indians in the Making: Ethnic Relations and Indian Identities around Puget Sound.* Berkeley: University of California Press, 1998.

Henri, Florette. *The Southern Indians and Benjamin Hawkins, 1796–1816.* Norman: University of Oklahoma Press, 1986.

Hershberger, Mary. "Mobilizing Women, Anticipating Abolition: The Struggle against Indian Removal in the 1830s." *Journal of American History* 86 (June 1999): 15–40.

Hewes, Gordon, and Minna Hewes, eds. "Indian Life and Customs at Mission San Luis Rey." *Americas* 9 (July 1952): 87–106.

Hildreth, James. *Dragoon Campaigns to the Rocky Mountains.* 1836. Reprint, New York: Arno Press, 1973.

Hill, Leonard U. *John Johnston and the Indians in the Land of the Three Miamis.* Piqua, Ohio: N.p., 1957.

Himmel, Kelly F. *The Conquest of the Karankawas and the Tonkawas, 1821–1859.* College Station: Texas A & M University Press, 1999.

Hinderacker, Eric. *Elusive Empires: Constructing Colonialism in the Ohio Valley, 1673–1800.* Cambridge: Cambridge University Press, 1997.

Hoig, Stanley W. *The Cherokees and Their Chiefs: In the Wake of Empire.* Fayetteville: University of Arkansas Press, 1998.

Holterman, Jack. "The Revolt of Yozcolo: Indian Warrior in the Fight for Freedom." *Indian Historian* 3 (spring 1970): 19–23.

———. "The Revolt of Estanislao." *Indian Historian* 3 (winter 1970): 43–54, 66.

Holton, Woody. "The Ohio Indians and the Coming of the American Revolution in Virginia." *Journal of Southern History* 60 (August 1994): 453–78.

———. *Forced Founders: Indians, Debtors, Slaves & the Making of the American Revolution in Virginia.* Chapel Hill: University of North Carolina Press in association with Omohundro Institute of Early American History and Culture, Williamsburg, Virginia, 1999.

Horsman, Reginald. *The Causes of the War of 1812.* New York: A. S. Barnes & Co., 1962.

———. *Expansion and American Indian Policy, 1783–1812.* East Lansing: Michigan State University Press, 1967.

———. *The Frontier in the Formative Years, 1783–1815.* New York: Holt, Rinehart and Winston, 1970.

Howard, James H. *Shawnee! The Ceremonialism of a Native Indian Tribe and Its Cultural Background.* Athens: Ohio University Press, 1981.

Howay, Frederick W. "Indian Attacks Upon Maritime Traders of the North-West Coast, 1785–1805." *Canadian Historical Review* 6 (December 1925): 287–309.

Hoxie, Frederick E., Ronald Hoffman, and Peter J. Albert, eds. *Native Americans and the Early Republic.* Charlottesville: University Press of Virginia in association with United States Capitol Historical Society, 1999.

Hudson, Charles M., ed. *Four Centuries of Southern Indians.* Athens: University of Georgia Press, 1975.

Hurt, R. Douglas. *Indian Agriculture in America: Prehistory to the Present.* Lawrence: University Press of Kansas, 1987.

———. *The Ohio Frontier: Crucible of the Old Northwest, 1720–1830.* Bloomington: Indiana University Press, 1996.

———. *Nathan Boone and the American Frontier.* Columbia: University of Missouri Press, 1998.

Hurtado, Albert L. *Indian Survival on the California Frontier.* New Haven, Conn.: Yale University Press, 1988.

Hutchinson, C. Alan. "The Mexican Government and the Mission Indians of Upper California, 1821–1835." *Americas* 21 (April 1965): 335–62.

———. *Frontier Settlement in Mexican California: The Híjar-Padrés Colony, and Its Origins, 1769–1835.* New Haven: Yale University Press, 1969.

Irving, Washington. *Astoria or Anecdotes of an Enterprise Beyond the Rocky Mountains.* New York: Hurst & Co., 1886.

Israel, Fred L. *The State of the Union Messages of the Presidents, 1790–1966.* 3 vols. New York: Chelsea House, 1967.

Jackson, Robert H. "Patterns of Demographic Change in the Missions of Central Alta California." *Journal of California and Great Basin Anthropology* 9, no. 2 (1987): 251–72.

———. *Indian Population Decline: The Missions of Northwestern New Spain, 1687–1840.* Albuquerque: University of New Mexico Press, 1994.

———. *Race, Caste, and Status: Indians in Colonial Spanish America.* Albuquerque: University of New Mexico Press, 1999.

Jackson, Robert H., and Edward Castillo. *Indians, Franciscans, and Spanish Colonization: The Impact of the Mission System on California Indians.* Albuquerque: University of New Mexico Press, 1995.

James, James Alton, ed. *George Rogers Clark Papers, 1771–1781.* Vol. 3, *Collections of the Illinois State Historical Library.* Springfield: Illinois State Historical Library, 1912.

Jennings, Francis. "The Indians' Revolution." In *The American Revolution: Explorations in the History of American Radicalism,* edited by Alfred F. Young, 319–48. DeKalb: Northern Illinois University Press, 1976.

Johansen, Dorothy O., and Charles M. Gates. *Empire of the Columbia: A History of the Pacific Northwest.* New York: Harper & Row, 1957.

John, Elizabeth A. H. "A Cautionary Exercise in Apache Historiography." *Journal of Arizona History* 25 (autumn 1984): 301–15.

———. "Nurturing the Peace: Spanish and Comanche Cooperation in the Early Nineteenth Century." *New Mexico Historical Review* 59 (October 1984): 345–69.

————. *Storms Brewed in Other Men's Worlds: The Confrontation of Indians, Spanish, and French in the Southwest, 1540–1795,* 2d ed. Norman: University of Oklahoma Press, 1996.

Jones, Oakah L., Jr. *Los Paisanos: Spanish Settlers on the Northern Frontier of New Spain.* Norman: University of Oklahoma Press, 1979.

Jones, Robert F., ed. *Annals of Astoria: The Headquarters Log of the Pacific Fur Company on the Columbia River, 1811–1813.* New York: Fordham University Press, 1999.

Kanon, Thomas. "'A Slow, Laborious Slaughter': The Battle of Horseshoe Bend." *Tennessee Historical Quarterly* 58 (spring 1999): 2–15.

Kappler, Charles J., ed. *Indian Affairs: Laws and Treaties.* 2 vols. Washington, D.C.: Government Printing Office, 1904.

Kavanagh, Thomas W. *Comanche Political History: An Ethnohistorical Perspective, 1706–1875.* Lincoln: University of Nebraska Press, 1996.

Kehoe, Alice Beck. *North American Indians: A Comprehensive Account.* Englewood Cliffs, N.J.: Prentice Hall, 1992.

Kellogg, Louise Phelps. *Frontier Advance on the Upper Ohio Frontier, 1778–1789.* Madison: State Historical Society of Wisconsin, 1916.

Kenner, Charles L. *A History of New Mexican-Plains Indian Relations.* Norman: University of Oklahoma Press, 1969.

Kessell, John L. *Friars, Soldiers, and Reformers: Hispanic Arizona and the Sonora Mission Frontier, 1767–1856.* Tucson: University of Arizona Press, 1976.

King, Duane H., ed. *The Cherokee Nation: A Troubled History.* Knoxville: University of Tennessee Press, 1979.

Kinnaird, Lawrence. *The New Frontiers of New Spain: Nicholas de Lafora's Description, 1766–1768.* Berkeley, Calif.: Quivira Society, 1958.

————. "Spanish Treaties with Indian Tribes." *Western Historical Quarterly* 10 (January 1979): 39–48.

Knollenberg, Bernhard. "General Amherst and Germ Warfare." *Mississippi Valley Historical Review* 1 (June 1954): 489–94.

Knopf, Richard C., ed. *Anthony Wayne: A Name in Arms: Soldier, Diplomat, Defender of Expansion Westward of a Nation.* Pittsburgh, Pa.: University of Pittsburgh Press, 1960.

Lambert, Joseph I. "The Black Hawk War: A Military Analysis." *Journal of the Illinois State Historical Society* 32 (December 1939): 442–73.

Langer, Erick D., and Robert H. Jackson. "Colonial and Republican Missions Compared: The Cases of Alta California and Southeastern Bolivia." *Comparative Studies in Society & History* 30 (1988): 286–311.

Lansing, Michael. "Plains Indian Women and Interracial Marriage in the Upper Missouri Trade, 1804–1868." *Western Historical Quarterly* 31 (winter 2000): 413–34.

Littlefield, Daniel F. Jr., and Lonnie E. Underhill. "Fort Coffee and Frontier Affairs, 1834–1838." *Chronicles of Oklahoma* 54 (fall 1976): 314–38.

Lumpkin, Wilson. *The Removal of the Cherokee Indians from Georgia, 1827–1841.* New York: Augustus M. Kelley, 1971.

Mahon, John K. *The War of 1812.* Gainesville: University of Florida Press, 1972.

Mason, William Marvin. "Fages' Code of Conduct Toward Indians, 1787." *Journal of California Anthropology* 2 (1975): 90–100.

Matson, Daniel S., and Albert H. Schroeder. "Codero's Description of the Apache—1796." *New Mexico Historical Review* 32 (October 1957): 335–56.

Mayhall, Mildred P. *The Kiowas.* 2d ed. Norman: University of Oklahoma Press, 1987.

McCarty, Kieran. *Desert Documentary: The Spanish Years, 1767–1821.* Historical Monograph No. 4. Tucson: Arizona Historical Society, 1976.

McCluggage, Robert W. "The Senate and Indian Land Titles, 1800–1825." *Western Historical Quarterly* 1 (October 1970): 415–26.

McClure, Charles R. "Neither Effective nor Financed: The Difficulties of Indian Defense in New Mexico, 1837–1846." *Military History of Texas and the Southwest* 10 (1972): 73–92.

McConnell, Michael N. *A Country Between: The Upper Ohio Valley and its Peoples, 1724–1774.* Lincoln: University of Nebraska Press, 1992.

McDermott, John Francis, ed. *The Spanish in the Mississippi Valley, 1762–1804.* Urbana: University of Illinois Press, 1974.

McLoughlin, William G. *After the Trail of Tears: The Cherokees' Struggle for Sovereignty, 1839–1880.* North Carolina: University of North Carolina Press, 1993.

McNitt, Frank. *Navajo Wars: Military Campaigns, Slave Raids and Reprisals.* Albuquerque: University of New Mexico Press, 1972.

Meighan, Clement W. "Indians and California Missions." *Southern California Quarterly* 69 (fall 1987): 187–201.

Minge, Ward Alan. "Mexican Independence Day and a Ute Tragedy in Santa Fe, 1844." In *The Changing Ways of Southwestern Indians: A Historic Perspective*, edited by Albert H. Schroeder, 107–22. Glorieta, N.Mex.: Rio Grande Press, 1973.

Moore, Mary Lu, and Delmar L. Beene. "The Interior: Provinces of New Spain: The Report of Hugo O'Conor, January 30, 1776." *Arizona and the West* 13 (autumn 1971): 265–82.

Moorhead, Max L. *The Apache Frontier: Jacobo Ugarte and Spanish-Indian Relations in Northern New Spain, 1769–1791.* Norman: University of Oklahoma Press, 1968.

———. *The Presidio: Bastion of the Spanish Borderlands.* Norman: University of Oklahoma Press, 1975.

———. "Spanish Deportation of Hostile Apaches: The Policy and the Practice." *Arizona and the West* 17 (autumn 1975): 205–20.

Morris, Grace P. "Development of Astoria." *Oregon Historical Quarterly* 38 (October 1937): 413–24.

Moulton, Gary E. *John Ross: Cherokee Chief.* Athens: University of Georgia Press, 1978.

———. *The Papers of Chief John Ross.* 2 vols. Norman: University of Oklahoma Press, 1985.

Nelson, Larry. *Men of Patriotism, Courage, & Enterprise: Fort Meigs in the War of 1812.* Canton, Ohio: Daring Books, 1985.

———. *A Man of Distinction Among Them: Alexander McKee and British Indian Affairs Along the Ohio Country Frontier, 1754–1799.* Kent, Ohio: Kent State University Press, 1999.

Nelson, Paul David. *Anthony Wayne: Soldier of the Early Republic.* Bloomington: Indiana University Press, 1985.

Neumeyer, Elizabeth. "Michigan Indians Battle Against Removal." *Michigan History* 55 (winter 1971): 175–88.

Nichols, Roger L. "The Black Hawk War: Another View." *Annals of Iowa* 36 (winter 1963): 525–33.

———. *Black Hawk and the Warrior's Path.* Arlington Heights, Ill.: Harlan Davidson, Inc., 1992.

Nobles, Gregory H. "Breaking into the Backcountry: New Approaches to the Early American Frontier, 1750–1800." *William and Mary Quarterly* 46 (October 1989): 641–70.

———. *American Frontiers: Cultural Encounters and Continental Conquest.* New York: Hill and Wang, 1997.

Noyes, Stanley. *Los Comanches: The Horse People, 1751–1845.* Albuquerque: University of New Mexico Press, 1993.

O'Brien, Warren Gregory. "Choctaws in a Revolutionary Age: A Study of Power and Authority, 1750–1801." Ph.D. diss., University of Kentucky, 1998.

———. "The Conqueror Meets the Unconquered: Negotiating Cultural Boundaries on the Post-Revolutionary Southern Frontier." *Journal of Southern History* 67 (February 2001): 39–72.

O'Donnell, James H. *Southeastern Indians in the American Revolution.* Knoxville: University of Tennessee Press, 1973.

———. "The World Turned Upside Down: The American Revolution for Native Americans." In *The American Indian and the American Revolution*, edited by Francis P. Jennings, 80–93. Chicago: University of Chicago Press, 1983.

Ogden, Adele. *The California Sea Otter Trade, 1784–1848.* Berkeley: University of California Press, 1941.

Onuf, Peter S. "'We shall all be Americans': Thomas Jefferson and the Indians." *Indiana Magazine of History* 95 (June 1999): 103–41.

Ostler, Jeffrey. "'They Regard Their Passing as *Wakan*': Interpreting Western Sioux Explanations for the Bison's Decline." *Western Historical Quarterly* 30 (winter 1999): 475–97.

Ourada, Patricia K. *The Menominee Indians: A History.* Norman: University of Oklahoma Press, 1979.

Owsley, Frank Lawrence, Jr. *Struggle for the Gulf Borderlands: The Creek War and the Battle of New Orleans, 1812–1815.* Gainesville: University Presses of Florida, 1981.

Parins, James W. *John Rollin Ridge: His Life & Works.* Lincoln: University of Nebraska Press, 1991.

Parsons, John E. "Letters on the Chickasaw Removal of 1837." *New York Historical Society Quarterly* 37 (July 1953): 273–83.

Pelzer, Louis., ed. "A Journal of Marches by the First United States Dragoons, 1834–1835." *Iowa Journal of History and Politics* 7 (July 1909): 331–78.

———. *Marches of the Dragoons in the Mississippi Valley.* Iowa City: State Historical Society of Iowa, 1917.

———. "Captain Ford's Journal of an Expedition to the Rocky Mountains." *Mississippi Valley Historical Review* 14 (March 1926): 550–79.

Perdue, Theda. *Cherokee Women: Gender and Culture Change, 1700–1835.* Lincoln: University of Nebraska Press, 1998.

Perdue, Theda, and Michael D. Green, eds. *The Cherokee Removal: A Brief History with Documents.* Boston: Bedford Books of St. Martin's Press, 1995.

Perrine, Fred S., ed. "Military Escorts on the Santa Fe Trail." *New Mexico Historical Review* 2 (April 1927): 178–93.

———. "Hugh Evan's Journal of Colonel Henry Dodge's Expedition to the Rocky Mountains in 1835." *Mississippi Valley Historical Review* 14 (September 1927): 192–214.

Pethick, Derek. *First Approaches to the Northwest Coast.* Vancouver, B.C., Canada: J. J. Douglas Ltd., 1976.

Phillips, George Harwood. "Indians and the Breakdown of the Spanish Mission System in California." *Ethnohistory* 21 (fall 1974): 291–302.

———. *Chiefs and Challengers: Indian Resistance and Cooperation in Southern California.* Berkeley: University of California Press, 1975.

———. *Indians and Intruders in Central California, 1769–1849.* Norman: University of Oklahoma, 1993.

Phillips, Paul Christopher. *The Fur Trade.* 2 vols. Norman: University of Oklahoma Press, 1961.

Pourade, Richard. *Anza Conquers the Desert: The Anza Expeditions from Mexico to California and the Founding of San Francisco, 1774–1776.* San Diego: Union-Tribune Publishing Co., 1971.

Powell, Philip Wayne. "Genesis of the Frontier Presidio in North America." *Western Historical Quarterly* 13 (April 1982): 124–41.

Price, Catherine. "The Comanches Threat to Texas and New Mexico in the Eighteenth Century and the Development of Spanish Indian Policy." *Journal of the West* 24 (April 1985): 34–45.

Prucha, Francis Paul. *American Indian Policy in the Formative Years: The Indian Trade and Intercourse Acts, 1790–1834.* Cambridge: Harvard University Press, 1962.

———. *The Sword of the Republic: The United States Army on the Frontier, 1783–1846.* Lincoln: University of Nebraska Press, 1969.

———. *The Great Father: The United States Government and the American Indians.* 2 vols. Lincoln: University of Nebraska Press, 1984.

———. *American Indian Treaties: The History of a Political Anomaly.* Berkeley: University of California Press, 1994.

Quaife, Milo Milton. *Adventurers of the First Settlers on the Oregon or Columbia River.* Chicago: R. R. Donnelley & Sons, 1933.

Rafert, Stewart. *The Miami Indians of Indiana: A Persistent People: 1654–1994.* Indianapolis: Indiana Historical Society, 1996.

Rawls, James J. *Indians of California: The Changing Image.* Norman: University of Oklahoma Press, 1984.

Reeve, Frank D. "Navaho-Spanish Diplomacy, 1770–1790." *New Mexico Historical Review* 35 (July 1960): 200–235.

Reeves, Carolyn Keller. *The Choctaw Before Removal.* Jackson: University Press of Mississippi, 1985.

Reff, Daniel T. *Disease, Depopulation, and Cultural Change in Northwestern New Spain, 1518–1764.* Salt Lake: University of Utah Press, 1991.

Remini, Robert. *Andrew Jackson and the Course of American Empire, 1767–1821.* New York: Harper & Row, 1977.

———. *Andrew Jackson and His Indian Wars.* New York: Viking, 2001.

Rhonda, James P. *Lewis and Clark Among the Indians.* Lincoln: University of Nebraska Press, 1984.

———. *Astoria & Empire.* Lincoln: University of Nebraska Press, 1990.

Richter, Daniel K. *The Ordeal of the Longhouse: The Peoples of the Iroquois League in the Era of European Colonization.* Chapel Hill: University of North Carolina, 1992.

Rickard, T. A. "The Sea Otter in History." *British Columbia Historical Quarterly* 11 (January 1947): 15–31.

Riley, Carroll L. *The Kachina and the Cross: Indians and Spaniards in the Early Southwest.* Salt Lake City: University of Utah Press, 1999.

Rollings, Willard H. *The Osage: An Ethnohistorical Study of Hegemony on the Prairie-Plains.* Columbia: University of Missouri Press, 1992.

Rooney, Elizabeth B. "The Story of the Black Hawk War." *Wisconsin Magazine of History* 40 (summer 1957): 271–83.

Ross, Alexander. *Adventures of the First Settlers on the Oregon or Columbia River.* Chicago: R. R. Donnelley, 1923.

Ross, Frank E. "The Early Fur Trade of the Great Northwest." *Oregon Historical Quarterly* 39 (October 1938): 389–409.

Royce, Charles C. *Indian Land Cessions in the United States.* 1900. Reprint, New York: Arno Press, 1971.

Ruby, Robert H., and John A. Brown. *The Chinook Indians: Traders of the Lower Columbia River.* Norman: University of Oklahoma Press, 1976.

Ruíz, José Francisco. *Report on the Indian Tribes of Texas in 1828.* Edited by John C. Ewers. Translated by Georgette Dorn. New Haven, Conn.: Yale University Library, 1972.

Salter, William. "Henry Dodge: Part IV, Colonel U.S. Dragoons, 1833–36." *Iowa Historical Record* 8 (April 1892): 251–67.

Santiago, Mark. *Massacre at the Yuma Crossing: Spanish Relations with the Quechans, 1779–1782.* Tucson: University of Arizona Press, 1998.

Satz, Ronald N. *American Indian Policy in the Jacksonian Era.* Lincoln: University of Nebraska Press, 1975.

Scheffer, Victor B. "The Sea Otter on the Washington Coast." *Pacific Northwest Quarterly* 31 (October 1940): 371–88.

Schilz, Frank, and Donald E. Worcester. "The Spread of Firearms Among the Indian Tribes on the Northern Frontier of New Spain." *American Indian Quarterly* 11 (winter 1987): 1–10.

Schroeder, Albert H., ed. *The Changing Ways of Southwestern Indians: A Historic Perspective.* Glorieta, N.Mex.: Rio Grande Press, 1973.

Schwantes, Carlos A. *The Pacific Northwest: An Interpretive History.* Lincoln: University of Nebraska Press, 1989.

Schwartzman, Grace, and Susan K. Barnard. "A Trail of Broken Promises: Georgians and the Muscogee/Creek Treaties, 1796–1826." *Georgia Historical Quarterly* 75 (winter 1991): 697–718.

Sheehan, Bernard W. *Seeds of Extinction: Jeffersonian Philanthropy and the American Indian.* Chapel Hill: University of North Carolina Press in association with Institute of Early American History and Culture, Williamsburg, Virginia, 1973.

Shipek, Florence. "California Indian Reactions to the Franciscans." *Americas* 41 (April 1984): 480–92.

Shirk, George H. "Peace on the Plains." *Chronicles of Oklahoma* 28 (spring 1930): 2–41.

Shriver, Phillip S. "Know Them No More Forever: The Miami Removal of 1846." *Timeline* 10 (November–December 1993): 30–41.

Simmons, Marc, ed. and trans. *Indian and Mission Affairs in New Mexico, 1773: By Pedro Fermin de Mendinueta, Governor of New Mexico, 1767–1778.* Santa Fe, N.Mex.: Stagecoach Press, 1965.

Skaggs, David Curtis, and Larry L. Nelson, eds. *The Sixty Years' War for the Great Lakes, 1754–1814.* East Lansing: Michigan State University Press, 2001.

Smith, F. Todd. *The Caddo Indians: Tribes at the Convergence of Empires, 1542–1854.* College Station: Texas A & M University Press, 1995.

———. *The Wichita Indians: Traders of Texas and the Southern Great Plains, 1540–1845.* College Station: Texas A & M University Press, 2000.

Smith, Ralph A. "Mexican and Anglo-Saxon Traffic in Scalps, Slaves, and Livestock, 1835–1841." *West Texas Historical Association Yearbook* 36 (1960): 98–115.

———. "Indians in American Mexican Relations Before the War of 1846." *Hispanic American Historical Review* 43 (February 1963): 34–64.

———. "The Scalp Hunter in the Borderlands, 1835–1850." *Arizona and the West* 6 (spring 1964): 5–22.

———. *Borderlander: The Life of James Kirker, 1793–1852.* Norman: University of Oklahoma Press, 1999.

Snapp, J. Russell. *John Stuart and the Struggle for Empire on the Southern Frontier.* Baton Rouge: Louisiana State University Press, 1996.

Sosin, Jack M. *Whitehall and the Wilderness: The Middle West in British Colonial Policy, 1760–1775.* Lincoln: University of Nebraska Press, 1961.

———. *The Revolutionary Frontier, 1763–1783.* New York: Holt, Rinehart and Winston, 1967.

Spaulding, Kenneth A., ed. *Alexander Ross: The Fur Hunters of the Far West.* Norman: University of Oklahoma Press, 1956.

Starkey, Armstrong. *European and Native American Warfare, 1675–1815.* Norman: University of Oklahoma Press, 1998.

Sugden, John. *Tecumseh: A Life.* New York: Henry Holt and Co., 1997.

———. "Tecumseh's Travels Revisited." *Indiana Magazine of History* 96 (June 2000): 151–68.

Swagerty, W. R., ed. *Scholars and the Indian Experience.* Bloomington: Indiana University Press, 1984.

Sword, Wiley. *President Washington's Indian War: The Struggle for the Old Northwest, 1790–1795.* Norman: University of Oklahoma Press, 1985.

Terrell, John Upton. *The Plains Apache.* New York: Thomas Y. Crowell Company, 1975.

Thomas, Alfred Barnaby. *Forgotten Frontiers: A Study of the Spanish Indian Policy of Don Juan Bautista de Anza Governor of New Mexico, 1777–1787.* Norman: University of Oklahoma Press, 1932.

Thomas, Alfred Barnaby, trans. and ed. *Teodoro de Croix and the Northern Frontier of New Spain, 1766–1783, from the original document in the Archives of the Indies, Seville.* Norman: University of Oklahoma Press, 1941.

Thomas, David Hurst. "The Native Response to the Colonization of Alta California." In *Archeological and Historical Perspectives on the Spanish Borderlands West,* edited by David Hurst Thomas, 377–94. Washington, D.C.: Smithsonian Institution Press, 1989.

Thornton, Russell. *The Cherokees: A Population History.* Lincoln: University of Nebraska Press, 1990.

Thwaites, Reuben Gold, and Louise Phelps Kellogg. "The Story of the Black Hawk War." *Wisconsin Historical Collection* 12 (1892): 217–65.

———. *Frontier Defense on the Upper Ohio, 1777–1778.* Madison: Wisconsin Historical Society, 1912.

———. *The Revolution on the Upper Ohio, 1775–1777.* 1908. Reprint, Port Washington, N.Y.: Kennikat Press, 1970.

———. *Documentary History of Dunmore's War, 1774.* Madison: State Historical Society of Wisconsin, 1974.

Trennert, Robert A. "A Trader's Role in the Potawatomi Removal from Indiana: The Case of George W. Ewing." *Old Northwest* 4 (March 1978): 3–24.

Tyler, Daniel. "Mexican Indian Policy in New Mexico." *New Mexico Historical Review* 55 (April 1980): 101–20.

Unser, Daniel H., Jr. *Indians, Settlers, & Slaves in a Frontier Exchange Economy: The Lower Mississippi Valley Before 1783*. Chapel Hill: University of North Carolina Press in association with Institute of Early American History and Culture, Williamsburg, Virginia, 1992.

———. *American Indians in the Lower Mississippi Valley: Social and Economic Histories*. Lincoln: University of Nebraska Press, 1998.

Utley, Robert M. *The Indian Frontier of the American West 1846–1890*. Albuquerque: University of New Mexico Press, 1984.

Valliere, Kenneth L. "The Creek War of 1836, A Military History." *Chronicles of Oklahoma* 57 (winter 1979–80): 463–85.

Van der Zee, Jacob. "The Neutral Ground." *Iowa Journal of History and Politics* 13 (July 1915): 311–48.

Vigness, David M. "Indian Raids on the Lower Rio Grande, 1836–1837." *Southwestern Historical Quarterly* 59 (July 1955): 14–23.

———. "Don Hugo Oconor and New Spain's Northeastern Frontier, 1764–1776." *Journal of the West* 6 (January 1967): 27–40.

Volwiler, A. T., ed. "William Trent's Journal at Fort Pitt, 1763." *Mississippi Valley Historical Review* 11 (December 1924): 390–413.

Wainwright, Nicholas B. *George Croghan: Wilderness Diplomat*. Chapel Hill: University of North Carolina Press in association with Institute of Early American History and Culture at Williamsburg, Virginia, 1959.

Wallace, Anthony F. C. *Prelude to Disaster: The Course of Indian-White Relations Which Led to the Black Hawk War of 1832*. Springfield: Illinois State Historical Library, 1970.

———. *Jefferson and the Indians: The Tragic Fate of the First Americans*. Cambridge: Belknap Press of Harvard University, 1999.

Wallace, Ernest, and E. Adamson Hoebel. *The Comanches: Lords of the South Plains*. Norman: University of Oklahoma Press, 1986.

Wardell, Morris L. *A Political History of the Cherokee Nation, 1838–1907*. Norman: University of Oklahoma Press, 1977.

Washburne, E. B., ed. *The Edwards Papers: Being a Portion of the Collection of the Letters, Papers, and Manuscripts of Ninian Edwards*. Chicago Historical Society's Collection. Chicago: Fergus Printing Co., 1884.

Webb, Edith Buckland. *Indian Life at the Old Missions*. Lincoln: University of Nebraska, 1952.

Weber, David J., ed. *New Spain's Far Northern Frontier: Essays on Spain in the American West, 1540–1821*. Albuquerque: University of New Mexico Press, 1979.

———. *The Mexican Frontier, 1821–1846: The American Southwest Under Mexico*. Albuquerque: University of New Mexico Press, 1982.

———. *The Spanish Frontier in North America*. New Haven, Conn.: Yale University Press, 1992.

Wells, Samuel H., and Roseanna Tubby, ed. *After Removal: The Choctaw in Mississippi*. Jackson: University Press of Mississippi, 1986.

Welsh, William Jeffrey, and David Curtis Skaggs. *War on the Great Lakes: Essays Commemorating the 175th Anniversary of the Battle of Lake Erie*. Kent, Ohio: Kent State University Press, 1991.

Whelan, Mary K. "Dakota Indian Economics and the Nineteenth-Century Fur Trade." *Ethnohistory* 40 (spring 1993): 246–76.

White, Richard. *The Roots of Dependency: Subsistence, Environment, and Social Change Among the Choctaws, Pawnees, and Navajos*. Lincoln: University of Nebraska Press, 1983.

———. *The Middle Ground: Indians, Empires, and Republics in the Great Lakes Region, 1650–1815* (Cambridge and New York: Cambridge University Press, 1991.

Wickwire, Franklin B. "Go On and Be Brave: The Battle of Point Pleasant." *Timeline* 4 (August–September 1987): 2–15.

Wike, Joyce Annabel. "The Effect of the Maritime Fur Trade on Northwest Coast Indian Society." Ph.D. diss., Columbia University, 1951.

Wilkins, Thurman. *Cherokee Tragedy: The Story of the Ridge Family and the Decimation of a People*. New York: Macmillan Co., 1970.

Williams, Robert A., Jr. *Linking Arms Together: American Indian Treaty Visions of Law and Peace, 1600–1800*. New York: Oxford University Press, 1997.

Worcester, Donald E., ed. and trans. "Advice on Governing New Mexico, 1794." *New Mexico Historical Review* 24 (July 1949): 236–54.

———. *The Apaches: Eagles of the Southwest*. Norman: University of Oklahoma Press, 1979.

Woodward, Grace Steele. *The Cherokees*. Norman: University of Oklahoma Press, 1963.

Wright, J. Leitch, Jr. *The Only Land They Knew: The Tragic Story of the American Indians in the Old South*. New York: Free Press, 1981.

———. *Creeks & Seminoles: The Destruction and Regeneration of the Muscogulge People*. Lincoln: University of Nebraska Press, 1986.

Young, Mary E. *Redskins, Ruffleshirts and Rednecks: Indian Allotments in Alabama and Mississippi, 1830–1860*. Norman: University of Oklahoma Press, 1961.

———. "Conflict Resolution on the Indian Frontier." *Journal of the Early Republic* 16 (spring 1996): 1–19.

Young, Otis E. *The First Military Escort on the Santa Fe Trail*. Glendale, Calif.: Arthur H. Clark Co., 1952.

———. "Dragoons on the Santa Fé Trail in the Autumn of 1843." *Chronicles of Oklahoma* 32 (spring 1954): 42–51.

———. "The Mounted Ranger Battalion, 1832–1833." *Mississippi Valley Historical Review* 41 (December 1954): 453–70.

Index

Page numbers in italics refer to illustrations.

Creek National Council: and Creek factionalism, 146; and land cessions, 145; and McIntosh, 147; and removal negotiations, 148–49; and U.S. diplomacy, 123

Creeks: alliance formation, 14; alliance with Spain, 119; and the British, 19–20, 23; and cession treaties, 121–22, 144–45, 255; and the Chickasaws, 124; and the Choctaws, 14, 20, 249; factionalism, 120, 123, 124, 146–47; at Fort Gibson, 201–3; at Fort Mims, 124–25; at Horseshoe Bend, 127–29; and land cessions, 144–45; location of, 2; peace with the U.S., 131–33; political organization of, 4; removal to Indian Territory, 151, 255; and the Shawnees, 18; spiritual revivalism, 122, 124; and Tecumseh, 123–24; and the Texans, 216; Treaty of Cusseta, 149–50; Treaty of Indian Springs, 146–47, 254; and the Treaty of Paris, 25–26; Treaty of Washington, 147–48; treaty with the U.S., 202–3; and white speculators, 150. See also Lower Creeks; Upper Creeks

Creek War, 255
Crockett, Davy, 127
Croghan, George, 13
Croix, Teodoro de, 40–41, 41, 67, 72–73
Crowell, John, 146
Crows, 190, 245
Cruzat, Francisco, 23
Cuchanec Comanches, 45
Cuerno Verde, 250
cultural exchange, 51, 102. See also acculturation
Cunning Chief (Char-a-cha-ush), 205
Cut Throat Massacre of 1833, 194, 255
Cuyahoga River, 114

the Dalles, 79, 83
Davis, Jefferson, 196
Dayton, Ohio, 135
Dearborn, Henry, 117, 123
de la Concha, Fernando, 46
Delawares: alliance formation, 14; and the American Revolution, 16–17; and the

Americans, 17–19, 111, 114, 116, 253; and the British, 6–7, 9–10; claims to land, 12; confederation of, 107; and disease, 8; at Fort Pitt, 250; guides for dragoons, 197; and Kirker, 227; location of, 2; migration of, 3–4; and the Ohio River, 112; political organization of, 4; and the Texans, 211–12, 216; Treaty of Fort McIntosh, 107, 251; Treaty of Fort Stanwix, 13; Treaty of Fort Wayne, 118

Detroit, 107; attack of, 7; defense of, 8; and trade, 6; during War of 1812, 134, 135, 253
Detroit River, 112
Díaz, Juan Marcelo, 69
diplomacy, 12–13, 17, 19–20, 72, 123. See also cession treaties
disease: at military forts, 194; at missions, 61, 63, 236; in the Pacific Northwest, 93; in the South, 153; in the Southwest, 45; in Texas, 213; in Upper California, 74–75; and warfare, xiii, 8, 247, 249
Dodge, Col. Henry M., 194, 196; and the dragoons, 195; as Maj., 181; meeting with Great Plains nations, 197–200; Rocky Mountain expedition, 203–4; and the Wichitas, 213
dragoons: along the Oregon Trail, 256; and the Comanches, 197–98; creation of, 194–95; expedition of 1834, 196–97, 197, 200–201, 202; and the Wichitas, 198
Dunmore's War, 15–16, 21, 249
Durán, Father Narciso, 73, 238, 239
Durango, Mex., 229

East India Company, 89, 91
Eaton, John, 141, 142, 193
Echeandía, Gov. José María, 238
Ecueracapa, 45, 46
Edwards, Ninian, 172, 174, 254
Eel Rivers, 116
Egushawa. See Blue Jacket
Eixarch, Father Thomas, 68
El Camino del Diablo, 67
Eldredge, J. C., 221
Elosúa, Antonio, 212
Emisteseguo, 19–20
Eneah Micco, 148, 149, 151